The Lunar Light of Whitman's Poetry

The Lunar Light of Whitman's Poetry

M. Wynn Thomas

Harvard University Press

Cambridge, Massachusetts, and London, England   1987

Publication of this book has been aided by a grant from the
Andrew W. Mellon Foundation.

This book is printed on acid-free paper, and its binding materials
have been chosen for strength and durability.

Library of Congress Cataloging in Publication Data
Thomas, M. Wynn.
   The lunar light of Whitman's poetry.

   Bibliography: p.
   Includes index.
   1. Whitman, Walt, 1819–1892—Criticism and
interpretation.   2. Whitman, Walt, 1819–1892—Political
and social views.   3. Social problems in literature.
4. United States in literature.   I. Title.
PS3238.T56   1987   811'.3   86-12141
ISBN 0-674-53952-4 (alk. paper)

I'm teulu
ac er cof am fy rhieni

✒ *Acknowledgments*

M Y INTEREST in Whitman goes back as far as my early student days at Swansea, when I heard George Dekker read the poetry in his rich American accent. But two people have been primarily responsible for encouraging me to write, and even to write at length, about Whitman's work. The first was my friend the late Brian Way. It was he who enabled me, through his own critical practice, to understand what Henry James meant when he said that "just in proportion as he reacts and reciprocates and penetrates, is the critic a valuable instrument." The second is Professor Helen Vendler. Without her repeated, and most generous, intellectual support, I would have been quite unable (as, at first, I was most unwilling) to sustain such an ambitious undertaking.

It is my pleasure to record my gratitude for the sabbatical term I was granted by University College, Swansea, to complete this book. My friend and colleague Andrew Varney read a draft with characteristic care, and I benefited from his scrupulous advice. My thanks go also to Rita Williams for turning an untidy draft into a beguilingly immaculate typescript and to Professor Frank Murphy, whose very kind assistance enabled me to obtain suitable illustrations for the book.

Parts of this book have previously appeared, in more rudimentary form, in the following journals: *American Quarterly, Delta* (France), *Journal of American Studies,* and the *Walt Whitman Review*. I should particularly like to thank the editors for the interest they have shown in my work.

Permission to quote from *Collected Poems of Wallace Stevens* (1965) has been granted by Alfred A. Knopf, Inc., and Faber and Faber Ltd.

Oxford University Press has allowed me to quote from Charles Tomlinson, *Selected Poems 1951–1975* (1978). The passage from Gary Snyder, *Myths and Texts* (copyright © Gary Snyder, 1960), is reprinted with the permission of New Directions Publishing Corporation. The extract from Charles Wright, "Dog Creek Mainline" (first printed in *POETRY*), is reprinted from *Hard Freight* (copyright © 1972 by Charles Wright), courtesy of Wesleyan University Press. Passages from Peter Redgrove, *Dr. Faust's Sea-Spiral Spirit and Other Poems* (1972), are included with the permission of Routledge and Kegan Paul. The passage from Charles Olson, *The Maximus Poems* (copyright © Charles Olson, 1960), is reprinted with the permission of University of California Press.

As for the dedication of this book, it both records my gratitude to my family and acknowledges my own country. To quote James again—or at least one of his characters—one can not, even as a critic, "give up one's country any more than one gives up one's grandmother. They're both antecedent to choice—elements of one's composition that are not to be eliminated." This is, therefore, in ways it would be tedious and inappropriate to explain here, very much a Welshman's book about an American.

Contents

✒ Illustrations

The Lunar Light of Whitman's Poetry

A NOTE ON SOURCES

Unless otherwise indicated, Whitman's prose is quoted from
Prose Works, 1892, ed. Floyd Stovall, 2 vols. (New York:
New York University Press, 1963, 1964), and cited by
volume and page. All selections from *Leaves of Grass* are
quoted from *Leaves of Grass: A Textual Variorum,* ed. Scully
Bradley, Harold W. Blodgett, Arthur Golden, and William
White, 3 vols. (New York: New York University Press,
1980), and cited by volume and page.

♆ Introduction

SINCE LUNAR LIGHT is after all pure moonshine, perhaps I had better try, at the outset, to establish the intended meaning of my title by referring the borrowed image to its source. It finds its origin in a passage from *A Backward Glance o'er Travel'd Roads,* the retrospective essay written by Whitman "in the early candlelight of old age" and first printed complete in *November Boughs:* "Also it must be carefully remember'd that first-class literature does not shine by any luminosity of its own; nor do its poems. They grow of circumstances, and are evolutionary. The actual living light is always curiously from elsewhere—follows unaccountable sources, and is lunar and relative at best . . . One needs only a little penetration to see, at more or less removes, the material facts of their country and radius, with the coloring of the moods of humanity at the time, and its gloomy or hopeful prospects, behind all poets and each poet, and forming their birth-marks" (2:717–718).

This lunar image incidentally possesses revisionist power. Writers, whether poets or critics, have grown accustomed to starting with the sun whenever they try to summon up a consummate image of Whitman. "In the far South the sun of autumn is passing / Like Walt Whitman walking along a ruddy shore," wrote Wallace Stevens famously;[1] and Whitman's hair and beard recently appeared as a blazing corona surrounding his face on the title page of *Walt Whitman: The Measure of His Song.*[2] It is natural enough, since Whitman himself made the image such an integral part of his mythologizing self-projections. To reject it for another, cooler trope—which is nevertheless still of Whitman's own making—is therefore to exchange one kind

of description he offers of himself for quite another, whose implications have perhaps been less thoroughly canvased. It is to lend an
ear not to the most familiar, and hypnotically raucous, claims he
makes, but to such asides and undertones as he recorded in passages
like the following: "The interrogative wonder-fancy rises in me whether
(if it be not too arrogant to even state it,) the 33 years of my current
time, 1855–1888, with their aggregate of our New World doings and
people, have not, indeed, created and formulated the foregoing leaves—
forcing their utterance as the pages stand—coming actually from the
direct urge and development of those years, and not from any individual epic or lyrical attempts whatever, or from my pen or voice,
or any body's special voice"(2:733).

It has naturally suited me to take Whitman at his notoriously unreliable word to the extent of hoping that such "little penetration"
as I possess would be enough to bring me to the "material facts"
concerning the poetry's relationship to its place and its period. I have
not, however, altogether trusted his own effusive explanations of that
relationship. Instead of accepting that his poems embody the essential
spirit of America, I have concluded that they are the products of what
was for Whitman, as it was for the artisan class with which he was
closely associated, a historically specific period of social crisis. In his
own case not only did poetry surface in him under this pressure, his
poems were also instrumental in enabling Whitman to adapt, or to
temper, his ideals (themselves partly historical in origin; the residue
of an earlier period) to the sometimes harsh requirements of a new
environment. At the same time, poetry was his indispensable means
of stating his *own* requirements, allowing him to address the contemporary situation in terms and tones that were, not infrequently in one
and the same poem, critical, celebratory, and visionary.

Or so they were roughly until the Civil War—that is, while changes,
however wholesale, in the socioeconomic order continued to be think-
able, with the aid of poetry, in terms derived essentially from a rapidly
disappearing phase of capitalist endeavor. After the war, though, such
a conception was entirely out of the question. Whitman was faced
with what had been the incipiently, or latently, foreign character of
the prewar American scene now made brazenly, exultantly evident
in a way that virtually rendered his poetry obsolete. The present was
removed from the grasp of his imagination; and since the vigor of
that imagination had been very much a function of his grappling with

the prewar present, it was inevitable his poetry should wane so markedly in strength. His rhetoric, increasingly, was all for the future; but such modestly genuine poetry as he was still capable of producing in those later years was almost all for the past.

That, then, is the implicit thesis of this book—implicit at least in the sense that the case is not systematically, or consistently or comprehensively, argued in the pages that follow. I have preferred to organize the book as a series of roughly chronological, semi-independent essays, which nevertheless I hope will supplement each other satisfactorily. There are a good couple of reasons for my choice of this loose, confederate structure. First, it corresponds to my actual, piecemeal manner of working; specific poems awaken an interest and thereby start a train of thought which I need to be free to follow. Second, it is guaranteed to invalidate any such claims to comprehensiveness of explanation as may be made in the heat of the rhetorical moment. These essays are manifestly no more than specimen studies, even of those limited aspects of Whitman's work which I have found personally congenial or relatively manageable.

Throughout my time of study, and particularly during my period of writing, I have been troubled and sustained by what, as a dutifully enlightened critic, I can only lamely describe as a necessary fiction. The fiction is that I have been dealing, through the poetry, with another person from a different century. In being the subject of my study, Whitman has therefore become for me a subject for concern, in the sense so finely recognized by Charles Tomlinson: "How to speak with the dead / so that not only / our but their / words are valid?"[3] The problem is one which cuts two ways, affecting both the modern reader and the dead author. Seeing my own words, thoughts, feelings assume in Whitman's presence the form that they do here, I am deeply grateful to him for what he has nurtured in me. But whether in the process he too has been allowed, or enabled, to find his own voice, or whether he has simply been struck dumb by it all, is an entirely different matter, and not for me to say.

I am in any case consoled by the thought that, whatever my shortcomings as a critic, Whitman would probably be predisposed to forgive them—at least if Traubel's report of him is a true one. A Boston man, who was obviously a twentieth-century critic before his time, once perplexed Whitman with his strange interpretations of *Leaves of Grass*. "I would ask: 'How do you get that?' " Whitman recalled later, "and he would say: 'Here they are—here they are': would himself have the most distorted versions—would find it hard to understand: even my explanations were mostly futile: text and all confessedly brought together in his hurly-burly head." The poet took it all in good part, however, deciding to "regard it as a study, a curio: instructive: it demonstrated by what a thin thread a writer holds his prestige: by the accident here and there of somebody understanding— in any case oftener misunderstanding—you. This man was a fair sample of the critics as critics go, good and bad (mostly bad)."[4]

Actually, Whitman himself has been very fortunate in this respect. The scholars and critics who have been attracted to his work during this century have mostly been good, and some of them have even been excellent. Indeed, such strength as this present study possesses is mostly a borrowed strength: or, to revert for the moment to the terms of this book's title metaphor, the light here shed on Whitman's work is probably no more than a faint reflection, or redirection, of the illumination I have myself received from the work of eminent scholars, from Allen to Aspiz, and from Holloway to Hollis. Most certainly, my project has depended at every point on the magnificent labors of those who have edited *The Collected Writings of Walt Whitman,* especially the recent *Textual Variorum* of the printed versions of *Leaves of Grass.* Such scholarly debts are, of course, openly acknowledged in my citations. By contrast, there are those invisible debts owed to the countless commentators on Whitman's poetry, whose influence on this present study undoubtedly extends far beyond those specific instances that are identified below in passing. Who, as Wordsworth put it, can tell what portion of the river of his, or her, mind comes from what source? What I do know, though, is that I worked throughout with many writers in mind. Not only did they enter both consciously and insensibly into what I was writing, they also represented for me an admirably settled achievement which I was very glad to take for granted, not least because it released me from the obligation of having to prepare a well-rounded, judicious, and comprehensive study of Whitman, and allowed me instead the welcome freedom to pursue my own, frankly limited line of inquiry. In other words, I think of this book as simply supplementing, as it in turn is supported by, the work of others who have already dealt with the many important aspects both of Whitman and of his poetry that are not properly considered here.

Having myself chosen a historical perspective, my closest affinities have naturally been with those who had adopted this same point of view before me. Of the Whitman scholars, I would therefore mention Joseph Jay Rubin as one whose detailed survey of the social and political background to the 1855 *Leaves of Grass* has particularly guided me. But help has come equally from a nonliterary quarter. It is no exaggeration to say that but for the work of pure historians of the caliber of E. K. Spann, Edward Pessen, and Sean Wilentz, this study could simply not have been written. My findings, at least in the first half of this book, are entirely dependent on theirs, and I am indeed grateful to them. They should not, however, be held responsible for what I have made of their conclusions. As Whitman himself very well knew, the most surprising things can happen once a text is brought together with all that goes on in a reader's "hurly-burly head."

Now that the critics who have had their say about Whitman run right through the alphabet from Arvin to Zweig, what possible excuse could there be for adding to their number? Apart from vanity, it is only, I think, the unanswered, and unanswerable, question which was definitively put by his brother George, that keeps teasing us into unavailing print: "Damn it, Walt, I think you have talent enough to write right: what are you up to, anyhow?"[5]

1 ✒ A Critical Situation

WHITMAN has his blessedly unguarded moments when truth will out. It slips out for instance in a sentence from "Song of Joys," which consequently encapsulates, better than does any other, Whitman's centrally divided feelings about his national mission: "To lead America—to quell America with a great tongue" (2:339). Whitman's wish to use his tongue to "lead" America is well known, having been greatly advertised by Whitman himself and vigorously proclaimed from the platform of his poetry. But the related inclination to "quell America," which arose from his obscure unease at the kind of society he saw developing all around him, was a violent impulse whose strength he, as a poet, could never comfortably admit. Yet during the 1850s not only was Whitman the queller of America very much the alter ego of Whitman the leader of America—the preferred poetic identity he so carefully cultivated—but this passionately critical disposition contributed directly to the well-being of the poet, since it was this deep concern with the social and political direction currently being taken by America that gave both impetus and substance to his poetry.

In his prose works Whitman was considerably less inhibited about displaying his dissenting anger, not only in substantial pieces like "The Eighteenth Presidency" and (later) *Democratic Vistas* but also in short explosive notes such as the following: "Go on, my dear Americans, whip your horses to the utmost—Excitement; money! politics!—open all your valves and let her go—going, whirl with the rest—you will soon get under such momentum you can't stop if you would. Only make provision betimes, old States and new States, for several thousand insane asylums. You are in a fair way to create a nation of lunatics."[1] Many years after it was written, Horace Traubel came across this note and read it out to the old man. While professing to be slightly baffled by such intemperate expressions of feeling, Whitman nevertheless refused to retract them: "That's old and kind o' violent—don't you think—for me? Yet I don't know but it still holds good."[2] Insofar as it is genuine, Whitman's mild bewilderment in old age is partly the measure of his distance from that younger, more politically impassioned and socially engaged, self from which the great poetry had come.

Yet that poetry itself was almost invincibly reluctant to admit its debt to anger, preferring to conceal the depth of its critical impulse. It is probably no coincidence that in "Song of Joys" Whitman displaces the impulse to quell America on to the separate person of the orator, rather than acknowledge it to be an intimate part of his own constitution as a poet. In fact only once, and then unforgettably, did Whitman ever give a poem over, entire, and in the process give himself up, entirely, to fierce disgust at his America, and that was in the piece entitled "Respondez." What makes that piece so unforgettable is not so much the quality of the poetry as the bitter quality of the emotion which pervades it, and the ghastly spectacle it seems to afford of a mind temporarily unbalanced, defeated by the American (and of course the world) scene. No wonder the marginal notes in the *Blue Book* describe the piece as "A cry in a dream I heard, with ironical taunting . . . we may as well say it, as think it."[3] Whitman hears not America singing, but America jeering.

It is in this respect one of the darkest of Whitman's dejection odes, although it has not been given nearly the amount or quality of attention that others, such as "As I Ebb'd with the Ocean of Life," have received. And in its wilder lines it seems to echo the maddened Lear's cry, "Let copulation thrive . . .":

> Let all the men of These States stand aside for a few
>   smouchers! Let the few seize on what they choose! Let the
>   rest gawk, giggle, starve, obey!
> Let shadows be furnish'd with genitals! Let substances be
>   deprived of their genitals!
> . . . . .
> Let the she-harlots and the he-harlots be prudent! Let them

> dance on, while seeming lasts! (O seeming! seeming!
> seeming!)
>
> . . . . .
>
> Let insanity have charge of sanity!   (1:263)

But there is a method in this madness—a methodical rage for disorder which is the demonic parody of the rage for order that customarily sustains Whitman's verse. On the cosmic scale (as Whitman is, of course, by vocation a cosmic poet) it manifests itself as a great nay-saying, or Fiat Nox which eclipses the Fiat Lux. Whitman deliberately abuses his poetic power by exercising it to speak the uncreating word, the unspoken, unspeakable, vocabulary of his society's actions: "Let the crust of hell be neared and trod on! Let the days be darker than the nights! Let slumber bring less slumber than waking time brings! / Let the world never appear to him or her for whom it was all made! / . . . Let the sun and moon go! Let scenery take the applause of the audience! Let there be apathy under the stars!" (1:261). On the social level the poem includes a series of demonically inspired variations on the cherished motto of economic individualism, "Laissez faire, laissez aller"—"Let there be money, business, railroads, imports, exports, custom, authority, precedents, pallor, dyspepsia, smut, ignorance, unbelief!" (1:262). While on a more personal and poignant scale the poem, in being structured out of "Lets," is a sad perversion of the indispensable grammatical structure of bridging imperatives upon which Whitman's optimistic poetry depends at every crucial juncture of faith ("Take my leaves, America," or "Incarnate me, as I have incarnated you").

There is also in the poem, however, an invigorating note of re-venge, which eventually turns the piece into a poet's curse—not that direct curse which occurs when a bardic and prophetic poet uses his magical verbal powers to blight his enemy ("Ruin seize thee, ruthless king!") but the indirect curse, which entails the withholding by the poet of those healing arts uniquely in his gift, from a society that is thus abandoned to its own catastrophically destructive devices. At the end of the *Apology for Poetry*, it will be remembered, Sir Philip Sidney pronounces just such a curse, with an air of whimsy certainly, but also as a wittily clinching proof of how indispensable the powers of poetry after all are to the human condition:

But if, (fie of such a but) you be born so near the dull-making *cataract of Nilus,* that you cannot hear the planet-like music of poetry, if you have so earth-creeping a mind, that it cannot lift itself up, to look to the sky of Poetry; or rather, by a certain rustical disdain, will become such a mome, as to be a *Momus* of Poetry: then, though I will not wish unto you, the asses ears of *Midas,* nor to be driven by a poet's verses, (as *Bubonax* was) to hang himself, nor to be rhymed to death, as is said to be done in Ireland: yet thus much curse I must send you in the behalf of all poets, that while you live, you live in love, and never get favour, for lacking skill of a *sonnet:* and when you die, your memory die from the earth, for want of an *epitaph.*[4]

"Respondez" is also, in its way, Whitman's defense of poetry in general, and of his own poetry in particular. Moreover, it qualifies as defense in two very different, even opposite, respects. First, it offers a negative definition and justification of what a poet can positively accomplish, through its demonstration of what happens when his saving action is suspended. And second, it functions as a defensive, or protective, fantasy for Whitman himself as a poet. It allows him to threaten his society in fantasy with the withholding of a service which will in reality never be missed, because it was never actually wanted.

This service, usually so readily performed by Whitman, is the service of praise, and its prevailing mode is not curse but rather the contrary, blessing. By imputing to contemporary, everyday American life a full measure of the ideal qualities he wishes it to possess, he represents it as already being the virtual embodiment of its Platonic conception of itself. This is, of course, one of the most ancient of those services the poet has rendered his community, formally recognized as constituting the important literary genre of eulogy. When, however, the term "poetry of praise" has been applied to Whitman's work its meaning has tended to be confined to the broadly religious or spiritual realm, whereas if the social features of traditional praise-poetry were to be recalled, Whitman's achievements in this style would be much more fully appreciated. In fact it would be useful to regard Whitman's praise of the spiritual order of the natural universe as a concealed form of inspirational praise of the premises upon which, in his view, the particular social and political order of the United States is based.

These and related aspects of the poetry will be examined in the succeeding chapters, but first more detailed attention needs to be given both to Whitman's expressed dissatisfaction, in some of his early poetry, with the current state of American affairs, and to the actual social grounds for this dissatisfaction. In the following passage from "Poem of You, Whoever You Are" Whitman's extravagant impulse to praise the unsung qualities of the nondescript American is based on the premise that the ordinary man presently lacks his full measure of self-respect:

> I will leave all, and come and make the hymns of you;
> None have understood you, but I understand you,
> None have done justice to you, you have not done justice
>   to yourself,
> None but have found you imperfect, I only find no
>   imperfection in you,
> None but would subordinate you, I only am he who will
>   never consent to subordinate you,
> I only am he who places over you no master, owner, better,
>   god, beyond what waits intrinsically in yourself.   (1:215)

When considering the attitude Whitman adopts towards the reader, critics have customarily resorted to several widely accepted kinds of explanation. Considered from a psychological point of view, Whitman is usually regarded as unconsciously wishing to associate others with those feelings of loneliness and insecurity from which he is commonly believed to have suffered, in an attempt to mitigate his own sense of isolation. If, by contrast, the critic refers to historical rather than personal circumstances, a whole cluster of ideas is likely to be invoked with the single aim of demonstrating that Whitman conforms, after his own admittedly peculiar fashion, to one or other of the features popularly supposed to typify his age. His anti-authoritarianism may for instance be (very properly) mentioned, and then coupled with his (undeniable) devotion to the common man so as to leave a vague and misleading impression of his preaching a version, at least, of the contemporary gospel of buoyant self-reliance.

But historians have recently been at work revising, and complicating, the previously accepted picture of mid-nineteenth-century American society, and some of their findings are proving to be of great assistance to the student of Whitman. When properly appreciated and attended to, theirs is an approach that can open the way to a reconsideration of the social climate within which the poetry itself took shape, thus providing an insight into the unique kind of social criticism—much subtler and more historically penetrating than that displayed in "Respondez"—which, at its best, the early poetry has to offer.

The most obviously important contribution historians have made in this connection has been their criticism of the prevailing idea that because prewar America was still largely a preindustrial, as well as an overwhelmingly rural, country, it had yet to experience the transition to urban-commercial capitalism which was to transform and galvanize society during the immediate postwar years. In fact it is now clear that from the 1820s on America was involved in a process of quiet but revolutionary change toward this postwar state, and that the liberal dream of individual freedom and equality came under extreme pressure during that time. The Locofocos and the Barnburners, informal political groupings that deeply influenced Whitman, were only the most dramatic of many responses to the serious threat expanding capitalism posed to the social, economic, and political power of the ordinary man, the average American. The political rights he had gained from the Jacksonian administration were proving to be ineffectual, as "mass-democracy . . . served only to shift power from a responsible political elite to the new breed of technicians, the politicians and journalists."[5] Simultaneously his economic freedom was seriously restricted by capitalistic constraints, which he was inclined to blame on corporate power grown monstrous through the connivance of a corrupt and excessively powerful central government.

There was in fact no way in which popular liberalism, with its noble dream of equal rights and opportunities spread throughout society, could prevent the appearance of the pronounced social and economic inequalities that were built into this expansive phase of capitalism. Ironically, several of the attempts made over a period of twenty-five years or more preceding the Civil War to return power to the democratic masses actually aggravated rather than improved the situation, as E. K. Spann has pointed out. In 1846 while the Barnburners "did not succeed in eliminating corruption from government, they did succeed in weakening government as a constructive power for the public good. In trying to expand the freedom of the individual, they left him naked before the new forms of power required to organize Americans in an increasingly massive democratic and capitalist society."[6]

But this pattern of events was to become clear only to the postwar generation, which was by then able to conceive a constructive form of central-government intervention that could actually protect the ordinary population against the depredations of monopoly. This notion of government as the defender rather than the enemy of popular rights was unthinkable to prewar Americans, since it lay outside their bitter historical experience of the prosperous alliance between government and big business. This was the oppressive partnership on which leading liberals fixed, not altogether correctly, the blame for the sharp decline in the individual's influence over economic and political affairs. As Spann has noted, Whitman's acquaintance William Cullen Bryant, "like Leggett, spoke for those unnumbered Americans who felt a sense of frustration and impotence before political and economic events beyond their control."[7]

Whitman also spoke for and to those very same Americans, which explains why his poetry so often presupposes a disaffected and demoralized readership. His special constituency was therefore this very large one of the dispossessed, and he nursed that constituency very carefully in his poems. His motives in so doing were confused. Had he been directly challenged on the subject, he would very probably have fallen back on arguments closely resembling those of liberal dogma. But then his prattlings about the soul were not exactly part of the daily currency of that tradition. Instead they bespeak his otherwise unspoken hope that in those "workers" disqualified as yet from participating fully in their society's opportunities, he would discover the tender growing points of an alternative consciousness. Needless to say he was sadly mistaken, but it was nevertheless a conviction that served him well as a poet.

THE UNTITLED second poem in the 1855 *Leaves of Grass* (eventually called "A Song for Occupations") offers several particularly good examples of Whitman's ability to enter with an intelligence that seems to have been largely intuitive into what was at that time the complex fate of so many unsuccessful individuals; to be led, imperceptibly, by circumstances, into self-estrangement and social alienation. The underlying concern of this poem makes itself known in the question that surfaces almost precisely midway through the piece: "Will the whole come back then?" (1:91). The loss of the conception of the complete human being is what Whitman vehemently charges his society with, and he exhorts it to make good that loss. That nebulous word "soul" is invoked to communicate to others his conviction that they have allowed themselves to be devalued, silently demoralized by accepting the current market prices for their lives and by relying on the crude descriptive terms of social classification for their self-identity. "Souls of men and women! it is not you I call unseen, unheard, untouchable and untouching; / It is not you I go argue pro and con about, and to settle whether you are alive or no" (1:85–86). Vague in meaning the word "soul" may very well be here, but it is by no means vacuous, as it is in his later poetry when used as part of a vapid vocabulary of spiritual transcendence. In the quoted passage it is a term transcendent in the historical rather than the metaphysical sense of the word. Its significance lies in its origin outside the universe of discourse within which American society has come to live, and therefore in its capacity to criticize that universe of discourse. It is for Whitman, at this stage of his poetic career, a key critical term, and what it signifies is nebulous only because of current society's false conception of what is real, substantial, and precise about human being.

By practicing such criticism, Whitman commits himself to pitting his ineffectual strength against the whole weight of the American predilection for respecting the power of money to decide personal worth and to dictate the terms of personal relations:

> Neither a servant nor a master am I,
> I take no sooner a large price than a small price . . . . I will
>   have my own whoever enjoys me,
> I will be even with you, and you shall be even with
>   me. (1:84)

Here he sets the pace and an example of how to define oneself in terms other than those of the cash nexus and of market relations. But this is only one of several ways he has of encouraging the contemporary reader to reassess the values he has allowed to govern his life.

Another, and very important, way derives from Whitman's realization that a person's self-image is crucially affected by his impression of how others perceive him and by their conduct toward him. Consequently, Whitman sets out to provide the very confirmation a person can find only in the eyes of others, while offering to supply it for experiences the person has never previously dreamt could be opened to public sanction: "I own publicly who you are, if nobody else owns . . . . and see and hear you, and what you give and take" (1:86). In fact, the unacknowledged purpose of much of Whitman's poetry in this vein is to break down the distinction between public and private life, for reasons which are simple but far-reaching. Public life, official society, works by relegating all those aspects of human need which present social organization cannot satisfy to the realm of private feelings and personal relationships. And in acceding to this arrangement people implicitly agree not to look to the one sphere of life to supply the satisfactions of the other. Thus is the "whole" man divided, and out of that self-division frequently come fundamental self-contradictions. It is, after all, not unusual for the conduct and character of the "self" in the public world to be, as Dickens demonstrated with Wemmick, the very opposite in substantial respects of the conduct and character of the self in the realm of "personal" relationships. What Whitman encourages, therefore, is the carrying of preoccupations that characterize private life into the wider public domain:

> If you are a workman or workwoman I stand as nigh as the
> nighest that works in the same shop,
> If you bestow gifts on your brother or dearest friend, I
> demand as good as your brother or dearest friend,
> If your lover or husband or wife is welcome by day or night,
> I must be personally as welcome. (1:84)

There is, on the face of it, something faintly ludicrous and even offensive about the way Whitman thrusts his unwanted attention upon these intimate situations. Two's company, three's a crowd, and he seems always to be insisting on being just that one person too many, whose presence is bound to alter the color and tone of the occasion. But if the effect is to violate the reader's privacy, it is perhaps what he intends, since in such privacy Whitman finds evidence of the disengagement of vital emotions from the activities of a public life that must therefore become increasingly bankrupt of serious human content.

During the forties and fifties Whitman had seen his hopes for the establishment of some version of direct democracy in America defeated by the emergence of a representative democracy in which the ideal of a *polis,* that is, of a genuinely self-governing community, was replaced by the actuality of party politics and professional politicians. Citizens had delegated the responsibilities of running their society to a few, and those few had constituted themselves into a power-class which thoroughly controlled and intimidated public opinion. The situation has been well summarized by Spann:

> As early as the 1820's the reign of the amateur, if it ever existed, was yielding to the influence of politicians, journalists, and the professional opinion-makers. Ironically, the very individualism for which the liberals were fighting contributed to this development, since professional organizers were required in order to form the mass of individuals into that force needed for effective popular government. Here was the paradox of individualism in a republic: effective government demanded organized efforts, yet such efforts brought into being technicians who specialized in manipulating people in defiance of the ideal of free individualism.[8]

The final triumph of this class of political operators stemmed from the fact that their answerability to the people, although frequently proclaimed, was no longer seriously believed by the generality of the population, which had come to regard its supreme governors as qualitatively different from themselves:

> Why what have you thought of yourself?
> Is it you then that thought yourself less?
> Is it you that thought the President greater than you? or the
>   rich better off than you? or the educated wiser than
>   you?   (1:85)

What Whitman is in fact reacting against, not altogether wittingly, is the development of a highly differentiated population that a rapidly expanding, constantly evolving, capitalistic society both requires and produces. Important areas of national life rapidly become the prerogative of those specialists and classes that make a profession out of the work of the political, economic, and even cultural sectors. His reaction is not directly to urge particular reforms, but to attempt to promote an outlook that will reclaim the whole of social life as the legitimate domain of every private individual's unremitting concern and attention:

> The sum of all known value and respect I add up in you
>   whoever you are;
> The President is up there in the White House for you . . . . it
>   is not you who are here for him,
> The Secretaries act in their bureaus for you . . . . not you here
>   for them,
> The Congress convenes every December for you,
> Laws, courts, the forming of states, the charters of cities, the
>   going and coming of commerce and mails are all for you.
>
> All doctrines, all politics and civilization exurge from
>   you.   (1:90).

Wherever he looks, Whitman sees signs that social, political, and economic life in America is increasingly so constructed as to offer the individual only a fragmented glimpse of his complete self, while persuading him that the fragment is the whole. One important instance, for Whitman, is the change in the whole ethos of work, as it becomes part of the new system of economic production inaugurated by a rapidly developing capitalistic system. Not only is the purpose and value of work no longer directly related to the exercise of the laborer's skills, but the very diversity of occupations valued by Whitman has in reality far less to do with the multiplicity of traditional crafts and trades (by which he was himself surrounded when young) than with the divisions of labor created by the complex, impersonal demands of an extensive continental and intercontinental market.

Whitman appreciates that as work and the products of work are ever more directly associated with the earning of money, they are in imminent danger of being reduced to economic transactions. Thus when he undertakes a comprehensive listing of occupations, it is under the impulse to reawaken a joyful wonder in people at the great richness of human significance that is discoverable in their everyday world of work:

> Shipcarpentering, flagging of sidewalks by flaggers . .
>   dockbuilding, fishcuring, ferrying;
> The pump, the piledriver, the great derrick . . the coalkiln
>   and brickkiln,
> Ironworks or whiteleadworks . . the sugarhouse . . steam-
>   saws, and the great mills and factories;
> The cottonbale . . the stevedore's hook . . the saw and buck
>   of the sawyer . . the screen of the coalscreener . . the mould
>   of the moulder . . the workingknife of the butcher.
>   (1:93–94)

He disconnects the working scene from its wider economic context—"What is it that you made money? what is it that you got what you wanted?" (1:91)—and reconstructs it as a valuable, self-contained social world of persons at work. Although this is an important regular practice of Whitman's in his poetry (as will be seen in Chapter 3), what is relatively unusual is to find him displaying such awareness of exactly what he's doing. At the end of this lengthy passage, in which he has been crusading to have "all trades, their gear and tackle and trim," as Hopkins put it, appreciated as part of the pied beauty of ordinary American life, he quietly reduces this to its bottom line— the making and spending of money:

> The column of wants in the one-cent paper . . the news by
>   telegraph . . . . the amusements and operas and shows:
> The cotton and woolen and linen you wear . . . . the money
>   you make and spend;
> Your room and bedroom . . . . your piano-forte . . . . the
>   stove and cook-pans,
> The house you live in . . . . the rent . . . . the other
>   tenants . . . . the deposits in the savings-bank . . . . the
>   trade at the grocery,
> The pay on Saturday night . . . . the going home, and
>   the purchases;
> In them the heft of the heaviest . . . . in them far more than
>   you estimated, and far less also,

> In them, not yourself . . . . you and your soul enclose all
>   things, regardless of estimation,
> In them your themes and hints and provokers . . if not, the
>   whole earth has no themes or hints or provokers, and never
>   had.   (1:96–97)

Not for the last time he tries to explain that his quarrel is not with money as such, but with the different, dominant role money is coming to assume in people's lives in what we can now, in retrospect, clearly identify as a revolutionary new phase of capitalist society.

In fact the underlying purpose of the whole of the passage has been to try to compensate for some of the damage to human awareness caused by this advance into urban–industrial capitalism. A single line can furnish a useful example of this: "The paper I write on or you write on . . and every word we write . . and every cross and twirl of the pen . . and the curious way we write what we think . . . . yet very faintly" (1:92). The effect of that line is to establish that paper and pen are as much the products, and therefore the record, of remarkable mental processes as is writing itself. It is exceptionally important for Whitman (like Blake) to emphasize the ideality of the physical world, because his whole environment is rapidly filling with things which no longer bear recognizable human signatures. Products are no longer self-evidently the end result of the human processes that actually produced them:

> The directory, the detector, the ledger . . . . the books in
>   ranks or the bookshelves . . . . the clock attached to
>   the wall,
> The ring on your finger . . the lady's wristlet . . the hammers
>   of stonebreakers or coppersmiths . . the druggist's vials
>   and jars;
> The etui of surgical instruments, and the etui of oculist's or
>   aurist's instruments, or dentist's instruments;
> Glassblowing, grinding of wheat and corn . . casting, and
>   what is cast . . tinroofing, shingledressing.   (1:92–93)

If in this way he invites the reader to reconnect material goods, through the instruments that fashion them, with the mental and physical processes that brought them into being, he also urges workers to look beyond the narrow confines of their independent occupations and to discover a solidarity with other workers which can give to their own efforts a revolutionary new pride in common purpose. Moreover, as Wilentz has pointed out, whereas "to upper and middle-class New Yorkers, the outset of metropolitan industrialisation appeared mainly as a dazzling cavalcade of new commodities, 'suited to every market,' " to "the craft workers it was the intensity of labour, the underpayment, and the subordination to the rule of another that was most apparent."[9] Whitman tries to counteract the effects of this segmentation and commodification.

In each of these respects he aims to provide the connecting tissue that will reconstitute his dismembered society into a whole, organic body. The poem is in fact haunted by images of dissociation, disjunction, and separation right from its very opening:

> Come closer to me,
> Push close my lovers and take the best I possess,
> Yield closer and closer and give me the best you possess.
>
> This is unfinished business with me . . . . how is it with you?
> I was chilled with the cold types and cylinder and wet paper
>   between us.   (1:83–84)

During the 1830s in America newspapers had developed into the first mass medium of democratic society, and Whitman, a newspaperman, had been part of that development. Subsequently—and indeed consequently—he became as disillusioned with journalism as he was with political management of public opinion in general, of which journalism was a part.[10] The widespread use of print as a medium of communication, therefore, naturally became expressive for Whitman of the obstacles preventing people from making immediate, unmediated contact with others. In the technical process of setting words in type he finds a suitably graphic illustration of the social and political mechanisms dividing individual from individual in the emergent America, and so preventing the emergence of a genuinely popular democracy.

There has been a pronounced tendency for critics to interpret the sentiments of lines such as these almost exclusively in terms of the peculiarities of Whitman's own psychology, and to overlook the extent to which he is accurately recording objective features of contemporary social relationships. These are commented on later in the poem as well: "I bring what you much need, yet always have, / I bring not money or amours or dress or eating . . . . but I bring as good; / And send no agent or medium . . . . and offer no representatives of value— but offer the value itself" (1:87). Again, individuals are perceived to be communicating with one another only indirectly, through the medium of social and economic signifiers, including a whole range of indicators of status, the most important of which, clearly, is money. Moreover, behind that promise of Whitman's to "offer no representative of value—but offer the value itself," there may very well lurk not only an objection to some of the dramatic social consequences of an advanced money economy, but also an awareness of the changing character of money itself. By the 1850s America had come to rely heavily on paper currency, in which a note was issued in lieu of gold. Indeed the socioeconomic structure of mid-nineteenth-century America depended directly on devices for producing financial flexibility and fluidity, of which paper money was a vital example.

Back in the thirties the country had seen a multitude of little banks, throughout the states, busily printing money that was not solidly backed by gold. This arrangement could, and did, bring bust as well as boom both to individuals and to virtually the whole community— indeed the disastrous collapse of the economy in 1837 was partly attributable to the recklessness of this practice. Rag money came to be identified in the eyes of aghast moderates (whose thinking in such matters was frequently, like Whitman's, a survival from a bygone age) with the untrustworthiness that resulted from the substitution of a token, which could fluctuate wildly in value, for the gold itself, the value of which was comparatively stable. In November 1846 Whitman devoted an editorial to this controversial issue, under the heading "Case of People vs. Paper." As he explained, he saw "the Paper Genius on the one side, and the Genius of a Republican People on the other, come in conflict."[11] He identified the former with the bullying Goliath of corporate business interests: "The manufactors, aiders and abettors of the present circulating medium of this country, (as great an incubus on its young energies, as impure air is to growing youth,) have gone on diffusing through the land all the circumstances of the paper system, until it has absolutely become unbearable—its tendency being to inflation, to derangement of the uniformity of value, to 'make the rich richer and the poor, poorer.' "[12] Behind the greenbacks he detected the gross alliance between banks and big business which, by fostering economic inequalities, threatened to damage the very fabric of democratic society.

It needs to be emphasized however that, as far as the poetry is concerned, these particular circumstances matter not in themselves, but only for what they suggested to Whitman about the direction society was taking. They were indicative of its departure from solid, reliable, proven standards of conduct. They were representative of everything that was involved in the mania for wealth. Unwilling to jettison the economic system, yet appalled at some of its consequences, Whitman preferred to blame the latter on those whom he regarded as unscrupulous exploiters of the economy and manipulators of the innocent American people. Banks and financiers were regarded as particularly dangerous ogres, as was the whole accursed race of speculators.

Yet in "Song for Occupations" Whitman correctly notes that in a rapidly growing, dynamic, capitalist society the speculative outlook is by no means confined to speculators. The credit arrangements, for example, upon which the American economy depended at every level, had speculation of sorts built into them both from the side of the borrower and from the side of the lender. Along with its diametric opposite, prudence (about which, as we shall see in Chapter 2, Whitman also discoursed at length), speculation is a basic ingredient in the complex psychology of economic liberalism, and as such is distributed throughout the whole striving, aspiring, population. Moreover, it consequently manifests itself well beyond the narrow field of economic endeavor, since it enters into and fashions every individual's response to life itself. As such, it is a fundamental characteristic of developing American psychology, which Whitman must directly confront and challenge:

> The sun and stars that float in the open air . . . . the
>   appleshaped earth and we upon it . . . . surely the drift of
>   them is something grand;
> I do not know what it is except that it is grand, and that
>   it is happiness,
> And that the enclosing purport of us here is not a speculation,
>   or bon-mot or reconnoissance,

> And that it is not something which by luck may turn out well
>   for us, and without luck must be a failure for us,
> And not something which may yet be retracted in a certain
>   contingency.   (1:88)

"Speculation" refers here in the first instance to a mental climate in which important ideas are lightly entertained on the supposition that, since the truth cannot be proven or disproven, they are only a form of pleasurable but inconsequential surmise. But the further, related, implication is that American society, predisposed to view life in terms of luck and gamble, renders itself incapable of making serious human choices and commitments. The passage thus offers a perfect example of Whitman's capacity to discover those underlying connections between apparently different spheres of activity that give the new American character its particular consistency and coherence.

Whitman's assessment of that character includes anomalies which directly betray the conflict of feelings that he, a transitional figure struggling to connect in his own person two very different periods of American history, was made to suffer. Like the majority of his countrymen, he particularly prized the American's freedom from the stifling gradations and stratifications of established European society and his freedom to determine his social fate by his own efforts. He was therefore apparently committed to regarding a man's worth as an unknown quantity to be decided by his actual achievements. But in America social status was by the middle of the century becoming a by-product of economic success, and so Whitman was confronted with the trend that under these circumstances a man's worth was liable to be measured in terms of money. Moreover, as capitalism developed apace, it was increasingly obvious that success in these terms was by no means directly related to personal effort, nor could it even be arranged that everyone begin with the same initial opportunities. Consequently, a central feature of Whitman's poetry is the insistence that human worth is totally independent both of social background and financial achievement. An individual's worth is constant, since it relates to his existence as a soul, and not to the vagaries of his life as a social and economic being. Personal value antedates social success and survives social failure: it inheres in the person himself and is inalienable.

> Because you are greasy or pimpled—or that you was once
>   drunk, or a thief, or diseased, or rheumatic, or a
>   prostitute—or are so now—or from frivolity or
>   impotence—or that you are no scholar, and never saw your
>   name in print . . . do you give in that you are any less
>   immortal?   (1:85)

The sentiment is a familiar one—Whitman is after all widely loved
as the consoler of the despised and rejected—but it should be noted
that this apparently timeless wisdom sprang from the experiences of
a particular historical epoch. This universal truth is, in Whitman's
case, very much the mature product of his involvement in a distinctive
set of social circumstances.

IN OTHER POEMS of this period even nature is occasionally felt by
Whitman to represent, in the scale of its operations, a serious threat
to the self-confidence which is necessary to the human individual,
who is urged to discover within himself, in reply, resources more
than equal to the elemental forces by which he is threatened:

> Whoever you are, you are to hold your own at any hazard,
> These shows of the east and west are tame compared to you,
> These immense meadows, these interminable rivers—you are
>   immense and interminable as they,
> These furies, elements, storms, motions of nature, throes of
>   apparent dissolution—you are he or she who is master or
>   mistress over them.   (1:216)

The immediate reference is, of course, to the outrageous size of
the American continent, where man is inescapably confronted with,
and his human dignity easily affronted by, the unaccommodated nature of Nature. The poetry therefore attempts to arrange an accom-
modation, a reconciliation of man and nature through the medium
of spirit.

Later on in his writing career, in "Passage to India," Whitman
specifically describes the poet's primary task as giving a humanly
intelligible voice to "this cool, impassive, voiceless earth" (3:568).
The story of Adam and Eve's expulsion from Eden is read as an

allegory of mankind's desperate intuition that human life is an accidental phenomenon, in which no clue can be found to Nature's larger, nonhuman purposes:

> Ah, who shall soothe these feverish children?
> Who justify these restless explorations?
> Who speak the secret of impassive Earth?
> Who bind it to us? What is this separate Nature, so
>   unnatural?   (3:567)[13]

The poet's particular responsibility, in this context, is to alleviate anxiety by using his poetry to reintegrate the natural and human orders, so that "Nature and Man shall be disjoin'd and diffused no more" (3:568). Such passages allow us to regard Whitman's optimistic poetry as the determinedly brave face put on things by a troubled Victorian mind, as it discovered, in the uncompromising character and extent of the American continent, disturbingly enlarged grounds for doubting the centrality of man's place in the universal scheme.

But in the present context it is not the spiritually vexed question of mankind's relationship to nature that is of immediate interest, but the social content of this relation. In the "Poem of You, Whoever You Are" the helplessness Whitman's contemporaries are prone to feel when faced by the might of natural processes is seen as simply one, albeit extreme, example of their general inability to believe that through their own attitudes and actions they can, to any significant degree, determine their own destinies. The inference is that their existential anxiety is partly a social symptom, and the work of recent historians has already enabled us to follow the aetiology of the underlying disease. Having been deprived by recent economic and political developments of effective control even over their limited personal affairs, the victims of change were left in a disorientated state which colored their whole outlook. In *Democratic Vistas* Whitman explicitly compares destructive natural forces with widespread social upheaval in terms of their disruptive effects on human life: "As I perceive, the tendencies of our day, in the States, (and I entirely respect them,) are toward these vast and sweeping movements, influences, moral and physical, of humanity, now and always current over the planet, on the scale of the impulses of the elements. Then it is also good to reduce the whole matter to the consideration of a single self, a man, a woman, on permanent grounds" (2:393). "Song of Myself" is an attempt to bring contemporary life under control in this way.

Social powerlessness produced, in those worst affected, intimations of their cosmic insignificance, inducing a fatalism which was itself a thoroughly characteristic symptom of that state of mental disorder which this changing society promoted. In the concluding lines of "Song for Occupations" Whitman uncovers further aspects of this disturbed social mentality:

> When the psalm sings instead of the singer,
> When the script preaches instead of the preacher,
> When the pulpit descends and goes instead of the carver that
>   carved the supporting desk,
> When the sacred vessels or the bits of the eucharist, or the lath
>   and plast, procreate as effectually as the young silversmiths
>   or bakers, or the masons in their overalls,
> When a university course convinces like a slumbering woman
>   and child convince,
> When the minted gold in the vault smiles like the
>   nightwatchman's daughter,
> When warrantee deeds loafe in chairs opposite and are my
>   friendly companions,
> I intend to reach them my hand and make as much of them as
>   I do of men and women.   (1:98)

Concealed within this calculated flight of apparently absurd fancy to a seriously unthinkable topsy-turvy world, is in fact a shrewd observation of the perverted social formations emerging in Whitman's own time. Considered from a Marxist point of view, what the passage offers, although in a spirit of play, is an almost classic description of the workings of the alienated mind, to which the products of human effort appear to possess a mysteriously self-generated and self-supporting life of their own. But whether or not the full Marxist explanation is accepted, in all its implications, what Whitman has unquestionably done is intuitively grasp one of the most significant structural features of the new capitalist psychology, namely, its reversal of cause and effect. Man understands himself with reference to the supposedly independent operations of a reality he has himself constructed. Depending partly on his social situation, the individual is either fascinated (like the possessive bourgeois) or dominated (like the laborer) by the commodified world of objects, and the commodified objective world, he has brought into existence.

Sensitive though he was to these changes in human consciousness, Whitman did not inquire too closely or analytically into their ultimate sources in the underlying economic assumptions of his society, as these were being practically demonstrated in his own period. To have done so would in any case have been to cast more than a shadow of a doubt on the economic foundations of a way of life whose essential character seemed to him to be indisputably natural, and self-evidently admirable. He regarded those threatening features of capitalism which were becoming apparent in mid-nineteenth-century America, not as consistent with, but as a departure from, the basic principles of American society, principles that were for him contained within the specifically political ideal of popular democracy as defined by writers such as Tom Paine.[14] In his pioneering pamphlet *Common Sense* Paine had, at the very moment when the new state was being independently established, given typically memorable expression to the political aspects of the negative liberalism on which he argued it was founded. He distinguished between "Society," which was the product of man's innate sociability, and "Government," which at best was but a necessary evil. "Government, like dress, is the badge of lost innocence; the palaces of kings [and also, he could have added, the parliaments of democratic societies] are built on the ruins of the bowers of paradise."[15]

In his poetry Whitman tried to recover, to recreate, those paradisal conditions. In his prose he argued fiercely for the minimum of government compatible with a defense of people's "life, liberty, and property." Officials of all ranks, even up to the President, were only "agents" of their "master," the people. "The citizen must have room. He must learn to be so muscular and self-possessed . . . This is the feeling that will make live men and superior women."[16] The 1856 "Poem of Remembrances for A Girl or A Boy of these States" made explicit these feelings, which were diffused throughout the early editions of *Leaves of Grass:* "Remember, government is to subserve individuals! / Not any, not the President, is to have one jot more than you or me, / Not any habitan of America is to have one jot less than you or me" (1:252).

Accepting Paine's fundamental distinction between Society and Government, Whitman followed him in regarding the latter, in its grossly overdeveloped form, not only as being inimical to economic freedom (the economic liberals' standard complaint), but also, more importantly, as disturbing the balance of what left to its own devices would have been a healthily self-regulating Society. As Government became centralized, so power passed into the hands of an unrepresentative few, whose exercise of it to consolidate and advance their own interests produced a socioeconomic situation over which the people as a whole had very little control. These were the primarily political circumstances to which Whitman looked for an explanation of what was unsatisfactory about American life, midway through the nineteenth century.

WHITMAN'S ADOPTION of this explanation, along with the outlook that went with it, was not an arbitrary matter. Nor was it his intention to preach a blithe version of the popular gospel of laissez-faire capitalism. Rather, his was a philosophy which flowed quite naturally from the historical experience of that specific social group to which Whitman belonged, both by origin and by conscious allegiance—an experience of being subject to social, economic, and political processes beyond their control, which eventually revolutionized every aspect of their lives, and to which the victims affixed the emotive term "monopoly." At the very end of his life, he pointedly drew Traubel's attention to what would nowadays be called the corporate authorship of *Leaves of Grass,* deliberately sinking his own personality, as he spoke, into the general character of the group with whose situation he closely identified:

> I resolved at the start to diagnose, recognize, state, the case of the mechanics, laborers, artisans, of America—to get into the stream with them—to give them a voice in literature: not an echoed voice—no: their own voice—that which they had never had before. I meant to do this naturally, however—not with apologies—not to lug them in by the neck and heels, in season and out of season, where they did belong and where they didn't belong—but to welcome them to their legitimate superior place—to give them entrance and lodgement by all fair means.[17]

Right up to the Civil War not only were the craft workers in the very vanguard of the labor movement, they also formed the actual numerical majority of the metropolitan workforce. And such had been the changes, over the preceding half-century, in their work conditions that they had been repeatedly forced into a radical reconsideration of those traditional values of their class which, until they were challenged, had seemed to them self-evidently central to the whole American enterprise. They "began to reinterpret their shared ideals of commonwealth, virtue, independence, citizenship, and equality, and struggled over the very meaning of the terms. In so doing, they also revealed the social meanings of republicanism for urban producers— and how they changed."[18] Whitman's poetry can itself be usefully regarded as a contribution to this struggle toward redefinition, since he too struggled, for the same reasons, to come to terms with the new American ethos.

The urban artisan class was that section of the American population which, during Whitman's formative years, was most dramatically affected by the transition to a new stage of capitalism, and especially by the far-reaching social and political consequences of this transition.[19] Under the advancing influence of commercial capitalism, the proletarian and the petty-bourgeois elements of the hybrid social personality of this class were gradually separated out, so that the original "artisan" tended to become either a thriving small entrepreneur and employer, or an employee whose largely obsolescent craft skills were devalued in being regarded, and rewarded, only as a form of skilled labor. The uneasy relationship between the two parts of this split social personality, further compounded by the confused reaction of the disadvantaged and partly proletarianized segment of the class, meant that anyone who tried to voice the artisan experience was almost bound to end up speaking with a forked tongue. It will accordingly be suggested over the next few chapters that this milieu contributed very significantly to the development of Whitman's notoriously ambivalent attitude toward his society.

It was, in any case, the milieu in which the Whitman family had— quite literally—been moving ever since the early-century urban prosperity had attracted Walter Whitman, Sr., like other migrants, from the rural hinterland to practice his craft. These all found a city where social, economic, and political life was dominated by the long-established aristocracy of urban capitalist wealth—the merchants and financiers. No wonder Walter Whitman, and later his son, turned not only to Tom Paine, but also to Fanny Wright and the vigorous agitators who were recasting the old artisanal dream of a free, egalitarian commonwealth into an aggressive new form.

Yet the economic base for so many of these social ideals was already antiquated by the 1820s and totally out of step with the giant strides of capitalist development. Most of the trades were still run on a small, local basis, employing the artisan system of labor, and not yet subject to vast impersonal market forces. Even the concept of the fixed, "just" price—the antithesis of market economics—had continued to operate, until very recently, in certain quarters. But everything was changing quite dramatically even as Walter Whitman, Jr., was growing into young manhood. Cheap labor, increased demand, and geographically expanding markets, led to a transformation first of the means of production and then of the social relations that were implicit in the economic process. The apprenticeship system broke down and was converted into a convenient form of child labor. And as some masters turned into increasingly distant employers, so journeymen became wage earners; and craftsmen (whose mature skills were superfluous to a system of division of labor and out-of-shop contracting) lost out in their unequal competition with cheaper, semiskilled and even unskilled workers.

Whitman's father was fairly typical of the disorientated artisan of this period, struggling to adjust to the new capitalist conditions. By turns a small-scale employer and a wage earner, he worked only fitfully while alternating between the kind of morose sense of isolation that drove many of his class to drink and the "rudimentary class awareness and sense of solidarity" that produced the working-class movements of the late twenties and early thirties, stimulating the passion for education and self-improvement that was evident in his young son.[20] So concerned have Walt's biographers been to ascribe a fixed temperament to his father, they have mostly failed to consider the part that circumstances undoubtedly played in the development of the father's character. Only recently have critics such as Justin Kaplan and Paul Zweig noted the air of social failure and defeat that seemed to surround Walter Whitman, as if he had never quite, to the very end, got the hang of entrepreneurial capitalism. His son Walt shared much of his bewilderment but was to find his own inimitable ways of coping with it, especially in his poetry. The boy who began his working life apprenticed to a printer of the old-fashioned, solid kind was to tell Traubel in old age that he had spent his whole working life as a poet "apprentice[d] to an ideal."[21] That ideal was in turn an amalgam of the two worlds Whitman had known—the mutuality which characterized artisan republican and commonwealth ideals being grafted (sometimes easily, sometimes distinctly uneasily) onto the expansive opportunities (but not the opportunism) of the competitive and libertarian free enterprise system.

Set against this background, "Song for Occupations" itself takes on a new significance. By means of his stately listing of the innumerable, proliferating occupations—and he was careful to update his list in later editions of *Leaves of Grass*—he created out of the mid-century, profit-orientated economy a sort of modern craft pageant similar to the grand parades of a bygone age. On such occasions trade iconography had traditionally been very colorfully in evidence, and with his little stylized vignettes Whitman fashions, out of the living materials and implements of working men and women, his own distinctive guild heraldry. Even the ideology advertised by the poem is similar to that publicized by the pageants—a display of craft solidarity to demonstrate "the common bond and mutual sympathy" existing among the proudly independent trades. Behind the sumptuousness of all that visual rhetoric had originally lain the solid corporate values professed by an artisan class who believed in what has been usefully called a "collective individualism."[22] But from the twenties onward this cooperative ethos came under increasing pressure from the discordant realities of the actual conditions in the shops and from the spirit of bourgeois individualism which was the presiding genius of the emerging capitalist order, committed as it was to the unfettered operations of the open market. Whitman's poem is therefore an intriguing mid-century attempt to infuse the spirit of the old, departed world into the different—and possibly opposite—character of the new America.

The fracturing of the original artisan system led to a whole spectrum of consequences, many of which formed part of the rich social and political experience from which the 1855 *Leaves of Grass* eventually came. True, Whitman was never directly associated with the working-class movements, the rudimentary unionism, reform campaigns, and political realignments of the early thirties. He was in any case too young.[23] But some of the heroes and heroines of that turbulent time, made vivid to him by the enthusiasm of a father who regularly subscribed to Robert Dale Owen's paper the *Free Enquirer,* remained favorites of his to the end of his days. So when Walt actually began to involve himself in politics it was natural for him to espouse a radical Democratic creed that eventually led to his applying to himself the old artisan label "Jeffersonian republican," and that soon prompted his enemies to call him "a well-known Locofoco."[24] As he told Traubel toward the end of his life, referring to his own childhood and youth, "the young radicals of that time have never had justice done to them." Most neglected of all had been their inspirational precursor, old Tom Paine, of whom "our people have been disgracefully oblivious." Furthermore, he added, "I determined I would some day bear my testimony to that whole group of slandered men and women."[25] And so indeed he did—not in the feeble, yet touchingly loyal, lectures he delivered in his old age, but in the gloriously radical vigor of the early *Leaves of Grass.*

Equally important was Whitman's appreciation of leading aspects of that working-class world which was a colorful by-product of all this economic change. In particular he became an honorary freeman of "the Republic of the Bowery," the "pungent" area of New York in which "things are in their working-day clothes, more democratic, with a broader, jauntier swing and in a more direct contact with vulgar life."[26] This was a new social world, fashioned out of the relative poverty of the small masters, journeymen, shopkeepers, mechanics, laborers, and immigrants of the metropolis, and it testified in its every ambiguous detail (including above all its clannishness) to the pressures of the powerful, dominant outside world which had brought it into being. Through its entertainments—from brothels to theaters, and from oyster halls to shooting galleries—it contrived a temporary escape for its members from the economic realities which oppressed them. Whitman particularly enjoyed the "real democratic lager element in the German beerhalls," observing that "there is lager enough on Broadway, but it is not imbibed as it is here, with the genuine working-man's thirst; nor associated, as here, with so many memories of friendship, and with the ideas of relief from toil, and with the social relaxations and pleasures of life."[27]

For the competitive culture of the bourgeoisie the Bowery substituted its own counterculture, a distinctive blend of insular camaraderie and internecine strife. The arrogant macho swagger of the working men of the feuding fire companies and of the young dandies in the street gangs was, moreover, in inverse proportion to their actual economic and social impotence. These were young men "out of step with the calculations of the marketplace or the union meeting, rebels without prospects other than those of the street corner or dance hall."[28] Whitman found it easy to sympathize with them and with the whole world they represented. Contemporaries were even more profoundly right than they supposed when they thought they detected something of the Bowery b'hoy in "Song of Myself." There is again the same defiant and slightly subversive assertiveness in "I Sing the Body Electric," whether Whitman is swimming with the swimmer, wrestling with wrestlers, or marching in line with the firemen "in their own costumes"—or, indeed, whether he is insisting very pointedly on the pure, uneconomic worth of the human body. Even the auction of a slave meant something much more general to Whitman than the insufferable plight of Southern blacks. It meant a system that threatened to degrade the beauty of the human body, and with it the dignity of human labor, to the status of an economic commodity.[29]

> A slave at auction,
> I help the auctioneer . . . . the sloven does not half know
>   his business.
>
> . . . . . .
>
> Examine these limbs, red black or white . . . . they are very
>   cunning in tendon and nerve;
> They shall be stript that you may see them.
>
> Exquisite senses, lifelit eyes, pluck, volition,
> Flakes of breastmuscle, pliant backbone and neck, flesh not
>   flabby, goodsized arms and legs,
> And wonders within there yet.   (1:128–129)

As his pamphlet "The Eighteenth Presidency" makes clear, the immediate fear behind this passage is that those who are economically powerful in the North share the belief of Southern landowners that "the workingmen of a state are unsafe depositaries of political powers and rights, and that a republic can not permanently exist unless those who ply the mechanical trades and attend to the farm-work are slaves, subordinated by strict laws to their master."[30] Although Whitman's analysis was not literally correct, it did nevertheless carry him very close to the heart of the capitalist society which America was developing at this time.

Whitman's rather inchoate mistrust of these developments made him naturally sympathetic to the Bowery. Disregarding the ugly side of the lower-class subculture, he recognized instead its "new ideological significance," namely, "a sort of republicanism of the streets that connected the working men's pride, resentments, and simple pleasures to the language of republican politics."[31] Here, and in the overlapping society of the cabdrivers, railway workers, and ferrymen, there appeared to his idealizing eyes to be the makings of the right American blend of traditional and modern virtues—rugged independence combined with social fellowship, a venturous spirit allied to a considerate nature. He particularly noticed, and approved of, the "openly loving" young couples he saw in the beer halls and the easy acceptance there of sexuality: "but their loving is unnoticed; there is great freedom of the individual permitted here."[32]

Just as Whitman himself moved incessantly between Broadway and the Bowery, so his poems restlessly explore different ways of relating this whole subordinate realm of debased artisan and working-class life to the dominant culture. Sometimes they appear as opposed worlds, alternative systems of values, locked in conflict. At other times the one, in Whitman's prejudiced account of it, seems to adumbrate the perfect or Platonic form of the other—and there are even occasions when they are seen as already being essentially identical, as the poetry is used to blur the distinction between the real and the ideal. At all times Whitman's equivocations gave him admission to the full, central ambivalence of American capitalism, a drama whose unfolding he graphically described as "the plunges and throes and triumphs and falls of democracy" (1:155).

APPROPRIATELY ENOUGH, the 1855 *Leaves of Grass* was itself the direct result of a plunging economic crisis that severely hit the bastard artisan class to which Whitman then loosely belonged. The earlier crises of 1852 had been precipitated by a strike for a living wage by carpenters, coach painters, cigar makers, masons, and other tradesmen, and it prompted Whitman to take steps to provide security for his family. As soon as the situation eased, he took advantage of the subsequent real estate boom to turn to speculative building, of sorts, on his own account. Like so many of the jerry-builders who had taken over the lucrative parts of the construction industry upon the collapse of the artisan system, he had served no proper apprenticeship in the building trades. But not only had he inherited the old-fashioned tradesman's conscience which had made his father such a reliable, and therefore such an impoverished, builder of frame-houses, he was also able to employ his father and two of his brothers as properly skilled carpenters, so the houses he erected were of solid quality.[33] Then, in the spring of 1854, came the slump that put his family, like thousands of others, out of work. Carpenters and printers, along with long-shoreman, laborers, and the rest of the New York work force, flocked in such numbers to the soup kitchens that charitable food supplies were quickly exhausted.[34] And it was during this period of enforced, but in his case welcome, idleness that Whitman, personally protected against the worst consequences of the depression, probably first seriously turned his attention to poetry. "Song of Myself," regarded in this context, is his equivalent to the *Eroica* symphony by Beethoven, which the Philharmonic orchestra defiantly played in the teeth of the depression.[35]

Indeed at least once, in the 1855 edition, this specific social context of the capitalist market economy with its concomitant strikes and dissatisfied labor force is directly mentioned. "To Think of Time" (as it was later called) includes a reference to

> The markets, the government, the workingman's wages . . . .
>   to think what account they are through our nights and days!
> To think that other workingmen will make just as great
>   account of them . . yet we make little or no
>   account.   (1:103)

Since one of the themes of the poem is Death as the great social leveler, there is a sense in which these lines read like a defensive philosophy of social quietism, developed in response to the artisan's chronically helpless situation in the new economy, and couched (as such a philosophy frequently is) in terms of transcendental enlightenment. By thinking loftily "of Time" (eternity), a man can drain the present of its painful urgency and cultivate an exalted indifference: "To take interest is well, and not to take interest shall be well" (1:104).

Whitman even implicitly includes his recent artisanal self in the time-ridden world of everyday affairs he now appears to be renouncing:

> To think how eager we are in building our houses,
> To think others shall be just as eager . . and we
>   quite indifferent.
>
> I see one building the house that serves him a few
>   years . . . . or seventy or eighty years at most;
> I see one building the house that serves him longer than
>   that.   (1:101)

But Whitman fights against the tendency of his poem to move in this acquiescent, socially quiescent, direction. There is indeed almost a kind of wit in the way he eventually puts this philosophy to a different, and militant, use. He turns instead into a social leveler, whose role is to humble the mighty and exalt the humble. And even though, with his customary panache, he proceeds to do this on a worldwide scale, it is clear he is reacting primarily to the economically induced inequalities of his own society, in which carpenters, masons, and laborers were indeed persuaded to translate their experience of social helplessness into a sense of personal worthlessness. To combat this he provides them, and other socially despised groups, with an honored place in the history of the continuing evolution of mankind:

> The interminable hordes of the ignorant and wicked are
>   not nothing,
> The barbarians of Africa and Asia are not nothing,
> The common people of Europe are not nothing . . . . the
>   American aborigines are not nothing,
> A zambo or a foreheadless Crowfoot or a Camanche is
>   not nothing,
> The infected in the immigrant hospital are not nothing . . . .
>   the murderer or mean person is not nothing,
> The perpetual succession of shallow people are not nothing as
>   they go,
> The prostitute is not nothing . . . . the mocker of religion is
>   not nothing as he goes.
>
> I shall go with the rest . . . . we have satisfaction.   (1:106)

It also becomes clear, as the poem proceeds, that "To Think of Time" engages with, and criticizes, the attitudes toward time that are implicit in, and necessary to, capitalist society. Since this is a subject which will be dealt with in the next chapter, there is no need to consider it here, but a more general point should be made. In its move away from a literalist depiction of social facts, and toward a resourceful criticism of contemporary social consciousness, "To Think of Time" is representative of *Leaves of Grass* as a whole, as the following chapters will attempt to show. The whole style of the poetry is, after all, ultimately directed to this very end. Even if the first and later editions of *Leaves of Grass* were, indeed, in a way and to an extent only partly recognized by Whitman himself, the "voice" of the artisans, nevertheless the "language" spoken by that voice—the grammar, as it were, of Whitman's thinking—is very decidedly not that of the mechanics and laborers. A serious attempt at measuring and theoretically explaining the distance, and difference, between the original social experience and its mature formulation in art, would involve a consideration of what has come to be called the "mediated" nature of the latter. Such an exercise lies outside the scope of this book. But insofar as the extremely complex point at issue is at some stage likely to involve the question of why Whitman's art is not mimetic and does not openly embrace the relevant social materials, then it may be worth briefly considering Whitman's reservation about the convention of descriptive realism.

That it is not neutral description, but a prejudiced convention, a literary style which secretly embodies and stealthily promotes an unacceptable set of extra-literary assumptions about the nature of the world, is what he wants to emphasize. Realism is not the presentation of substantive reality—it is a particular construction placed on reality, and a misconstruction from Whitman's point of view. His objections are usually couched in militantly idealist terms, and involve the advancing of spirit's claims against those of reductive materialism. But what he is actually doing is refusing the positivist categories of bourgeois thought and denying the validity of the kind of significance it finds in things and in lives. And poetry, as he made clear in *Democratic Vistas,* is (at least in this respect) for him a vital means, a medium, of subversion:

> Fearless of scoffing, and of the ostent, let us take our stand, our ground, and never desert it, to confront the growing excess and

arrogance of realism. To the cry, now victorious—the cry of sense, science, flesh, incomes, farms, merchandise, logic, intellect, demonstrations, solid perpetuities, buildings of brick and iron, or even the facts of the shows of trees, earth, rocks, etc., fear not, my brethren, my sisters, to sound out with equally determin'd voice, that conviction brooding within the recesses of every envision'd soul—illusions! apparitions! figments all! (2:417–418)

This dismissal of the physical world is, however, only a prologue to the readmission of it on different terms. Whitman envisages the poet recovering it by presenting it as a scene "in which power transacts itself." By "power" he means spiritual purposiveness, and he describes the poet's role as being to construct, out of the actual materials, and in the very image of the present time, a world which will be the embodiment of the serious purposes and possibilities of human life. "The poet, the esthetic worker in any field, by the divine magic of his genius, projects them, their analogies, by curious removes, indirections, in literature and art. (No useless attempt to repeat the material creation, by daguerreotyping the exact likeness by mortal mental means.) This is the image-making faculty, coping with material creation, and rivaling, almost triumphing over it" (2:419).

The value, and the danger, for Whitman of this influential aesthetic lies in the equivocal relationship it establishes between the ideal and the real. Writing to this aesthetic, Whitman is, to his great psychological relief, able to discover the ideal to be immanent in many aspects of contemporary life, so rendering it once more fit (as the America of "Respondez" is not) for proper human habitation. And indeed the early Whitman's work is distinguished by its success in translating the fact of America, in all the density and quiddity of its current forms of existence, into a different realm of meaning: "O to teach! to convey the invisible faith / To promulge real things" (2:291). But he can also, the victim maybe of his own "magic," mis-take the simply existent for the substantially ideal. Then again, at other times, he can find it extremely difficult to produce out of himself the considerable confidence necessary to raise the inert weight of present circumstances aloft into vision—and yet, unlike writers such as Blake and Shelley, unless he carries the detailed present with him, he cannot authentically enter the condition of vision at all. At their best, as for instance in the lambent passages in "Song of Myself," his augmented perceptions can indeed seem as natural and as self-validating as eyesight—"Eyes of my Soul, seeing perfection, / Natural life of me, faithfully praising things, / Corroborating forever the triumph of things" (2:302).

On other occasions, though, he is by no means so hospitably disposed toward the existent, but works instead with defensive aggression to regulate a maverick world, anxious to corral it within the parameters of the spiritually manageable. The following extract from "Starting from Paumanok" is notable for the several aspects of Whitman's plight as an "envision'd" American soul which are here collected into a single passage:

> See! steamers steaming through my poems!
> See, in my poems immigrants continually coming and landing;
> See, in arriere, the wigwam, the trail, the hunter's hut, the
> flat-boat, the maize-leaf, the claim, the rude fence, and the
> backwoods village;
> See, on the one side the Western Sea, and on the other side the
> Eastern Sea, how they advance and retreat upon my poems
> as upon their own shores,
> See, pastures and forests in my poems—See, animals, wild
> and tame—See, beyond the Kanzas, countless herds of
> buffalo, feeding on short curly grass;
> See, in my poems, old and new cities, solid, vast, inland, with
> paved streets, with iron and stone edifices, and ceaseless
> vehicles, and commerce.   (2:288)

"See! steamers steaming though my poems!" A great deal is comprehended within the use of the word "through" in that line. If, as the second line indicates, it can simply mean "in my poem," it will also bear a rather different, more ambitious interpretation. The point is that Whitman's poems are the unique *means* whereby (that is, "through" which) the steamers, and all the other distinctive features of present and future American life, are not simply seen in the customary way, but are reconstituted so that they stand revealed in their true purpose and significance.

If truth, however, be told, what he sees here is by no means as arresting as the delight he so evidently takes in the very achievement of such seeing—the euphoric relief of finding he has after all been able to engage with contemporary life without being subdued by it;

that he has been able to produce out of its unpromising materials, in the name of the future, something that can be regarded as "the present raised aloft." Then, of course, there is also hidden within his exultant "See" a soliciting, beseeching "Look," inviting his reluctant countrymen to enter along with him into this substantive world of imagination in which alone true responsibilities can begin—to recognize their world as reflected in his achievement. His poem is a refracting medium which does not, like water, bend things out of true, but bends them toward the truth. Yet in the fact that these are only words in a poem which refer the reader's attention to other words in other poems ("See! steamers steaming through my poems!") there lies a prophetic irony. In spite of Whitman's wishing to affirm that his poetry participates in, and contributes to, the teleological process of American history, the lines bespeak Whitman's fear that his writing will simply be autotelic, self-referential rather than referential, self-enclosed rather than debouching onto and affecting the real world.

Words like "vision" are perennially useful when one is discussing Whitman's poetry and have been freely used in the preceding paragraphs, but they are terms which lend themselves rather readily to the cult of the charismatic personality who is uniquely percipient. Therefore the following chapters attempt to continue the corrective work already tentatively begun in this one. They try to illustrate some of the special constituents of Whitman's imagination, and to suggest the way even its most intimate and personal characteristics derive, in a sense, from shared historical experience. Vision is seen as complementing criticism within Whitman's precariously integrated response to what was for him, as it was for the artisan class with which he was closely connected, a disturbing period of social transition. Poetry was his indispensable way of coping with the critical situation brought about by change.

2 ❧ Self-Possession and Possessive Individualism

I F WHITMAN was quite simply disturbed by the confidence-sapping effect on people, particularly the artisan class, of discovering they lived under a new social, political, and economic dispensation which allowed them only marginal control over the course of their own lives, then his reaction to the ethos of self-confidence which was also a product of this expansive stage of liberal capitalism was much more mixed. He was both excited and disconcerted by it, and in "Song of Myself" he discovered the perfect means of simultaneously idealizing and indicting it.

"I celebrate myself." The beginning of "Song of Myself" has become so disastrously familiar that it has lost its original brash power to provoke the reader into a constructive misinterpretation. By failing nowadays to recognize and react to Whitman's perfect imitation of the tone of voice characteristic of a struttingly aggressive individualism, we may also fail to appreciate how subtly he suggests the limitations of that tone and that voice. But he goes further than this. By means of the lines that follow, he incorporates the phrase into a sentence which, read complete, puts a very different complexion on this "self" that is celebrating and being celebrated. That solitary, egotistical phrase, placed in this redeeming social context, is reclaimed for use in the service of a radically different conception of the glories of individual existence:

I celebrate myself, and sing myself,
And what I assume you shall assume,

> For every atom belonging to me as good belongs to
> you.   (1:1)

The last line is encouraged by the rest of the poem to bear two different but corroborative meanings. It tells us that "your atoms are every bit as good as my atoms"; just as later Whitman speaks of "opposite equals advanc[ing]" and instructs us that "All I mark as my own you shall offset it with your own" (1:25). But it can also be understood as making us an extraordinary offer, in the same spirit as the one made later in the poem when the thoughts of great men are described as being "yours as much as mine" (1:22). Whitman is actually offering to share every atom of himself with us.

These two meanings, brought like a single pair of eyes to bear upon the opening phrase, give a stereoscopic prominence to its hitherto concealed meaning. Thomas Stone, writing in *The Dial*, complained that in contemporary society "the permanent *I* subjects and enthrals itself to the changeful MINE, all which can be brought within the compass of this same MINE is sought rather than the being and growth of the MYSELF."[1] It is precisely this distinction which Whitman is implicitly making at the very beginning of what is very pointedly a "Song of MYSELF." And it is a distinction by which the whole poem is significantly governed. In the modern terms suggested by Erich Fromm it could be described as a poem written to demonstrate and to celebrate the "being" mode of existence and to distinguish it from the "having" mode. So that, borrowing a phrase from Shelley, we could say that here Whitman "wantons in endless being."[2] "The quality of BEING in the object's self, according to its own central idea and purpose" was what he primarily valued, he later explained in *Democratic Vistas,* adding that this seemed to him to be under threat in his society, and in need of poetic protection: "under the luminousness of real vision, it alone takes possession, takes value. Like the shadowy dwarf in the fable, once liberated and look'd upon, it expands over the whole earth, and spreads to the roof of heaven" (2:394). Hence the fabulous expansiveness and giantism of "Song of Myself."

Later in his essay Stone deplored the psychological and social effects of the system of private ownership: "Property is not only appropriation but exclusion; in what proportion it holds, in that repelling, what it keeps in itself that keeping away from all others." Whitman likewise recorded in his 1847 notebook his own dislike of "the orthodox proprietor [who] says this is mine, I earned or received or paid for it,—and by positive right of my own I will put a fence round it, and keep it exclusively to myself."³ "Song of Myself" both implicitly and explicitly attacks the contemporary tendency (deriving from as well as expressed in, actual socioeconomic practice) to view the self—in its relations to itself, to others, and to the world at large— overwhelmingly in possessive, proprietorial, and therefore inevitably competitive terms.

There is indeed a particular appropriateness to this being the opening poem of the 1855 *Leaves of Grass,* when one bears in mind the reason given by Whitman to Traubel, in his old age, for having published that first edition anonymously. "It was deliberate—not an accident. It would be sacrilege to put a name there—it would seem just like putting a name on the universe. It would be ridiculous to think of Leaves of Grass as belonging to any one person: at the most I am only a mouth-piece. My name occurs inside the book—that is enough if not more than enough. I like the feeling of a general partnership—as if the *Leaves* was anybody's who chooses just as truly as mine."⁴

The word "myself" in "I celebrate myself" can then be understood as existing in what structuralists would call a "vertical" or "associative" relationship with the word "mine," which had in contemporary life effectively usurped its place at the center of people's conception and definition of themselves. The word "mine" has a kind of absent presence in the first sentence, which "partly creates and certainly winnows and refines the meaning of [the word] that *is* present."⁵ But that term "myself" is further charged with an additional discriminatory force which Emerson can this time help us to feel. "Men," he remarks in "Self-Reliance," "have looked away from themselves and at things so long that . . . they measure their esteem of each other by what each has, and not by what each is."⁶ In such a social context, to "celebrate myself" on Whitman's terms is indeed therefore to look in a radically new direction and to speak in a new way. And a reader can probably best educate himself to notice these accents in "Song of Myself" by taking note of what Whitman has elsewhere and more prosaically to say about those who are "demented with the mania of owning things" (1:42).

Sometime probably toward the end of the 1850s, Whitman assembled a substantial collection of notes with a view to preparing a lecture, or series of lectures, on the subject of religion. These scatterings of remarks are not systematically organized, let alone arranged to form the rudiments of an argument, but they do spontaneously assume the form of clusters of reflections on several more or less distinct topics. Of these, the topic which is relevant here is ownership; and since Whitman's observations, somewhat Thoreauvian or Emersonian in tone, on this important subject are still relatively little known, they should be worth examining carefully in connection with "Song of Myself."

"What is it to own anything?—It is to incorporate it in yourself, as the primal god swallowed the five immortal offspring of Rhea and accumulated to his life and knowledge and strength all that would have grown in them."[7] In this almost Blakean fashion Whitman uses myth to carry him beyond the apparent rationality and respectability of the social institution of property into the darkly complex psychology of possession. Kronos in his malignant aspect represents not only ruthless greed, but the savage anxiety and fear that, devouring the individual, makes him a compulsive devourer of his fellowmen as Kronos devoured his own children. It is noteworthy that Stone, in the aforementioned essay, believed his age to be the age of Cain, who killed his brother Abel out of jealousy. But Kronos also has a benign aspect, corresponding to that pristine impulse in man of which rampant possessiveness is the ugly, dangerous, and sadly common perversion. "Song of Myself" is itself written by such a latter Kronos; a "primal god" who "incorporate[s] gneiss and coal and long-threaded moss and fruits and grains and esculent roots," (1:41) as well as human beings and living things.

The malignant Kronos is insatiable because he has a void where his heart should be. He is selfish precisely because he lacks authentic selfhood. Self-alienated, he nevertheless persists in believing that what he lacks can eventually be acquired. Conversely, the benign Kronos knows that "No one can realise anything unless he has it in him . . . The animals, the past, light, space—if I have them not in me, I have them not at all."[8] Whitman accordingly offers a redefinition of the term "affluence": "the affluent man is he who confronts the show and sees by an equivalent or more than equivalent from the grander wealth of himself."[9] The circumambient universe is no longer merely the appetitive self's vital source of supply: a significant part of its value lies in its ability to call forth all of a man's powers and resources, and so to give him back the self that he hadn't known he was. "Here is realization, / Here is a man tallied—he realizes here what he has in him" (1:230). Satisfaction lies in the simultaneous discovery of such a world and such an augmented self, and "Song of Myself" is a demonstration and celebration of this transactional process.

In the possessive self the impulse to have is inseparable from the impulse to hold. Conversing with Traubel, late in life, Whitman was still capable of eloquence on this particular subject. Adhering to his lifelong, idealistic belief in free trade as the sine qua non of all other freedoms, whether in social, political, or economic fields, he resumed his attack upon the selfish protectionism of "tariff sneak-thieves": "it's when they seem most sure, sufficient, self-satisfied, prosperous, that there comes the smash-up: heap-up your treasure—gold, goods: heap them up high—way up: then beware! The Greeks—nearly all of them: the writers, the race traditions: are full of this idea: the idea that the gods hate prosperity—this sort of prosperity: the idea that when men sit heaped all round with possessions, loot, then the end is near—then look out!"[10] It is a fine example of one of Whitman's fundamental strategies for dealing with any of the unacceptable elements in the new capitalist character. He isolates it, and then attributes it to a single un-American sector of society.

Emerson, also alarmed by the cupidity of the America which was coming into being, explored the psychology of the hoarder through the character of Saturn in his debate with Uranus. Saturn, having successfully created an oyster, wants to do nothing but go on "creating the race of oysters," repeating himself indefinitely. His reason, born of fear, is that in this way "I hold what I have got; and so I resist Night and Chaos." Conversely, Uranus argues fiercely that "Thou canst not hold thine own, but by making more. Thy oysters are barnacles and cockles, and with the next flowing of the tide, they will be pebbles and sea foam."[11] Whitman's muse and guiding spirit is Uranus and not Saturn. He holds only by making, and not simply taking, more. His style of self-presentation in "Song of Myself" is the very antithesis of self-preservation. His Self exists in a fundamentally different relation to Time from that of the possessive individual in its hoarding aspects: "The past and present wilt . . . . I have fill'd them and emptied them, / And proceed to fill my next fold of the future" (1:81). Whitman echoes and obeys Emerson's injunction not to identify himself with his obsessively retentive memory, and not to fear "lest you contradict somewhat you have stated in this or that public place. Suppose you should contradict yourself; what then? . . . bring the past for judgment into the thousand-eyed present, and live ever in a new day. Trust your emotion . . . Leave your theory, as Joseph his coat in the hands of the harlot and flee."[12] "Let it out then" could be the motto of "Song of Myself," and the economic context of the injunction is made perfectly clear in the 1855 preface: "This is what you shall do: Love the earth and sun and the animals, despise riches, give alms to every one that asks, stand up for the stupid and crazy, devote your income and labor to others" (2:440). Whitman particularly likes to represent his openness, his "giving out," as a form of liberality and of frankness. These are qualities which significantly suggest and repudiate their opposites; the prudence, parsimony and secretiveness which are three important constituents of the acquisitive self. "Behold I do not give lectures or a little charity, / What I give I give out of myself. / . . . And any thing I have I bestow" (1:62). The earth itself is his great teacher in this: "Prodigal! you have given me love! . . . . therefore I to you give love! / O unspeakable passionate love!" (1:28). Here, as elsewhere, attitudes toward love become for Whitman (as for Blake) an important guide to selfishness and selflessness. By implicitly exposing the possessive aspects of conventional love-relationships, Whitman reveals the prudential, calculating spirit which governs the passional life. By contrast, his own sympathies are defiantly promiscuous. He provocatively represents himself as an easy pick-up: "Adorning myself to bestow myself on the first that will take me" (1:16)—the opposite, in short, of someone holding out for a good catch. Although he stops well short of Blake's attack on "the marriage hearse," Whitman certainly knew of the close connections that could and did exist between marriage and property. Even the relationship between husband and wife could be governed by the spirit of ownership. He protested in his 1847 notebook that a man is "no owner" of his friend or wife "except by their love, and if anyone gets that away from him, it is best not to curse, but quickly call the offal cart to his door and let physical wife or friend go, the tail with the hide."[13]

   A lack of generosity, even a jealous regard for one's own, may well be recognized as an inevitable corollary of possessiveness: but what about secretiveness? It is Emerson who best brings out this connection. "The general system of our trade," he complained in his lecture "Man the Reformer," is "a system of selfishness . . . is a system of distrust and concealment, of superior keenness, not of giving but of taking advantage."[14] The logic of such a situation can readily be appreciated. In a society based on competitive individualism there is a distinct advantage in concealing one's assets and one's intentions. Whitman's frankness, in itself an appeal for a reciprocal frankness, is an open challenge to this closed, clam-tight "system of selfishness." "The great poets," it is said in the 1855 preface, "are also to be known by the absence in them of tricks and by the justification of perfect personal candor. Then folks echo a new cheap joy and a divine voice leaping from their brains" (2:451). In that last sentence Whitman practices his revisionary wit on one of the sacred pecuniary terms which are crucial to his society's market values. He also does something else of particular interest. Conflating the radical Protestant doctrine of the indwelling Word with the Greek story describing the birth of Pallas Athene, the Goddess of Wisdom, from the head of Zeus, he constructs his own myth of personal liberation. Social masquerade, in the form of conventional language, may so come to occupy the tongue that a man inescapably alienates himself from his true self in the very act of speaking. But by means of Whitman's poetry, or so the myth runs, the living thought of the reader's unique personality, locked up in the brain's dumbness following the tongue's defection, is made directly vocal.

What emerges clearly and decisively from the lecture notes on religion and from "Song of Myself" is Whitman's understanding of how the impulse of ownership, fostered by the ethos of the age, had in his time been allowed to operate in utterly inappropriate areas and directions. For a man to own a house was one thing: for him to think and to act as if he owned the earth was quite another. "There is," as Whitman saw, "no such thing as ownership here anyhow—one of the laws being that from the moment a man takes the smallest page exclusively to himself, and tries to keep it from the rest, from that moment it begins to wither under his hand and its immortal hieroglyphics presently fade away and become blank."[15]

Another of the "laws" for which Whitman was profoundly grateful, as he records in "Song of Myself," is that the earth will always be proof against man's every attempt to possess and overpower it by knowledge. It is partly in this spirit that in "Song of Myself" he rejoices in the variety, unpredictability, and above all the simple mystery, of the animal, vegetable, and mineral world. It is his way of demonstrating how, in Hugh MacDiarmid's superlative phrase, "the prodigiousness of the universe is a safeguarding excellence." Its prodigiousness is guaranteed to defeat man's grandiose yet mean-spirited ambition to subject it to his own purposes and to subjugate it to his own perfect satisfaction. "This great earth that rolls in the air, and the sun and moon, and men and women—do you think nothing more is to be made of them than store-keeping and books and produce and drygoods and something to pay taxes on?"[16] And by safeguarding itself—through its prodigiousness, its protean energies and inscrutable ends—against all such misguided human enterprise, the universe performs the inestimable service of safeguarding man from himself. It prevents him from imprisoning himself beyond all possibility of release or escape within cripplingly narrow conceptions of the purpose of human existence.

The same service of prevention is performed in "Song of Myself" by Whitman's making so much of the "puzzle of puzzles," the mystery of life, of which death is our ultimate reminder. "To be in any form, what is that?" (1:38). "A child said, What is the grass? fetching it to me with full hands; / How could I answer the child? . . . . I do not know what it is any more than he" (1:6). Referring to Conscience and Reason, the transcendentalist Theodore Parker wrote that man can claim "no property in them. They have been shot down into us without our asking and now stand unmanageable in our minds."[17] Whitman says much the same thing, not only of the powers of the soul, but also of all the attributes of the body and therefore of the human being complete. All of Whitman's celebration of himself is, paradoxically, designed to demonstrate that, like Lawrence's Tom Brangwen, he knows that he does not belong to himself; that he is not his own, let alone any other man's property. And it is precisely in this concept that we should locate the origins of Whitman's transcendentalism. It has been fashionable to seek a narrowly psychological explanation for the genesis of the "Me myself" and this peculiar insistence that "Apart from the pulling and hauling stands what I am" (1:5). But such a Self is better seen as a creative response to social pressure than as a neurotic or pathological symptom. A contrast central to the transcendentalists' own conception of the cosmic Self is identified blandly but effectively by G. K. Newcomb in the *Dial*. The individual should realize that he is "A form called self which Life has taken. Life is the unpersonaliser of persons," whereas removed from this context and "left to itself, the vital becomes a centred isolation in the individual, like water in anything whose pores are closed."[18] Emerson likewise spoke of two kinds of "subjectiveness": the first was but another name for "intellectual selfishness"; the second described "The great man [who] even whilst he relates a private fact personal to him, is really leading us away from him to an universal experience."[19] The spread of this spirit would, he significantly remarked, facilitate "the descent of love into Trade." In other words, the transcendental Self is partly the product of social circumstances similar to those which Dickens imagined as producing, in England, Little Dorrit's almost pathological selflessness. In a world full of jostling egos, "pulling and hauling," a sensitive person is driven either to renounce self altogether or else, like Whitman, to renounce egotistical selfhood in the name of an utterly different, authentic Self.

Whitman, however, complicates things by borrowing the language of "having" in order to speak about living in the "being" mode. How consciously and how successfully this is done is something about which there may well be legitimate disagreement. Denis Donoghue has identified and defended this habit particularly well: "Whitman spent most of his life sponsoring an affluent society, with this admonition, that our possessions should include sympathies, accords, pleasures, marriages, pains, passions, the sun and the stars as well as gadgets. But judged simply as an aesthetic . . . Whitman's creed was uncannily faithful to the dominant metaphors of his place and time."[20] What is, however, overlooked in such an account is the unmistakable element of satire, subversion, and redefinition in Whitman's use of these metaphors. There is his humorous parody of Yankee shrewdness: "What is commonest and cheapest and nearest and easiest is Me, / Me going in for my chances, spending for vast returns" (1:15); or again, "I or you pocketless of a dime may purchase the pick of the earth" (1:79). And there is surely also a measure of irony in saying "I see through the broadcloth and gingham whether or no, / And am around, tenacious, acquisitive, tireless . . . . and can never be shaken away" (1:9), as there is in "I have embraced you, and henceforth possess you to myself" (1:63). Again when he proclaims "I think I will do nothing for a long time but listen, / And accrue what

I hear into myself . . . . and let sounds contribute toward me" (1:36) he is, as surely as Thoreau in his chapter "Sounds," orientating himself by reacting against the kind of active, acquisitive individualism which was so admired, produced, and promoted by his society.

He is, after all, the most disgraceful idler, loafer, and loiterer. In fact, in a whimsical essay he wrote in 1840 Whitman early announced his love for genuine loafing (as distinct from a mongrel laziness, in which there was an unfortunate admixture of work) and his rebellious intention of establishing "an entire loafer kingdom": "Talk about your commercial countries, and your national industry, indeed! Give us the facilities of loafing, and you are welcome to all the benefits of your tariff system, your manufacturing privileges, and your cotton trade."[21] Whitman is a "caresser" rather than a possessor "of life wherever moving" (1:14). For some time now, critics have been in the habit of casually referring to Whitman's lists as "inventories," while failing to relish the ironic appropriateness of the term, when applied to the work of a poet who can pointedly ask: "Shall I make my list of things in the house and skip the house that supports them?" (1:29).

"Me going in for my chances, spending for vast returns" is a sentence particularly worth returning to. "Spend" was at this time the popular term for reaching orgasm, and in his brilliant essay "The Spermatic Economy," G. J. Barker-Benfield has examined in dazzling detail the interconnections between sexuality and economics in the thinking of American capitalist society during this period. Males were assumed to be biologically designed for the strenuous competitiveness of the social life that awaited them. Their manifest sexuality was regarded as the vital source of a limited supply of energy, which therefore had to be carefully conserved until it could be effectively expressed—not in sexual intercourse, but in the fruitful industriousness that bred success. Actual sexual activity (as opposed to the economic activity that was powered by the rechanneling of the sex drive) was therefore regarded with considerable suspicion and anxiety, since energy expended in this way was energy lost to industry. Masturbation was thought to be criminally wasteful, particularly since the loss of sperm was supposed to be similar in effect to the loss of blood, leaving the body physically depleted and seriously weakened. As Barker-Benfield points out, such doctrines anticipated Freud's theory of sublimation, and when it is referred to in this context, Whitman's

"Song of Myself" appears to be a work of deliberate desublimation, which resexualizes the body by recovering for it the energy wasted in economic competition.[22]

But if Whitman attacks impotent hoarding, he also attacks its companion vice, impotent display. American bards, says Whitman in the 1855 preface, "shall not be careful of riches and privilege . . . they shall be riches and privilege" (2:446). On this basis "Song of Myself" could be said to include Whitman's parodic and revisionist version of conspicuous consumption. Repeatedly he demonstrates his lavish powers of acquisition and puts on display the "possessions" he has amassed. But in his demonstration of what he means by "possession" he challenges his contemporaries to the empty center of their own self-display: "To see no possession but you may possess it! enjoying all without labor or purchase—abstracting the feast, yet not abstracting one particle of it; / To take the best of the farmer's farm and the rich man's elegant villa, and the chaste blessings of the well-married couple, and the fruits of orchards and flowers of gardens!" (1:235). Tucked away there, in that apparently gratuitous remark about the well-married couple, is perhaps another sly dig at the smug, proprietorial aspects of prosperous middle-class marriage. Although it would be 1899 before Thorstein Veblen published his psychosociological study of the elaborate display-rituals of the leisured classes, their empire of fashion was, to Whitman's democratic disgust, beginning to be established in New York during the 1840s and 1850s. From the forties onward, such events as fancy-dress balls became fixtures in the rapidly developing social calendar of the superwealthy, while the opulent department stores of Broadway provided them with satisfactorily expensive jewels, clothes, and furniture. Elsewhere could easily be obtained those works of art essential to what Spann has aptly called their "cultural consumerism." Whitman's animus against the preciosity and snobbishness of "culture" is at least partly due to the artistic pretensions of this social elite. When, in "Song for Occupations," he attacks the economic functionalism which pervades his society's outlook on life, his disapproval is deliberately widened to embrace the new predatory enthusiasm of the pampered rich:

> The wonder every one sees in every one else he sees . . . . and the wonders that fill each minute of time forever and each acre of surface and space forever,

Have you reckoned them as mainly for a trade or farmwork?
  or for the profits of a store? or to achieve yourself a
  position? or to fill a gentleman's leisure or a lady's leisure?

Have you reckoned the landscape took substance and form
  that it might be painted in a picture?
Or men and women that they might be written of, and songs
  sung?   (1:88)

Given his awareness of such a social context, it may be suggested
that the conception and genesis of Whitman's Self should be sought
not only in his efforts to avoid becoming a possessive self, but also
in his determination to avoid being appropriated by others. In "Song
of the Open Road" he presents himself as "gently but with undeniable
will divesting myself of the holds that would hold me" (1:228), and
his attacks on authority and conformity could be usefully regarded
in this light. Knowing that he will never be recognized as a prophet
in his own country, he pronounces himself to be of mysterious foreign
extraction. He refuses to be his temporal father's son, for the father
is in this respect always Kronos, the devourer. He rejects society's
attempts to control him by first bestowing upon him, and then con-
fining him to, a familiar, approved identity. He will not submit to
being described in terms of "the effect upon me of my early life . . . . of
the ward and city I live in . . . . of the nation" (1:4). And in these
respects he is like the baby in Blake's "Infant Sorrow," "struggling
in my father's hands, / Striving against my swaddling bands," because
they represent the "dangerous world" which tries to restrain and
appropriate him.[23] There is something of the "fiend hid in a cloud"
in Whitman's transcendental Self, after all. Perhaps both Blake and
Whitman became Platonists for similar social reasons.
  Regarded as a carefully constructed verbal portrait of an alternative,
ideal, American Self, "Song of Myself" finds its visual counterpart
in the famous portrait of Whitman, casually dressed like a working-
man, which served as frontispiece to the 1855 *Leaves of Grass*. This
engraving has attracted a great deal of illuminating attention from
the critics over the years. Perceptions of it have naturally varied according to the preconceptions of the viewer, and since emphasis has
most recently been placed on its sexual provocativeness, it is worth
redressing the balance a little by noting its socioeconomic features.

In his 1851 address to the Brooklyn Art Union, Whitman contrasted the Greek ideal of manhood (which in his hands took on a distinctly Locofoco character) with the "orthodox specimen of the man of the present time." For the contemporary man, success in business is all. He feels nothing but "contempt for all that is in the world, except money can be made of it," and his dress is an eloquent statement of the values by which he lives:

> Then see him in all the perfection of fashionable tailordom—the tight boot with the high heel; the trousers, big at the ankle, on some rule inverting the ordinary ones of grace; the long large cuffs, and thick stiff collar of his coat—the swallow-tailed coat, on which dancing masters are inexorable; the neck swathed in many bands, giving support to the modern high & pointed shirt collar, that fearful sight to an approaching enemy—the modern shirt collar, bold as Columbus, stretching off into the unknown distance—& then to crown all, the fashionable hat, before which language has nothing to say, because sight is the only thing that can begin to do it justice—& we have indeed a model for the sculptor.[24]

Such a businessman is a "mean and bandaged spirit," as tightly swathed in self-protective secrecy as Tite Barnacle, while his spikily aggressive shirt collar is a weapon to be wielded in the fight for social and economic supremacy. In what might be called a "pointed" contrast, Whitman's shirt is left trustingly, fraternally, open at the neck—not so casually, perhaps, after all.

In poem as in portrait Whitman fights against his social identity, not least because he recognizes that his own society seeks to promote by theory and practice the idea that men are by their very nature limited, competitive individuals; and it does this because its very continuing existence, in its present form, depends upon maintaining this illusion. Stone, in the aforementioned essay, saw this quite clearly: "[True] Society, instead of being as political fiction-makers would have us think, a cunning device, a thing of compact, grounded on a self-interest ascertained by experience, is in fact the first natural growth of the human instinct."[25] Stone is here not simply bringing the language of religion to bear upon politics, he is appealing to alternative social and political theories which had traditionally been well respected in America, but had lately been ignored. Their origins are in Shaftesbury's denial of "the Hobbesian and Lockeian proposition that self-interest and self-love were the dominant passions of man."[26] He asserted that man's inborn sociability, his deep passion for fellowship, made him a naturally social creature. And it is high time that Whitman's own language of comradeship and "adhesiveness," which has come to be considered almost exclusively in psychological terms, should be related to this social and political tradition. Even Emerson, after all, was so disgusted by the contemporary American reliance "on the power of the dollar," and so alarmed by the incipient class conflicts in his society, that he proclaimed love to be "the one remedy for all ills, the panacea of nature. We must be lovers."[27] "Song of Myself," seen in this context, is indeed a love song. As such it has its Prufrockian aspects, but it is also unmistakably the work in which Whitman, aware of the centrifugal forces in his society, acts out an American version of the poet's duty as defined by the quintessentially English Romantic, Wordsworth: "the Poet binds together by passion and knowledge the vase empire of human society."[28]

Whitman's poem is also conceived and presented in terms of the act of love it can perform for the reader. The first evidence of this love is negative—Whitman's refusal to let his poem provide the reader with the kind of acquirable content of meaning and message that other books provide. Negatively considered, then, "Song of Myself" frustrates the reader's wish to make the content of books, like the books themselves, a form of what Wemmick in *Great Expectations* memorably called "portable property." It is interesting to note that, despite all critics have said about Whitman's approaches to the reader, insufficient work has been done on "Song of Myself" from the point of view of the difficulties and challenges with which, in the name of love, it confronts that reader. Instead, it has been readily taken at its face value—as the proclamation and demonstration of a unique self—and discussed chiefly in terms of expressive theories of literature. But passages such as the following seem rather to invite a different kind of approach:

> The smoke of my own breath,
> Echoes, ripples, and buzzed whispers . . . . loveroot,
>   silkthread, crotch and vine,
> My respiration and inspiration . . . . the beating of my

> heart . . . . the passing of blood and air through my lungs,
> The sniff of green leaves and dry leaves, and of the shore and
>   darkcolored sea-rocks, and of hay in the barn,
> The sound of the belched words of my voice . . . . words
>   loosed to the eddies of the wind,
> A few light kisses . . . . a few embraces . . . . a reaching
>   around of arms,
> The play of shine and shade on the trees as the supple
>   boughs wag,
> The delight alone or in the rush of the streets, or along the
>   fields and hillsides,
> The feeling of health . . . . the full-noon trill . . . . the song of
>   me rising from bed and meeting the sun.   (1:2).

The point and power of this verse paragraph lies in its not having a main verb—which is, of course, something the unwary reader is likely, on a first reading, to spend his time expecting in vain. The discovery when it finally comes, and the rereading that must hastily follow, involve much more than the noting of a grammatical peculiarity. They involve a realization that these descriptive phrases are not simply a preparation for action, subject to and therefore subordinate to the directing presence of the verb. They are grammatically an end in themselves, thereby creating a physical world in which experiences such as "The smoke of my own breath . . . The sniff of green leaves and dry leaves . . . The sound of the belch'd words of my voice" become vividly foregrounded. Filling the whole picture, they become significant and satisfying experiences in themselves. In other words, as the reader adjusts so as finally to find meaning in the verbless "sentence," so too does he simultaneously reorient himself in relation to himself and his world, and engage in a revaluation of life itself. It is a fine example of the quiet subversiveness of Whitman's writing—the way the "new free forms" of the poetry constitute what he himself called a "silent defiance" (*Prose Works* 2:445).

This section (like the whole poem in relation to, say, traditional epic) could be described as a sort of "shaggy dog" story, where the listener or reader keeps expecting something to happen which will "justify" the time spent in listening or reading, quite literally waiting for the "pay-off" line, which never comes. Blake uses a very similar device for an almost identical purpose in *Songs of Innocence* (for example, "The Ecchoing Green" and "Spring"). Although the first verse of the latter is not actually verbless, the completing verb is so long delayed that the reading mind, prompted by rhyme and rhythm, begins to function like the mind of a child. It starts making nouns (like "Nightingale") into verbs, thereby investing the mere existence of things with an active life normally appreciated only when they are doing something and not simply being.

> Sound the Flute!
> Now it's mute.
> Birds delight
> Day and Night;
> Nightingale
> In the dale,
> Lark in Sky,
> Merrily,
> Merrily, Merrily, to welcome in the Year.[29]

So, too, on April Fool's day, 1846, Whitman devoted an entire *Daily Eagle* editorial to the holiday spirit and the want of it among the "toilers & burrowers for superfluous wealth." Mocking their preoccupation with business, Whitman waxes positively biblical: "Oh, Fool! The little birds, & the sheep in the field, possess more reason than thou; for when once their natural wants are satisfied, they repose themselves and toil no more. The lambs gambol. The birds sing, in joy and gratitude, as it were, to the good God; and you will do nothing but plod, and plod. Go to, Fool! It is not well to labor in servile offices, while the great banquet is spread in many princely halls, and all who would partake are welcome."[30]

"I," says Charles Olson, "dazzled / as one is, until one discovers / there is no other issue than / the moment of / the pleasure of / this plum." "These things," he adds, "which don't carry their end any further than / their reality in / themselves."[31] Whitman, too, provides the poetic means that enable the reader to escape from his usually end-directed thinking, in which the present is always being seen in terms of the future. That, for Whitman as much as Thoreau, is a waste of time to which the acquisitive man is addicted in the name of spending time profitably. That is false economy; true economy being always to live in the very nick of time, the present. F. H. Hedge

complained of his period that "On all hands man's existence is converted into a preparation for existence . . . like that king of Epirus,
who was all his lifetime preparing to take his ease, but must first
conquer the world. The end is lost in the means . . . We cannot get
to ourselves." And he goes on to yearn "for some moral Alaric . . . who
should sweep away, with one fell swoop, all that has been in this
kind."[32]

Whitman is precisely that "moral Alaric," living (*pace* Santayana)
with a *calculated* barbarism in the present:

> I have heard what the talkers were talking . . . . the talk of the
>   beginning and the end,
> But I do not talk of the beginning or the end.
>
> There was never any more inception than there is now,
> Nor any more youth or age than there is now;
> And will never be any more perfection than there is now,
> Nor any more heaven or hell than there is now.   (1:3)

As he nicely put it elsewhere, drawing his image this time not from
pastoral convention but from the escapist dream-fantasy of the Bowery theater: "The ignorant think that to the entertainment of life they
will be admitted by a ticket or check, and the dream of their existence
is to get the money that they may buy this wonderful card."[33]

It is surely significant that specifically in "Song of Myself"—and
not, sadly, in most of his poetry thereafter—Whitman is supremely
Lawrence's poet of "the quivering nimble hour of the present," rev-
elling "in the sheer appreciation of the instant moment, life surging
itself into utterance at its very well-head."[34] He is addicted to the
present tense and the present participle, and his descriptions of people
always catches them in the very act of living. "The pavingman leans
on his twohanded rammer . . . The canal-boy trots on the tow-
path . . . / The drover watches his drove, he sings out to them that
would stray . . . / Off on the lakes the pikefisher watches and waits
by the hold in the frozen surface" (1:extracts from 18 and 19). By so
catching them and isolating their actions from questions of motive,
purpose, and consequence, he manages to recreate an idealized form
of the comfortably blended urban and rural worlds of his childhood.
Yet the whole panorama is implicitly presented as a celebration of

the free spirit of economic liberalism, the laissez-faire capitalism of the mid-nineteenth century. It is of course nothing of the sort. Whitman replaces the pleasure of acquiring and the acquiring of pleasure which was becoming the real business of his time, with the pleasure of simply being and living. His poem translates a having world into a being world, which appears to obey the biblical injunction to "serve the Lord your God with joy and gladness of heart, in the midst of the fullness of all things" (Deut. 28:47). America so transfigured becomes a psalm of life.

IT IS IN "Song of Myself," then, that Whitman enters most completely, and captivatingly, into the "swimming shape of today," repeatedly committing himself "to the representation of this wave of an hour and this one of the sixty beautiful children of the wave" (*Prose Works*, 2:455). Yet, as the 1855 preface, from which these phrases are taken, makes plain, it is certainly not his intention to advocate a frantic, time-ridden hedonism. One important reason why he seeks to place himself on "the present spot" is his desire to be fully "present," in every sense of the word, at the very instant when life conveys itself "from what was to what shall be" (2:455). This simple remark cracks open directly to reveal the vertiginous depths of the formidable subject of temporality. This, however, is not germane to the present discussion, since I am concerned not to examine the nature, or to assess the adequacy, of Whitman's philosophy of time, but rather to draw attention to its immediate social implications. When Whitman insists upon the full significance of the living moment, he does so partly by way of measured dissent from everything his contemporaries understood by the word "prudence."

As Emerson had already famously demonstrated, "prudence" was clearly a keyword in the social discourse of mid-nineteenth-century America; a term placed at what Whitman might have called the dead center of the network of interconnections between moral values and economic practice upon which the respectable self-image of the emerging bourgeois world depended. Whitman therefore proceeded to honor it with his very particular attention. In 1855 he devoted several paragraphs of the preface to an attempt at restoring, by redefining, a precious term he regarded as having been defaced and devalued by contemporary use. The following year he resumed his work of rehabilitation, converting this prose matter into number seventeen of *Leaves of Grass,* 1856, and entitling it "Poem of the Last Explanation of Prudence." As the opening lines make clear, the title does more than record Whitman's provocative claim to provide the last word on the subject. It refers to his contention that the only person who genuinely deserves to be called "prudent" is he who shows true wisdom and foresight by always suiting his conduct to the ultimate requirements of his soul.

Thus paraphrased, the notion may seem intolerably vague, and even sanctimonious, but it gains considerably in coherence, as it does in interest, when seen for what it really is—a militant reaction, born indeed of revulsion, against the new kind of economic thinking which had come to prevail in America. By then, the word "prudent," which once had signified the cardinal virtue of wisdom aforethought, had been abducted, removed from its original, extensive sphere of meaning, and prostituted to the pragmatic interests of the developing economic order. In this connection it was performing a currently indispensable, but also an infinitely self-demeaning (and Self-demeaning) service as Whitman noted with disapproval in the 1855 preface: "It has been thought that the prudent citizen was the citizen who applied himself to solid gains and did well for himself and his family and completed a lawful life without debt or crime" (2:452).

Therefore, the narrower sense given to the word "prudent" in nineteenth-century America seemed to Whitman covert evidence of his age's debased philosophy for living. But there were other terms, of course, much more openly implicated in the process of constructing a materialistic ideology, and Whitman proceeded to question the economic values they too normally embodied, by employing the terms in a different, challengingly spiritual sense:

> Charity and personal force are the only investments
> worth anything.

> No specification is necessary—all that a male or female does,
> that is vigorous, benevolent, clean, is so much profit to him
> or her, in the unshakable order of the universe and through
> the whole scope of it forever.

> Who has been wise, receives interest . . .   (1:245)

Perhaps the best social gloss on these lines is provided by a remark Whitman made to Traubel over thirty years later. "We are so commercialized in this country that we will do nothing without the pay is in sight—nothing, nothing: the profits must be near enough to grab: we seem to lack that great faculty of wait, wait, wait, which distinguishes and accounts for the world-power of the English merchant. Yet there are signs of an awakening. We may soon have to revise our notions on this score. Some day we may rise to the standards of moral, spiritual, profit, letting all the base standards fall into disuse."[35] The really important feature of this prose passage, though, is not the inverse relation it proposes between a concern for material gain and an increase in spiritual awareness, but rather the understanding Whitman here shows of the strikingly different character of two separate phases of capitalism. A product of this is the critical insight he gains into the distinctive dynamic of his own capitalist period. Of course, by the time he made this comment to Traubel, Whitman had lived through the Gilded Age and could be under no illusions regarding the unsavory social consequences of the system of liberal capitalism and monopoly capitalism operating in the second half of the nineteenth century. Yet even thirty years earlier, in 1855–56, during the relatively innocent inaugural stage of this economic development, he had sensitively observed the disturbing change it wrought in general consciousness. And time, or rather attitudes towards time, was of the essence in this change, as Whitman correctly saw.

Although "Song of Myself" is, in a way, concerned throughout with this temporal crisis, the subject is broached only rarely. One of the most notable of these occasions occurs toward the end of the poem, when Whitman reviews the "immense preparations" made over millions of years, first for the genesis of human life on earth, and then for the refining of it in each new individual case:

> Cycles ferried my cradle, rowing and rowing like
>   cheerful boatmen;
> For room to me stars kept aside in their own rings,
> They sent influences to look after what was to hold me.
>
> Before I was born out of my mother generations guided me,
> My embryo has never been torpid . . . . nothing could
>   overlay it;

> For it the nebula cohered to an orb . . . . the long slow strata
>   piled to rest it on . . . . vast vegetables gave it sustenance,
> Monstrous sauroids transported it in their mouths and
>   deposited it with care.
>
> All forces have been steadily employed to complete and
>   delight me,
> Now I stand on this spot with my soul.   (1:72)

Yes, of course, this is only a new twist given to a very familiar American story. The providential view of a human history, in which America has been chosen to play the leading modern part, is here neatly translated into pre–Darwinian evolutionary terms. Equally noticeable, though, is that by drawing upon Lamarck, as well as perhaps upon the remarkable discoveries made by early nineteenth-century geologists such as Lyell, Whitman fashions a philosophy which, in bestowing the dignity of great antiquity upon the Self, also makes it responsible for the potential it has been freely given in gift, and in trust, by the past: "in the universe of the material kosmos, after meteorological, vegetable, and animal cycles, man at last arises, born through them, to prove them, concentrate them, to turn upon them with wonder and love" (*Prose Works,* 2:425).[36]

This version of evolutionary history serves many purposes in Whitman's thinking. But what matters most at this juncture is the profoundly critical relation in which this passage stands to the temporal philosophy promoted by the practices of capitalism. If man's whole experience of time is governed by his constantly pressing need (out of hope and fear) to be clairvoyantly attuned to the rapid fluctuations of the economic market, then he has no time to give to measuring or regulating his life by the larger spans and more leisurely rhythms which also obtain. Even more important, perhaps, is the basic lack of trust, the wariness, which corrodes man's being when he has to live daily by his wits, striving always to stay just that one step ahead of the game. In this connection Whitman's evolutionary theory is altogether less important for what it actually says than for what, at least in "Song of Myself," his belief in it enables him to be and to do. He comes up with a rather fine Wordsworthian phrase for this in the 1855 preface. "Eternity," he says, "is the bond of time" (*Prose Works,* 2:454), and in evolutionary theory he found a satisfactory disclosure of the terms of this bond. This supplies the security, on the strength of which he is able to relax into self-exploration, since he knows his continuing existence in time as a self does not depend upon the constant maintenance of the established ego, and its conscious, guarded advance from moment to moment.

Some psychiatrists have argued that this capacity in the adult to relax, to return to an unintegrated state, is itself an important prerequisite of personal maturity. This, in turn is seen as a product of the support given, at an early stage, to the nascent self by a sympathetic mothering environment which continued to hold it steadily in mind as a person even when (as in sleep, or when overwhelmed by emotions) the child failed to sustain for itself a continuing sense of its own identity.[37] Although Whitman certainly does not work within any such specific theory of personal growth, he does implicitly deal, in "Song of Myself," with the *social* environment in which the self develops.

Since that socioeconomic environment is radically unstable, it induces an anxious instability in the Self, against which the ego precipitately constructs its defenses: "Were mankind murderous or jealous upon you my brother or my sister? / I am sorry for you . . . . they are not murderous or jealous upon me; / All has been gentle with me . . . ." (1:71). By contrast, therefore, Whitman imagines a different kind, and place, of nurture for his Self. Out of the materials made available to him by contemporary evolutionary theory, he fashions an extraordinary myth, or fabulous history, of personal gestation, in which the emphasis is squarely on a facilitating environment provided by love. Love becomes the bond of time, as the constancy of adaptive care carries the embryonic self safely through every violence of internal and external change:

> Afar down I see the huge first Nothing, the vapor from the
>   nostrils of death,
> I know I was even there . . . . I waited unseen and always,
> And slept while God carried me through the lethargic mist,
> And took my time . . . . and took no hurt from the
>   foetid carbon.
>
> Long I was hugged close . . . . long and long.
> Immense have been the preparations for me,
> Faithful and friendly the arms that have helped me . . . .

> Monstrous sauroids transported [my embryo] in their mouths
> and deposited it with care.   (1:71)

The positive outcome of this fostering is the creative experience of personal omnipotence on which "Song of Myself" is founded. In Freudian theory, "omnipotence [is] conceived of as a quality of feeling accompanying a denial of impotence of helplessness in the face of reality (external or internal)."[38] Many critics (including myself, in later chapters of this book) have drawn consciously or unconsciously on this psychological model in order to identify Whitman's boosterism and to explain it. But surely the distinguishing feature of "Song of Myself" is that the poetry of omnipotence here is qualitatively different from what it is elsewhere, which suggests it represents a fundamentally different psychological condition. The relevant model is therefore not to be looked for in Freud, but may instead be found in the work of certain other psychiatrists—particularly those, such as D. W. Winnicott, who trace the early growth in the child of a creative imagination.[39] When viewed in this setting, the omnipotence appears as the successful outcome of an early phase, when the mother (or surrounding environment) has so empathized with the child as to anticipate its every instinctual and emotional need, so providing its fragile ego with maximum support. Consequently, it appears to itself to be the satisfier of its own needs—the creator, as it were, of its own world. This habit of confidence then forms the primitive basis of all the subsequent creative functioning which alone can produce a personally meaningful world.

Whitman is not simply regressing, in an infantile way, to this omnipotent stage in "Song of Myself." What he is doing is not only seriously exercising and demonstrating the power of play, but deliberately dramatizing it, by employing ancient rhetorical devices—boast, hyperbole, conceit, and so on—sanctioned by countless cultures for this very purpose. "Play your muscle," he urged in the 1847 notebook, "and it will be lithe and caoutchouc and strong as iron—I wish to see American young men, the working men, carry themselves with a high horse."[40] He was thinking of more than actual muscles. Like Shelley, he regarded the human imagination as a limb in constant need of exercise and believed the future of democracy depended on the provision of suitable gymnasiums, such as he so dramatically offered in "Song of Myself."[41]

In an adult, it is true, this putting forth of one's strength is bound, sooner or later, also to involve a trial of strength—the testing to the limit of the precarious ability to imagine what we know, as Shelley put it. That, too, is acknowledged in "Song of Myself"—for instance, "Dazzling and tremendous how quick the sunrise would kill me, / If I could not now and always send sunrise out of me" (1:35). But the primary emphasis is on the rootedness of authentic selfhood in the capacity to play, and so to dwell anew in possibility. And this becomes an indictment of the self-protective limitations and fixities of the prudential mind.

In a section of the 1855 preface, and again in "Song of Prudence," Whitman builds up, mostly by opposites, a critical profile of the social mentality emerging out of the new economic conditions. His handling of the material is tamely decorous, however, compared with the outrageous vitality displayed in the subtly varying treatment of the same subject in "Song of Myself." Witness the following episode, which deals with the grotesque perversion of the gift of life into a market commodity.[42]

> I am satisfied . . . . I see, dance, laugh, sing;
> As God comes a loving bedfellow and sleeps at my side all
>   night and close on the peep of the day,
> And leaves for me baskets covered with white towels bulging
>   the house with their plenty,
> Shall I postpone my acceptation and realization and scream at
>   my eyes,
> That they turn from gazing after and down the road,
> And forthwith cipher and show me to a cent,
> Exactly the contents of one, and exactly the contents of two,
>   and which is ahead?   (1:4)

Prudence is farcically exposed here as a neurotically inadequate philosophy for living, adopted by an insecure ego. The ego's anxiety in the face of internal pressure from those instincts which it has completely failed to integrate is expressed as a shrill, frightened intolerance of the incalculable, because it is uncontrollable. Against such a desperately defensive attempt to foreclose the question of where mankind is to find its proper satisfactions, Whitman sets not the localized impulse of sexual need but the diffused, plastic, unsubduable power of the erotic. If those baskets covered with white towels "mean" anything, then *that* is what they mean—the environment progressively charged with libidinal energy, as the imagination is sensually aroused. To the mingled fury and fear of that desiccated calculating machine, the prudent mind, the eyes desert its service. Being organs of sense, they revel in an instinctual delight, which is a revelation in itself while leading to the discovery of a vastly augmented internal and external world. As Whitman suggests, such an aggrandizement is the product not of immediate sexual gratification but of sexuality sublimed (instead of being sublimated) into the erotic. The sexual sublime is the counterpart of the spiritual sublime, in that both are experiences in which man, revived and revivified by wonder, recovers a sense of himself as infinite possibility rather than as a known, fixed quantity.

The fixations characteristic of the psychopathology of prudence are vividly brought out in a section from the 1855 preface:

> The premises of the prudence of life are not the hospitality of it or the ripeness and harvest of it. Beyond the independence of a little sum laid aside for burial-money, and of a few clapboards around and shingles overhead on a lot of American soil own'd, and the easy dollars that supply the year's plain clothing and meals, the melancholy prudence of the abandonment of such a great being as a man is to the toss and pallor of years of money-making with all their scorching days and icy nights and all their stifling deceits and underhanded dodgings, or infinitesimals of parlors, or shameless stuffing while others starve . . and all the loss of the bloom and odor of the earth and of the flowers and atmosphere and of the sea and of the true taste of the women and men you pass or have to do with in youth or middle age, and the issuing sickness and desperate revolt at the close of a life without elevation or naivete, and the ghastly chatter of a death without serenity or majesty, is the great fraud upon modern civilization and forethought, blotching the surface and system which civilization undeniably drafts, and moistening with tears the immense features it spreads and spreads with such velocity before the reach'd kisses of the soul.   (2:452–453)

It is a revealing passage in several respects. For one thing, it opens by nostalgically invoking the primitive American dream of a nation of small-scale property owners (whether rural yeomen or urban artisans), for whom property would be no more than a simple means of subsistence and a noble guarantor of personal freedom.[43] For another, it brings out very clearly the hidden adversary element in Whitman's poetic stance. If the "premise" of "Song of Myself" is the need to show hospitality to the chances of life, then that is by way of deliberate, combative opposition to the very different presuppositions underlying the prudential conduct of business affairs. Similarly, Whitman's repeated exploration, in his poetry, of the relation between self and world in terms of the figure of love and of sexual passion has, as its usually unspoken counterpart, the view here broadly hinted at, that intense commercial activity is powered by repressed or misdirected sexual energy ("icy nights").

Indeed, the passage treats the acquisitive spirit of capitalist enterprise as a composite, corporate form of neurosis. The phrase "melancholy prudence" may be Whitman's way of saying that in his eyes the vigorous commercialism of modern America is but a melancholy sight. But there is also the implication that prudence is itself a symptom of melancholia. Dickens, it will be remembered, found in the extremes of mood that typified the melancholic character a perfect model for the manic, purposeless energy and bleak despair of which the contemporary social world seemed to him to be compounded. The "melancholy-mad elephants" of the cotton looms in *Hard Times;* the ennui that paralyzes the will of many in *Bleak House,* while Trooper George runs a shooting gallery where suppressed violence may safely explode; the hollow Merdle and neurotically restless Fanny; this pattern of contrasts, suggesting a profoundly disordered social psychology, recurs in "the toss and pallor . . . the scorching days and icy nights" of a "melancholy prudence" which is a travesty of true "forethought."

Many years earlier than either Dickens or Whitman, Blake had recorded, in the *Book of Urizen,* the emergence of man in his own period as a gross, appetitive self. The devastating image he offered for this monstrous social birth was the coming into being of the body as a crude collection of sensory organs, each with its unassuageable craving:

> In ghastly torment wide,
> Within his ribs bloated round
> A craving Hungry Cavern;

Thence arose his channel'd Throat,
And, like a red flame, a Tongue
Of thirst and of hunger appear'd.[44]

The innocent body is thus deformed, remade in the very image of greed. Yet, behind this dominion of sense lies fear. The deep-set eyes, and down-turned nostrils are the product of defensive anxiety, while man's whole corporeal being stiffens self-protectively into a calcified rigidity: "A vast Spine writh'd in torment / Upon the winds, shooting pain'd / Ribs like a bending cavern / And bones of solidness Froze / Over all his bones of joy."[45] Whitman's attempts, in "Song of Myself," to unfreeze this body and to nerve it again for joy, is part and parcel of his anatomy of psychic health:

> If I worship any particular thing it shall be some of the spread
> of my body;
> Translucent mould of me it shall be you,
> Shaded ledges and rests, firm masculine coulter, it shall
> be you,
> Whatever goes to the tilth of me it shall be you,
> You my rich blood, you milky stream pale strippings of
> my life;
> Breast that presses against other breasts it shall be you,
> My brain it shall be your occult convolutions,
> Root of washed sweet-flag, timorous pond-snipe, nest of
> guarded duplicate eggs, it shall be you,
> Mixed tussled hay of head and beard and brawn it shall
> be you,
> Trickling sap of maple, fibre of manly wheat, it shall be you;
> Sun so generous it shall be you,
> Vapors lighting and shading my face it shall be you,
> You sweaty brooks and dews it shall be you,
> Winds whose soft-tickling genitals rub against me it shall
> be you,
> Broad muscular fields, branches of liveoak, loving lounger in
> my winding paths, it shall be you,
> Hands I have taken, face I have kissed, mortal I have ever
> touched, it shall be you.   (1:33)

This is a dramatic substantiation of his creed: "I believe in the flesh and the appetites, / Seeing hearing and feeling are miracles, and each part and tag of me is a miracle" (1:32–33). Accordingly, there is indeed a naming of parts—not by repeating the familiar terms of physical identification so as to draw up an inventory of the commonplace, but by finding a language of wonder that can express his body's own intricate, independent existence, and so bring him to a fuller identity. What Whitman is doing in joyfully tracing the mysterious contours, excrescences, and organic processes of this "foreign" body is accepting the spread of his personal being beyond the area dominated and controlled by the ego. The "I" extends itself to, and through, a recognition of this "you" which nevertheless is still decidedly "*my* body." Here the "my" is clearly not a simple possessive. It does not mean this body belongs to the "me." Rather, as the whole passage makes clear, Whitman is communicating a satisfying experience of the self as indwelling everywhere in the body. Whereas the passage starts by registering details of the body as if they were features of the natural environment, it then proceeds to treat the natural world as if it were sentient and sensuously organized like the human body, so that it is through the body that man best gains entry to an understanding of the real nature of his world. Moreover, Whitman's corporeal identity is strengthened by the world's delighted physical recognition of *him*. Nor is its response only one of intimate sexuality. The sexuality is integrated with other aspects of the world's approaches to Whitman. And in its conduct towards him it, too, recognizes his body (inclusive of its sexuality) as having the status of a person. The sun is generous, the vapor implicitly considerate, and the liveoak is a "loving lounger in my winding paths." Even his sweat is provided with new meaning in being seen as the counterpart of brooks and dew. That it is misleading to talk dismissively of all this as "narcissism" (at least in the ordinary sense of the word) is shown by its outcome in the final sentence: "Hands I have taken, face I have kissed, mortal I have ever touched, it shall be you." The affectionate, sympathetic relationship with another, does not simply follow what has preceded: it flows directly from it. Whitman's security of personal being—incorporated as it is in a complex state of physical well-being—leaves him free to reach out, literally and metaphorically, to acknowledge the being of others. By rejecting possessiveness, with all its aggressions and defenses, he has entered into fuller possession of himself.

WHITMAN'S observations on the proprietorial and acquisitive self, whether in his notes or in "Song of Myself," are frequently infused with the values and expressed in the language of a venerable Christian and biblical tradition. But they are also addressed very directly to, and deeply affected by, the special circumstances of his own age. Emerson characterized that age as one in which "A selfish commerce and government have caught the eye and usurped the hand of the masses. It is not to be contested that selfishness and the senses write the laws under which we live, and that the street seems to be built, and the men and women in it moving not in reference to pure and grand ends, but rather to very short and sordid ones."[46] And contemporary observers, domestic and foreign, almost without exception seconded Emerson's opinion, seeing the average American of this period as one "straining every fibre to accumulate the things he covets and amoral about the methods to be used."[47]

It is true that Whitman will ostensibly have none of this. Whenever he raises the question of American materialism, it is in order to exonerate the average American, and to place the blame as squarely as possible on the cupidity of the wealthy business class. Yet such is the resourceful passion displayed in "Song of Myself" against the psychopathology of possession, that it becomes clear the malaise is far too insidiously infectious ever to be credibly confined to the quarantine of a single class. Whitman had himself explicitly conceded this in the editorial he wrote in 1846 for the Brooklyn *Daily Eagle* entitled "Morbid Appetite for Money." Whereas religious fanaticism might abate with time, "the mad passion for getting rich does not die away in this manner. It engrosses all the thoughts and the time of man. It is the theme of all their wishes. It enters into their hearts and reigns paramount there." Although this obsession was chiefly promoted by the banks and other "immense moneyed institutions," it radiated outward until it "enter[ed] into every transaction of society, and more or less taint[ed] its moral soundness. And from this it is that the great body of the working-men should seek to guard themselves."[48]

It is obviously true that "Song of Myself" does not concern itself with the detailed socioeconomic causes and results of Jacksonian capitalism; but it is a reaction—and as valid and constructive a reaction as the political radicalism in which the younger Whitman engaged— to the widespread human world produced by this process. Those anti-acquisitive aspects of "Song of Myself" that have already been identified can be better understood if something is known not only about Whitman's cultural and religious vision but also about that social and political criticism of his age, which his own earlier experiences produced in him.

As the previous chapter has shown, the early Whitman lived through and was closely identified with a decisive transformation in the social character and structure of New York and Brooklyn. From the twenties onwards, the work conditions of the self-employed craftsmen, artisans, and tradesmen—the solid bulk of the population of the cities— changed very markedly in what has been variously described as a period of "epochal historical transformations," or, quite simply, "the great transformation."[49] This was due to the advance from the artisanal to the post-artisanal phase of capitalist production.[50] Under the former, the producer, although ultimately subject to local market forces, is still able to retain a considerable amount of control over his work, including the eventual terms and conditions of sale. Consequently the process is one not easily construed by the participants as a purely financial transaction, as there is much more at stake, at every stage, than the accumulating of capital. Marx himself drew attention to the paradox of a situation where the workshop was run by a man who was at once a capitalist, of a minor kind, and a "master" who, in being a master *craftsman,* was primarily an artist, initiating his apprentices into the mysteries of his craft. His relationship to them was more like that of a professor to his pupils than of an employer to employees.[51] But in the post-artisanal phase the function (and with it the whole status) of the producer is fundamentally altered. He now produces for a middleman who deals in a complex, increasingly remote, and demanding market. In the first instance this intermediary may be only the distributor of the product, but even then he soon comes to dictate the terms of production. Alternatively, he may himself be a large producer, who uses the small producer only as a profitable source of supply. Under this arrangement the former artisan, now effectively a supplier or hirer of labor in return for money, finds himself deeply implicated in a system of relations which alter his whole conception of himself and his work. In short, his consciousness is changed in the ways Whitman explores so critically in "Song of Myself." He lives by the competitive accumulation of capital, rather than by virtue of what he produces through the exercise and public demonstration of patiently acquired skills.

The change from the artisanal to the post-artisanal system of production contributed very largely toward the making of a commercially dynamic mid-nineteenth-century America. But from the beginning this transition caused a serious, and in some cases traumatic, upheaval, whose effects continued to be very widely felt throughout the fifties, not least in Whitman's poetry. The late twenties and thirties saw labor movements and disturbances with which Whitman and his family were fairly closely associated. Workingmen's parties and later the Equal Rights (or Locofoco) movement were important symptoms of, and interesting reactions to, the changing labor conditions and social distress of those decades.[52] There was, however, no solid front maintained by the various social groups affected, because it was for them a complicated situation of gains and losses. There were those who thrived under these new conditions, while even the losers remained hopeful the very developments which had downgraded them would eventually benefit them spectacularly. By the fifties the industrial and social revolution was virtually complete, although different trades were affected to differing degrees, and at variable rates of change, as huge firms came to coexist alongside thousands of small shops and establishments in "a metropolitan labyrinth of factories and tiny artisan establishments, central workrooms and outworkers' cellars, luxury firms and sweatwork strapping shops."[53] At one extreme was the shockingly exploited sweated labor of the clothes trade, with its elaborate system of subcontractors, in-shop workers, garret masters, out-workers, and operatives. At the other extreme were such trades as blacksmithing and butchering, which, although they were relatively unaffected by the new manufacturing system, were firmly locked into the new capitalist economy.

Exceptionally sensitive to all the different issues involved, and to the different levels of those issues, Whitman turned to poetry to resolve him of his ambiguities. In "Song of Myself" he makes contemporary capitalism, with all the freedom and variety of existence it quite genuinely seems to him to promise, the ostensibly simple subject of his celebrations; while at the same time he attacks the very spirit of selfhood, which in historical fact animates and agitates this new world—pulling down its vanity by means of his very different pride in himself. It is almost as if he were trying to bring the artisanal and post-artisanal phases he had known together into a single imaginative synthesis, in which each of the two elements is used to criticize and transform the other. In this he is perhaps a fascinating example of how poetry made a visionary out of "the schizophrenic Jacksonian, the man who looks backward while plunging forward."[54] And it was this visionary who, in "Song of Myself," produced his own distinctively American view of what Marx, at virtually the same time and with tragic splendor, was calling the simultaneous "birth and decline" of the individual.

3 ✎ Inhabiting the Kosmos

"WALT WHITMAN, an American, one of the roughs, a kosmos" (1:31). Ever since the anonymous author of the 1855 *Leaves of Grass* revealed his identity in that braggart line, he has himself been identified as the poet of the "kosmos." The word is instantly recognizable as his trademark, and as the very distillation of his creed. It announces his belief in a complete world discoverable within every individual (body and soul), equal and answering to the world without, the plentitude and diversity of the created universe. These worlds are, moreover, assumed to be governed by identical principles of natural order; spiritual laws which establish the internal coherence that distinguishes kosmos from its necessary antithesis chaos. The world-making poet, in his turn, develops his own little verbal realm, the heterocosm of his poetry, by means of creative powers continuous with those that inform and advance the macrocosm of the organic universe. His poems are accordingly possessed of organic form. A "kosmos" of sorts themselves, they thereby offer, by virtue of their form as well as their content, a revelation of the original Kosmos.

This much is obvious to anyone who knows anything about Whitman. Yet these and related implications of the word "kosmos" continue to attract critical notice, to the detriment of other, less prominent but extremely interesting, connotations of the word as used by Whitman.[1] Perhaps it is therefore time to examine a rather different aspect of this familiar term. "I find the contemporary substitution of society for the cosmos captive and deathly," said Charles Olson not so long ago.[2] But critics of Whitman's poetry have tended towards the opposite extreme—choosing to disregard the social aspects of the kosmos he so lovingly tended. A useful point of entry into his kosmos, on these terms, is to be found in the following passage from the preface to the first edition of *Leaves of Grass:* "The American bards shall be mark'd for generosity and affection, and for encouraging competitors. They shall be Kosmos, without monopoly or secrecy, glad to pass anything to any one—hungry for equals night and day" (*Prose Works,* 2:446).

What is immediately striking is the context in which the word "Kosmos" is here placed and by which it is significantly defined. It is proferred as the antithesis of a prevailing state of affairs, deplored by Whitman, for which he uses the term "monopoly." This by now vague and innocuous word was, for mid-nineteenth-century America, a highly charged social and political term with an interesting political history. Most interpreters of Whitman have gladly assumed "Kosmos" to be a completely nonpartisan word, untainted by political associations and relating only to Whitman's spiritual convictions: and yet here it is, being clearly, even aggressively used, to criticize important socioeconomic trends in contemporary America—developments summed up in that single, controversial word "monopoly." Clearly, therefore, this latter word is well worth investigating for whatever new light it can throw on Whitman's polemical Kosmos.

The passage quoted from the preface allows some rapid progress to be made in these directions. "Monopoly" is, as inference makes clear, synonymous with secrecy, niggardliness, dislike of competition, possessiveness, and domination. Whitman thus composes a psychological picture of what was for him a familiar social type. But he does not explicitly mention the economic assumptions that at this point underlie and inform his thinking. These nevertheless appear in the natural bias of such words as "competitors" and "monopoly," terms which clearly indicate that Whitman's thoughts are guided by a belief in the economic egalitarianism of the free market and a hostility to any form of artificial restraint on trade.

His views on monopoly could be seen as a commonplace of Democratic party rhetoric of the 1850s.[3] The party had committed itself publicly to an assault on all forms of privilege and found popular economic targets in the banks and other powerful business corporations. Democrats loved to contrast financiers, and related parasites, with the honest toiling masses who were, they argued, economically disadvantaged since they were prevented by monopolies from gaining their fair share of economic opportunities and rewards. Whitman's attitude towards monopolies is, then, very much in line with that of the Democrats of the fifties, and his remarks could be read as an innocent version of their somewhat cynical populism. But this is extremely unlikely, given Whitman's open disgust, by this time, with party politics in general and with the Democratic party in particular. What is much more probable is that he is doing what he repeatedly did throughout this antebellum decade: invoking the stirring idealism of the recent political past in order to expose the seedy corruption of those ideals in the present. And the period which Whitman then, as later, regarded as the age of the political giants before the flood was that of his own childhood and early manhood; the period when it was still possible to regard Jacksonianism as a natural and desirable development of Jeffersonian democracy.

"As the term was commonly understood in the Jackson era," Edward Pessen has written, "a monopoly was a corporate charter granted a group of individuals by a special legislative enactment."[4] Opposition to this practice was widespread, but especially vocal among the workers and the radicals, the two overlapping groups with whom Whitman tended—however romantically—to identify himself. When the workingmen's movements finally collapsed in the face of the 1837 recession, many of their ideas, particularly those relating to monopoly, were carried into the Democratic party by the Locofocos, who campaigned for equal social, political, and (most important in this context) economic rights. Whitman himself came to be associated with this faction and was a particular admirer of William Leggett, the leading socioeconomic theoretician and campaigner of the movement.[5]

The agitation for equal rights grew out of labor's resentment at the great economic and therefore social power rapidly accruing to the wealthy few. More specifically, the movement originated—at least as far as Whitman's New York was concerned—in the ever-widening gap between those masters who were able to capitalize (literally) on the breakdown of the old artisanal system of production, and those other small masters and journeymen whose whole way of life was profoundly altered, and downgraded, by these shattering developments. Reluctant to adopt a revolutionary, and un-American, terminology of working-class interests, they clung to the hallowed theory that in egalitarian America every man could, with very little capital, make his own independent, successful way in the world. But in contemporary practice this starting capital was extremely difficult, indeed virtually impossible, to secure. Again unwilling to blame the economic system for this, they fixed their resentment on the most obvious immediate targets. The banks were the first objects of attack, as a prime example of what Whitman called "those immense moneyed institutions which have so impudently practised in the face of day, frauds and violations of their engagements, that ought to make the cheek of every truly upright man burn with indignation. Reckless and unprincipled—controlled by persons who make them complete engines of selfishness—at war with everything that favours our true interests—unrepublican, unfair, untrue and unworthy."[6] They were a natural target, because in the new commercial climate of the mid-century, when the transport revolution had already opened up vast new markets in the West, only those with the necessary capital could take advantage of the expanding economic opportunities; and the banks were accused of restricting their credit facilities to those with the necessary security—that is, the already rich. For this reason they attracted the resentment of the rising small entrepreneurs, as well as the artisans who had virtually been debased to the status of labor. There was also the related grievance that profit-making corporations of any effective size were required by law to obtain special monopoly charters from the state legislature. These were invariably granted only to wealthy groups of applicants who were already possessed of sufficient capital. It was, in the eyes of the Locofocos, a perfect example of the unholy alliance between government and privilege. Moreover, the consequent economic inequalities resulted inevitably in further social inequalities, and so undermined the very principles of egalitarianism upon which the American republic was supposedly founded.

Whitman's debt, even as a poet, to the Locofoco movement has been very well demonstrated by Joseph Jay Rubin, who has pointed out that "the singer of 'Song of Myself,' like a veteran Locofoco, annuls special privilege; he is of all ages, colors, religions; he demands esteem for each bodily function and for all God's creation: grass, pismire, star. He insists upon equality of time and of rank."[7] The 1855 preface even sees miracles as being a species of elitism which would be totally unacceptable to an egalitarian deity: "The whole theory of the special and supernatural and all that was twined with it or educed out of it departs as a dream. . . . The great master has nothing to do with miracles. He sees health for himself in being one of the mass. . . . he sees the hiatus in singular eminence. To the perfect shape comes common ground" (2:447–449).

Moreover, the term "Kosmos" is itself, at least in part, of Locofoco extraction, in that it is negatively derived from Whitman's hatred of what seemed to him to be unnatural, un-American, and antidemocratic monopolies. The social world regarded as kosmos appears, therefore, to be composed of those "natural" free-trade relations which are, for Whitman, the prerequisites and guarantee of all other forms of egalitarianism. (Even poets are expected to conduct their verbal trade, and to regulate the economy of their poetry, accordingly.) His passionate belief in free trade, evident from the very beginning of his journalistic career, never faltered, even during his declining years. He continued to the end to regard it not only as safeguarding equality of opportunity, but also as leading to equality of social conditions: "Protectionism, one nation against another nation, property all of it in a few hands, none of it in the many hands—such things, conditions, ask questions which America must answer—yes, answer in the right voice, with the right decision (answer for democracy's sake) or leave our republic to go to hell for its pains. . . . the protection of profit— the protection of the swell proprietors—I guess I don't care a shucks for that: I guess I'd just whip it out of the temple with cords any day if I could."[8]

Time after time, in his conversations with Traubel, he returned to the same subject:

> As things are the working classes as such belong to neither party— are not billed to either. I am glad to see that it is getting through their wool that the tariff, for instance, is more for capital than for labor—always has been so. The great country, the greatest country, the richest country is not that which has the most capitalists, monopolists, immense grabbings, vast fortunes, with its sad, sad foil of extreme, degrading, damning poverty, but the land in which there are the most homesteads, freeholds—where wealth does not show such contrasts high and low, where all men have enough—a modest living—and no man is made possessor beyond the sane and beautiful necessities of the simple

body and the simple soul. The great country, in fact, is the country of free labor—of free laborers: negro, white, Chinese, or others.[9]

In spite of the contemporary references, and the occasionally up-dated phrasing, what is actually being heard here, in 1888, is the voice of the disadvantaged artisans of the 1830s.

But a moment's thought at this point, plus the briefest of backward glances at the original passage quoted from the 1855 preface, will bring out the queer mismatch between Whitman's economic and his social theories. Somehow or other a system of untrammeled economic competition is supposed to produce a harmoniously cooperative and egalitarian social order.[10] In this extraordinary world individuals will actually welcome competition and will even actively seek to promote it, "glad to pass anything to any one," dedicated it would seem to the proposition that social stability depends on a permanent balance between equals.

What is significant, then, is that Whitman here seeks to construct, on the basis of an artisanal version of the orthodox economic theory of his time, a superstructure of human qualities and of social relations that is manifestly at odds both with what that economic system humanly and socially requires in order to function, and with what, in these respects, it is actually likely to produce.[11] Therefore, while apparently championing a system of free commercial enterprise, Whitman is in fact rejecting the whole ethos of such an undertaking. It is a contradiction which lies at the very heart of Whitman's convictions and which manifests itself in everything he writes, including his poetry. And it is a contradiction that can already be discovered in the ambivalent rhetoric of the Locofocos, and in the confused aims of the original workingmen's movements during the thirties.

Pessen has concluded, from his examination of this period, that whereas most of the antimonopolists simply wanted to extend to everyone the capitalistic opportunities they believed had been restricted to the few, some of the workingmen were by contrast critical of the very nature of the economic system itself—"the commercial profit system within which they operated."[12] They disliked the greed of the new entrepreneurial spirit (of which monopolies were, after all, only a prominent expression) and sought to reestablish a respect for labor in place of the encouragement given by the new commercial order to speculativeness and innovation. Marvin Meyers has shown how this difference of opinion about Jacksonian capitalism, which is evident among antimonopolists of the thirties, becomes dramatically foreshortened into contradiction in the writings of William Leggett. Although Leggett apparently welcomed the new capitalism, provided everyone was given an equal opportunity to participate in it, he instinctively looked "for political and moral support . . . not to the enterprising 'new men' of America but to the 'producers of the middling and lower classes': farmers, laborers, mechanics and shopkeepers."[13]

In Whitman's case a comparable mixture of feelings issued, or so I have suggested in the previous chapter, in similar inconsistencies. In spite of his careful mention, for inclusiveness's sake, of financier and connoisseur, he instinctively turned from poetic and political preference to "butchers, sailors, stevedores, and drivers of horses—to ploughmen, wood-cutters, marketmen, carpenters, masons, and laborers,—to workmen in factories—and to all in These States who live by their daily toil! Mechanics!"[14] Ostensibly embracing the whole (and the whole ethos) of his society, he in fact dealt very selectively with it, and thereby refashioned it poetically.

A selective representation of the life of his time was not Whitman's only poetic strategy for dealing with its unattractive realities. Even more effective was his ability to translate the aggressive socioeconomic energies which actually galvanized his society into animating principles of a qualitatively different kind. In other words, he changed his nineteenth-century world into kosmos by displacing social materials from the relatively uncongenial historical milieu of his own time into the preferred realm of a supposedly eternal and universal natural process. His poetry was of course the means whereby, as well as the place wherein, this alchemy or legerdemain of displacement took place.

But if "kosmos" thus involved a poetic transmutation of the socioeconomic facts of mid-nineteenth-century American life, it was also a concept that allowed Whitman to save some of the crude power of that world for his poetry—and thereby to save the poetry itself; because Whitman as poet was deeply dependent, for the strengh and vigor of his creative effort, on his involvement in the hectic disorderliness of the contemporary scene. It was in fact only while "kosmos" functioned, under the pressure of need, as this enabling concept that Whitman was at his greatest as a poet. Its decline into a purely spiritual term left Whitman grasping at air, and building the cloud castles of the future.

"Do I contradict myself? Very well then . . . I contradict myself" (1:82). This, probably the most famous and the most indulgently quoted of all of Whitman's rhetorical flourishes, is also the one that has been taken least seriously. Few critics have attempted patient identification of those contradictions, and fewer still have tried to analyze them so as to discover not only their psychological, but more important perhaps their social, antecedents. The ideological character of one of the most significant of these contradictions has already been identified: Whitman's willingness on the one hand to approve and even to sponsor the vigorously expanding American society of his time, while on the other continuing to have serious reservations about the uncompromisingly competitive origins of its exciting energy.

He resolved this conflict in his poetry by desocializing and "naturalizing" this energy. Instead of acknowledging the social origins and goals of people's actions, he represented them in vitalistic terms, and reconstituted them into a kosmos. The following passage from "Song for Occupations" beautifully illustrates some of the successful poetic strategies employed by Whitman to transfigure his particular historical society into kosmos, so as to minimize its for him disquieting characteristics:

> The usual routine . . . . the workshop, factory, yard, office,
>   store, or desk;
> The jaunt of hunting or fishing, or the life of hunting
>   or fishing,
> Pasturelife, foddering, milking and herding, and all the
>   personnel and usages;
> The plum-orchard and apple-orchard . . . .
>   gardening . . . . seedlings, cuttings, flowers and vines,
> Grains and manures . . marl, clay, loam . . the subsoil
>   plough . . the shovel and pick and rake and
>   hoe . . irrigation and draining;
> The currycomb . . the horse-cloth . . the halter and bridle and
>   bits . . the very wisps of straw,

> The barn and barn-yard . . the bins and mangers . . the mows
> and racks;
> Manufactures . . commerce . . engineering . . the building of
> cities, and every trade carried on there . . and the
> implements of every trade,
> The anvil and tongs and hammer . . the axe and wedge . . the
> square and mitre and jointer and smoothingplane.   (1:91)

The very syntax there ensures that such controversial features of the contemporary social landscape as "workshop, factory, yard, office," and others are quickly naturalized by being integrated, through parallelism, with "plum-orchard and apple-orchard . . . gardening" and other apparently timeless rural pursuits. Then, the formidable economic machinery for producing the new capitalist power—"manufactures . . commerce . . engineering," and so on—is honored with only a brief mention, before being swamped by the traditional materials of the disappearing world of independent artisans and craftsmen.[15] And the catalog rhetoric works throughout, as so frequently in Whitman's poetry, to represent American society not as a particular historical phenomenon, but as the supreme expression of the inexhaustible vitality of nature.

This catalog rhetoric has been most fully analyzed, and its several functions best explained, by Lawrence Buell. In a penetrating aside he suggests that the device was Whitman's way of preventing the world from disintegrating, as for him it constantly threatened to do, into a spectacle of endless mutability and into the chaos of a meaningless succession of experiences. His catalog technique allows him "to move so fast through the circuit of forms that no catastrophe can touch him. The spirit triumphs over chaos by sheer energy."[16] For Buell's psychological analysis of the origins and mode of operation of this literary technique I would, in the context of the present discussion, substitute a social explanation. It is catalog rhetoric that enables Whitman to move so fast through the circuit of social phenomena that the catastrophe of the underlying logic cannot touch him. Through the energy of his writing he imbues his social world with "Kosmic" energy, and manages, for the duration of his poems, credibly to transform the capitalist spirit by which his society was in fact animated into the indwelling spirit of the living universe.

As suggested in the last chapter, Whitman was able to achieve this integration of the human world of work into the natural kosmos by imparting idealized artisanal qualities to the post-artisanal world. In his late conversations with Traubel he spelled out, fairly clearly, what he had been doing with his early poetry in this respect: "In business it is too much the custom to sink labor in money values: which is all the more reason why I should break through the custom—show that I put quite another estimate upon work, product."[17] He was indeed obsessed—it is not too strong a word—with the world of work, perhaps because he intuitively recognized its increasingly problematical character. Again he discussed with Traubel the fascination the subject held for him:

> I sat there—learned a few new words—words of trades and they are poems to me—a word is a poem of poems! In my early years I had a great fondness for names in trade—names among carpenters, bricklayers, transportation men—always learned, always retained them. If I knew one and forgot it, I would be much worried. But as time wore on, while my curiosity remained, its direction changed somewhat. Instead of minor names—names of objects—I now hungered for names of trades themselves, occupations: so much so that Dr. Bucke now vaunts that he knows no trade or occupation that is not in some way mentioned in *Leaves of Grass*—though *I* do—many of them. But Bucke declares he has tried to detect one, but never found it.[18]

In actual economic fact the multiplication of trades after, say, 1850 was largely the result of the breakdown of the earlier craft structure and the advent of "money values." Whitman, however, treated it all as a glorious extension (rather than destruction) of artisan values, witness the enthusiasm with which he listed, in one of his pieces for the *Standard* (1862), the "Annual Manufactures and Products of Brooklyn, According to the State Census, 1855."[19] Aspects of the artisanal world writ heroically large provided him with his model of the "natural" state of free enterprise:

> O muscle and pluck forever for me!
> O workmen and workwomen forever for me!
> O farmers and sailors! O drivers of horses forever for me!
> O I will make the new bardic list of trades and tools!

. . . . . .

> O for native songs! carpenter's, boatman's, ploughman's
> songs! shoemaker's songs!   (2:291)

As far as possible he describes people going about their independent business, expressing themselves in work as completely as in leisure, deriving immediate satisfaction from whatever it is they do, exercising their unique skills in living, simply acting out their existences. And the market economy is nowhere in sight:

> The crew of the fish-smack pack repeated layers of halibut in
> the hold,
> The Missourian crosses the plains toting his wares and
> his cattle,
> The fare-collector goes through the train—he gives notice by
> the jingling of loose change,
> The floormen are laying the floor—the tinners are tinning the
> roof—the masons are calling for mortar,
> In single file each shouldering his hod pass onward
> the laborers;
> Seasons pursuing each other the indescribable crowd is
> gathered . . . . it is the Fourth of July . . . . what salutes of
> cannon and small arms!
> Seasons pursuing each other the plougher ploughs and the
> mower mows and the wintergrain falls in the ground;
> Off on the lakes the pikefisher watches and waits by the hole
> in the frozen surface.   (1:19)

Even as social beings, such people—regardless of whether they are urban or rural—seem to live in a state of nature, the human inhabitants of the natural kosmos. That it does seem so is partly due, however, to another of Whitman's poetic achievements—his creation of nature in the very image of American society as he would wish it to be. If in his poetry American society seems to be the living kosmos incarnate in human flesh, that is only because previously the kosmos has, in the first place, been conceived of in specifically American terms. But this is a point best left for discussion in Chapter 5.

Whitman's kosmic approach to the socioeconomic life of his times also had the advantage of denying the conflicts which were built into the actual economic structure of society. Whitman was certainly disturbed, throughout his life, by social conflict. Speaking to Traubel of "the strain of American life" he declared that "every man is trying to outdo every other man—giving up modesty, giving up honesty, giving up generosity, to do it; creating a war, every man against every man: the whole wretched business falsely keyed to money ideals, money politics, money religions, money men."[20] Likewise earlier in his career, shortly indeed after the first two editions of *Leaves of Grass* had appeared, he conceded that in the America of his day "the brotherhood of humanity is looked upon as a fine phrase signifying but little or nothing." Nor would he dispute that "it may seem so, in the jostle and attrition of conflicting elements that make up the life-battle; it may seem that selfishness is the universal rule, and sympathy only the rare exception." But he did argue that great disasters roused the very best in people and revealed "that mysterious sympathy which is the universal bond underlying all mankind" even "in these days, stigmatised as matter of fact and materialistic."[21]

In "Song of the Answerer," the poem constructed out of materials from the 1855 preface, the language of his poetry is proffered as the Pentecostal tongue which will resolve the Babel of voices, arising from the American world, into unity:

> Every existence has its idiom . . . . every thing has an idiom
> and tongue;
> He resolves all tongues into his own, and bestows it upon
> men . . and any man translates . . and any man translates
> himself also:
> One part does not counteract another part. . . . He is the
> joiner . . he sees how they join.   (1:139–140)

In his office as kosmic poet, Whitman acts (without acknowledging it) as mediator, reconciler, and "joiner" (the craftsman-carpenter's term is singularly appropriate).[22] This is possible because the mode of his kosmos is simultaneity, where everyone is conceived of as acting together in a single moment of time which therefore takes on the attributes of space. Only in this space, perhaps, could the various conflicting interests within Whitman's society, and the many contradictory impulses within Whitman himself, be happily accommodated through justaposition, and thereby apparently be reconciled. "Kosmos" allows these opposing elements to appear, as they do in Whitman's famous catalogs, and as they do within the magic "space" of his poems, "inseparable together":

> The squaw wrapt in her yellow-hemmed cloth is offering
>   moccasins and bead-bags for sale,
> The connoisseur peers along the exhibition-gallery with
>   halfshut eyes bent sideways,
> The deckhands make fast the steamboat, the plank is thrown
>   for the shoregoing passengers,
> The young sister holds out the skein, the elder sister winds it
>   off in a ball and stops now and then for the knots,
> The one-year wife is recovering and happy, a week ago she
>   bore her first child,
> The cleanhaired Yankee girl works with her sewing-machine
>   or in the factory or mill,
> The nine months' gone is in the parturition chamber, her
>   faintness and pains are advancing;
> The pavingman leans on his twohanded rammer—the
>   reporter's lead flies swiftly over the notebook—the
>   signpainter is lettering with red and gold,
> The canal-boy trots on the towpath—the bookkeeper counts
>   at his desk—the shoemaker waxes his thread.   (1:17–18)

The socially significant differences of race, sex, class, and religion are very much part of the point of this spatial composition, the effect of which is to impute to American society the unity in diversity Whitman believed characterized the life of the natural order. It is a signal—if ambiguous—achievement, and one for which Whitman has not really been given due credit by the critics. The reason for this is simple. Literary critics have still not properly registered what recent historians of mid-nineteenth-century America have repeatedly emphasized; namely, the presence of serious divisions and conflicts within antebellum Northern society. Nowhere were these more marked than in Whitman's own city, described by Sean Wilentz as "a city that ranked second to none as a disaster of laissez-faire urban development."[23] The growth of commercial New York, centering on Wall Street, Broadway, and South Street, was matched by that of "its sordid twin, a seemingly alien social and political city, associated with crime, disorder, dirtiness, political deceit, governmental corruption, and burdensome taxes." In fact, the metropolitan geography of New York City "was crudely organized on the basis of economic class."[24] The actual urban space of New York, clearly subdivided as it was into rich and poor areas, was a very different affair from the socially inclusive agora or space of Whitman's poetic kosmos.

This schizophrenic city was in part the product not of mental but of social breakdown—the breaking up of the artisanal class, under the impact of metropolitan capitalism, into two vividly contrasting social groups, the one being increasingly absorbed into the successful middle class, the other forming part of a social continuum that included the laboring masses. Viewed from below, from the point of view of this recently created working class, whose numbers were swollen daily by the arrival of immigrants in the thousands, New York society was anything but harmonious. What genuine community of interests, other than those of crude economics, could there be to bind together the exploiter and the exploited—the underpaid piece-rate workers, say, who toiled to meet the requirements of garret masters, themselves subject to the demands of major contractors, manufacturers, and wholesalers? Division was the very name of the economic game—from the subdivision of labor to the social segmentation of the previously relatively homogeneous artisan class, and the creation of definite class boundaries.

But if Whitman's kosmos in these respects stands in an opposite and corrective relationship to the actual New York society of his time, in other respects, indeed, it closely approximates that society's most favorable (mis)conception of itself. One of the seminal points made by Spann is that "New York was *the* American metropolis precisely because, unlike Boston or Philadelphia, it both encouraged individuality and accommodated cultural diversity . . . New York, therefore, became a confederation of individuals each seeking to live his own life in his own way. This individualism was balanced by each man's recognition that he depended on others to achieve his goals."[25] "The city," Spann concludes, summarizing the public rhetoric of the time, "would become a cosmos of human diversity where in public all could meet as brothers in disregard of the diversity of the private worlds from which they came."[26]

The social reality was, however, as Spann points out, rather different from this official rhetoric. It involved "real ethnic, religious, and racial tensions." It also involved rampant selfishness: "Materialism, corruption, ruthless individualism, an indifference to the plight of the weak, the sense of individual helplessness—these formed the negative side of any large city, but perhaps nowhere more than in New York were they so closely aligned with the prevailing ethos."[27] And just as, in the passage originally quoted from the 1855 preface, Whitman's attack on monopoly, and his use of a laissez-faire language to characterize human relations obtaining within his kosmos, brought him very close to the party rhetoric of the fifties, so too does his creation in his poetry of a naturally harmonious society of extreme individualists closely accord with the dominant public rhetoric of his time. There is a poignancy laced with irony to this recurring situation, where Whitman's urgent improvement of social fact into visionary kosmos should, in certain crucial respects, so closely resemble the concealment of fact by a conservative rhetoric which complacently represents existing mid-century American society as "a cosmos of human diversity."

WHITMAN is sometimes liable to behave in his poetry as if his kosmos were not only incipient but actually immanent in the existing scheme of things. At other times he acknowledges the considerable distance there is between his ideal of a harmoniously individualistic society and the contemporary scene. Conflicting interests are acknowledged to be the order of the day, so that, according to the 1855 preface, an important function of the American poet is to act as a "common referee":

> Of all nations the United States with veins full of poetical stuff most need poets and will doubtless have the greatest and use them the greatest. Their Presidents shall not be their common referee so much as their poets shall. Of all mankind the great poet is the equable man. Not in him but off from him things are grotesque or eccentric or fail of their sanity. Nothing out of its place is good and nothing in its place is bad. He bestows on every object or quality its fit proportions neither more nor less. He is the arbiter of the diverse and he is the key. He is the equalizer of his age and land . . . he supplies what wants supplying and checks what wants checking. (2:743)

Whitman may very well be guided at this point in his thinking by a familiar observation made by Emerson in his essay "The Poet." The artist, he there explains, "is said to see through the earth, [to turn] the world to glass and show us all things in their right series and procession."[28] But to acknowledge, on Whitman's behalf, this debt is also to realize how he sharpens this metaphysical comment into specific, and acute, social perception. The fissiparous diversity of America; the continuing inequalities within this professedly egalitarian society; the "grotesque" and "eccentric" features of the current way of life; these are acknowledged to be the subject of the poet's corrective attention. Nevertheless, Whitman is committed, as a good, believing American, to the proposition that his society is structurally sound.

Kosmos is the product of his need to revolutionize, or at least reform, society without either his, or its, knowing it. The reordering, adjusting, and redistributing he refers to actually entails a fundamental revaluing and restructuring; and the strain of effecting this revolution by stealth shows itself periodically even when Whitman is in his prime. Take, for instance, the following extract from the 1855 preface: "Obedience does not master him, he masters it. High up out of reach he stands turning a concentrated light . . . he turns the pivot with his finger . . . he baffles the swiftest runners as he stands and easily overtakes and envelops them. The time straying toward infidelity and confections and persiflage he witholds by his steady faith . . . he spreads out his dishes . . . he offers the sweet firmfibred meat that grows men and women. His brain is the ultimate brain. He is no arguer . . . he is judgment. He judges not as the judge judges but as the sun falling around a helpless thing" (2:437).[29]

The tone of the passage is ultimately rather odd, because Whitman wavers betwen professions of faith, or trust, and the urge to compel. It is as if he wished to invest himself as poet with the power denied him in life—bestowing upon his poetry the capacity to deliver those social realities, to which he is normally so humiliatingly subject, into his power. There may also very well be humiliating memories of the years spent on ineffectual polemical journalism behind the fantasy of being no "arguer" any longer but "judgment" itself. Sunlight's effortless mastery of "helpless thing[s]" becomes Whitman's trope for the nonchalant power over the world he needs to imagine that, as a poet, he possesses. It is a moment answering to that in Emerson's work when he dreams of the coming of the poet "with tyrannous eye," who will "know the value of our incomparable materials."[30] That phrase "the tyrannous eye" wonderfully betrays Emerson's awareness of precisely what he is up against. He is testily responding to the bumptiousness of an American society which is rampantly vulgar and offensive in its unrepentant self-sufficiency. For the space of a word Emerson dreams Platonically of a spiritual dictator who will subdue this world to order, by dictating uncompromising terms to it.

The dream is sometimes shared by Whitman, except that in his case it takes the form of an imaginary journey to the sun. As used by him, the image is the perfect one for expressing the ambivalence of his relationship to the American scene. It allows him secretly to admit that his judgment of America is made from a point of view outside of the socioeconomic field of American activity, while at the same time it allows him to say the opposite. His use of the image of light ensures his judgments appear not as an indictment from without, but as a disclosure, and an endorsement, of the fundamental good order of contemporary American life.

This strange, ambiguous, flight to the sun exactly corresponds to the process by which Whitman creates his kosmos. It also highlights a fundamental difference between the American and the English Romantic. Think of "Religious Musings," the poem written by Coleridge in his very early days, before the great years of his illustrious association with Wordsworth.[31] It is the product of Coleridge's anxiety at the character of the emerging economic order, an anxiety sufficiently acute to cause him, as early as 1794, to undertake his own flight to the sun:

> There is one Mind, one omnipresent Mind,
> Omnific. His most holy name is Love.
> Truth of subliming import! with the which
> Who feeds and saturates his constant soul,
> He from his small particular orbit flies
> With blest outstarting! From himself he flies,
> Stands in the sun, and with no partial gaze
> Views all creation; and he loves it all,
> And blesses it, and calls it very good![32]

The reference is, of course, via Milton, to the angel in the sun in the Book of Revelation, and to God's satisfaction with His Creation, as expressed in the Book of Genesis. Nor are these references incidental, since Coleridge's journey outward, sunward, is a trope for the adventure of discovering and becoming inward with a religious language which creates life anew in very different terms from those deployed by the rational discourse of the dismal science. The resulting revelation implies an accompanying psychological revolution of Copernican proportions: a decentering of the self-centered social personality, to allow unprecedented excursions of the imagination that break out of the confines of self-interest. These "blest outstartings" are doubly blessed: they are instances of a person being so carried away by, and being so caught up in, the wonders of existence, that, like the Ancient Mariner, he blesses life unawares, thereby himself incurring an unexpected blessing. Such experiences are, for Coleridge, truly "subliming":

> 'Tis the sublime of man,
> Our noontide Majesty, to know ourselves
> Parts and proportions of one wondrous whole!
> This fraternises man, this constitutes
> Our charities and bearings.[33]

"The sublime of man," and "noontide majesty" are phrases eminently suited to aspects of "Song of Myself." The particular value of Coleridge's poem, though, is not that it provides us with new terms for familiar aspects of Whitman, but that it supplies us with the hidden terms of Whitman's major poetic equation. It identifies the social and economic circumstances that, when added together, produce (by way of criticism and reaction) the nonpossessive Self examined in the previous chapter, and the alternative society, the human kosmos of his poetry.

Coleridge frankly pictures his society as given over entirely to "embattling interests," lashing himself into a fury at the ubiquitous and murderous trade wars of the eighteenth century. As he surveys the revolting spectacle of the dissolution of "the moral world's cohesion" he speaks with the anguish of outrage:

> we become
> An Anarchy of Spirits! Toy-bewitched,
> Made blind by lusts, disherited of soul,
> No common centre Man, no common sire
> Knoweth! A sordid solitary thing,
> Mid countless brethren with a lonely heart
> Through courts and cities the smooth savage roams
> Feeling himself, his own low self the whole;
> When he by sacred sympathy might make
> The whole one Self! Self, that no alien knows!
> Self, far diffused as Fancy's wing can travel!
> Self spreading still! Oblivious of its own,
> Yet all of all possessing![34]

A similar reaction—necessarily unspoken, because unadmitted—against related tendencies in his own commercial society, may be the original impulse underlying and directing Whitman's famous excursiveness—the "blest outstarting" which so distinguishes his poetry. Still, he could never knowingly subscribe to the grim view taken by Coleridge of an economic individualism which Whitman's own historical and social training had prepared him to regard as a necessary precondition of political democracy and social egalitarianism. He was therefore less able than Coleridge to strike directly at the root causes of the selfish materialism for which he felt such a pronounced yet somewhat perplexed antipathy. Instead, by constructing in his poetry his own version of a Self "oblivious of its own / Yet all of all possessing," he succeeded in the critical task of substituting a very different kind of individualism for the egotism at the center of American existence. (His poem "Kosmos" is a studied portrait of this New Man.) And, at the same time, by interweaving selected, idealized aspects of the artisanal and the natural worlds, he produced a human kosmos which credibly appeared to be an evolved form of the existing free enterprise system—and which could be conveniently mistaken for the status quo on occasion.

Whitman could never distance himself openly from the existing premises, as well as practices, of his society in the way Coleridge did by his revolutionary flight to the sun. And in any case even had he undertaken such a flight, he could never have survived poetically there. The devices of "Self" and "kosmos" provided him with what he most needed both as a man and as a poet. They allowed him to continue to partake, on his own, recreative terms, of the energies of prewar America. But with the war the country accelerated into an advanced state of commercial and industrial capitalism. It was impossible for Whitman any longer to read artisan-related qualities into this America, and so he could not refashion this new environment into a kosmos. But even then he did not take a Coleridgean flight to the sun. Instead, he took flight, disastrously, to the future. While not "condemning the show" in *Democratic Vistas* he nevertheless urges "every envisioned soul" to "migrate" to "what we can already conceive of superior and spiritual points of view." "Conceive," be it noted, and not "perceive." The new, migratory Whitman openly (and disastrously for his poetic career) took off into theoretical space, "to make observations for our Vistas, breathing rarest air" (2:417). It is a far and desperate cry from the exultant 1855 endorsement of contemporary American life; "the theme is creative and has vista."[35] But then at that time the kosmos had been everywhere in sight, whereas his hopes had since vanished into thin air.

4 ❧ Crossing Brooklyn Ferry

DEVICES such as the kosmos and the transcendent self allowed Whitman to avail himself of the energies of this period without on the whole inquiring too closely into their economic origins, or condoning, to any serious degree, their social consequences. As a result not only did he survive in, but he thrived on, the excitement of his turbulent milieu. Yet always in the vibrancy of his celebrations there is a slight tremor of unease, the shadow of a doubt concerning whether his poetic act, a verbal deed that is also a histrionic performance, will work this time. Taking pleasure in "moving in these broad lands as broad as they" (2:308), he nevertheless needs to feel that the world depends on his benediction: "Have I forgotten any part? / Come to me, whoever and whatever, till I give you recognition." What surely lies behind this characteristic gesture is neither arrogance nor complacency, but fear: fear of some part of the American character that carries on an anarchic life of its own, beyond his kosmos; fear even, that the quintessential America may exist totally independently of him, and beyond his recognition.

Although this feeling is probably constant in his work, it runs at different levels and pressures, sometimes making itself very evident, at other times seeming actually to inspire confidence ("Song of Myself"), or, as in "Crossing Brooklyn Ferry," lending serenity a deeper hue—whether darker or richer depending perhaps on the angle at which the scene is held to the light. Light permeates "Crossing Brooklyn Ferry," as also it fills the canvases of some splendid American paintings of the very same period, a coincidence that is well worth pursuing. Even the contrast between the cosmic exuberance of "Song of Myself" and the quieter tones of "Crossing Brooklyn Ferry" is strikingly mirrored in the two main kinds of landscape painting produced by the outstanding artists of mid-nineteenth-century America. One of the greatest examples of the first school is the familiar, but still astonishing, picture of Niagara Falls (1857) by Frederick Edwin Church, a painting which perfectly answers in style to Whitman's sweeping vistas. A revolutionary work, its main features have been summarized by John Wilmerding:

> Church's version presented something new, an aspect placing it distinctively in the second half of the nineteenth century—the close-in vantage point and the horizontality of the composition. Rather than standing back from the subject, the spectator has to move in to the very precipice of the falls. He is confronted with its pulsing power. The water sweeps in from one side of the canvas and out the other, as if the dimensions of the picture cannot contain this great event. Church also emphasizes the horizon, placing rising clouds just above it to suggest that the scene extends even beyond the sight of the viewer.[1]

The painting bursts its elongated frame in every direction. Most remarkable of all is the way it violates, does deliberate violence to, artistic convention by cutting away the solid ground customarily left in the foreground of pictorial prospects to provide a reassuringly solid, fixed point of view from which the observer regards the panorama. In Church's painting the water laps right up to the very front of the canvas, so that the observing eye seems itself to be a drop of water raised up, as Whitman said of himself, "to buoyancy and vision." Not that the vision this eye glimpses of the energies by which it is itself ineluctably propelled is merely exhilarating. The painting is balanced between the majestic horizontal sweep of the eye around the horseshoe line of the falls and the precipitous drop of the cascade, which is a white magnificence in the distance. In the foreground is only a sinister darkening of the water immediately ahead of us, where it disappears from view over the edge. "What afterlife for the vehemence of sheer-fall?" asks Peter Redgrove, the "Taliesin" poet of our own time who has obsessively explored the coursing energies of a metamorphosing universe.[2]

Whitman is also a writer in the "Taliesin tradition"[3]—Taliesin, the great shape-shifter who is honored in his land of Wales as the father of poetry. Even Whitman's boasting is part of this tradition. When asked "who are you?" Taliesin invariably replies by listing his prodigious exploits of metempsychosis: "A thunderharvest of twinkling grain. / A vivid gang of molten pig-iron. / The great man-eating skull that opens against the sky. / A whistle made from the wingbone of an eagle."[4] But in human beings the response to the vertiginous energies of which they are themselves composed is always deeply equivocal. And in Whitman's case this unease was, as I have already noted, intrinsic to his response to the seething, swirling social environment in which he was immersed. One of his favorite images for the democratic masses was water, and there is no need to distort Whitman into the thundering antidemocrat of *Shooting Niagara* in order to believe that in his poetry, as in Church's painting, the water rushing to display itself proudly in a torrential cataract is also the water darkening towards a plunge into an invisible abyss.

Of course, Wordsworth memorably referred to the "stationary blasts of waterfalls," but when Whitman wanted to intimate an eternal, unchanging state of being that underlay all motion, he turned to the permanent currents of the East River, with its associated human flow. Just as "Crossing Brooklyn Ferry" is a quiet, contemplative poem, constructed on a much more intimate scale than the roving cosmic poetry, so its closest painterly analogue is not the great baroque machinery of the Hudson River school, but the serene calm of some of the time-arresting canvases produced by the luminists, in which water is indeed forever wedded to meditation.[5]

The term "luminist" was first applied in the 1940s to what had until then been the neglected work of a number of remarkable painters. They were not an organized group, but a handful of individuals all of whom, during the third quarter of the nineteenth century, developed a brooding interest in rendering light-suffused landscapes and seascapes. The four major figures have gradually been accepted to be Fitz Hugh Lane (1804–1865), Martin Johnson Heade (1819–1904), John F. Kensett (1816–1872), and Stanford Robinson Gifford (1823–1880), although Church himself may also, but more arguably, qualify for inclusion by virtue of his fascination with atmospheric light. The lingering doubt in his case arises from the kind of light which is present in his work, because the luminists are distinguished not simply by their treatment of light per se, but by the very particular, limpid quality of the light in their paintings. Noting that "the smooth glow of luminist light" is rarely found in European paintings, Barbara Novak has argued that the style is essentially indigenous to the United States, much more so in fact than the "grand opera" manner of Church and Bierstadt in those theatrical panoramas they produced to depict the vastness of the Rockies and the wilderness.[6] She further points out that in luminist paintings "light, because of its silent, *unstirring* energy, causes the universe, as Emerson would have it, to become 'transparent, and the light of higher laws than its own' to shine through it. For Emerson, the soul in man 'is not an organ . . . not a faculty, but light. . . . From within or from behind, a light shines through us upon things and makes us aware that we are nothing, but the light is all.' "[7]

While not disputing the transcendentalist connection, another influential historian of the movement, John Wilmerding, has supplemented this explanation of the origin and significance of luminist light with a social reference. According to him, the "crystallising pictures of the 1850's stand as supreme manifestations of Jacksonian optimism and expansiveness," while the actual or impending Civil War experience accounts for the ominous light which fills some later canvases, such as Martin Johnson Heade's famous painting *Approaching Storm, Beach Near Newport* (1860).[8]

It remains for the following discussion to attempt some sort of commentary on the way light is used in "Crossing Brooklyn Ferry," but a few general points should be made here at the outset. Like the luminists, Whitman was undoubtedly sensitized to light by the spiritual attention it received from the transcendentalists; but, as was also the case with the painters, he used this spiritual vocabulary to express a social vision that was (very broadly speaking) Jacksonian in character. At this point, however, the simple parallel between the painters and the poet begins to grow intriguingly complicated. For whereas the dark side of luminism in no way compromises its spiritual and social optimism, since the one is an unqualified affirmation of the fifties, and the other is the legacy of the Civil War years that followed, Whitman by contrast incorporates both light and dark into a single poem which thereby epitomizes his equivocal relationship with "Jacksonian" America.

Furthermore, there is one clear area of difference separating Whitman from the luminists. Although they, too, are fond of periods like sunset, when the sun is in its axial position and light comes across water in a steady glow, the painters invariably prefer a coastal scene, often a seascape with a ship or two, that is totally empty of human figures and drained of all suggestion of movement. But for Whitman, stillness exists as a paradoxical aspect of movement, and natural process brings human energy irresistibly to mind. Therefore, although in the supreme works of mature luminism—such as Fitz Hugh Lane's *Ship 'Starlight' in the Fog* (1860)—light radiates a permanent calmness very powerfully corresponding to Whitman's experience in "Crossing Brooklyn Ferry" (1856), it is to an earlier work of Lane's, *Boston Harbor* (1850), or to the even busier canvases of Robert Salmon, a precursor of the luminists, that we have to look in order to find human beings, in the very midst of their activities, transfixed and preserved by light. If Salmon's *Wharves of Boston* (1829), or more especially his *Boston Harbor from Constitution Wharf* (1833), could only be supplied with the richer glow that light gives out in the paintings of the mature luminists, then we would have in them a very fair visual approximation of the tranquil surface experience, at least, of "Crossing Brooklyn Ferry."

FROM THE BEGINNING, Whitman's approach to his fellow New Yorkers is rather wary and circumspect:

> Flood-tide of the river, flow on! I watch you, face to face,
> Clouds of the west! sun half an hour high! I see you also face
>   to face.
>
> Crowds of men and women attired in the usual costumes,
>   how curious you are to me!   (1:217)

The phrase "face to face" is conspicuous here in being applied not, as would be expected, to a meeting between human beings, but to an encounter between Whitman and the natural world. The crowd, by contrast, remains unfaced and faceless, and even allowing for the probability that by the word "curious" Whitman means "fascinating," or "mysterious" (as, for instance, he does in "There Was a Child Went Forth"), an impression remains of his detachment from his fellowmen.

But this detachment is not admitted by Whitman, even to himself.

The structural parallelism between the opening two lines and the third is his attempt to heal, or rather to conceal, syntactically, the breach between himself and others. It nevertheless appears that his relationship with them is certainly not like the unmediated, immediate contact he has with flood tide and with clouds. In fact it is partly through the mediating office of the sky, of the water whose flow provides him with acceptable terms for contemplating flux, and above all of the sun, that Whitman is eventually able to approach more closely to "the hundreds and hundreds that cross" (1:217). A particularly significant part is also payed by "you that shall cross from shore to shore years hence" (1:217) in enabling this to happen.

Before the future is brought into play, however, there are intimations of bafflement. The word is Whitman's own, except that it occurs much later, in the penultimate section of "Crossing Brooklyn Ferry," where at last he obliquely acknowledges the unsettled, confused state of mind which is the dark side of this light-filled poem: "Throb, baffled and curious brain! throw out questions and answers!" (1:224). This concealed psychological disturbance does leave its verbal marks very early, though. Its secret history can, for instance, be intriguingly traced in the ubiquitousness of the mentally troubled, equivocating word "curious," and the throbbing of the baffled and curious brain can be sensed, at the outset, in the somewhat disjointed vagueness of his original declarations of faith:

> The impalpable sustenance of me from all things at all hours
> of the day,
> The simple, compact, well-joined scheme—myself
> disintegrated, every one disintegrated, yet part of the
> scheme,
> The similitudes of the past and those of the future.   (1:218)

When Whitman does next turn to "you men and women of a generation, or ever so many generations hence" (1:218), one remarkable feature emerges. Contrary to his usual practice, he conceives of the future not as progress, not as being spiritually well in advance of the present, but in terms of the infinite perpetuation and confirmation of certain forms of the present. The paradox is that only by looking at his surroundings like this, through the imagined eyes of the future, can Whitman sustain the psychological process of meditation by which he gradually achieves security of tenure in his present world. When he assures us, dwellers in the future, "you are more in my meditations than you might suppose" (1:217), we might now reply that we are also more in his meditatons than he himself supposes. Not only are we the subject of his thoughts, we are actually the means by which he maintains his meditative concentration. By thinking of "the certainty of others" who are to follow him, "the life, love, sight, hearing of others" (1:218), he is unconsciously encouraged to turn his own random private impressions ("The glories strung like beads on my smallest sights and hearings") into dependable public observations, so fashioning controlling images out of the unsettling, unpredictable background of change represented by contemporary New York and Brooklyn:

> Just as you feel when you look on the river and sky, so I felt,
> Just as any of you is one of a living crowd, I was one of
> a crowd,
> Just as you are refreshed by the gladness of the river, and the
> bright flow, I was refreshed,
> Just as you stand and lean on the rail, yet hurry with the swift
> current, I stood, yet was hurried,
> Just as you look on the numberless masts of ships, and the
> thick-stemmed pipes of steamboats, I looked.   (1:219)

In collaboration with the future, Whitman gradually orders his perceptions according to an inner, invisible principle of coherence, of which light is the outward and visible sign. In recognition, perhaps, of this, the poem was specifically called "Sun-Down Poem" when it was first published—a reference not only to a time of day, but to the distinctive quality of light by which sun and mind together hold the scene steady. The process is partly one whereby the surrounding world is carried alive and whole into the mind by light: "Just as you are refreshed by the gladness of the river, and the bright flood, I was refreshed"; "I watched the December sea-gulls, I saw them high in the air floating with motionless wings oscillating their bodies, / I saw how the glistening yellow lit up parts of their bodies, and left the rest in strong shadow"; "The scallop-edged waves in the twilight, the ladled cups, the frolicsome crests and glistening" (1:219–220). At

the same time the mind is invested with a reciprocal power of illumination:

> [I too] saw the reflection of the summer-sky in the water,
> Had my eyes dazzled by the shimmering track of beams,
> Looked at the fine centrifugal spokes of light round the shape
>   of my head in the sun-lit water.   (1:219)

This is not narcissism but an act of self-perception utterly central
to Whitman's social philosophy. Genuinely egalitarian democracy
entails, for Whitman, the organizing of society in accordance with
the perception that its center is everywhere, and its circumference
nowhere. One of his favorite images for the equal, fraternal unique-
ness of every human being is the democratic halo, as he explains in
"Poem of You, Whoever You Are":

> Painters have painted their swarming groups, and the centre
>   figure of all,
> From the head of the centre figure spreading a nimbus of
>   gold-colored light,
> But I paint myriads of heads, but paint no head without its
>   nimbus of gold-colored light,
> From my hand, from the brain of every man and woman it
>   streams, effulgently flowing forever.   (1:215)

Nevertheless it may be indicative of his relative lack of social confidence at this point in "Crossing Brooklyn Ferry" that he makes
himself out to be both the democratic perceiver and the democratic
subject of perception, thus completing a defensively closed circuit of
faith. Only later, at the very end of the poem, does he discover the
confidence to include others in, and to associate them with, the same
perception: "Receive the summer-sky, you water! faithfully hold it
till all downcast eyes have time to take it from you! / Diverge, fine
spokes of light, from the shape of my head, or any one's head, in
the sun-lit water!" (1:224). This enlargement of perception comes
through a process of meditation, substantially developed under the
auspices of the future, which allows Whitman to consolidate an integrated, spiritually egalitarian view of the (mostly natural) world to

a point where, by extension, he can virtually believe his vision to be a widely established, socially accomplished fact.

As the occasion is evening, the objective correlative of this meditative vision is light. In his poem to the sun Whitman typically coupled a tribute to the fructifying energies of the "orb aloft full-dazzling" with a particular mention of the light that enfolds all impartially (3:690); and it is to the harmonizing and equalizing powers of light he quite literally looks in "Crossing Brooklyn Ferry." The 1855 preface makes it explicitly clear that for Whitman this natural phenomenon had profound social and political implications—as indeed it had for one of the greatest of the earlier, English generation of Romantic poets. From the Euganean Hills, north of the Lombardy plain, Shelley looks down in 1818 on a post-Napoleonic Italy returned to reactionary tyranny. But as the sun rises, it first works its transforming magic on his immediate surroundings (" 'Till all is bright, and clear, and still, / Round the solitary hill"), and then proceeds to fill the distant prospect of Venice with a radiance which seems, to Shelley, like the advent of democratic liberty, since "the universal light seems to level plain and height." By mid-day the triumph of light is briefly complete, even over Shelley's darkness of spirit, so that the features of both the inner and the outer scene

> Interpenetrated lie
> By the glory of the sky;
> Be it love, light, harmony,
> Odour, or the soul of all
> Which from heaven like dew doth fall
> Or the mind which feeds this verse
> Peopling the lone universe.[9]

The vision begins already to fade in those last two doubting lines, which question its general validity by referring it back to its origins in Shelley's isolation.

In certain crucial respects "Crossing Brooklyn Ferry" can be regarded as the evolved, or revisionist, form of "Lines Written from among the Euganean Hills." This evolution is the counterpart of the social and political revolution which had supposedly made Shelley's lonely libertarian dream an American reality. Both poets speak the language of light, and for both it is a coded form of social discourse;

but the difference between their respective situations seems to be signified in every detail of their chosen locations. Shelley abandons the populous plains and removes to the distant hills, whereas Whitman positions himself on a ferry, plying between two great cities. Shelley's imagination is excited by the sheer opulence of light and kindled by its effortlessly spectacular power to revolutionize an impoverished landscape: "the legioned rooks" are "grey shades" until they are irradiated, and then "their plumes of purple grain, / Starred with drops of golden rain, / Gleam above the sunlit wood."[10] By contrast, Whitman watches seagulls, noticing "how the glistening yellow lit up parts of their bodies and left the rest in strong shadow," and so seems to see light as acting only in solid confirmation of the actual. Hence his preference for the settled light of evening, and Shelley's for inflammatory sunrise and high noon. The choice of hour, like the choice of location, is an index of social perspective, and seems to highlight the difference between a prerevolutionary and a postrevolutionary outlook.

The difference between Shelley and Whitman is indeed unmistakable: and yet in "Crossing Brooklyn Ferry," too, light comes to remedy deficiencies in the surrounding social landscape, except that Whitman is adept at affirming that it (and he) is doing no more than presenting the actual scene in a favorable light. By so doing, he protects the sources of his strength, because whereas Shelley's poetic gifts were an aspect of his adversary relationship to his reactionary age, Whitman's are deeply implicated in his devotion to the American way of life. Whereas Shelley dramatizes the ideological distance between himself and contemporary Europe, the drama in "Crossing Brooklyn Ferry" arises from Whitman's rhetorical efforts to conceal the distance between his vision of democracy and the imperfect reality. In this he is very largely successful, even, as we shall see, when his suppressed, "baffled" sense of isolation eventually demands, and is duly given, more urgent expression.

In "Crossing Brooklyn Ferry" light is presented as the natural democratic medium. But it actually acts as a democratizing medium. Therefore, light is here to Whitman's meditative achievement what energy is to the making of kosmos in his other poetry: it is the vital agent that allows vision secretly to infiltrate and to inhabit historical facts. "Love, like the light, silently wrapping all! / Nature's amelioration blessing all!" (3:681). Consequently, its influence is by no means confined to specifically mentioned light effects, since it permeates the mind and sets the very tone and tempo of observation:

> I too saw the reflection of the summer-sky in the water,
> Had my eyes dazzled by the shimmering track of beams,
> Looked at the fine centrifugal spokes of light round the shape
>   of my head in the sun-lit water,
> Looked on the haze on the hills southward
>   and southwestward,
> Looked on the vapor as it flew in fleeces tinged with violet,
> Looked toward the lower bay to notice the arriving ships,
> Saw their approach, saw aboard those that were near me,
> Saw the white sails of schooners and sloops, saw the ships
>   at anchor,
> The sailors at work in the rigging or out astride the spars,
> The round masts, the swinging motion of the hulls, the
>   slender serpentine pennants,
> The large and small steamers in motion, the pilots in their
>   pilot-houses,
> The white wake left by the passage, the quick tremulous whirl
>   of the wheels,
> The flags of all nations, the falling of them at sun-set,
> The scallop-edged waves in the twilight, the ladled cups, the
>   frolicsome crests and glistening.   (1:219–220)

By giving them equal attention, and full, appreciative consideration, the mind renders democratic justice to all the specific particulars of the scene, while integrating them into a single perception. When it occurs in luminist painting this effect has been aptly described by John Baur as "pantheistic realism."[11] Every detail in turn bulks large in experience, each displacing an equal amount of mental space while it occupies the imagination. Although varying in length, the phrases are nevertheless of roughly equivalent duration, and Whitman directs his attention with meditative deliberation so that seeing ("Saw . . .") proceeds from a conscious looking (Looked . . .") until eventually the observer is lost (and lost sight of) in contemplation. And yet always it is the light that seems to compel this quality of attention, investing every detail with a singularity of being, rather in the way described by Henry James in his early short story "A Landscape Painter"

(1866): "How color and sound stood out in the transparent air! . . . The mossy rocks doubled themselves without a flaw in the clear, dark water . . . There is a certain purity in this Cragthorpe air which I have never seen approached—a lightness, a brilliancy, a *crudity,* which allows perfect liberty of self-assertion to each individual object in the landscape."[12] James concludes, however, by seeing this "prospect" as being "more or less like a picture which lacks its final process, its reduction to unity"; whereas what distinguishes the Whitman passage is the way in which he achieves an integrated effect without having to "reduce" individual objects to unity.

By this point in the poem Whitman's deployment of a future perspective is also beginning to pay important dividends. It allows him, for instance, to blend several seasonal impressions of the ferry crossing, gathered from different occasions in the past, into a single composite picture. This achievement exactly anticipates, and so corroborates in advance, the continuity between present and future which he is predicting. Since he is already using the past tense even for present experience, as if it were being imaginatively viewed in retrospect from some point in the distant future, then there is no way of clearly distinguishing when, to immediate impressions, Whitman is adding material from memory of previous summer and winter crossings. Thus is the limited, changeful prospect of the historical present silently improved into an ideal, timeless conspectus, and once again it is light which unifies these different timescapes into a single landscape: it yellows the December seagulls, dazzles Whitman's eyes in midsummer, and picks out the scallop-edged waves in the (presumably) present twilight.

Moreover, having first employed the fictional ferry passenger of the future as a device for inaugurating, sustaining, and validating what amounts to a social vision, Whitman now proceeds to put him to rather different, yet related, use. By imagining himself as identifying sympathetically with a future listener who is inwardly troubled, Whitman constructs a scenario in which confession not only seems good for his soul, but positively becomes a fraternal obligation. In this way he overcomes whatever reluctance he himself may originally have felt to confront his own darkness, and finds the relief of an outlet for the repressed feelings that have made his use of light so vibrant.

He is, however, as cunningly adept as any practiced confessor at revealing only surrogate secrets, while contriving to conceal the core issue even from himself. Whitman finds it relatively easy (judging by his glibness) to accuse himself of a whole range of familiar human failings, in a poignant attempt to avoid confronting the reality of his isolation. Rather than admit that the human world by which he is surrounded stands at an appreciable distance from anything he could genuinely accept and participate in, Whitman prefers to take the blame on himself in a glib ecstasy of self-accusation.

In 1855 in the poem eventually called "Faces," he had briefly tapped the real darkness within him (which is also one of the real sources of the light in "Crossing Brooklyn Ferry"). He noted at the time how "Sauntering the pavement thus, or crossing the ceaseless ferry, faces and faces and faces, / I see them and complain not, and am content withall" (1:133). Mixed in with the "pure," "spiritual prescient," or simply "common benevolent" faces, there were others. These assumed animal forms in his tortured imagination; a dog's snout, a mouth filled with snakes, and "the tangling fores of fishes or rats."[13] Although in that poem he found ways of controlling this nightmare, it is not surprising that a year later, in "Crossing Brooklyn Ferry," he should for so long avoid looking the crowd in the face and prefer this time to regard himself, rather than others, as the maverick animal: "The wolf, the snake, the hog, not wanting in me" (1:221). It is not authentic introspection. Rather, it is the act of introjection which, together with a corresponding act of projection, constitutes Whitman's chief means, in "Crossing Brooklyn Ferry," of handling the formidable psychological difficulties arising from his devotion to a New York which was as untrustworthy as it was essentially unworthy of his affections. "I project myself a moment to tell you," Whitman informs the future reader, who is thereby made the custodian of a vision of Brooklyn-New York that Whitman cannot fully share with, or entrust to, his contemporaries.

In WHITMAN'S EXPERIENCE the ferries remained the focal point of modern, democratic city life, and so his several, clearly distinguished kinds of reactions to what he saw on his innumerable travels aboard the boats provide a very useful glossary of the complex terms in which his relationship with contemporary America was conducted. Moreover, the crucial part the ferries played at this time in the social and economic affairs of New York is a consideration that enters inevitably, if invisibly, into everything Whitman wrote on the subject, and yet this factor has seldom been adequately appreciated by critics of his work. Crossing Brooklyn ferry was, after all, not only a deeply cherished and familiar personal experience for Whitman, it was also one of the occasions when he participated most directly, most enthusiastically, and most doubtfully in the traffic of his time.[14] The original meaning of the word "traffic" was "a trade in commodities," the carrying on of commerce; and from thence it derived its secondary meaning of a coming and going of persons and of goods. As they developed around the middle of the century into one of the chief arteries of trade, the Brooklyn ferries carried an enormous volume of traffic, in every sense of the word.

"Despite its grandeur," says Spann, the notable recent historian of mid-nineteenth-century New York, "the soul of the city could best be told not in poetic images but in numbers, since the source of its being was far less a striving for the awesome than a humbler though more complex instinct for money." He adds that there was no mistaking the main business of the three hundred thousand or so people "who clustered at the southern end of Manhattan Island. Except for its graceful bayfront promenade at the Battery on the tip of the island, the city's waterfront was solidly devoted to trade."[15] Crossing the East River, the ferries connected Brooklyn with what was known as "the golden toe" of Manhattan Island, and the traveler on board had a commanding view of what at that time was probably the greatest area of concentrated commercial power in the world. Whether he looked toward the New York wharves and piers, with their immediate financial and business hinterland of South Street, Broadway, and Wall Street, or whether he looked around him on the water at some of the three thousand and more ships annually arriving there from several hundred foreign ports, he was ideally situated to appreciate the real, uncompromising character of the great metropolis.

Journeying this route, Whitman was confronted by the alienating signs of his society's passion for wealth not only as distantly profiled in the New York skyline, but also, much more troublingly, in the circumstances and the demeanor of his fellow passengers. The presence of marked inequalities of wealth and status within his society, although it made him crusadingly angry, was a welcome diversion of sorts for Whitman. It allowed him to separate the sheep very clearly from the goats, to excoriate the privileged few while exonerating the many. It enabled him to preserve, and to dramatize, his faith in the purity of the masses. Circumstances were, however, conspiring by the mid-fifties to make the massed passengers on the Brooklyn ferry a microcosm of a society in which the relatively rich and the relatively poor were indiscriminately mixed, equalized by their shared, crude ambition for an increase in wealth.

When he was editor of the *Brooklyn Daily Eagle,* back in the forties, Whitman liked to think of the ferry as existing only to serve the needs of the average American, the ordinary working man and woman in whose name he mounted several modest campaigns for a reduction in fares.[16] Yet, during the same period and later, New York aldermen were, ironically enough, requesting that fares be dramatically increased (from three cents to twenty-five cents) in order to discourage passengers from crossing Brooklyn ferry. The reason was simple. The ferry was becoming an important commuter service for wealthy citizens who had left New York for the attractions of Brooklyn Heights and its environs, not only to live among more salubrious surroundings, but to take advantage of the lower rate of taxation in Brooklyn. So important was this "traffic" that huge companies like the Union Ferry Company, which ran the Brooklyn ferries (it was capitalized as $776,200 in 1853) operated in close, lucrative conjunction with real estate promoters. The net result was that they enjoyed a massive turnover in terms both of profits and of passengers (over 32 million people traveled on the East River boats in 1860 alone).[17]

The Brooklyn ferry in 1855 was clearly big business, and it catered to big business. Therefore, as he crossed, Whitman didn't have to look very far, not even as far as the prodigiously growing twin cities of New York and Brooklyn, in order to be deeply troubled, or "baffled," by the direction in which American life was so rapidly flowing. No wonder his initial "curiosity" in the poem about "the hundreds and hundreds that cross, returning home," is charged with a considerable amount of uncertainty. But he chooses and uses that word "curiosity" very carefully, so that it allows for a trusting, self-forgetting wonder, which is the attitude Whitman works to produce throughout "Crossing Brooklyn Ferry." The poetry is itself an important means of production, since it allows him to alter social experience, reproducing it in terms of light and water: and it is by so composing a scene that Whitman composes his troubled mind.

Changeful movement is benignly associated with "the gladness of the river and the bright flow" (1:219), a use of light in conjunction with water which is very much in keeping with the practice of luminist painters during the same period, the aim being to bring a central stillness into the very heart of movement without actually arresting it completely. Novak has argued that "luminist silence, in the repose of inaction, represents not a void but a palpable space, in which everything happens while nothing does. We have here a visual analogue of Eckhart's 'central silence,' and Thoreau's 'restful kernel in the magazine of the universe.' "[18] Whitman similarly creates an occasion when things and persons seem to shed their harassed temporality and assume the calm existence that is theirs when they are worthy of themselves. It is at an opposite remove from the noise and frenzy that actually accompanied the daytime excursions of the ferry— a frenzy which, as Whitman gloomily observed in some of his editorials, was symptomatic of the feverish hurry of American society. People rushing to embark or to disembark used not infrequently to fall into the water, where they were extremely fortunate if they weren't caught and crushed "between the landing and the prow." Protesting against the mad, careless haste by which New Yorkers seemed to be possessed, Whitman ironically speculated "perhaps it is a development of the 'indomitable energy' and 'chainless enterprise' which we get so much praise for," before remarking that "if the trait is remembered down to posterity and put in the annals, it will be bad for us."[19] When he addresses posterity in "Crossing Brooklyn Ferry," it is specifically in order to fill its memory, and his own, with calmer images to remember America by.

Entitling one of his *Eagle* editorials the "Philosophy of Ferries," he paid particular attention to his favorite, the Fulton, "which takes precedence by age, and by a sort of aristocratic seniority of wealth and business, too." In the process he (most unusually and revealingly) turned the inexorable mechanical power of the ferry into an image of the darker, questionable aspects of the philosophy of American progress in which he elsewhere so clamorously protested his faith:

> It moves on like iron-willed destiny. Passionless and fixed, at the six-stroke the boats come in; and at the three-stroke, succeeded by a single tap, they depart again, with the steadiness of nature itself. Perhaps a man, prompted by the hell-like delirium tremens, has jumped over-board and been drowned: still the trips go on as before. Perhaps some one has been crushed between the landing and the prow—(ah! that most horrible thing of all!)

still, no matter, for the great business of the mass must be helped forward as before . . . How it deadens one's sympathies, this living in a city![20]

"Crossing Brooklyn Ferry" is therefore, in this respect, an attempt to construct a "philosophy of ferries" antithetical to that by which the Fulton Ferry, in company with America itself, actually operated.

Yet it would be extremely misleading to suggest that the poem is simply a sort of reversed image of historical reality. Whitman's actual social experience contributed in a positive as well as in a negative fashion to the forming of the final poetic image of "Crossing Brooklyn Ferry"; and it is no accident that the confluent where his misgivings meet his hopes should be a poem about the East River, because that was precisely the geographical location where he felt most baffled, perhaps, but also where he felt very particularly at home. "Yes, yes; for some of the nicest of the 'happy ten minutes' that glitter in one's experience, have we been indebted to the Fulton Ferry."[21]

That may be a private, personal response, but behind it lies a social philosophy. The river ferries, along with the omnibus and horsecar services, were the earliest form of mass transportation, an amenity which was indispensable to the economic development of New York, but which could also be seen as a striking instance of how, in a democracy, what used to be a privilege of the few was now being made available to all. Whitman certainly liked to think of the ferries as a valuable public service that was being provided, as was right and proper, by private enterprise. So regarded, the arrangement appeared in every respect to be the absolute apotheosis of the idealistic Jacksonianism in which Whitman believed. In his eyes of faith a competitive system of individual free enterprise assumed the aspect of a spiritual community of free spirits. Even when campaigning, on behalf of the working population, for a reduction in fares, he was exaggeratedly careful not to accuse the Union Ferry Company of being extortionate. Instead, he most particularly commended their public-spiritedness, fulsomely declaring that passengers were "indebted to the desire of the present ferry company to subserve the interests of the public instead of their own purposes."[22]

As will be more clearly seen in chapter 6, there were even occasions when his description of Brooklyn itself ("Brooklyn the beautiful")[23] could make that city seem like a veritable artisan's paradise. He could persuade himself that the glory of the new Brooklyn lay in the provision it made for "the middle class, the man of moderate means."[24] The ferry carried them quickly and easily from overcrowded New York to the cheap, solid housing which was so plentiful across the river. So when it suited him—as, for instance, when addressing an open letter to the city authorities in 1854—he could represent consolidated Brooklyn as the prototype of the American cities of the future, and as the antithesis of existing American cities (diplomatically left unnamed!) which "are huge aggregates of people, riches and enterprise." Yet in spite of all his protestations to the contrary, it is clear that Brooklyn is not exempt from the anxious criticism he makes (anticipating *Democratic Vistas*) of American commercialism: "To encourage the growth of trade and property is commendable; but our politics might also encourage the forming of men of superior demeanour . . . Every one should be possessed with the eternal American ideas of liberty, friendliness, amplitude and courage."[25] In his poem, two years later, he was to turn this Brooklyn dream into a landscape.

When, therefore, in "Crossing Brooklyn Ferry" Whitman (reversing Spann's modern dictum) translates the dollar sign, the money figure which actually stimulated urban activity, into the poetic figures of water and sun, and so instills soul into his city, he does so by way of reasserting, against his own doubts to the contrary, an exalted faith in the masses; a faith which is at least to some extent underwritten by his own selective version of current affairs. So uncertain, though, are the objective historical grounds for declaring such a faith, that he has to rely on his poetry to find alternative means of supporting his democratic vision. And hence a landscape of meditation is developed in the light of, and under the eye of, the future. The maintaining of hope then becomes very much a poetic achievement, in that it is accomplished by means which can be fully employed only in poetry. Nevertheless, Whitman does use related means elsewhere, outside the poetry, for dealing with American society as it appears on board, and from on board, the ferry; and although the results are by definition less satisfactory, some of the methods he uses are correspondingly more clearly visible there, and conveniently open to our examination.

"Scenes on Ferry and River—Last Winter's Nights" is the title of a section from *Specimen Days*. The ferry in question is no longer the Brooklyn but the Camden ferry, Whitman having transferred his affections from the one to the other when, in his declining years, he settled permanently in New Jersey. Along with his affections went his whole complex reaction to ferry travel and ferry traffic, which had originated in his old, daily crossings of Brooklyn ferry, but was now focused on the Delaware crossing. And in the prose passage the different strands of feeling on this subject, so closely intertwined in the poem, are separated out for our inspection.

Whitman is at pains to distinguish between the passengers and the ferrymen proper, and in the process admits that it has been his long-standing practice to bring his melancholy to the ferries for relief and reassurance: "the ferry men—little they know how much they have been to me, day and night—how many spells of listlessness, ennui, debility, they and their hardy ways have dispell'd" (1:183). While the remark illuminates "Crossing Brooklyn Ferry," the immediate reference is undoubtedly to the mental prostration from which Whitman suffered following his physical breakdown in 1872. Physical frailty again makes him especially grateful for the strong young arms proffered by the pilots, "so often supporting, circling, convoying me over the gaps of the bridge, through impediments, safely aboard" (1:183), but the incident also encapsulates that sense of solidarity triumphing over the forces of disintegration which is the essence of Whitman's vision while crossing Brooklyn ferry, and which ultimately derives from his exalted view of ferrymen, omnibus drivers, and the like. In turn, his attachment to them goes right back to childhood, to the "Old Brooklyn Days" he recalls in a short piece written in 1890, when he used to wander the ferries and be "petted and deadheaded by the gatekeepers and deckhands (all such fellows are kind to little children)" (2:688).

Compared to the warm intimacy of his relations with the ferrymen, Whitman's attitude towards his fellow passengers is coolly appreciative, amused as he is by what, presumably following Balzac, he calls "the comedy human" (1:185). Among the "queer scenes" mentioned are childbirth in the waiting houses, masquerade parties, and entertainingly large families. American life is here "illustrated thoroughly" in a series of living pictures ranging from vivacious theatergoers, to "domestic pictures, mothers with bevies of daughters (a charming sight—children, countrymen—the railroad men in their blue clothes and caps . . .)" (1:184–185), until finally "all the various characters of city and country" seem to have been "represented or suggested"

(1:185). The point is that Whitman is simply responding to the surface energy, the diverting busyness of the scene. As I will discuss more fully in Chapter 6, he always finds this superficial aspect of human affairs immensely stimulating and attractive, but in the long run it is insufficiently substantial for him either to rely on or to satisfy his deepest needs. Hence the attempt, in his poetry, to convert the mere vitality of New York life into cosmic energy, or, in the case of "Crossing Brooklyn Ferry," into a "bright flow."

Poetry is an essential agent in that conversion process, and when the catalyst is missing the chemical reaction which accomplishes this alchemy cannot occur. Consequently all we are left with in the prose passage is the stark antithesis of those separate elements which the poetry so magnificently brings into synthesis: "Then the Camden Ferry. What exhilaration, change, people, business, by day. What soothing, silent, wondrous hours, at night, crossing on the boat, most all to myself—pacing the deck, alone, forward or aft. What communion with the waters, the air, the exquisite *chiaroscuro*—the sky and stars, that speak no word, nothing to the intellect, yet so eloquent, so communicative to the soul" (1:183). Daytime bustle is simply contrasted, here, to the profounder nighttime experience, when the "river affords nutriment of a higher order" (1:185). Whereas in the poetry the evening crossing of Brooklyn ferry blends "the human stream" with "the sheeny track of light in the water, dancing and rippling."

Just as the prose passage is distinguished from the poetry by its failure to make anything very significant out of the liveliness of human movement, so too is it unable to make spiritual capital out of that aesthetic sensitivity which, in the poem, forms an invaluable basis for Whitman's meditation. That a ferry crossing did awaken all his artistic sensibilities, is as evident in the following passage as it is in the poetry: the crows "play quite a part in the winter scenes on the river, by day. Their black splatches are seen in relief against the snow and ice everywhere at that season—sometimes flying and flapping—sometimes on little or larger cakes, sailing up or down the stream. One day the river was mostly clear—only a single long ridge of broken ice making a narrow stripe by itself, running along down the current for over a mile, quite rapidly. On this white stripe the crows were congregated, hundreds of them—a funny procession—('half mourning' was the comment of someone)" (1:184). What is missing in this description is the deeper social compulsion that such sensibility is made so gloriously to serve in the poetry, and that transforms aesthetic sensitivity into a powerful human vision. It is yet another example of Whitman's inability to bring one part of his experience to bear upon another in the prose, in the way he constantly does in his matchless crossing of Brooklyn ferry.

PERFECT though Whitman's radiant vision in "Crossing Brooklyn Ferry" may seem to us to be today, there are striking indications in the text that it came, or rather was constructed, at a time when the unilluminated, unresponsive reality of American society was beginning to depress him, and threatening to extinguish his creative faith:

> It is not upon you alone the dark patches fall,
> The dark threw patches down upon me also,
> The best I had done seemed to me blank and suspicious,
> My great thoughts, as I supposed them, were they not in
>   reality meagre? Would not people laugh at me?   (1:221)

Beset by such doubts, he first reacts by choosing to take the blame upon himself, both for breaking faith with his true, Manhattan self, "friendly and proud," and for breaking rank by withholding a part of himself from social contact. He makes his isolation appear to be due to his own culpable reserve, since he "Saw many I loved in the street, or ferry-boat, or public assembly, yet never told them a word" (1:222). The lack of mutuality in his relations with others is put down to a self-consciousness about role playing which inhibits him from losing himself entirely in his social role.

His long-term purpose in confessing all this is not to appear as a freak, an isolato, or an Ishmael, it is rather the opposite. By associating the reader with the same experience, Whitman is actually able to turn these disturbing feelings of inadequacy and isolation into common ground between human beings. They become the inevitable corollary of social involvement, a reflex of social activity, and are therefore accepted as an immutable aspect of social experience. The historically specific problems Whitman experienced in participating in mid-nineteenth-century American life are in the process subtly translated into existential problems that are an eternal part of the human condition.

It follows that his obscure unease and dissatisfaction are no longer to be regarded as a reflection on his beloved society, or as indicating a serious flaw in the great democratic chain of being. Self-consciousness is seen as an unavoidable consequence of human consciousness; isolation becomes an inescapable aspect of individuated being; and so those experiences that threatened to be divisive, by separating Whitman from his contemporaries (or rather by revealing his separation from them), are themselves turned against the odds into strong social adhesives.

On the new strength of this remarkable discovery of solidarity in weakness, he confidently proceeds, without fear of laughter, to reassert his "great thought" that each individual is a unique part of a coherent whole; "that each came, or comes, or shall come, from its due emission" (1:222), from what in 1871 he specified as "the general centre of all, and forming a part of all" (1:222). He returns with sharpened appetite to the landscape which his meditation, by its labor of love, had made the veritable embodiment of this perception:

> Now I am curious what sight can ever be more stately and
>   admirable to me than my mast-hemm'd Manhatta, my river
>   and sun-set, and my scallop-edged waves of flood tide, the
>   sea-gulls oscillating their bodies, the hay-boat in the
>   twilight, and the belated lighter,
> Curious what gods can exceed these that clasp me by the
>   hand, and with voices I love call me promptly and loudly
>   by my nighest name as I approach,
> Curious what is more subtle than this which ties me to the
>   woman or man that looks in my face,
> Which fuses me into you now, and pours my meaning into
>   you   (1:223).

That "now" is alive with the wholehearted enthusiasm of a new beginning, a fresh start, as Whitman reclaims and repossesses what is unmistakably *his* world, an America that he has rescued for vision just when it seemed he might lose it. Securely established within his own very moving rhetoric, he leaves to us the poignant observation that "his" mast-hemm'd Manhattan is not in fact New York. Instead of suffering from "curiosity," he is now enthusiastically consumed by it, and uses the word to stitch together a whole tapestry of wonders.

Proceeding to (re)count the glories strung on his sight like beads, Whitman appears to be blessing the world exactly as he finds it. But his joy is clearly infused with a telltale relief at having, by means of poetry, successfully reconstructed and thus reconsecrated a profane world. The restoration of faith is primarily marked by a restoration of trust in the sheer physical process of existence. Masts grow tall, the sunset is gorgeous, the rail becomes firm over the hurrying water, as Whitman urges the scene to assume full body, color, and energy. Yet by means of the ambiguous terms on which he gives his peculiar blessing, he simultaneously relinquishes his hold over the objects of his perception and retains control over them. As he willingly releases life, and allows it to go its way, so Whitman wills, and verbally ensures, its specifically spiritual continuation. A Prospero who breaks his staff but does not burn his books, he concludes by magicking the world itself into a poem, an *envoi*. Irresistibly invested with the full glory of their materiality, objects become the spiritual signifiers which together comprise a semiotic system that is the secret language of the soul. Consequently the world can at any point be reliably tested, or "arrested," tapped for meaning without interrupting its flow.

Whitman's previous doubt about America, his reluctant suspicion of its materialism and its social inequalities, is now finally attributed by him to a failure to read these signs (or, as we might prefer to put it, an inability to live always within the sacred confines of his own poetry). Understood on his terms, this failure was partly due to the intrinsic difficulty of the task, and partly to be regarded as a betrayal by Whitman of America's trust. The spiritual aspects of the materialistic American world did indeed play hard to catch and prove slippery to hold—"Not you any more shall be able to foil us, or withhold yourselves from us" (1:225)—but it also waited until the faithless, unfaithful prodigal returned: "you faithful solids and fluids, / . . . You have waited, you always wait, you dumb beautiful ministers! you novices! / We receive you with free sense at last, and are insatiate henceforward" (1:225).

Guilt blends with gratitude in this thanksgiving, and Whitman feels pleasure at the restoration of "free sense" because the understanding and the senses are both free of misgivings at last, and can be safely relied on to report only a spiritually coherent, meaningful world.

Earlier, he had experienced particular difficulty with his senses, which kept providing him with unwelcome evidence of materialism. Even his use of the senses in meditation was then guarded, deliberate, as he worked them, and himself, free from bondage to doubt. Hence his rapturous injunction now: "Gaze, loving and thirsting eyes, in the house or street or public assembly!" (1:224) and his relief that in his own eyes at least the appearance of things is no longer such as to call their spiritual reality into question: "Burn high your fires, foundry chimneys! cast black shadows at night-fall! cast red and yellow light over the tops of the houses! / Appearances, now or henceforth, indicate what you are! / You necessary film, continue to envelop the soul!" (1:224).

There is no mention of the meditative observer in the penultimate section of "Crossing Brooklyn Ferry," so completely does what Wallace Stevens called "the world as meditation"[26] appear to have ousted the objective world and appropriated its factuality. Whitman locates himself within the scene, as one of the receptive "gazers," rather than a detached contemplator. Again the analogy holds with luminist paintings in which the artist absents himself so completely that the canvas seems not covered with paint but simply given up to light. Novak has commented shrewdly on the way such painters avoid leaving evident brushmarks in the picture: "Stroke lessens the hyperclarity of object penetration . . . In luminism the absence of stroke heightens the textural properties of natural elements beyond the compass of normal vision . . . The medium itself is subsumed by the illusively hyper-real image. The linear edges of reality are pulled taut, strained almost to the point of breaking. This is why I have called luminism a kind of impersonal expressionism."[27]

Whitman's poetry near the end of "Crossing Brooklyn Ferry" aspires to this condition, and in his concluding section he outlines, in effect, the spiritual poetics of the style of writing he has so movingly essayed. If, nevertheless, he is not one hundred percent successful in eliminating from his writing the poetic equivalent of stroke, the telltale rhetorical signs of the author's presence, then that is by no means to be considered a failure in the poetry. The verbal "stroke" is present as a poignantly unintentional signature, identifying this depicted world as being, after all, of Whitman's own making and indicating that his unconditional trust in the actual is much more apparent than it is real.

As is appropriate, "Crossing Brooklyn Ferry" displays, to the very end, reluctant but graphic signs of the particular historical conditions under which, and because of which, it was written. They are its secret raison d'être, in the decisive sense that they propose the unacknowledged problems which the poetry comes into existence to solve. And the chief problem is obviously the avid materialism predicated by a free enterprise society, which minutely determined the circumstances of American life. Nineteenth-century America may certainly seem to provide ample confirmation of Byron's sly remark about "circumstance" being life's "unspiritual god," but in "Crossing Brooklyn Ferry" Whitman tries heroically to spiritualize circumstance and to prove that no "Gods can exceed these that clasp me by the hand, and with voices I love call me promptly and loudly by my nighest name as I approach" (1:223).

Boston Harbor from Constitution Wharf, painting by Robert Salmon, 1829. His interest in rendering the even spread of light throughout a scene made Salmon a precursor of the luminists. Unlike them, however, and rather like Whitman, he favored settings crowded with human activity.

Boston Harbor, painting by Fitz Hugh Lane, n.d. As is the case with all the best luminist pictures, time seems to have been arrested by light in Lane's painting. In "Crossing Brooklyn Ferry," Whitman's poetry achieves a comparable effect.

Niagara Falls, painting by Frederick Edwin Church, 1857. The pictorial frame serves only to emphasize the uncontainable nature both of the falls and of the American landscape itself. Many of Whitman's poetic devices serve a similar purpose.

The Woodcutter, painting by Eastman Johnson, 1857. The woodman, with his ax, was a significant figure for nineteenth-century Americans. A hero to most, but a villain to a few, he acted as a focus for America's mixed feelings about its treatment of the continental "wilderness."

Brooklyn Street Scenes, drawing by Charles Dana Gibson. These tasteful vignettes, exercises in the suburban picturesque, show how areas of Whitman's Brooklyn had, by the second half of the nineteenth century, become a fashionable, lush, middle-class retreat.

The Life of a Fireman—the Ruins, lithograph by Nathaniel Currier, n.d. The fires that so regularly brought ruin to both individuals and companies in nineteenth-century New York also provided the public with spectacular street theater. Exploiting the popularity of the subject, Currier and Ives produced a series of lithographs depicting the fireman's life.

The Field Where General Reynolds Fell, photograph by Timothy H. O'Sullivan and Alexander Gardner, 1866. "Faces ghastly, swollen, purple . . . the dead on their backs with arms toss'd wide": this photograph is grim testimony to the accuracy of Whitman's memory of carnage.

Portrait of Walt Whitman, photograph attributed to Thomas Eakins, 1887. This study of the old man in his somewhat cramped living quarters touchingly suggests the way Whitman's world had contracted in his old age, in spite of his unflagging energy of mind.

5 ❧ The Nature of American Society

W HITMAN CONCLUDES *Specimen Days* with a short section in which he characteristically urges both democracy and art to model themselves on nature. It is an interesting illustration of the truth of Raymond Williams's observation that "the idea of nature contains an extraordinary amount of human history. What is often being argued, it seems to me, in the idea of nature is the idea of man, and this not only generally, or in ultimate ways, but the idea of man in society, indeed the Ideas of kinds of societies."[1]

Whitman's lifelong obsession with nature is surely best understood in this context, which reveals him to be conducting, through the medium of nature, an argument with his society about the kind of society it should be. With a subject as rich and as central to Whitman's poetry as this, it would be foolish even to attempt to encompass it in a single chapter. Therefore all that is here offered is a series of three short studies which provide glimpses into several different aspects of the subject: first, Whitman's use of nature to develop his own refined version of the individualist philosophy on which the social, political, and economic life of the United States depended; second, the argument he conducted through his poetry with fashionable art, art in which the misrepresentation of nature seemed to him both to reflect and to reinforce the inadequate social life of his times; and third, his preoccupation not only with America's idea of nature, but with Americans' conduct towards nature, in which so much was revealed about the actual, existent state of U.S. democracy.

THE TRANSCENDENTALISTS would certainly have agreed that man's intense preoccupation with external nature arises from his concern with his own essential or ultimate nature. But they could not possibly have accepted the view that nature is a historically variable idea, which has only ever existed in the intellectual eye of the constantly changing social beholder—although they might well have appreciated the spectacle of man demonstrating in his social history an ability to rival nature itself in the fertile variety of his conceptions of it.

Whitman was deeply indebted (to put it mildly) to the transcendentalists for his natural faith, and so any attempt today to treat his outlook on nature as a mirror of his circumscribed historical period can take place only over his dead body. Or so one naturally supposes, before coming across the following surprising passage:

> Not only is the human and artificial world we have establish'd in the West a radical departure from anything hitherto known— not only men and politics, and all that goes with them—but Nature herself, in the main sense, its construction is different. The same old font of type, of course, but set up to a text never composed or issued before. For Nature consists not only in itself, objectively, but at least just as much in its subjective reflection from the person, spirit, age, looking at it, in the midst of it, and absorbing it—faithfully sends back the characteristic beliefs of the time or individual—takes, and readily gives again, the physiognomy of any nation or literature—falls like a great elastic veil on a face, or like the molding plaster on a statue.   (2:484–485)

This comes from "Poetry Today—Shakespeare—the Future," an essay written when Whitman was an aging paralytic, thoroughly bogged down in the social morass of the postwar period. His language was by then so undermined by suppressed doubt that, despite increasingly elaborate syntactical underpinnings, his rhetoric had become hollow, and his phrases were liable to internal collapse whenever he tried, as he tries here, to place any substantial reliance on them. Clearly his intention, at this point, was to reaffirm an old faith in the new world of the American West, and its "*al fresco* physiology" (2:603), but by emphasizing nature's infinite malleability he also inadvertently calls its ultimate dependability, its spiritual constancy, into question, and by giving prominence to the subjective element in perception he virtually eliminates objective reality in all but name. In its semantic unsteadiness the writing testifies unwillingly, therefore, to Whitman's growing inability to keep faith with himself, and there is even a mournful poetic justice about the way nature becomes implicated in his frailty, the partner in his fall. "What is Nature?" he proceeds to ask, in this same essay. And if even the most elaborate critical study must fail to offer a comprehensive account of what the concept meant to Whitman himself, it is precisely because in his work nature continued faithfully to reflect every twist and turn of his Byzantine relationship with an American society he nevertheless artlessly insisted was simple and open in character.

From the first, Whitman had used nature in his poetry to explore the ideal meanings of the preconceptions upon which actual American practice in the social, political, and economic fields depended. He had also tried from the beginning to explain in his prose that America should pay particular attention to the internal organization, as well as the impressive scale, of its natural environment. But his prosaic understanding of what he was doing in his poetry fell appreciably short of the full marvel of the achievement. Only gradually, over a period of years, was he able to distinguish some of the many different personal impulses—of criticism, doubt, dismay—that had, without his noticing, been consistently feeding into and filling out the image of nature that appeared in his poetry.

It was 1871, for instance, before he consciously registered, in *Democratic Vistas,* his concern that America was in serious danger of becoming a monotonously uniform society. Fortunately for his own peace of mind he did not see that this new single-mindedness, this grim unanimity of commercial purpose on which he was commenting, was a translation into civilian terms of the military discipline Americans had learned during the Civil War. He was therefore spared the tragic irony of seeing the wartime solidarity he had celebrated under the name of comradeship reduced in the end to this. Instead Whitman looked elsewhere to explain this unwelcome conformity, blaming mechanization and industrialization, and referring to "the long series of tendencies, shapings which few are strong enough to resist, and which now seem, with steam-engine speed, to be everywhere turning out the generations of humanity like uniform iron castings" (2:424). The obvious, if implicit, contrast is with the life of the natural order described by Whitman earlier in the same essay. If the first law of nature is equality, he there argues, then the second law is "individuality, the pride and centripetal isolation of a human being in himself—identity—personalism. Whatever the name, its acceptance and thorough infusion through the organizations of political commonalty now shooting Aurora-like about the world, are of utmost importance, as the principle itself is needed for very life's sake. It forms, in a word, or is to form, the compensating balance-wheel of the successful working machinery of aggregate America" (2:391–392).

The explanation is a disappointingly familiar one—and that in a way is the salient point. Because what is significant is that Whitman does not need to reconsider, or to rejigger, his established working definition of nature in order to meet what appears to be a new challenge. The reason for this is simple. The threat of conformity may indeed be one which, under the pressure of immediate historical circumstances, Whitman is now, in the postwar years, forced consciously to consider for the first time, but the poet has long since unconsciously divined that this was a danger inherent in the process of democratic leveling, especially when it was aimed at producing a single commercial class. His poetic imagination, which was also a profound social imagination, had constantly taken this paradoxical aspect of economic individualism into account when developing through the poetry an integrated, variegated view of nature that was very much a corrective (as well as an inspiration) to contemporary American society. It was a process that, as we have already seen, also included an attempt to present American trades as highly differentiated examples of creative (and not simply "free") enterprise.

Indeed, as he admits in "A Backward Glance o'er Travel'd Roads" (1888), this anxiety about conformity had contributed very substantially toward his creation of the two deliberately magnified and idealized figures of the Westerner and the Working Man. He states the case quite baldly: "I have allow'd the stress of my poems from beginning to end to bear upon American individuality and assist it—not only because that is a great lesson in Nature, amid all her generalizing laws, but as counterpoise to the leveling tendencies of Democracy" (2:726). His diagnosis at this point is primarily a political one: "Democracy has been so retarded and jeopardized by powerful personalities, that its first instincts are fain to clip, conform, bring in stragglers, and reduce everything to a dead level. While the ambitious thought of my song is to help the forming of a great aggregate Nation, it is, perhaps, altogether through the forming of myriads of fully develop'd and enclosing individuals. Welcome as are equality's and fraternity's doctrines and popular education, a certain liability accompanies them all, as we see" (2:726).

A few lines earlier, however, he had also identified the economic roots of the problem: "As for native American individuality, though certain to come, and on a large scale, the distinctive and ideal type of Western character (as consistent with the operative political and even money-making features of United States' humanity in the Nineteenth Century as chosen knights, gentlemen and warriors were the ideals of the centuries of European feudalism) it has not yet appear'd" (2:726).

Throughout the first half of the nineteenth century, travelers to the United States and observers of the brave new democratic experiment there, frequently remarked on the lack of variety in American society. De Tocqueville's views on the subject are by now too well known to be worth repeating, but surprisingly little attention has been paid to John Stuart Mill's perceptive comments.[2] Between 1835 and 1840 Mill wrote three long articles on the state of American society, two of them reviews of de Tocqueville's *Democracy in America.* In the second of these he focused particularly on what he called "the democracy of the middle class."[3] He had quickly realized something that Whitman had always uneasily intuited in his poetry but was only able to confront rationally, reluctantly, and belatedly in *Democratic Vistas,* namely, that the distinguishing characteristics of the United States were owing not, as was usually supposed, to its much-vaunted democratic system, but to "the commercial state" of its society. The American people, Mill concluded, resembled "nothing so much as an exaggeration of our own middle class" and precisely therein, rather than in democracy per se, lay the danger. The preponderance of a single class, "the unbalanced influence of the commercial spirit," prevented the development of a healthy variety of outlook and of conduct.[4]

Relatively unknown though this minor review-essay continues to be today, it was while preparing it, and reflecting at leisure on de Tocqueville's work, that Mill was able to develop the ideas that eventually appeared in his great, mature essay *On Liberty* (1859). Whitman refers to this major study in the opening paragraph of *Democratic*

Vistas, and although critical attention in this connection has traditionally concentrated on Carlyle's *Shooting Niagara,* since that was clearly the negative inspiration for Whitman's essay, there are also grounds for arguing that *On Liberty* may have been an equal but answering, because positive, inspiration to Whitman at this time. Certainly he would have warmed to Mill's opening account of the struggle throughout human history "between Liberty and Authority" which culminated in the establishment, in modern times, of popularly elected governments. Whitman would have also agreed with Mill's refusal to trust even this democratic form of social control, and his insistence on the need to secure extensive individual rights which could not, under any circumstances, be infringed by government. But most important of all, from the present point of view, is Mill's argument that in a democracy the most insidious, and therefore the most dangerous, threat to the individual is likely to come not from government action, but from "the tyranny of the prevailing opinion and feeling," which stealthily promotes conformity and inhibits development of true individuality: "Society itself is the tyrant."⁵

This theme is taken up and expanded by Mill in chapter 3, where he argues for "Individuality, as One of the Elements of Well-being." The result is a discussion which would certainly have commanded Whitman's entire assent and respect. It is here, above all, that Mill lives up to the exalted claim made on his behalf in the extract from William Humboldt's work he had chosen as an epigraph for *On Liberty:* "The grand, leading principle, towards which every argument unfolded in these pages directly converges, is the absolute and essential importance of human development in its richest diversity." The arguments are, in fact, too fine and too far-ranging to be conveniently summarized here: they include a reasoned preference for the original over the traditional; a spirited appreciation of "individuality of desires and impulses"; an explanation of the way authentic self-development blends with self-government; and an attitude toward "exceptional individuals" (such as Whitman's Poet) which, although respectful, is nevertheless carefully distinguished from Carlyle's "hero-worship." Something, at least, of the flavor of this deeply attractive writing is captured in the following passage: "Among the works of man, which human life is rightly employed in perfecting and beautifying, the first in importance surely is man himself . . . Human nature is not a machine to be built after a model, and set to do exactly the work prescribed for it, but a tree, which requires to grow and develop itself on all sides, according to the tendency of the inward forces which make it a living thing."[6]

But the interest of Mill for a student of Whitman lies not so much in the part his work may possibly have played in enabling Whitman to organize a reasoned account of what he meant by democracy, as in Mill's clear demonstration that the real threat to the individuality he and Whitman regarded as the most quintessential of human qualities, was now coming from the very quarter they had trusted implicitly. Both Mill and Whitman had supposed that the political individualism embodied in democracy, and the economic individualism intrinsic to liberal capitalism, were not only necessary but sufficient causes of that individuality which was, in their opinion, the real end of human existence. Not only was this proving not to be the case, but these individualisms, as they became established in current economic and political practices, seemed actually to inhibit and thereby to imperil the development of a society of authentic individuals. If competition was one serious problem in this respect, then conformity was another; and if the situation had been clearly dissected by Mill's analytical mind, then it had also been grasped, after a different but equally intelligent fashion, by Whitman's poetic imagination.

The imagination is, however, always liable to work in a very different way from the discursive reason. It was through his poetry that Whitman set out to save America from uniformity, and it was the vista of the American landscape which provided him with the language for exploring and advertising the redeeming miracle of variety. So successful indeed was he in using the vast continental space in this way that the achievement now seems to us not only natural but inevitable. Yet space has in fact been known to speak to men in very different, and even opposite, terms, as D. H. Lawrence demonstrated when reviewing Frederic Carter's book *The Dragon of the Apocalypse.* Referring to the unboundedness of outer space as demonstated by modern science, Lawrence noted, with considerable psychological acumen, that "when science extends space *ad infinitum,* and we get the terrible sense of limitlessness, we have at the same time a secret sense of imprisonment." The problem, he realized, lay in the homogeneity, and therefore the monotony, of the phenomenon. In being "a mere extension of what we know," it failed to give an extension to our own beings, since that required a "real release of the imagination" which alone "renews our strength and our vitality." He pointed out that "in astronomical space one can only *move,* one cannot be," whereas in "the ancient zodiacal heavens, the whole man is set free, once the imagination crosses the border."[7]

Similarly, Whitman's response to nature in his poetry is an attempt to create a society that will not simply move its customary self across the great continental space of America, but will be brought into new, authentic being by the experience. His poetry exists not to advance the existing frontier, but to help the imagination cross the border, and one of the greatest sections of the 1855 preface deals with precisely this journey:

> When the long Atlantic coast stretches longer and the Pacific coast stretches longer he easily stretches with them north or south. He spans between them also from east to west and reflects what is between them. On him rise solid growths that offset the growths of pine and cedar and hemlock and liveoak and locust and chestnut and cypress and hickory and limetree and cottonwood and tuliptree and cactus and wildvine and tamarind and persimmon . . . and tangles as tangled as any canebrake or swamp . . . and forests coated with transparent ice and icicles hanging from the boughs and crackling in the wind. . . . and sides and peaks of mountains. . . . and pasturage sweet and free as savannah or upland or prairie. . . . with flights and songs and screams that answer those of the wildpigeon and highold and orchard-oriole and coot and surf-duck and redshouldered-hawk and fish-hawk and white-ibis and indian-hen and cat-owl and water-pheasant and qua-bird and pied-sheldrake and blackbird and mockingbird and buzzard and condor and night-heron and eagle.   (2:742)

The relish of the diversified life of the earth is there in the heightened individuality, the bodily weight of single words—hickory and limetree and cottonwood and tuliptree—which seem themselves to rise like solid growths out of the page. Yet the dynamic is provided by the subtle discriminations between related sounds, which form a latticework of delicate yet sinewy energy: "Hemlock and liveoak and locust"; "blackbird and mockingbird and buzzard." By the simplest of means Whitman achieves a verbal density and aural texture comparable to that found in Charles Wright's "Dog Creek Mainline," a notable poem of our own time:

> Dog Creek: cat track and bird splay,
> Spindrift and windfall; woodrot;
> Odor of muscadine, the blue creep
> Of kingsnake and copperhead.[8]

Words, said Edward Thomas, are dear as the earth they prove that we love. And to Whitman, also, they are precious in being the living proof of that: "Great is language . . . / It is the fulness and color and form and diversity of the earth. . . . and of men and women" (1:157). As a poet in an age of dirth he avails himself of the human richness that is stored in words, causing them, as Stevens put it, to "add to the senses" of his shrunken contemporaries; "The words for the dazzle / Of mica, the dithering of grass, / The Arachne integument of dead trees, / Are the eye grown larger, more intense."[9]

When therefore he presents himself, in his writing, as one who incarnates the land, it is not just a vivid figure of speech for his attachment, however intense, to the natural landscape. It is a passionate, yet practical demonstration of what it would be like for men in his time to be created anew by what they, with their whole body, saw—an experience synonymous with coming alive in language. This is not a matter of personal indulgence, nor is he simply advocating some form of private mystical enlightenment: rather, it is an event of profound historical significance, in which is implied an act of social criticism and transformation. In Raymond Williams's terms, what Whitman is doing is using nature as an argument—an argument about the real aims, as opposed to the existing, accepted character, of the democratic capitalist society of the United States. As Whitman himself put it, addressing his fellow countrymen: "You have not learn'd of Nature—of *the politics of Nature*" (2:416, my italics).

To REALIZE that an idea of society is contained within Whitman's approach to nature is also to appreciate the social significance of the distinctions between his treatment of nature and that of some of his artistic contemporaries. Throughout the century a ruthlessly practical, even exploitative attitude toward nature was balanced, in American culture, by an enthusiastic taste for the picturesque, and the relationship between Whitman's poetry and this writing in the picturesque tradition is worth some further consideration at least. It is a complex, changing, and ambivalent relationship, very much as Wordsworth's had been half a century before. Early in their lives both Whitman and Wordsworth seem to have been sufficiently attracted to the picturesque to have adopted some of its techniques, and even some of its vocabulary. (Whitman refers to "vista" as well as to the "picturesque," loves to employ an artful chiaroscuro in some of his miniature scenes, arranges tableaux vivants, and so on.) Both, too, during their declining years, and as their creative energies subsided, settled fairly comfortably at times into the picturesque habit. Wordsworth even prepared a *Guide to the Lakes,* and as for Whitman, who could with confidence distinguish the following passage from the entry called "Manhattan from the Bay" in *Specimen Days?*

> New York rises before us from the sea, in the centre of the picture; the city of Brooklyn, on Long Island, to the right, spreads a far and measureless sea of roofs, with endless sky-aspiring spires; the shores of New Jersey extend along the far western border of the picture, on the left, with faint markings of Jersey City a little beyond, on the shores of the Hudson. The picture cannot easily be excelled for beauty; but one or two bays in the world are finer, and none are more animated with stirring and picturesque life. Here are the tall, white-sailed ships; the swift, black-funnelled steamers; the stately steam-boats from the Hudson or the Sound; the graceful, winged pleasure-yachts; the snorting, bull-dog tugs; the quaint, tall-masted, and broad-sailed schooners; flotilla of barges and canal-boats; the crab-shaped but swift-motioned ferry-boats, all coming, going, swiftly or slowly, amid fleets of anchored ships, from whose gaffs fly the flags of nations.

Yet this comes from an essay on picturesque New York and Brooklyn by the delightfully named O. B. Bunce.[10]

But in their prime both Whitman and Wordsworth seemed to intuit that an unacceptable personal and social psychology was frequently concealed within this popular aesthetic, and they consequently developed an independent approach to nature, which in certain respects constituted a serious criticism, if not a complete repudiation, of the picturesque.[11] Whitman never made his objections explicit, but Wordsworth did, in book 12 of *The Prelude.* There he deprecated the practice of applying "rules of mimic art . . . To things above all art," and of assuming a detached, superior, judicious stance toward natural scenes. But above all he deplored the despotism of "the bodily eye," over the comprehending, imaginative mind:

> . . . my delights
> (Such as they were) were sought insatiably,
> Vivid the transport, vivid though not profound;
> I roamed from hill to hill, from rock to rock,
> Still craving combinations of new forms,
> New pleasure, wider empire for the sight,
> Proud of her own endowments, and rejoiced
> To lay the inner faculties asleep.[12]

The pursuit of novelty is there realized to be the destructive antithesis of real imaginative innovation. The picturesque approach turns the natural world into an infinite, yet shallow, source of undifferentiated and therefore monotonous pleasure.

But the most important thing to note is how sociopolitical terms such as "despotism" and "empire" occur involuntarily, even inevitably to Wordsworth as he analyzes what purports to be a purely personal state of mind. It signifies Wordsworth's realization that the possessive psychology of the middle class manifests itself as certainly in what that class likes to regard as a private realm of aesthetic experience as it does in its public conduct of economic, social, and political affairs. Translated into mid-nineteenth-century American terms, it means that the continuing cult of the picturesque is liable to have much in common, after all, with that hard-headed working and business world to which it seems so totally and fastidiously contrasted.

American interest in the picturesque probably reached its zenith with the publication of works like *Picturesque America* (1872–1874), edited by William Cullen Bryant.[13] An impressive, lavishly illustrated tome, it looks very much like what it is, the substantial product of that prosperous class which Whitman rejected as un-American. Although hardly designed to appeal either to the eyes or to the pockets of his own beloved workingmen and women of the states, the book does nevertheless indirectly reflect the entrepreneurial spirit which, in spite of Whitman's blandishments, they continued to share with their richer compatriots. As such, it certainly offers one or two useful points of reference for considering Whitman's relationship to the picturesque.

Given the attention already paid in this chapter to Whitman's socially significant delight in the diversity of natural forms—especially as expressed in the great continent-embracing passage from the 1855 preface—it is convenient that specific reference should be made in the preface to *Picturesque America* to the varied scenery so prized by the picturesque traveler. "Our country borders on two oceans," the editor writes, "and comprises within the vast space that lies between them a variety of scenery that no other people can boast of . . . No country in the world possesses a succession of such varied pictures."[14] The use of the word "possess" in this context is no doubt entirely innocent, and one wouldn't want to make too much of it, except that it does seem indicative of a proprietorial bias in the picturesque outlook. So too does the habit of viewing the continuous landscape as a discontinuous "succession of . . . varied pictures." It will be remembered that Whitman specifically devised poetic techniques which allowed him to treat a land whose "push of perspective spreads with crampless and flowing breadth and showers its prolific and splendid extravagance."

Picturesque writers liked to appear to be remote from the crudeness of American society, preferring beauty to utility and favoring sensibility over practical common sense. And yet, as Wordsworth had foreseen in an English context, they too were tainted with what was fundamentally a proprietorial attitude toward the land, and therein discovered to be, after all, very much the children of their own society. "The lover of Nature," observed W. C. Richards with approval when writing about the valley of the Connecticut River, "may be sure of finding abundant material to gratify his taste for the sublime and the beautiful all through this picturesque region."[15] It is not surprising that the publication of *Picturesque America* coincided with the increasingly rapid colonization of New Jersey by wealthy New York businessmen who preferred to "live in the midst of these picturesque scenes, an hour's ride serving to convey them from the turmoil of city occupations to the serene quiet and sylvan charms of rural life."[16] And it was again the railway which made it possible by 1872 for writers to treat the whole continent as a single tourist area and to speak credibly of picturesque America. It was hardly what Whitman had intended when in 1855 he had called on writers to incarnate the geography of America; but it was the sort of development he had perhaps feared when insisting that even an appreciation of beauty was not in itself enough, and that the poet must indicate the path between reality and the human soul.

If the picturesque writer did not indicate this path, neither did the picturesque tourist travel the open road. "There is," the judicious writers inform us, "a great deal in knowing how to find the picturesque,"[17] and a great deal of time and energy is duly expended first on carefully selecting a location, and then on finding the right outlook from which to view it. During his visit to Charleston, Bunce tells us that "the search for the picturesque that would meet the necessities of our purpose was not expeditious. It is only after walking around a place, and surveying it from different situations, that an artist can settle upon his point of view. We were three days in Charleston ere Mr Penn [the artist who accompanied him] discovered the prospect from St. Michael's belfry, and to this the reader's attention is solicited. If he does not think it very good, we shall be tempted to denounce his artistic appreciation."[18] In turn one of the essential services provided by the book is to offer the discerning reader a carefully designed itinerary, which allows him or her to approach the recommended scenes from the most advantageous angles, and so to maximize the emotional profit, as it were, that can be extracted from the visits.

Whitman found these aesthetic discriminations offensive because not only did they reek of effete gentility, they also translated into ominously anti-egalitarian terms. To privilege one scene, as "scenery," over and above the claims of the land in general, was in his opinion to indulge in antidemocratic practice. Furthermore, in assuming the right to accept and to reject at will, the artist places himself in a position of power over the natural world. The arts, too, are therefore guilty of fostering the attitude identified by Whitman as central to his society. "Modern society, in its largest vein, is essentially intellectual, infidelistic—secretly admires, and depends most on, pure compulsion or science, its rule and sovereignty—is, in short, in 'cultivated' quarters, deeply Napoleonic" (2:532). By contrast, Whitman places himself in a totally different and "affectional" relationship to nature—a relationship which is, in his poetry, an accomplishment of style. It can be seen particularly clearly in the opening lines of "Protoleaf" (later "Starting from Paumanok"), the first and keynote poem of the 1860 *Leaves of Grass.*

Whereas the birth of the nonpossessive self is trumpeted throughout "Song of Myself," its existence is taken for granted in "Protoleaf." The distinctive mode of being of this new individuality is inscribed from the beginning in the very syntax of the writing, which is composed according to the rules of what Whitman would doubtless regard as natural, rather than conventional, grammar:

> Free, fresh, savage,
> Fluent, luxuriant, self-content, fond of persons and places,
> Fond of fish-shape Paumanok, where I was born,
> Fond of the sea—lusty-begotten and various,
> Boy of the Mannahatta, the city of ships, my city,
> Or raised inland, or of the south savannas,
> Or full-breath'd on Californian air, or Texan or Cuban air,
> Tallying, vocalising all—resounding Niagara—resounding
>   Missouri.   (2:273)

Conventionally analyzed these lines prove to consist of a series of adjectives and adjectival phrases loosely, almost reluctantly, related to the eventual personal pronoun which accompanies the main verb— "Solitary, singing in the west, I strike up for a new world" (2:274). But the whole point lies, of course, in the relative grammatical disorder of the verse, and it amounts to a criticism, of sorts, of customary syntax—a criticism which calls the dormant psychology of ordinary word order into question. Usually in English the personal pronoun is fitted in to the basic sentence pattern of subject-verb-object, which allows the "I" a self-sufficient grammatical existence prior to, and independent of, the adjectives which may then be attached to it and qualify it. ("I am proud, happy, sad," and so on.) This structure also discourages the attribution of two or more adjectives simultaneously to the subject pronoun. It is this assumption of a unitary subject, standing apart from those constantly metamorphosing emotions and experiences which in fact constitute its very existence, that Whitman is rejecting. And with good reason, since it was this dominant self propounded by grammar that functioned so effectively as the "Napoleonic" social unit of his day.

Illuminating analogies are available in Romantic painting for these verbal techniques, and the use to which Whitman puts them. In his brilliant recent book on nineteenth-century American painting, Brian Jay Wolf contrasts the calculatedly conservative technique of the American portraitist John Allston with the radical experimentation in Romantic British portraiture, which anticipates Whitman's poetic innovativeness:

> The self was understood less as character or consciousness than as energy linked to a world of natural forces. The bravura style of Allston's contemporaries programmatically flattened the canvas, de-emphasised realistic three-dimensional modeling, frustrated the viewer's desire to read interior character, and drew his attention instead to the brushwork and surface brilliance of the canvas. Technique and brushstroke were not only central to this mode of portraiture, but became in fact the unstated subject of the painting. They did so not simply as a protomodern concern for the painting as a two-dimensional object, but in order to break out of the traditional concept of the self as a container of individual properties, and to replace it with a self less centered, less defined by character and consciousness, and more a confluence of unbound energies.[19]

In similar fashion, Whitman's handling of syntax is the unstated subject of the "Protoleaf" passage, and the unspoken means by which he cracks that tough nut, that "container of individual properties," the American personality.

This revolutionizing of syntax, along with the concomitant redefinition of individual existence, continues to occur on a smaller scale within the large unit of the opening passage, witness the following example:

> Far from the clank of crowds, an interval passing, rapt
> and happy,
> Stars, vapor, snow, the hills, rocks, the Fifth Month flowers,
> my amaze, my love,

> Aware of the buffalo, the peace-herds, the bull, strong-
>   breasted and hairy.   (2:273)

Here it is the middle line of the three that is worth noting. Conventionally interpreted, and translated into the syntax of "common sense," the line can clearly be understood to affirm that the stars, vapor, and so on, are a source of amazement and love to Whitman. But by mentioning "my drink" and "my diet" a few lines previously he has prepared the mind to construe "my amaze" and "my love" not as reactions to "stars" and "vapor" but as additional phrases in a continuing list. The experiences signified by these phrases thus appear as an extension of a natural order which itself then seems, by backward extension, to comprehend what Shelley called the "loves and hates . . . that variegate the eternal universe."[20] So interpreted, the structure of the line closely corresponds to Whitman's earlier description of himself as "tallying, vocalising all—resounding Niagara—resounding Mississippi" (2:273). Just as resounding Niagara is resounded, vocalized, in Whitman, so "Stars, vapor, snow, the hills, rocks, the Fifth Month flowers" are resounded in the "amaze" and love that are as much a human extension of this active and activating existence as a reaction to it.

Even when, in later editions, he rearranged the syntax of this passage, he was careful to retain its ambiguities. Notice, for example, how in the following version he represents himself not only as being aware of the "Fifth-month flowers," but also as being aware of his awareness ("experience") and of his "amaze." He thus treats his own emotions as an objective feature of the world at large, a natural phenomenon:

> Aware of the buffalo herds grazing the plains, the hirsute and
>   strong-breasted bull,
> Of earth, rocks, Fifth-month flowers experienced, stars, rain,
>   snow, my amaze . . .   (2:273)

In being a "language experiment," then, *Leaves of Grass* is also a psychological and social experiment, since the responsibility for establishing that true self which is to be the antonym of the false self, and the antidote of selfishness, is entrusted to syntax. "When man changes his state of being," said D. H. Lawrence, "he needs an entirely different description of the universe, and so the universe changes its nature to him entirely."[21] In "Protoleaf" Whitman's "changed state of being" is both reflected in and confirmed by the "different description of the universe" which is developed in and by the poetry itself—a "description" radically different from that offered by picturesque literature.

Whitman's social and political argument with the picturesque could occasionally be conducted in relatively complicated and initially confusing terms, as appears in one of his finest landscape poems. Although eventually entitled "Our Old Feuillage" it began its public life as number four of *Chants Democratic,* in the 1860 *Leaves of Grass,* and included several little vignettes which, had they been encountered in a different context, could easily have been mistaken for working sketches from a picturesque artist's notebook: "On interior rivers, by night, in the glare of pine knots, steamboats wooding up"; "The shadows, gleams, up under the leaves of the old sycamore-trees—the flames—also the black smoke from the pitch-pine curling and rising" (2:294–295).[22] Furthermore, the family resemblance between this and picturesque writing extended to the metaphor chosen by Whitman to explain and justify the scatter of scenes comprising the poem. He represented himself as mentally gathering "bouquets of the incomparable feuillage of these States" (2:299)—a trope which threatened to add a hint of preciosity and of self-conscious deliberateness to the proceedings.

These features were not removed when the poem was revised, but their effect was modified and counterbalanced by the changes Whitman introduced. And other passages were omitted. The original, 1860 version had opened with the clamant self very much to the fore—a foregrounding that immediately placed the land within a containing human perspective, while relegating it to the middle distance: "America always! / Always me joined with you, whoever you are! / Always our own feuillage! / Always Florida's green peninsula . . ." (2:293). To remove that opening, as Whitman chose to do, was to turn the poem more directly over to the land, and to turn the reader loose into a poem that does not immediately provide him with bearings:

Always our old feuillage!
Always Florida's green peninsula—always the priceless delta of
    Louisiana—always the cotton-fields of Alabama and Texas,

> Always California's golden hills and hollows, and the silver
>   mountains of New Mexico—always soft-breath'd Cuba,
> Always the vast slope drain'd by the Southern sea, inseparable
>   with the slopes drain'd by the Eastern and Western
>   seas.   (2:293)

When the figure of the speaker is eventually introduced, he appears
in a subordinate position, not as the unique organizing consciousness
of the whole, but simply as a passing part of the changing scene:

> All characters, movements, growths, a few noticed,
>   myriads unnoticed,
> Through Mannahatta's streets I walking, these
>   things gathering,
>
> .   .   .   .   .
>
> In a lonesome inlet a sheldrake lost from the flock, sitting on
>   the water rocking silently,
> In farmers' barns oxen in the stable, their harvest labor done,
>   they rest standing, they are too tired,
> Afar on arctic ice the she-walrus lying drowsily while her cubs
>   play around,
> The hawk sailing where men have yet sail'd, the farthest polar
>   sea, ripply, crystalline, open, beyond the floes,
> White drift spooning ahead where the ship in the tempest
>   dashes.   (2:294)

"As they emit themselves," Whitman observed in 1855, "facts are
showered over with light," and even when his perceiving self does
intrude into this poem, he tries to make himself as transparent as
possible, so that the world's lustrous factuality should not be re-
fracted, as it is by the picturesque observer, into mere charm:

> The setting summer sun shining in my open window,
>   showing the swarm of flies, suspended, balancing in the air
>   in the centre of the room, darting athwart, up and down,
>   casting swift shadows in specks on the opposite wall where
>   the shine is.   (2:297)

Such indeed is his mistrust of the actual observer's distorting presence within a scene, that he much prefers the invisible presence of

the imaginary participant: "Northward, on the sands, on some shallow bay of Paumanok, I with parties of snowy herons wading in the wet to seek worms and aquatic plants" (2:298). In the early version, however, this device rather backfired, since it seemed to signal the reappearance of the commandingly omnipresent self with which the poem at that time somewhat peremptorily opened. So into the revised version Whitman inserted a significant phrase, entered as a saving clause at this crucial juncture:

> O lands! all so dear to me—what you are, (whatever it is,) I putting it at random in these songs, become a part of that, whatever it is. (2:298)

By adding the phrase "I putting it at random in these songs," Whitman draws attention to what his revision of the poem has, up to this point, accomplished. As a result of removing those original lines which had established from the outset the presence of an appreciative, implicitly selective self, he has created the impression of things coming to him and leaving him of their own free will, confirmed in their inalienable right to independent existence. The initiative now appears to come from the American land, not from Whitman, and the song arises from his completely trusting obedience to this muse of randomness.

But the application of the additional phrase is prospective as well as retrospective. It confers a randomness on the succeeding lines as well as confirming the randomness of the preceding ones, and in so doing it goes some way at least toward controlling the increasingly intrusive and potentially coercive presence of Whitman's powerful self in the later stages of the poem. It also helps us to realize that when Whitman refers, as he still does in the concluding line, to "collect[ing] bouquets of the incomparable feuillage of these States" (2:299), he is speaking not, as the picturesque writers did, of culling a few choice blooms of American scenery, but of gathering a bouquet of leaves of grass at egalitarian random from the "free range and diversity" of this "continent of Democracy" (2:293). (Had he not, after all, even objected to a belief in miracles on the novel grounds that "any miracle of affairs or persons [is] inadmissible in the vast clear scheme where every motion and every spear of grass and the frames and spirits of men and women and all that concerns them are unspeakably perfect miracles, all referring to all and each distinct and in its place"? [2:448]) In other words, the poem, in its revised form, is much more clearly revealed for what it always was: a work which touches on the picturesque only by way of criticism, in order to define itself as unpicturesque, and even as an antipicturesque form of writing. As such, it has affinities with George Eliot's famous radical critique of the picturesque in chapter 17 of *Adam Bede:* "Yes! thank god; human feeling is like the mighty rivers that bless the earth: It does not wait for beauty—it flows with resistless force and brings beauty with it."

But still it *is* beauty which human feeling brings with it—and that, too, is part of the point of "Our Old Feuillage." Because if, regarded from one point of view, the poem censures the picturesque, then seen from another it argues a case *for* beauty against mere utility.[23] In other words, the poem is as much a comment on the insensitivity to beauty of the average pragmatic American, as it is a repudiation of fashionable aesthetic tastes. Bernard Rosenthal has very thoroughly demonstrated the indifference most mid-nineteenth-century Americans felt to the glories of their continent.[24] They possessed an eye only for its commercial possibilities, with an accompanying talent for the commodification of nature. Words like "bouquet," therefore, clearly signal Whitman's intention to consider this landscape under the alternative rubric of beauty, as, throughout the piece, he cunningly interweaves references to the material prosperity which the land promises with ecstatic appreciation of "the large black buzzard," as it floats "slowly high beyond the tree tops" (2:294).

In spite of taking issue, in this indirect way, with the acquisitive mentality of bourgeois America, and despite his attempts to modify it, Whitman himself shared—albeit on his own distinctive, and virtually dissenting terms—his society's expectation that nature should ultimately minister to human needs. The problem in this connection was, of course, how to distinguish need from greed. Perhaps it was Whitman's uneasiness on this score that led him to change the doubly possessive phrase "our own feuillage" to "our old feuillage" when revising the poem (2:293). Still, the fact remains that in the opening lines the landscape is valued for, and described in terms of, what it yields—but with Whitman's reservations perfectly registered in the equivocal meaning of the word "priceless": "Always the priceless delta of Louisiana—always the cotton-fields of Alabama and Texas, / Always California's golden hills and hollows, and the silver mountains of New Mexico" (2:293).

In that last astonishing line the rip-roaring goldrush of 1849 and the scarring of the land by the search for wealth are commuted to romance. The very words "gold" and "silver" cease to be the metallic nouns that were in Whitman's actual time and country so closely connected with the hard, aggressive verbs "to mine," "to grab," "to grow rich quick," and revert to being the soft, poetic adjectives traditionally associated with pastoral landscape. Whitman thus appears to do a splendid cosmetic job on the unacceptable face of American free enterprise. It certainly gives one pause. Is he being totally naive? Or is there incriminating evidence here of the dangerous consequences of a self-deludingly optimistic philosophy? Has he even, maybe, been exposed at last as the Skimpole of the United States?

What certainly has been exposed is the (perhaps extreme) lengths to which Whitman is prepared to go in order to discover the potential good of virtually every American practice, and to renovate the ideal which has been obscured, but not obliterated, by the actual. It is a hazardous undertaking, liable at any time to become a chimerical pursuit, or to turn into unintentional propaganda for the existing state of society, and certain to prove especially difficult whenever Whitman is confronted by a particularly blatant example of the real, unreconstructed character of nineteenth-century American individualism.

In particular there is, or rather for him there was, the problem of what to make of pioneer and frontier life—the point at which the heroic yet deeply questionable nature of American society was most dramatically exposed through that society's treatment of nature. Everyone of course knows that Whitman idolized the Westerner, seeing in him the autochthonous democratic American and contrasting him with Easterners who continued to be infected by social diseases imported from the Old World. But this idol could prove to have feet of clay, particularly when he had an ax in his hands. The ax was quite literally the cutting edge of American capitalism, as it made capital out of, while simultaneously making a home in, the western wilderness. In this respect the ax was double-edged, as Novak has pointed out: "a double-edged symbol of progress, the axe that destroys and builds, builds and destroys." Such indeed was its power as "the appropriate symbol of the early American attitude towards nature" that fascinated artists throughout the nineteenth century.[25] When in 1856 Whitman composed his own "Song of the Broad-Axe," he followed the "long varied train of an emblem" (1:176) which had been accumulating significance for almost a century before he wrote, and to which new meanings continue to accrue even today. Improved methods, however, have been developed for the mass murder of trees, and so Gary Snyder, in the "Logging" section of *Myths and Texts,* has had to vary the emblem slightly in order to ensure the perpetuation of its meaning:

San Francisco 2X4s
   were the woods around Seattle:
Someone killed and someone built, a house,
   a forest, wrecked or raised
All America hung on a hook
   & burned by men, in their own praise
  . . . . .

"Pines grasp the clouds with iron claws
like dragons rising from sleep"
250,000 board-feet a day
If both Cats keep working
& nobody gets hurt.[26]

It sounds like an extravagant amount of timber, as only a modern mind could think up and only modern machinery could bring down, yet Novak quotes a railway report of 1865 as estimating that 40 million feet of lumber came annually "from the inexhaustible forests of California."[27] Already by mid-century the land had been cleared to such an extent that a chorus of voices was being raised in alarm at what was vanishing. When the English singer Henry Russell toured America between 1835 and 1841, his most popular song was "Oh, Woodman, Spare that Tree."[28] The settlers, by contrast, continued to set about the felling of trees with a will, and with a relish, that some observers deemed to be in excess of what was strictly necessary to the progress of civilization. Traveling in the West, Basil Hall noticed the "singular degree of pleasurable excitement attending this process of clearing waste lands; for it is apparently not so much the end, as the means, which afford this gratification."[29]

Writers such as Cooper and Thoreau are by now well known for having demurred at the wholesale axing of the wilderness, but only in the recent work of Novak and Nicolai Cikovsky, Jr., has it become apparent that landscape painters were equally concerned during this period with the price being paid in trees for the advance of civilization. Novak has pointed out that paradoxical feelings about the progress westward are captured in the iconography of nineteenth-century landscape painting, where they are most particularly represented by the figure of the ax. The talented Thomas Cole was one of the first, and remains one of the best, explorers of this pictorial device for commenting on his society's intemperate conduct. The prominent stump in *River in the Catskills* translates into the symbolic language of painting those warm feelings against "tree destroyers" which led him, in a letter of 1836, to visit "maledictions on all dollar-godded utilitarians."[30] Following Novak's lead, Cikovsky has resourcefully demonstrated that the cut stump motif was used extensively by American painters throughout the century as a symbol of ravaged nature. It even appears in the pediment designed (1854–1856) by Thomas Crawford for the United States Senate, where a backwoodsman is depicted hacking away at the remains of a tree trunk, while an Indian family looks on, reading its own doom in his vigorous actions.

When studied exclusively in this context, "Song of the Redwood Tree" (1874) seems to be a crudely ingenious, or possibly ingenuous, attempt to justify, even to incite, indiscriminate felling. Either way it is discreditable. There is also, regarded from this point of view, a measure of sadness about the way Whitman here abuses one of the most potent, imaginative devices in his poetry. In several of his greatest poems the means of resolving a serious psychological crisis is offered to Whitman in the form of a song from some natural source, which his soul humbly acknowledges and "tallies." In "Song of the Redwood Tree" this device seems to be reduced to a convenient propaganda trick, involving a psychological process of rationalization rather than of initiation. Under the repeated impact of the woodman's ax the "mighty dying tree" is imagined by Whitman as speaking not an elegy but a benediction and a prophecy. It recognizes that its own noble qualities are reflected, in enhanced form, in the "superber race" by whom it is now being superceded: "For them we abdicate, in them ourselves ye forest kings! / . . . These huge precipitous cliffs, this amplitude, these vallies, far Yosemite, / To be in them absorb'd, assimilated" (3:675–676). This is the sinister side of his theory of evolution.

At this point Whitman is virtually the bland spokesman for that commonplace progressivist philosophy of his time, which Rosenthal has discussed under the broad heading of the "city of nature." He quotes the Frenchman Gustave de Beaumont as remarking that "the Americans . . . regard the forest as a symbol of the wilderness, and consequently of backwardness; so it is against the trees that they direct their onslaughts."[31] In Rosenthal's opinion Beaumont is being simultaneously acute and obtuse: "Beaumont attributed to the Americans a kind of monomania against trees that can only be equated with Ahab's feeling about the whale. But for all its indignant exaggeration, Beaumont's discernment is telling. Like the almost ubiquitous wooden fences that surrounded American homes, the transformed trees symbolized the impulse to turn the wilderness into an artifact of civilization." Rosenthal is surely right in insisting that in its ideal form of the aspiration to turn a "wilderness" into fertile "nature" the dream is an ancient one, and worthy of respect; while at the same time he acknowledges that the reality of American western expansion marred the dream and left a great deal to be desired. This discrepancy is very much Whitman's inspiration and dilemma as a poet.

If there is more to "Song of the Redwood Tree" than appears, it can, I am convinced, emerge only when the poem is examined—as for example it has been by Gay Wilson Allen—in a personal context, and also perhaps if it is specifically connected to Whitman's wartime experience.[32] Considered simply as a "frontier" poem, it is an endorsement of the "new society . . . clearing the ground for broad humanity" that succeeds only in functioning as a repugnantly naive apologia for the old society's rapacious clearing of the wilderness. But precisely here, where it fails, is also where this work is most interesting, because it exposes a fact that better poems by definition obscure; namely, that poetry is the intricate mechanism by means of which Whitman tries to lift the unsatisfactory facts of American individualism onto an entirely different plane. Where a poem actually succeeds in accomplishing this considerable task, then the effort involved has been transformed into creative energy, and so, in a way, concealed. Yet the process of transformation is still eminently worth attending to, as can be seen in "Song of the Broad-Axe."

A much earlier poem than "Song of the Redwood Tree," composed in 1856, when Whitman's engagement with his society sustained and was sustained by an alert and flexible imagination, it opens in a most extraordinary way:

> Broad-axe, shapely, naked, wan!
> Head from the mother's bowels drawn!
> Wooded flesh and metal bone! limb only one and lip only one!
> Gray-blue leaf by red-heat grown! helve produced from a little
>   seed sown!
> Resting the grass amid and upon,
> To be leaned, and to lean on.   (1:176)

It is, to begin with, unique among Whitman's mature poems in employing end-rhymes—and intricate end-rhymes at that, including internal rhyme, eye-rhyme, a masculine-feminine combination, and elaborate slant rhyming. The total effect is spellbinding—as it is surely meant to be, since the lines are the modern, democratic equivalent of the baptismal spell chanted by primitives to confer sacred power upon a newly fashioned weapon.[33] In this case it is presumably part of a ceremony of rebaptism, since a weapon traditionally associated with the violent wars and summary class justice of "feudal" times has been refashioned as the American broadax, re-formed into an innocent domestic instrument: "I see the blood washed entirely away from the axe, / Both blade and helve are clean" (1:185). Even more remarkable, however, are the terms in which the ax is here democratically reconceived, and out of this its poetry born. Shorn of its ferocious masculine associations, it is viewed as a fetchingly helpless baby, drawn from its mother nature's womb. The literal reference is to the metal that was mined to make the axhead—but to make the referential connection is to break the spell Whitman has so carefully woven. This spell performs a dual function by a single means: by mythologizing the process of nineteenth-century technology that produced the ax, it bestows an ancient dignity on a modern practice, while simultaneously softening the harsh realities of contemporary mining work. It is therefore a perfect example of the economy of Whitman's imagination when that is working at full power.

The technology of mining had, of course, been described in tropes before. The most celebrated occasion in literature is undoubtedly that in *Paradise Lost,* when the devils discover that in hell's "womb was hid metallic ore." The "pioneers" (in Milton's intriguingly different sense of the word) hurry there, led by Mammon:

> by him first
> Men also, and by his suggestion taught
> Ransack'd the Center, and with impious hands
> Rifled the bowels of their mother Earth
> For Treasures better hid. Soon had his crew
> Opin'd into the Hill a spacious wound
> And digg'd out ribs of Gold.[34]

Clearly there is a considerable amount of complicated, if unintentional, interplay between these and Whitman's lines. Whitman's "pioneers," he would have us believe, are not led by Mammon. They do not (in this instance at least) grub for gold, they utilize a humbler, more serviceable metal, and instead of incestuously raping nature, they assist her to give birth. This last image is, for Whitman, a particularly crucial one to establish, since it allows him to represent man not as conspiring to seize the fruits of nature, but as assisting to bring nature to full fruition, a theme cleverly continued in the following line: "Gray-blue leaf by red-heat grown! helve produced from a little seed sown!" The humanly devised technological process for extracting crude ore and transforming it first into metal, and then into axhead, is turned by a witty conceit into a fantastic example of natural, organic growth.

Thus does Whitman brilliantly falsify the facts of the extractive process that Ray Allen Billington, a recent historian of the West, forthrightly described as "a dangerous, dirty, exploitive industry," which not only damaged the land but "exploit[ed] the human beings who worked it." The graphic example he offers is the huge Butte copper mine: "Wily, boisterous Butte, killing or maiming a man a day in her mines, crippling with silicosis those whose arms and legs stayed secure, was the ultimate of nineteenth-century new country laissez-faire industrialism."[35]

Equally worth noting is the outrageously bold suggestion that the ax helve has been grown directly from seed—without the dubious benefit of human intervention: "helve produced from little seed sown." Whitman thus cuts out the middleman, and so excludes the questionable stage in the production of what is after all not a natural but an artificial object, a human artifact. An ax begins in fact with what is for Whitman at this point the unmentionable—that is, with the felling of trees; and as it begins, so must and will it continue, since in American hands its primary function is to turn trees into timber. This poetic spell operates therefore as a brilliantly constructed social euphemism. The lines are a palimpsest where Whitman's images overlay, so as virtually to conceal both the specific embarrassing realities of mining and felling and the more general reality of the American social character as revealed in such activities.

The final touch is also the final triumph of simplified image over messy fact. With the studied care of an experienced portrait painter, Whitman places the completed ax against a background carefully chosen to advertise its harmlessness and its rustic homeliness: "Resting the grass amid and upon / To be leaned, and to lean on." A nicely turned couplet, it also beautifully balances the naturalness of the ax against its serviceableness to man. Furthermore "to lean on" can, in this context, either mean the familiar pose of the ax idly leaning against the woodman's shoulder, or the woodman leaning on his faithful ax; and so the one phrase knits man and tool together into a partnership which is so close that each takes on something of the character of the other. Indeed, the very presence of an ax within a natural setting is itself sufficient to signify the human, and Whitman takes advantage of this when he lays the ax to rest in the grass.

So, its reputation now safely established, the ax lies there ready for Whitman to take up and put into action in succeeding sections. Predictably it is the masculinity of the ax that is next evoked: "Strong shapes, and attributes of strong shapes" (1:176). This association of "shapes" with "strong" only serves to emphasize in retrospect the peculiarity of the opening line, where the full-formed ax is seen as "shapely, naked, wan." Indeed throughout the opening verse the ax is curiously invested with attributes that not only emasculate it, but also incline to feminize it by rendering it in passive rather than active terms. Thus is it shorn of its strength, and along with that deprived of its aggressiveness, which is surely part of the point of the elaborate poetic exercise.

Wordsworth, in "Nutting," had already exposed the aggression, the fundamental drive to power and domination which were attaining respectability in the agricultural, commercial, and industrial sectors of the emerging economy. For him, too, this perversion of masculine energy showed itself in man's misconduct toward nature. The young boy in "Nutting" is unconsciously persuaded by his social environment that the rite of passage to full manhood involves a demonstration of his virility through the greedily violent deflowering of the natural scene, the "dragging to earth both branch and bough with crash and merciless ravage." Nature then disconcerts, and eventually educates him, by responding to this outrage not with an equal violence of anger and reproof, but in patience and silence. Wordsworth's final words are therefore addressed to a "Maiden" who is at once an actual girl, and also now an admitted part of his own maturely masculine self:

> move along these shades
> In gentleness of heart; with gentle hand
> Touch—for there is a spirit in the woods.[36]

At first glance the contrast is a striking one between the English and the American landscapes, the English and American experience. In America aggression seemed, after all, to come initially from nature, not from man, who had to struggle to "tame" and "conquer" a "wilderness." The quintessential image is not that of a sheltered "bower" deformed and sullied by a guilty intruder, but rather the familiar picture of the log cabin in a clearing hacked out of supposedly dense forest: "The sylvan hut, the vine over the doorway, the space clear'd for a garden" (1:177). But that in turn is only one side of the complete American picture. Even at the beginning of the century several observers noticed a wanton urge, common to pioneers, farmers, and woodsmen, to destroy the forests that once had covered about forty percent of the states. In *The Pioneers* Cooper's woodsman Billy Kirby maintains that trees are "a sore sight at any time, unless I'm privileged to work my will on them"—a masculine sentiment very much in the spirit of "Nutting." Moreover, the really serious and profitable work of despoliation was very soon being done not by individual farmers and woodsmen, but by the great lumber companies, employing thousands of workers, who rapidly consumed most of the timber in New England and New York, before moving on to the even more productive, and therefore more lucrative, regions of Wisconsin, Michigan, and elsewhere. But all this is turned, by Whitman's poetry, into idyll:

> Lumber-men in their winter camp, day-break in the
>   woods, stripes of snow on the limbs of trees, the
>   occasional snapping,
> The glad clear sound of one's own voice, the merry song, the
>   natural life of the woods, the strong day's work,
> The blazing fire at night, the sweet taste of supper, the talk,
>   the bed of hemlock boughs, and the bear-skin.   (1:178)

Timber was actually one of the most important raw materials of the American economy.[37] Consequently, the lone axman was already, like these lumbermen, less of an American archetype than he was, to all intents and purposes, a social anachronism. Whitman here resumes in places his fight to recover the world for his immensely magnified version of the free artisan, as well as for the equally idealized pioneer or woodsman whose innocently "natural" energy is uncontainable and unsubduable by the economic and political powers that be: "The beauty of wood-boys and wood-men, with their clear untrimmed faces, / The beauty of independence, departure, actions that rely on themselves" (1:178). Such idealizations—and they extend elastically to include butchers, sailors, raftsmen, and so on—are the product of his struggle with what he elsewhere called "the operative political and even money-making features of United States humanity in the Nineteenth Century": in other words, that rapidly developing form of the capitalist system of which the actual lumberman, and for that matter the woodsman, were ultimately as much a part as was the eastern businessman.

The ax is ingeniously used throughout "Song of the Broad-Axe" as an organizing symbol which allows him to restructure society drastically, so as to make it into a nonprofit association of purely heroic adventurers and spirited workingmen, in anticipation of the brave New Jerusalem, the heavenly city, to be built eventually on American soil. He uses the tool to link the "adventurous and daring persons" of the West with the heroic trades of the urban East. The result is that the poem includes some of the best, and most comprehensive poetry written by Whitman (outside of "Song for Occupations") on the subject of work; and the emphasis is predictably as much on loving skill and expertise as it is on physical vigor:

> The huge store-house carried up in the city, well under way,
> The six framing-men, two in the middle and two at each end, carefully bearing on their shoulders a heavy stick for a cross-beam,
> The crowded line of masons with trowels in their right hands, rapidly laying the long side-wall, two hundred feet from front to rear,
> The flexible rise and fall of backs, the continual click of the trowels and bricks,
> The bricks, one after another, each laid so workman-like in its place, and set with a knock of the trowel-handle,
> The piles of materials, the mortar on the mortar-boards, and the steady replenishing by the hod-men.   (1:178–179)

But perhaps the most remarkable poetic achievement in "Song of the Broad-Axe" is the conversion of those modes of production, and the complex system of socioeconomic relations associated with them— which were characteristic of his America—into entirely natural forms of metamorphosis:

> The axe leaps!
> The solid forest gives fluid utterances,
> They tumble forth, they rise and form,
> Hut, tent, landing, survey,
> Flail, plough, pick, crowbar, spade.   (1:185)

Even the unmistakably new world—the world as revolutionized by the technological advances greedily financed by industrial capitalism—is assimilated, through the symbol of the working ax, to this "natural" process:

> The shapes arise!
> Shapes of factories, arsenals, foundries, markets,
> Shapes of the two-threaded tracks of railroads,
> Shapes of the sleepers of bridges, vast frame-works, girders, arches.   (1:186)

Ultimately, his ax—the ax he has poetically fashioned—strikes, almost without his consciously aiming it, at the root of his society's practices. Yet it is still the homely American broadax. In other words, as was the case with the kosmos, and the nonpossessive self, he has developed an ingenious image of the ideal, which he can conveniently confuse, or at least credibly connect, with the existing state of affairs. And the crucial factor in all this is the way he subtly transforms the American's working relationship to nature. "The axe leaps! / The solid forest gives fluid utterances." The ax is not even seen to strike a blow. In the careful parallelism of these lines man does not touch, let alone attack, nature. As if by a form of sympathetic magic, the dumb forest is persuaded to deliver itself in speech—in the human terms of implements and commodities—by the sheer articulate energy of the ax. The trees do not die, they are brought to fuller, more abundant life, as the leap awakens an answering fluidity in previously inert wood. Although the philosophy is virtually identical with that preached in "Song of the Redwood Tree," the underlying crisis has here, at least, registered itself not only in, but even in a sense as, poetry, whereas in the later poem it produces only flat assertion. By the eloquence of its hard-won omissions, as much as by what it consequently has to say, "Song of the Broad-Axe" becomes one of the most resounding comments Whitman ever made on the nature of his society.

6 &ᵉ *Mannahatta–New York*

CRITICS generally recognize Whitman's special attachment to urban life. Morton and Lucia White, for example, in *The Intellectual versus the City,* see Whitman as a notable exception to the general nineteenth-century rule that American intellectuals were both hostile to and critical of the American city.[1] Oscar Handlin, in criticizing rural idealists who emphasized "the personal hardships of adjustment to city life," states his preference for those like Whitman and "other observers, whose gaze was fastened on the residents as human beings, [and who] made out a somewhat different pattern."[2] More recently, Spann, himself almost daunted by the way New York City's "concentrated population and its trade generated a vast array of business roles," concluded that "perhaps only the magnificent eye of Walt Whitman was capable of perceiving the totality of the city-building insect, and then only by translating a list of occupations and activities into a great hymn to the equality of man."[3]

Whitman was certainly capable of finding the pattern of urban life he encountered in Brooklyn and New York absorbing, even stimulating. Whoever was tired of the city seemed to him to be tired of life, as he explained to Traubel with specific reference to the case of Thoreau: "The great vice in Thoreau's composition was his disdain of the universe—his disdain of cities, companions, civilization. I have very little room for the man who disdains the universe."[4] The equation here between "cities" and "companions," "civilization," ultimately even "the universe" itself, seems to be a firm one. But at bottom his feelings toward what he liked to call, with a characteristic mixture of confidence and anxiety, "my city," were ambivalent. The ebb and flow of this tense relationship contributed to the energy of the poetry in which Whitman's passionate involvement with New York is most fully and compellingly disclosed. Thus this chapter first considers the terms on which Whitman felt at home in the city and examines some of the ways he was consequently able to respond positively and creatively to urban life; and then it explores the strains that led eventually to the breaking of that contact with the living city on which his poetry so deeply depended.

IN SOME of his best work Whitman draws implicitly on his early experience of the city that was his home for most of the first forty years of his life. During that period New York grew fom a burgeoning town of less than 125 thousand to a vast metropolitan complex with a population approaching 1.5 million by 1870. The young Whitman, a working journalist and editor, was closely involved with the changing life of his city. He understood the social and political consequences of such a radical transformation of its character and was familiar with the successive waves of workers' movements (parties and unions) that characterized the New York of the twenties and thirties.[5] These were primarily a reaction to the gradual breakdown of the old social pattern whereby an apprentice could advance to master craftsman and eventually to small entrepreneur. As has already been seen, this pattern was destroyed by economic conditions that produced new social classes and divided the population more rigidly into laborers, semiskilled workers, small enterprisers, white collar workers, businessmen, and so on. But very little of all this upheaval is at least directly reflected in Whitman's poetry or gathered into his prose recollections. Instead he fuses idealized aspects of the old urban order with the new economy so as to make features of his growing, changing city comprehensible and acceptable to him.

And by 1855 New York was indeed growing very rapidly. Recently emerged from a ten-year slump, the city was, in spite of occasional setbacks, leading America into a new phase of commercial activity. It was only after the Civil War that the extreme social consequences of industrial and commercial capitalism seriously came to occupy Whitman's conscious attention. Then he reacted with alarm to "the immense problem of the relation, adjustment, conflict, between Labor and its status and pay, on the one side, and the Capital of employers on the other side." It meant "many thousands of decent working people, through the cities and elsewhere, trying to keep up a good appearance, but living by daily toil, from hand to mouth, with nothing ahead, and no owned homes—the increasing aggregation of capital in the hands of the few . . . the advent of new machinery, dispensing more and more with hand-work."(2:753).

But his best poetry was written before the war, and by concentrating on the free play of human energies it suggests a harmonious society in which traditional crafts continued to be practiced and honored. Even the "tear-down and build over again" spirit of the emerging commercial metropolis was ultimately seen only as giving greater scope for familiar activities, even though it could temporarily unnerve him, as he glimpsed in it the undiscriminating fervor of the philistine commercial spirit: "Then they communed with themselves, and said in their own hearts, 'Let us level to the earth all the houses that were not built within the last ten years; let us raise the devil and break things!' "[6] When the old Brooklyn graveyard was replaced by magnificent new streets, humming with life and glittering with gas jets, Whitman greeted the transformation not as another manifestation of beneficent cosmic energy, but, rather grimly, as "a fit illustration of the rapid changes of this kaleidoscope of alteration and death we call life."[7] But of course one of the primary functions of his poetry was to protect him from precisely this nightmarish vision of mutability to which the radical social changes of his period threatened to expose him.

Whitman's father was a carpenter, Whitman himself a builder as well as printer, and, as has already been argued, this artisanal background influenced his depiction of ordinary, city working life in his poems. This is most evident in set pieces where Whitman is presumably drawing directly on his own experience:

> The house-builder at work in cities or anywhere,
> The preparatory jointing, squaring, sawing, mortising,
> The hoist-up of beams, the push of them in their places,
>   laying them regular,
> Setting the studs by their tenons in the mortises, according as
>   they were prepared,
> The blows of mallets and hammers, the attitudes of the men,
>   their curved limbs,

Bending, standing, astride the beams, driving in pins, holding
    on by posts and braces.   (1:178)

But the same appreciation of the way physical action can become
so absorbing as to command, and therefore express, the vital energies
of a human being is evident wherever he describes people bending
to and blending with their work: "The spinning-girl retreats and
advances to the hum of the big wheel, / . . . The jour printer with
gray head and gaunt jaws works at his case, / He turns his quid of
tobacco, his eyes get blurred with the manuscript" (1:16). Although
such observations are rooted in the particular social, and indeed, political, experiences of Whitman's youth and early manhood, they
grow here into a spiritual vision that values people not for conventional reasons but for that precious singularity of life each one possesses. The city is for Whitman the place in which this natural equality
of men in their "abundance of diversity" most torrentially and therefore irresistibly displays itself.[8]

Seeing people at work in this way allows Whitman to interweave
urban and agricultural work into one magically seamless garment of
description. The whole of human society seems, in its harmonious
variety, to be a microcosm of the miraculously integrated living universe. City and country are not hostile opposites or stark alternatives.[9]
They naturally complement each other. Whitman is by turns a "dweller
in Mannahatta my city" and "withdrawn to muse and meditate in
some deep recess" (2:273). Both kinds of experience are needed to
satisfy the generous scope of man's energies and needs. This approach
has the strengths of its considerable weaknesses. It makes no attempt
to consider the underlying structure and internal character of an urban
society full of growing divisions and conflicts, but it is admirably
suited to the uninhibited evocation of the excited and exciting surface
of contemporary life. And yet Whitman never really participates in
this unpredictable turbulence. He remains an impassioned observer,
sustained by the conviction that this disorder is more apparent than
real.[10]

He preferred not to use the name "New York," partly because it
originated with the "tyrant" Duke of York, later James II: "a pretty
name, this, to fasten on the proudest and most democratic city in the
world!"[11] Instead he adopted whenever possible the aboriginal name—
Mannahatta—which seemed to him to offer a reassuring guarantee

of the naturalness and appropriateness of the life of the modern city.[12] "My city's fit and noble name" faithfully evokes the spirit of the geography of the place: "A rocky founded island—shores where ever gayly dash the coming, going, hurrying sea waves" (3:695).

> Now I see what there is in a name, a word, liquid, sane,
>   unruly, musical, self-sufficient,
> I see that the word of my city, is that word up there,
> Because I see that word nested in nests of water-bays, superb,
>   with tall and wonderful spires,
> Rich, hemmed thick all around with sailships and
>   steamships—an island sixteen miles long, solid-founded,
> Numberless crowded streets—high growths of iron, slender,
>   strong, light, splendidly uprising toward clear
>   skies.   (2:419)

In this, Whitman's most spontaneous and best sustained celebration of his city's vigorous diversity, the flood of sights and sounds throughout the seasons (of the soul as well as of the year) are both released and controlled in him by the word, the "specific" name Mannahatta, which "perfectly" comprehends and commands the whole of the city's life. He is thus able to see this thronging, variegated life as simultaneously uniquely modern and primevally old; an expression of the procreant urge of the world, the restless breed of life, but in the evolved form of a contemporary, proudly democratic society. That society he sees in *Democratic Vistas* as composed of "an infinite number of currents and forces, and contributions, and temperatures, and cross purposes, whose ceaseless play of counterpart upon counterpart brings constant restoration and vitality" (2:362). Viewed in this way even the sordid, ugly, and brutal aspects of city life, acknowledged by Whitman to exist, are redeemed by the energy flowing in and around them, providing what Whitman calls "ventilation."[13] The city epitomizes nature as evolutionary process, "the Great Unrest of which we are part" (2:289). By so treating it as kosmos he is mostly able to avoid the main thrust of Horace Greeley's grim perception that "the gorgeous rainbow that spans the whirling torrent of metropolitan life rests its base on such dark depths of misery and crime as it makes one shudder to think of."[14]

Whitman's celebration of New York under the poeticized pseudonym of Mannahatta inevitably breeds its own ironies. Since 1811, when the state plan of gridiron streets was adopted, the development of New York had required the wholesale relandscaping of Manhattan Island.[15] Nature was changed to fit in with man's plans. New Yorkers "transformed the landscape to conform to their rigid geometry, leveling hills and filling in ponds, swamps, marshes and portions of the waterfront."[16] New York rose, and rose to eminence, on the ruins of Mannahatta, as the Indians had known it. The bays, it is true, were largely untouched, but that was only because these natural features were probably the most important single reason for the commercial preeminence of New York. They were the natural advantages it availed itself eagerly of.

Whitman also took advantage of these sea approaches to the city. They offered him another important perspective on New York, another avenue of approach to its meaning for him. "My own favorite loafing places have always been the rivers, the wharves, the boats," he informed Traubel. "I like sailors, stevedores. I have never lived away from a big river."[17] No wonder, therefore, that the "city of hurried and sparkling waters" was also the "city of spires and masts! / The city nested in bays! my city!" (2:420). City life always fell most happily into place for Whitman around his beloved port. About this vigorous, exciting, and adventurous side of commerce he could be unequivocally enthusiastic. New York could be seen across wide water, beyond the movement and the masts, the merchandise and the beauty of the ships which directly contribute, and lend an impressive character to its vibrant power and energy. In such a beguiling setting it is easy to believe Tom Paine's old prediction that international trade would promote world peace. "Commerce," he had explained, "is a pacific system, operating to cordialise mankind, by rendering Nations, as well as individuals, useful to each other."[18] Upon the departure of the steamer *Atlantic* from New York in 1850, a New York minister was moved to declare: "These pillars of cloud by day and of fire by night are heralding our modern civilization to conquests and results not possible before. The fast-flying gigantic shuttles are weaving the nations inextricably together in the bonds of mutual acquaintance, friendship, and commercial intercourse. They will soon make war impossible . . . They will lift the masses . . . They will make—are making—a highway for our God."[19]

In the scene Whitman paints in *Specimen Days,* the foreground is "thick" with ferries, coasters, "great ocean Dons, iron-black, modern," and "those daring, careening, things of grace and wonder, those white and shaded swift-darting fish-birds . . . ever with their slanting spars, and fierce, pure, hawk-like beauty and motion," the sloops and schooner yachts. Beyond, "rising out of the midst, tall-topt, ship-hemm'd, modern, American, yet strangely oriental, V-shaped Manhattan, with its compact mass, its spires, its cloud-touching edifices group'd at the centre," all well blended "under a miracle of limpid delicious light of heaven above and June haze on the surface below" (1:170–171).

This strategically chosen vantage point is convenient both for what it allows Whitman to see and what it allows him not to see. It discourages the nearer acquaintance that might lead to uncomfortable reflections on the motivating force of all that power and beauty. But it does allow him successfully to reconcile two different, and to him equally important, aspects of Manhattan. New York, in such a romantic vision, rises up effortlessly like a natural form. But it is also recognized and honored as having been raised up, constructed by men, a monument to the ingenuity and endeavors of the masterful modern spirit. It is all obliquely suggestive of "the divine mind of man, or the divinity of his mouth, or the shaping of his great hands" (*Leaves of Grass,* 1:246).

By so conceiving the city, Whitman is able, contrary to the experience of many of his contemporaries, to appreciate how it afforded men a physical environment that was neither spiritually oppressive nor dead. Buildings are for him dwellings saturated with human experience. They have absorbed, and can exude, the essence of the life they have known: "You flagged walks of the cities! you strong curbs at the edges! / . . . From the living and the dead I think you have peopled your impassive surfaces, and the spirits thereof would be evident and amicable with me" (1:227). The urgent presentness, the jostling coexistence of things and lives in space that characterize city living, stimulate Whitman to produce superbly impressionistic passages of poetry. After all, the city is the natural domain of a poet whose favorite device is parataxis: the arranging of perceptions side by side in what Hayden White has called "a democracy of lateral coexistence, one next to another."[20]

The blab of the pave . . . . the tires of carts and sluff of
   bootsoles and talk of the promenaders,
The heavy omnibus, the driver with his interrogating thumb,
   the clank of the shod horses on the granite floor,
The carnival of sleighs, the clinking and shouted jokes and
   pelts of snowballs. (1:9)

Such profusion and ceaseless ripple of energy is irresistibly attractive
to a poet who loves life to be "thick in the pores of my skin" (1:73).
It is what makes the city for him the very epitome of modern democratic life: "The present, now and here, / America's busy, teeming,
intricate whirl" (3:658).

He loves the simply spectacular and thrilling elements of urban
living; the melodrama of the streets is to Whitman as delicious as the
drama of the Broadway theaters he frequented. "I sometimes think,"
he wrote in a letter in 1868, "I am the particular man who enjoys the
show of all these things in New York more than any other mortal—
as if it was all got up just for me to observe and study."[21] There is
that in Whitman which relishes the yeast of insobriety in great city
life and celebrates its exciting unpredictability. "There have been some
tremendous fires," he wrote to Pete Doyle in October 1868, "the
[one] in Brooklyn—eight or ten first-class steam engines."[22] The zest-
fulness of the remark is appropriate to a man who loved "to see the
sights. I always enjoy seeing the city let loose and on the rampage."[23]
And, "among the sights of New York city . . . few possess a vivider
interest for the time, than the public fires. Alarming as they are, too,
there is a kind of hideous pleasure about them."[24] Introducing readers
to the Bowery, he warned them that "here, if there happens to be an
alarm of fire in the Seventh or Eighth District, you will, in its fullest
extent (and with joy, if you accept strong sensations, and take the
precautions to brace yourself by an iron lamp-post,) realize the practical meaning of the phrase, "h—l broke loose.' "[25] "The sight of the
flames," he wrote in "A Song of Joys," "maddens me with pleasure"
(2:335). This, as much as suppressed homosexuality, surely accounts
for his sharing the popular enthusiasm of his time for those modern
epic heroes, the urban firemen, described in 1857 by the English
jounalist Charles Mackay as "young men at the most reckless and
excitable age of life, who glory in a fire as soldiers do in a battle."[26]

Whitman loves to be one of "the crowd with their lit faces watching, the glare and dense shadows":

> The city fire-man, the fire that suddenly bursts forth in the
> close-packed square,
> The arriving engines, the hoarse shouts, the nimble stepping
> and daring,
> The strong command through the fire-trumpets, the forming
> in line, the echoed rise and fall of the arms forcing
> the water,
> The slender, spasmic blue-white jets—the bringing to bear of
> the hooks and ladders, and their execution,
> The crash and cut away of connecting wood-work, or through
> floors, if the fire smoulders under them.   (1:179)

It is a powerfully idealized social (as well as sexual) image. Intrepid individualists voluntarily submit to discipline as they use their daring in the service of the community. No wonder firemen became popular idols. Even the typical Bowery b'hoy (not to be confused with the Bowery Boys, who were a violent street gang) liked to dress in fireman's red, to give the finishing touch to his swaggeringly macho image.

At times, the younger Whitman seems almost predisposed to regard fires as a natural product, and even a welcome dramatic expression, of the electricity being generated by his hyperactive society. In view of this, there is real poignancy in the old man's reaction, as reported by Traubel, to a disastrous blaze. "I have been incessantly thinking of that fearful, frightful tragedy in New York—that terrible fire in the tenements last night. I often wonder how the people in those foul rookeries manage to exist anyhow in such weather. I have often been accused of turning a deaf ear to that side of my life—of being too unconcerned—of treating it as if it was not. Lately, as I have sat here thinking, it has come upon me that there must be some truth in the charge—that I should have studied that strata of life more directly— seen what it signifies, what it starts from, what it means as a part of the social fabric. I have seen a lot of the rich-poor—of the people who have plenty yet have little—of the miseries of the well-to-do, who are supposed to be exempt from certain troubles."[27] In old age Whitman not infrequently liked to think of himself as Lear, and this is an authentically Lear-like moment. "Oh! I have ta'en too little care of this"—"this" in the present context being the wretched lives of the urban poor in their "foul rookeries."

Encouraged by these self-accusations, Traubel, as was his wont whenever opportunity presented itself, tried to get Whitman to think in terms of social and economic conditions, and to nudge him gently in the direction of a vague sort of socialism. Whitman's response— characteristic of many such exchanges between them over the months— was to agree in general terms, without ever showing any real interest in, or understanding of, the specific terms Traubel was anxious to employ. After all, Whitman had spent his best years, and his greatest creative energies, as a poet, trying to avoid having to make the openly critical, radical kind of analysis of his society which Traubel later advocated.

In his recent study Spann has emphasized that "poverty was a major presence in New York, but it was a presence which successful New Yorkers ignored whenever possible. The poor, tucked away in side streets, alleys and cellars, and behind almshouse walls, were easily forgotten, despite such reminders as street beggars, chiffoniers, hot-corn girls, and the concentrated riffraff of the notorious Five Points."[28] Whatever his dark doubts on the subject in his old age, Whitman was not, and never had been, one of these "ignorers." In fact he had inveighed against those who did ignore "that region down below," and all "the gaunt physical want and heathenish spiritual ignorance that make the city's stews and purlieus hideous."[29] In a peroration reminiscent of his great favorite, Dickens, he raged against the tinsel and trappings that engaged public attention: "Nobody wishes to look deeper—it is unpleasant and inconvenient. It is not pleasant to grope among the muck and slime. Cover it up! Do you say that pestilence will arise? Never mind—cover it up—never look 'Down below.' "[30] Most of New York's poor were tucked away in slums, to the una-vailing horror of humane observers and city reformers, who for two decades and more conducted innumerable campaigns to try to remedy the situation.[31] Following the Tenement Housing Commission of 1856, Whitman launched an eloquent attack on the dreadful conditions in which people lived in the cheap boarding houses that were then proliferating in New York—those perfect breeding grounds for chol-era, typhoid, and other epidemics, as well as for a multitude of social abuses, including incest. He denounced this "wicked architecture" and demanded that these rack-rent tenements be torn down and replaced by decent accommodations.[32]

So, too, his poetry goes "down below" to visit prostitutes and drunkards, seamstresses, draymen, and many other representatives of the vast, socially depressed, laboring force of New York. In the process he bestows upon them not sentimental sympathy, but explicit recognition of their inherent worth as human beings, and with that goes an implicit acknowledgment of their social rights. It is, however, only implicit, because Whitman isn't really clear what can be done—whether, indeed, anything should be done—immediately to remedy their situation. Instead of a crusading program of reform, he relies on the richly suggestive, but endlessly ambivalent image of the kosmos. Perhaps that is why he felt, toward the end, a twinge of guilt, at not having done enough to change the urban underworld of crime and desperate poverty.

There is no doubting his sympathy for the laboring poor, or his concern at sudden fluctuations in the economy that threatened to turn workers into paupers and beggars. For years he pleaded in his columns on behalf of the "sweated" seamstresses,[33] and countered the Panic of 1857, which he foresaw would throw as many as twenty-five thousand out of work, with a sonorously biblical lament: "Vainly the laborer cries out in the market-places and at the corners of the streets—'No parish money or loaf, / No pauper badges for me, / A son of the soil, by the right of toil, / Entitled to my fee.' "[34] If, though, there was a limit to his sympathy it is to be detected precisely here, and thus to be understood as a characteristic of his class solidarity. Like any "decent," "self-respecting" artisan he feared genuine poverty and was therefore liable to treat the poor not as economic casualties, but as a class apart, shiftless, chronically idle, and generally culpable. An editorial which considered "how to diminish pauperism" (1858) supported a proposal to amend the poor law so as to discontinue relief outside the poorhouse and to make its conditions less attractive by separating husband from wife, and both from their children. As Whitman noted, with prim approval, the main aim was "to render the situation of the able-bodied recipient of the public charity so unpleasant a one, that it will not be courted by the dissipated or indolent as a means of escaping from that toil which the community may justly call on each of its members to undergo, who has not means wherewith to support himself in idleness." He went on to pour scorn on the "palatial mansions" built by New York for the poor—the grounds of his bitter objection becoming clear when he argued that these poorhouses "support the pauper in a style sumptuous in comparison with that in which the hard-working laborer lives."[35]

The all-embracing, socially undiscriminating sympathy registered by the poetry is certainly genuine, and Whitman has become renowned for it. But it might be proper to suggest, without reductive cynicism, that this sympathy could to some small degree be the reflex of anxiety—an anxiety that remained submerged during the prewar years and which was therefore indistinguishable from other, stronger, and more positive emotions, but which later developed into a distinct, and even prominent, part of Whitman's reaction to postwar America. In *Democratic Vistas* he firmly pronounced "the aggregate of its middling property owners" to be the bulwark of American democracy and emphasized that ("ungracious as it may sound") "democracy looks with suspicious, ill-satisfied eyes upon the very poor, the ignorant, and those out of business" (2:383–384). The equivocal phrasing exactly records the ambivalence of feeling within Whitman on this subject. In one way he is saying, unexceptionably enough, that in a democracy poverty is not to be endured and must be eradicated as soon as possible. But in another way he is suggesting that the helpless, hopeless poor represent a serious threat to democracy, both because they have no vested interest (such as property) in supporting it, and because they have, through their circumstances, been positively alienated from it. This was the crisis scenario he outlined in his fascinating fragmentary remarks "The Tramp and Strike Questions," where for the first time he openly admitted that "beneath the whole political world, what most presses and perplexes to-day, sending vastest results affecting the future, is not the abstract question of democracy, but of social and economic organization, the treatment of working-people by employers, and all that goes along with it—not only the wages-payment part, but a certain spirit and principle, to vivify anew these relations" (2:527).

By 1876 Whitman was seriously concerned by developments. Could anything be more alarming, he asked, "than the total want of any such fusion and mutuality of love, belief, and rapport of interest, between the comparatively few successful rich, and the great masses of the unsuccessful, the poor? As a mixed political and social question, is not this full of dark significance?" (2:533). By then it most certainly was, and it was what made the postwar city essentially unintelligible to Whitman and poetically unmanageable by him. Of course, before the war the problem was by no means as acute, nor therefore did he see it so starkly and clearly. But the destructive side of New York City's new capitalism was nevertheless already there, embodied in the plight of the immigrants, the unemployed, the sick, the laboring poor, and the paupers. In his journalism Whitman's remedies might vary according to his diagnosis of the social disease, but in his poetry he offered the one nostrum of sympathy allied to an evolutionary philosophy.

Disregarding for the moment the genuine humanity of this impulse of fellow feeling, we can see it as an instrument of social control. By assuring the social unfortunates of his sympathy, Whitman performs a kind of holding operation—of several kinds. He surrounds them with concern and reassurance while waiting for time to remedy their ills; he binds them into a kosmos, the ultimate ends of whose processes are benign, whatever its incidental indignities; and he attaches them securely to the existing social, political and economic order—sympathy being a kind of social cement which prevents the disaffected from splitting off into a hostile, adversary group or class. (It will be remembered that Whitman even disapproved of fledgling unionism.) This was, after all, the period when George Eliot, working of course under much more extreme conditions, wrote her famous review entitled "The Natural History of German Life," in which she spelled out the moral principles on which her novels were shortly to be constructed: "The greatest benefit we owe to the artist, whether painter, poet, or novelist, is the extension of our sympathies . . . a picture of human life such as a great artist can give, surprises even the trivial and the selfish into that attention to what is apart from themselves, which may be called the raw material of moral sentiment."[36] Alarmed at the developing class alignments of her time, and at the turn contemporary politics was taking, she used her art specifically to practice and to preach the socially conservative and conciliatory gospel of sympathy. Whitman attempted something similarly soothing and reconciling in the much less sharply divided but still unequal society of the United States.

When he isn't singling them out for sympathetic attention, he prefers to see the poor as part of the crowd. He always values crowded city life, for its colorful vitality, and for the sustaining fellowship it offers, which generates a correspondingly heightened sense of separate identities. The milieu prompts man to confront his essential existence as a soul, and this self-realization, when properly matured, permeates and enriches his relationships with his fellowmen and his world. Furthermore, the city advances men to related insights into the paradoxical nature of that world. The human currents of the streets suggest the coincidence of fluidity and permanence, as do the flowing river and its tides. Yet it is precisely those features of New York which Whitman lovingly regards as possessed of distinctive spiritual significance that more hard-headed observers attributed to its obsession with trade. Daniel Curry argued in 1852 that "the essential character of the city derived from its having been settled by individuals seeking commercial opportunity rather than by an organized group with common goals. In such a society, no single group had the power to assimilate all others . . . New York therefore became a confederation of individuals each seeking to live his own life in his own way."[37]

Whitman never really identifies with the enthusiastically pecuniary spirit of this new, explosive version of free enterprise. Yet his continuing identification, in some respects, with an older, artisanal stage of capitalism does not make him (as it makes Wordsworth in "Michael," for instance) the elegist of a dying community. He actively likes what other writers deplore: the fact that human beings in the city are not embedded in deeply traditional forms of life that shape their personal identities and determine the course of their own existence—as continued for some time to be the case in other American cities, such as Boston and Philadelphia. He likes the approachability of new, urban man, his relative freedom from binding contracts or commitments of relationship, the way in which he remains malleable enough to receive the stamp of new impressions, and free enough to be moved in new directions.[38] "Perhaps in no other city were even citizens so much strangers to each other," concludes Spann of the New York of this period.[39] The very tone of Whitman's poetry presupposes a milieu in which strangers are at least free to become friends: "I do not ask who you are. . . . that is not important to me, / You can do nothing, and be nothing, but what I still infold you" (1:62). For him, city life does usually represent an advance on country living. He is not one of those who automatically regard the metropolis as an un-American phenomenon. Instead, he belongs to the other contemporary group, for whom Greeley spoke when he claimed rural areas were inescapably backward because "their excessively sparse and scattered population . . . denied them the concentrated power and concerted effort which had made the cities centers of wealth and culture; the result was ignorance, dullness, and inefficiency."[40] Whitman expresses similar views in his essay "Some Poetic Comparisons between Country and City," which appeared in *Letters from a Travelling Bachelor* (1849). There he sees fewer strengths than weaknesses in rural life. Coarse and insular, it causes people to age prematurely, and to harden, through enforced isolation, into a "singular sort of egoism." Country life is fully as wicked as urban life, with the additional disadvantage that "out of cities the human race does not expand and improvise so well morally, intellectually, or physically."[41]

YET WHITMAN'S MASTERY of this urban world was perhaps not as complete as it appeared to be: and as he found it increasingly difficult to cope with the dramatic extremes in New York's disturbingly headstrong character, so he turned to the more manageable, and ideologically malleable, prospect of his hometown of Brooklyn— a totally independent city until its merger with New York in 1898. This attachment to Brooklyn was not only sentimental, it was also a profitable matter of professional interest, since so many of the papers edited by him at this time were specifically Brooklyn based and oriented. Already in the forties Whitman was used to entering, with gusto, into the spirit of seemingly friendly rivalry that existed between the twin cities. New York papers, he complained, overlooked Brooklyn completely—just like the lantern in the Chinese proverb, which cast its light far and wide, but failed to illuminate the pole upon which it was hung.[42] By the mid-fifties Brooklyn had grown into a city of over two hundred thousand souls, rapidly heading for the million Whitman was already anticipating, and it was already the third largest city in the United States. Many factors had contributed to its phenomenal rise, but one of the most important of its attractions was the opportunity it offered both the wealthy and the middle classes to escape the squalid overcrowding of New York, and "find a superior place for dwelling."[43] Brooklyn Heights became the favored residential area of the rich, while outlying, semirural areas like Williamsburgh were quickly overrun by the cheaper housing built in great quantities for the much more moderately well-off. The social pattern of this commuter development was relatively simple to comprehend, compared to the untidy, unnerving, complexities of New York. Moreover, this growth of an extensive suburbia in pleasant surroundings was eminently amenable to idealization: it offered Whitman practical grounds for hope.

He devoted several editorials in the Brooklyn *Daily Times* (1857–58) to the development of what was becoming known as "Consolidated Brooklyn," and contributed a series of twenty-five articles on its glories, past and present, to the Brooklyn *Standard* in 1861–62. Mindful of his readership, he advertised the city's advantages in terms that were clearly related to the promotional material of real estate agents, making much of the natural beauties of the site, the picturesque charms of Long Island, the excellent transportation facilities and manufacturing prospects. Civic pride was further strengthened and refined by his account of Brooklyn's noble history, from its Dutch beginnings, through the ordeals it suffered during the struggle for independence, to its amazing growth in a matter of decades, during the first half of the nineteenth-century, from village into city. But what Whitman was clearly trying to do, through all this, was to supply the citizens of Brooklyn with a pride of place, an exalted image of their city which would direct future developments and control conduct. His aim was to bring the "citizens and government" to "accept the spirit of its old days, and calculate our future on those large and patriotic premises."[44] Therefore, through his account of Brooklyn's history, he sought to attach the modern citizens to the robust egalitarianism of the early Dutch, the heroically defiant libertarianism of the prisoners in the British prison ships, and "a hundred other of the precedents and preparations which have so rapidly been gone through within the last thirty years, and left for signs of themselves the present advanced condition of this noble, wealthy, intelligent, cultivated, populous, and every way remarkable and to be proud of Brooklyn of ours."[45]

But even while he, as editor and journalist, approximated the language of the real estate hustlers and the hard-headed business community, he tried to build into it a dimension of the ideal. In this way he attempted to capture the business ethic for his own distinctive vision of democracy. A vital case in point was his effort to make Brooklyn out to be the city of actual thousands, and prospectively a

million, of what, by implication, was an artisanal middle class. This
was his theme whenever he waxed lyrical on the subject of his hometown: "*Our* architectural greatness consists in the hundreds and thousands of superb private dwellings, for the comfort and luxury of the
great body of middle-class people—a kind of architecture unknown
until comparatively late times, and no where known to such an extent
as in Brooklyn, and the other first-class cities of the New World."[46]
That last phrase, however, was not characteristic of his general conclusions. Indeed, he customarily contrasted Brooklyn to other American cities in this very crucial respect, pointing out that in Brooklyn
"men of moderate means may find homes at a moderate rent, whereas
in New York there is no medium between a palatial mansion and a
dilapidated hovel."[47] There we have it again—Whitman's fear of a
metropolitan society that was becoming polarized and was, by various
means, squeezing out all those social, political, and economic elements
in which he had been able to place at least a degree of reassuring faith.
In this respect Brooklyn provided him with a temporary refuge—
with continuing grounds, in short, for visionary hope. If he could
resonantly conclude, in 1854, that "there is indeed nowhere any better
scope for practically exhibiting the full-sized American idea, than in
a great, free, proud, American city,"[48] then it was explicitly and
almost exclusively of the potential of Brooklyn that he was thinking.
But even then, there was more than a tinge of desperation in his
rhetoric, as he went on to recognize disconsolately that "most of our
cities are huge aggregates of people, riches, and enterprise. The av-
enues, edifices, and furniture are splendid; but what is that to splendor
of character? To encourage the growth of trade and property is commendable; but our politics might also encourge the forming of men
of superior demeanor, and less shuffling and blowing."[49]

So, too, in his poetic handling of the city, Whitman clearly shows
the different and sometimes dangerously contradictory elements in
his conception of contemporary America. In the early *Leaves of Grass*
Whitman's hospitality toward all manifestations of energy tends to
facilitate his apparently uncritical acceptance of urban life. The impulse is rooted in the Romantic delight in the plenitude, mystery,
and variety of the benignly evolving universe. God is imagined as
committed to the promotion of a diversity of life, even at the cost
of allowing evil to exist. Whitman's genius lies in his accommodating
city life within this vitalistic Romantic philosophy. And when he is

possessed by such a faith he can, particularly in "Song of Myself," trustingly accept "each day's flux and lapse" of city life, confident of discovering "a music of constancy behind / The wide promiscuity of acquaintanceship."[50] It becomes a field of energy entered by Whitman and explored on the same generous and uninhibited terms that he explores his own bodily self. Whoever "having consider'd the body, finds all its organs and parts good; / . . . understands by subtle analogies, the theory of a city, a poem, and of the large politics of These States" (2:432).

Yet only at his most optimistic is Whitman able to sustain this mode of seeing. It takes a white heat of faith to weld the randomness of the quotidian to the transcendental, so as to fashion a credible and durable vision. The 1860 *Leaves of Grass* particularly shows the strain.[51] True, it not only continues but augments Whitman's theme of urban pride: "for I think I have reason to be the proudest son alive—for I am the son of the brawny and tall-topt city" (1:243). The edition features, in "Mannahatta," Whitman's single most memorable and unequivocal act of homage to his city. Yet at the end of *Chants Democratic* he reveals significantly qualified terms of belief in "the approved growth of cities and the spread of inventions": "They stand for realities—all is as it should be" (2:318). These realities are "the visions of poets, the most solid announcements of any," the spiritual values whose social and political manifestations are freedom and democracy. For and by these standards the city is to stand—or, perhaps, to fall. In trying to knit the visions of poets to the actual growths of cities Whitman is eventually to find himself (in Auden's sardonic phrase) sitting in an expanding saddle. Material and spiritual realities are revealed by time to be inexorably diverging rather than converging.

In *Enfans d'Adam* Whitman is consistently looking away from the present scene and turning toward nature, the West, and the future. The city is securely placed in these redeeming contexts. New inland cities are predicted: "I, chanter of Adamic songs, / Through the new garden, the West, the great cities, calling" (2:363). Whitman wanders through these cities of the future, including his own Mannahatta, satisfied that he has anticipated their development and that they will find him "unchanged" (2:362). But, significantly, in "Once I Pass'd Through a Populous City" memory can no longer recall the "ephemeral [urban] shows, architectures, customs, traditions": "now, of all that city, I remember only a woman casually met there, who detained me for love of me" (2:360).

This is of course one of the main themes of *Calamus*. There are occasions in that collection when Whitman, fiercely rejecting the public world of the city in favor of his private relationship with his lover, sounds surprisingly like the Arnold of "Dover Beach." The sacred is everywhere besieged by the profane. "City of Orgies" and "A glimpse" both turn on a dramatic distinction between, on the one hand, a world of "shifting tableaux," "interminable rows of . . . houses," "drinking and oath and smutty jest," and on the other, the "swift flash of eyes offering me love" (2:388).

Whitman seems to draw two different conclusions from these recurring situations in the course of *Calamus*. One is that the world must be accepted, and therefore effectively abandoned, as being of uncertain and perhaps unredeemable character. So Whitman concedes in "Of the Terrible Doubt of Appearances" and "Long I Thought That Knowledge Alone Would Suffice" (2:378). The other is the determination (sometimes a buoyant conviction) that he can "give an example to lovers, to take permanent shape and will through The States" (2:367). His "brotherhood of lovers" (2:397) then becomes a saving remnant, what Hart Crane would later call a "visionary company of love," through whom the modern world, frequently identified with its cities, will eventually be redeemed: "I will make inseparable cities, with their arms about each other's necks" (2:375). It is an ideal which naturally seeks refuge in (or derives strength from) a dream: "I dreamed in a dream, I saw a city invincible to the attacks of the whole of the rest of the earth, / I dreamed that was the new city of Friends" (2:400–401). Such a Philadelphia is not, of course, a future structure entirely without foundation in the present. Whitman is building shakily upon those intermittently urban examples of passionate (and therefore inherently exclusive) masculine love commemorated in *Calamus*.[52] Yet there is no avoiding the impression that his future hopes are raised as much on the grounds of disenchantment with the urban present as on his mistaken faith in its potential for growth.

The immediate social source of this dissatisfaction by the end of the fifties was almost certainly, as poems in *Drum-Taps* show, New York's reluctance to tackle the problem of the South. A deeper, underlying, and unacknowledged cause was surely Whitman's suspicion that the drift of the modern (as discernible in its most representative city) was not toward, but away from, democracy as he conceived of it. There are occasions when his faith in the city as a natural democratic force fails completely, and he can see New York only as the very antithesis of everything he believes in. "The cities I loved so well, I abandon'd and left—I sped to the certainties suitable to me" (2:485). The "Nature" to which he then, in mind if not in body, temporarily retreated, was not really a substantial place in which his imagination might settle permanently and thrive. It was insufficiently social to satisfy the multitudinous needs of his simultaneously solitary and gregarious nature. It was invariably with relief—definitively expressed in "Give Me the Splendid Silent Sun"—that he patched up his quarrel and resumed city life: "wherever humanity is most copious and significant—let it all filter into me" (*Prose Works*, 1:354). "New York loves crowds—and I do too," he wrote with disarming simplicity and frankness. "I can no more get along without houses, civilization, aggregations of humanity, meetings, hotels, theatres, than I can get along without food." He rejected as misanthropic and shallow his previously recorded wish to "live absolutely alone" and "to hear nothing but silent Nature in woods, mountains, far recesses" (1:354–355).

But his outbursts against, and removal of his sympathy from, the city were not simply demonstrations of pique, nor romantic misanthropy. They were rather the result of chronic disappointment, both bitter and sorrowful, at what his city was becoming. Whitman deplored, but reluctantly accepted, the undemocratic fact that city life had produced an aristocracy of wealth. The unrepresentativeness and ineffectuality of such a class was evident in the unease and self-consciousness with which it tried to ape the artifices and conventions of the European gentility. But there were other, unmistakably indigenous social forces that posed a very different and grimly serious threat to democratic values as Whitman understood them. He wrestled with the energetic commercialism and dedicated materialism that had made New York what it was by mid-century.[53] Attracted as he was to so many aspects of the life generated and sustained by these energies, Whitman was in no position to condemn them roundly. He was quite unable and unwilling to renounce and denounce commercial capitalism and all its works, as Carlyle, for instance, had done. His own mixed, sometimes muddled, and constantly changing reactions to his urban world were the result of not objecting to it on principle, and having therefore to strive repeatedly to discriminate, not always successfully or convincingly, between the shifting positives and negative in its mercurial character. Whitman's envious admiration of the strength and clarity of Carlyle's unambiguous, untrammeled, and unremitting hostility to modern life was therefore understandable. "His rude, rasping, taunting, contradictory tones—what are more wanted amid the supple, polish'd, money-worshipping, Jesus-and-Judas equalising suffrage-sovereignty echoes of current America?" (1:285).

As the following chapter will demonstrate more fully, it was the outbreak of war which brought Whitman's own internal civil war to a head, and then apparently to an end. He could at last openly admit to himself his nagging doubts about his society: "Long had I walk'd my cities, my country roads, through farms, only half satisfied; / One doubt, nauseous, undulating like a snake, crawl'd on the ground before me" (2:485). And he could do so because he now believed himself to be confident that, like Simeon, his eyes had seen the salvation of his people, Israel:

> But now I no longer wait—I am fully satisfied—I am glutted;
> I have witness'd the true lightning—I have witness'd my
>   cities electric;
> I have lived to behold man burst forth, and warlike America
>   rise. (2:485–486)

In "Song of the Banner," a pre-Sumter poem, he is openly anxious that his city's first and last loyalty might prove to be to prosperity, and therefore peace, at any price. When the North eventually declared war, it also, in Whitman's eager eyes, declared itself to be firmly for democracy and the union. His relief is evident in the rapture of his welcome for New York's mobilization in "First O Songs for a Prelude." Thereafter he continues to protest his pride in his martial city and his excitement at its aroused and purposeful energy: "Manhattan streets, with their powerful throbs, with the beating drums, as now" (2:499). After going to Washington, the "big-city boy" in him comes out occasionally: "this city is quite small potatoes after living in New York."[54] Even the frankly commercial spirit of his home city now seems to him healthy compared with bureaucracy-ridden Washington, whose grand public buildings are white elephants. He yearns for "the oceans of life and people" that characterize New York. Yet on his occasional return visits to Brooklyn he is quickly made uneasy: "Here in this place & New York, I go around quite a good deal—it is a great excitement to go around the busiest parts of New York, Broadway & the wharves, & great ferries—The oceans of people, the trucks & omnibuses, go all jammed together, & such bustle & noise—I like it much for a few hours now and then—but don't want to be continually in it."[55]

His misgivings were too fundamental and substantial ever to evaporate completely. New York trade thrived callously on the war. Whitman noted on a wartime visit home how "here in all this mighty city, every thing goes with a big rush & so gay, as if there was neither war nor hospitals in the land. New York & Brooklyn appear nothing but prosperity & plenty."[56] And it is noticeable that even in the poem where the current of his pride in wartime New York runs most strongly, there is still a considerable undertow of doubt about the way in which it might choose to use its prodigious strength:

> City of ships!
> (O the black ships! O the fierce ships!
> O the beautiful, sharp-bow'd steam-ships and sail-ships!)
> City of the world! (for all races are here;
> All the lands of the earth make contributions here;)
> City of the sea! city of hurried and glittering tides!
> City whose gleeful tides continually rush or recede, whirling
> in and out, with eddies and foam!
> City of wharves and stores! city of tall facades of marble
> and iron!
> Proud and passionate city! mettlesome, mad, extravagant
> city!   (2:490)

No passage from Whitman's poetry better captures his fascination, amounting almost to a hopeless infatuation, with the beauty and dangerous energy of his city. The hyperbolic phrases are designed to flatter and appease, to secure its morally ambivalent power for the democratic cause in the war.

Whitman emerged from the war sure that he had been convinced of the glory of the American future. This optimism was different from, more willed than, the visionary idealism that produced the great poetry of the fifties. A contributing factor may have been the imperative need Whitman felt after 1865 to believe beyond a shadow of a doubt that all the pain and suffering which he had helplessly witnessed had not been in vain; that the death throes of soldiers were also the birth pangs of a forthcoming, united, democratic nation. Most of Whitman's diminished energy during the last twenty years of his life must have gone into the effort of preserving, in the face of a disfigured rather than transfigured world, the equilibrium of this optimism that was for him a matter of life or death. The price he paid was the severing of that vital connection between his visionary imagination and the "rude, coarse, tussling facts of our lives, and their daily experiences" (*Prose Works*, 2:479) upon which his poetry so deeply depended and to which his involvement with his city had contributed so much. He retired, as *Specimen Days* shows, to nature, "the only permanent reliance for sanity of book or human life" (1:120). Self-exiled from New York, he continued to anguish, in general terms, over the state of the American city: "Since the war, I have no longer had the least fear but an eventual issue of freedom was secure. Since the war I have sat down contentedly, convinced that we were to be righted at last. Oh! there is no doubt of it! And not the most to this end is to come of the civilizee himself—the man of cities, knowing as he is, and prosperous—for civilization, cities, are also a great curse. I know in the armies the clearest-brained, cleanest-blooded, of all the soldiers—were the farmer-boys. In them was the future—democracy—America."[57]

* * *

And you, Lady of Ships! you Mannahatta!
Old matron of the city! this proud, friendly, turbulent city!
Often in peace and wealth you were pensive, or covertly
　frown'd amid all your children;
But now you smile with joy, exulting old Mannahatta!
　(2:455–456)

In calling New York by the name of Mannahatta, Whitman was doing much more than exhuming the old poetic device of personification. Mannahatta was New York as it revealed its essential self to the favorite son who was, at least in his creative fantasy, on such lovingly familiar and uniquely intimate terms with it. Insofar as it is often for Whitman a kind of redeeming and long-suffering archetype of New York, Mannahatta has something of the imaginative status of Blake's vision of transfigured London, as Jerusalem. It is appropriate that Whitman should, out of his own family struggles as well as his poetic needs, have imbued his city with such a personality precisely at the time when many Americans were beginning to identify themselves with their cities in a new way. Urban historians have noted how, around the middle of the century, "notions of the 'general interest' emerged in debates about the proper competitive course for their city to pursue; the railroad or the canal was desired, or was talked about as desired, not just by this or that group of aggressive Baltimore or Philadelphia businessmen but by 'Baltimore' or 'Philadelphia.' In this way the cities acquired public images, indicating that they possessed one or another set of individual characteristics."[58] Whitman's Mannahatta would seem to stand in an interesting and challenging relationship to such calculated processes of "community personification," motivated more by commercial ambitions than by real love. But after the war Mannahatta grew increasingly distant from the actual New York; since that no longer bore any resemblance, even to the eye of faith, to the humanely liberal, artisan-based economy which was the nearest historical correlative of Whitman's visionary democracy.

"Human and Heroic New York" Whitman called it in *Specimen Days;* and the eulogistic passage so entitled was a convenient summary of the quintessential Americanness of that city, as, in his increasingly willful optimism, Whitman was capable of seeing it even as late as the 1880s. He found "the human qualities, of those vast cities . . . comforting, even heroic, beyond statement" (1:171), the citizens possessed of "alertness, generally fine physique, clear eyes that look straight at you, a singular combination of reticence and self-possession, with good nature and friendliness—a prevailing range of according manners, taste and intellect, surely beyond any elsewhere upon earth" (1:171–172). Blank assertion reinforced by blustering rhetoric seemed to be the order of the day as Whitman tried, with a desperation more often comic than poignant, to convince himself by first convincing others that contemporary New York was a city animated by the spirit of democratic comradeship.

His idealism was no longer manufactured out of the very materials of contemporary life. It existed only in simple, empty defiance (or perhaps obdurate ignorance?) of the facts. Unlike Blake or Shelley, Whitman could not make great poetry out of the glowing materials provided by the visionary imagination alone. He was no constructor of alternative worlds. More literal-minded than they, he remained dependent on the inspiring eloquence of real life; even "the hard, pungent, gritty, worldly experiences and qualities in American practical life."[59] When those ceased to speak to him, or at least when they began to speak in a foreign language, Whitman was left marooned in dreams, incapable of writing authentic poetry and driven to barren prophecy.

By the time Whitman came to write "Human and Heroic New York," the passion had gone from his affair with the city and had been replaced by pious, wishful sentimentality. He himself sensed the change early. "I am well as usual," he wrote in September 1867 to friends in Washington, "& go daily around New York & Brooklyn yet with interest, of course—but I find the places & crowds and excitements—Broadway, etc.—have not the zest of former times— they have done their work, & now they are to me as a tale that is told."[60] Yet powerful poetry had arisen from the violent psychological pattern of his longstanding lover's relationship with New York, from his bitter, periodic revulsions against the city and his subsequent reconciliations, and from his alternating feelings of trust and betrayal.

There was, however, one fine, poignant poem born even of this cooling passion—and born to Whitman in what was, in a sense, his old age as a poet, an old age that preceded his actual physical aging by some few years. This poem is the 1871 "Sparkles from the Wheel," a riveting little piece which is the culmination of those mistrustful views of the city Whitman had sketched out in *Calamus,* over a decade before:

1

Where the city's ceaseless crowd moves on, the live-long day,
Withdrawn, I join a group of children watching—I pause aside
    with them.

By the curb, toward the edge of the flagging,
A knife-grinder works at his wheel, sharpening a great knife;
Bending over, he carefully holds it to the stone—by foot
    and knee,

With measur'd tread, he turns rapidly—As he presses with light
but firm hand,
Forth issue, then, in copious golden jets,
Sparkles from the wheel.

2

The scene, and all its belongings—how they seize and affect
me!
The sad, sharp-chinn'd old man, with worn clothes, and broad
shoulder-band of leather;
Myself, effusing and fluid—a phantom curiously floating—now
here absorb'd and arrested;
The group, (an unmindful point, set in a vast surrounding;)
The attentive, quiet children—the loud, proud, restive base of
the streets:
The low, hoarse purr of the whirling stone—the light-press'd
blade,
Diffusing, dropping, sideways-darting, in tiny showers of gold,
Sparkles from the wheel.   (3:602)

Significantly enough, this miracle of ephemeral beauty is a sort of
Arabian Nights entertainment produced by a "sad" poor man practicing his socially disregarded but still arresting craft. Behind all the
enchantment is his concentration, his physical delicacy, his skill:
"Bending over, he carefully holds it to the stone—by foot and knee, /
With measur'd tread, he turns rapidly—As he presses with light but
firm hand." A displaced person, who cannot be accommodated within
the modern city, he inhabits a marginal, and therefore slightly magical, world ("By the curb, toward the edge of the flagging"), which
makes him an American version of a Wordsworth solitary, a figure
who seems to span two different levels of experience. Drawn by him
thus "aside" from the anonymous flow, Whitman finds his reactions
sharpened, whetted like the "great knife" itself. To his heightened
sensations everything seems suddenly much more clearly defined—
"The sad, sharp-chinn'd old man, with worn clothes, and broad
shoulder-band of leather." And in the process he himself acquires a
sharper self-definition—"now here absorb'd and arrested"—much as
in 1856 he thanked "you faithful fluids and solids" for enabling him
to "realize the soul" (1:225).

But what precisely is it that becomes clear to Whitman, and to what kind of insight is he conducted by the old man? When it comes to these questions, the power of the poem is discovered to lie in its evasiveness. The language and the images he finds himself using are sufficiently similar to those used in other poems to satisfy him, perhaps, that here is no disturbing new departure. On this reading the contrast the poet perceives between, say, "the city's ceaseless crowd" and "the attentive, quiet, children," is precisely what superior insight discovers to be false: the citizens, although they do not know it, are themselves all "sparkles from the wheel," and the whole of city life is itself, to the eye of revelation, centered on what had previously appeared to be this "unmindful point set in a vast surrounding." But it must surely be admitted that the antithesis between absorbed group and indifferent city which is set up by the poem is in fact too strong and uncompromising to be thus comfortably resolved, whatever Whitman's conscious intentions. If the pathos of these contrasts is attended to, what emerges from the poetry is not a visionary version of the contemporary city, but a visionary alternative to it, hauntingly centered on a "sad" old craftsman who, like an artist—certainly like *this* artist—creates his arabesques of beauty, and so gathers around him a rudimentary fellowship. If the poem does indeed incline toward this latter meaning, then Whitman has taken a sizable step in the direction of the impression of the city, which is established in the graphic opening scene of *An American Tragedy*. There a tiny family group, dwarfed by "the tall walls of the commercial heart of an American city of perhaps 400,000 inhabitants," set up their little organ, and raise their thin voices in praise of God and "against the vast skepticism and apathy of life."[61]

"Sparkles from the Wheel" is all the more memorable a poem because it is a magnificent exception to the general rule: after the war it was prose which became Whitman's primary medium of expression as his poetry faltered and failed. In *Democratic Vistas* he made his supreme effort to reconcile his aspiration for, and belief in, a golden age of American democracy, with what he permitted himself to see of the cynical opportunism of the Gilded Age. And when he came to balance the pros and cons of his contemporary society, to take the weight of its character and try justly to estimate its quality, he turned to his most recent experiences of New York, confident that it would, as always, faithfully epitomize for him both the strengths and weaknesses of contemporary America. The result is a splendidly full disclosure—honest even perhaps beyond Whitman's conscious intentions—of his conflicting feelings about his city.

He shows remarkable self-knowledge when he remarks how the vigorous, ample life of the great cities "completely satisf[ies] my senses of power, fullness, motion, etc., and gives me, through such senses and appetites, and through my aesthetic conscience, a continued exaltation and absolute fulfillment." Kindled, his rhetoric swells to a diapason of praise: "I realize (if we must admit such partialisms,) that not Nature alone is great in her fields of freedom and the open air, in her storms, the shows of night and day, the mountains, forests, sea—but in the artificial, the work of man too is equally great—in this profusion of teeming humanity—in these ingenuities, streets, goods, houses, ships—these hurrying, feverish, electric crowds of men, their complicated business genius, (not least among the geniuses), and all this mighty, many-threaded wealth and industry concentrated here" (2:371).

But then aesthetic appreciation is ousted by the moral sense. Whitman obeys its stern injunctions to shut his eyes "to the glow and grandeur of the general superficial effect." He searches minutely for "*men* here worthy the name," for "crops of fine youths, and majestic old persons," for the arts and manners of a "great moral and religious civilisation—the only justification of a great material one." His conclusion is "that to severe eyes, using the moral microscope upon humanity, a sort of dry and flat Sahara appears, these cities, crowded with petty grotesques, malformations, phantoms, playing meaningless antics" (2:371–372).

As in this passage the moral eventually prevails over the "aesthetic," so too in Whitman's life did the thwarted idealist quench the poet. New York, one gradually realizes as one reads, was judging Whitman as surely as Whitman was passing judgment on New York. The poet's ideal men and women are thin and anemic creatures compared to so "thick and burly" a world of unregenerates as that magnificently established in the first paragraph.[62] A note originally included in *Democratic Vistas* (1871) reveals the same dichotomy between actuality and dream, couched this time in terms of the hopeless present and the hopeful future—the contrast upon which Whitman's postwar optimism was usually dependent. "New York, of which place I have spoken so sharply, still promises something, in time, out of its tremendous and varied materials, with a certain superiority of intuitions, and the advantage of constant agitation, and ever new and rapid dealings of the cards" (2:525). The forlorness of Whitman's prediction is only too evident from the gambling image which has here supplanted the vatic confidence of the prewar poetry.

Still, he remained theoretically committed, to the end, to the discovery of good democratic material for the future in present-day New York. When his friend Chubb inquired of the big cities whether they did not militate against America, Whitman responded: "I think I can say without hesitating about that—*no:* I accept all the cities—all that America so is—then ask for more."[63] His enthusiasm for the colorful life of the streets long outlived his ability to make profound sense of what he saw there. "Oh! I can see it all," the aged cripple told Traubel, "I have gone through it all; many, many a time have I enjoyed such crowds—experienced the thrill of the crowd: for what, from what, who can tell? I am at home in such places: I respond sensitively to the life of the street—its almost fierce contagion: it seizes you in spite of yourself, even against your sympathies, your dreams: I remember the big affairs on Broadway, many of them memorable, all of them historic: I never missed one of them. What you tell me goes to confirm my old faith in the masses. The good nature, the nonchalance, of the people—what may not come of that? I hope for all things from the crowd—the crowd needs no saviour: the crowd will be its own saviour."[64]

At the same time, the new, uncontrollable character of postwar New York was known to him, and he realized the threat it posed to everything he valued in democracy. "He described 'the big cities, the immense accumulations of peoples, the squalid poverty: the danger of our experiment: hunger; madness to make money whatever happens': all of that had 'to be skillfully piloted through if we are finally to come out safe.' "[65] He himself no longer felt equal to the struggle of the encounter with the present at its most brutal. Hearing that Ingersoll had gone to New York to live, a friend welcomed it as good news, since " 'it's the Lord's own country.' 'But say, Tom,' retorted Whitman, 'isn't it a sort of delirium tremens?' Then he reflected: 'I used to love it. Perhaps it'll do from seven or eight to fifty or sixty— but not before, not after!' "[66] Yet, well over sixty himself, he liked to remember the times he had spent in various cities—Brooklyn, Washington, New Orleans, St. Louis, New York. Camden, too, he loved, "but Washington, New Orleans, Brooklyn—they are my cities of romance. They are the cities of things begun—this [Camden] is the city of things finished.' "[67] And in the poem he sent in December 1887 to greet Whittier on his eightieth birthday, he touchingly adopts the old, familiar posture: "So I aloft from Mannahatta's ship-fringed shore" (3:727).

Whitman's tragic dilemma as a postwar poet is clear. His imagination intuitively recognized its true home ("I don't wonder you like and are exhilarated by New York and Brooklyn—They are the only places to *live*," the crippled Whitman wrote from Camden in 1878).[68] It craved that uninhibited, but not indiscriminate, contact with the teeming life of the city and the times that produced the gloriously fresh poetry of the early years. But the older Whitman, ailing as well as aging, and (in spite of his protests to the contrary) palpably mistrusting the energies that animated contemporary life, could no longer give his imagination his unqualified support and blessing. He retreated to the consolations of the ideal under the pretense of advancing to the future; or else he turned, like so many disappointed social revolutionaries before and after him, away from the recalcitrant material of a social and political world to the much more amenable world of the spirit. And somewhere along the road leading away from his estranged city he lost his shaping spirit of imagination.

There is, however, a touching postscript, which comes in the form of a remark made in a letter written in 1889, very near the end of his life. "Suppose you and Nelly have rec'd your big book by this time— I can hardly tell why, but feel very positively that if any thing can justify my revolutionary utterances it is such *ensemble*—like a great city to modern civilisation, and a whole combined paradoxical identity a man, a woman."[69] Although it was to the rank profusion of natural life that Whitman had, with a sure instinct, turned for a title for his life's work, he could not, at the end, forbear from also thinking of *Leaves of Grass* as a kind of city. It is perhaps his last, unconscious, and most appropriate tribute to the hold of "tumultuous, close-packed, world-like New York" over his creative imagination.[70]

7 ❦ The Other Civil War

"I CONSIDER the war of attempted secession, 1860–1865, not as a struggle of two distinct and separate peoples," wrote Whitman in *Specimen Days and Collect,* "but a conflict (often happening, and very fierce) between the passions and paradoxes of one and the same identity" (2:426–427). He interpreted the Civil War as a violent expression of the persistent conflict between democratic and broadly antidemocratic tendencies within the one "identity" of American republicanism; and he emphasized that this conflict was as much a subtle feature of social and political life in the North as it was in more blatant form the underlying cause of the war between North and South.

The antebellum years had seen the political life of the North dominated by Democrats against whom, in "The Eighteenth Presidency," Whitman had directed some of his coarsest and most unforgiving (if unpublished) invective: "Office-holders, office-seekers, robbers, pimps, exclusives, malignants, conspirators, murderers, fancy-men . . . deaf men, pimpled men, scarr'd inside with the vile disorder, gaudy outside with gold chains made from the people's money and harlots' money twisted together; crawling, serpentine men, the lousy combings and born freedom-sellers of the earth."[1]

The democratic mass of Americans had become "the helpless supplejacks of a comparatively few politicians." Invoking his modified and magnified version of the artisanal dream, in the face of all the powerful contemporary forces which were accomplishing its destruction, he predicted the coming of the day "when qualified mechanics and young men will reach congress and other official stations, sent in their working costumes, fresh from their benches and tools, and returning to them again with dignity." Rhetorically asking "where is the real America?" he provided his own answer in the anachronistic terms of what we have already seen was a largely vanishing world of modestly independent labor and decent self-reliance—"the laboring persons, ploughmen, men with axes, spades, scythes, flails . . . the carpenters, masons, machinists, drivers of horses, workmen in factories."[2]

As entrepreneurial capitalism took its irresistible course, America was carried in a direction very different from the broadly Jeffersonian republic of workmen-cum-small-producers Whitman had envisaged. And in his bafflement he blamed government in general, and the party system in particular, for being the nursery of corruption. His conclusion, that "America has outgrown parties; henceforth it is too large, and they too small," has convincingly been interpreted as a significant example of the anti-institutionalism of that period. There were many who believed that "if the people could be sufficiently aroused or uplifted," then "all or most of the traditional agencies of authority could be cast aside, to make way for *man himself* in his natural perfection, free for the first time in history from the burden of privileged classes, oppressive governments, and outworn creeds."[3] This was one natural outcome of the Jacksonian democratic and egalitarian sentiments of the twenties and thirties, and Whitman would seem to be only one of the many disappointed Jacksonian idealists who sought extrapolitical means for the realizing of their quasi-religious ideals.[4] But the serious limitation of this view is that it seeks to remove Whitman too completely from his political background. It posits a dramatic contrast between Whitman the "good party man" of the forties and his "quasi-mystical" concept of democracy of the fifties. Both Whitman's inveighings against the corruptions of government and his radical mistrust of political institutions were after all strictly consistent with, if more extreme than, the views he had taken throughout his earlier career as a politically committed editor and working journalist. He had always adhered to the position of William Leggett, the revered New York politician who was the inspiration of the Locofocos with whom Whitman had been deeply involved in his youth. Leggett passionately believed that the government governs best which governs least; he warned that parties could become monopolists of poitical power and should therefore be resisted like all other monopolies. "Parties," Whitman came to see, "usurp the government."[5] In the forties Whitman attacked the Whigs along these lines, charging them with "regarding men as things to be governed" and claiming that he, as a "Democratic-Republican," wished conversely "to deal liberally with humanity, to treat it in confidence and give it a chance of expanding, through the measured freedom of its nature and impulses."[6] But already by the beginning of the fifties he felt that in this substantial respect the Democrats had gone the way of the Whigs.

Whitman had never been an orthodox Democratic party member. He had always campaigned, within the party, for radical egalitarian, antimonopolist, broadly humanitarian policies. His views, and the whole inclination of his ardent temperament, made it natural, indeed inevitable, that he join the Free Soil movement as soon as it was formed. No sooner had he arrived back in New York from New Orleans in the summer of 1848, than he was off again, this time as Brooklyn delegate to the Free Soil Convention at Buffalo.[7] It was a heady occasion, likened by some who attended it to the European revolutions of that year, and with at least one of the gathering suggesting the movement adopt the motto "Liberty, Equality, Fraternity."[8] From then on, through all the turbulence of the succeeding years—including the collapse of the Free Soil party, the passing of the Fugitive Slave Act, the Kansas-Nebraska Bill, and the Burns affair—Whitman held firm to the beliefs he had enunciated most clearly in an 1847 editorial, almost a full year before he went to Buffalo. "The question whether or no there shall be slavery in the new territories which it seems conceded on all hands we are largely to get through this Mexican War, is a question between the *grand body of white workingmen, the millions of mechanics, farmers, and operatives of our country,* with their interests, on the one side—and the interests of the few thousand rich, 'polished,' and aristocratic owners of slaves at the south, on the other side."[9] For him, as for many others who were to become ardent free soilers, the main point at issue was not the fate of "the Negro," but the fate of artisans and farmers.[10] If the new West and Southwest went slave rather than free, then in those states (and ultimately, perhaps, throughout the whole of the United States, as George Henry Evans warned) the white workingmen would be reduced to the status of "owned goods, and driven cattle." Warming to his alarming theme, Whitman rallied all the members of the threatened class, addressing them by their individual callings, as he was later to do in his poetry:

We call upon every mechanic of the north, east and west—upon the carpenter, in his rolled up sleeves, the mason with his trowel, the stone-cutter with his brawny chest, the blacksmith with his sooty face, the brown-fisted ship-builder, whose clinking strokes rattle so merrily in our dock yards—upon shoemakers, and cartmen, and drivers, and paviers, and porters, and millwrights, and furriers, and ropemakers, and butchers, and machinists, and tinmen, and tailors, and hatters, and coach and cabinet makers—upon the honest sawyer and mortar-mixer, too, whose sinews are their own—and every hard-working man—to speak in a voice whose great reverberation shall tell to all quarters that the *workingmen* of the free United States, and their business, are not willing to be put on the level of negro slaves."[11]

This makes it perfectly obvious that for Whitman the struggle for free soil was part of the general struggle by the "workingmen," that is the artisans, to rescue their republic from those political and economic forces—which they identified with the rich and the powerful—that threatened to monoplize it and "enslave" them. Whitman's editorial is typical of the rhetoric of the late forties and fifties when such spokesmen for the artisans as Greeley and Evans were busily at work adapting the old yeoman cult, beloved of Crèvecoeur and Jefferson, to the crisis facing many of the urban workingmen. According to this dramatic scenario, government should make tracts of western land available, which would enable the oppressed labor force of the cities to migrate there and regain the economic and social independence they had lost under the incoming phase of capitalism. At the same time, their departure would benefit those of their class who remained behind, since a relative scarcity of labor would mean higher wages for those in cities, and greater economic security. This dream of a new western society, which would also incidentally help rescue the old urban world from the nightmare that had gripped it, had a pervasive influence on the political movement with which Whitman was most actively involved in the years leading up to 1855—the Free Soil movement—as also it played a crucial part in the success of the Republican party during the late fifties, and on to the passing of the Homestead Act of 1862.[12]

In view of all this, it is somewhat surprising that literary critics have not treated Whitman's "Western" poetry, from 1855 through

1860, as a contribution to what Henry Nash Smith has aptly described as the ideological "struggle for the West." "Solitary, singing in the West, I strike up for a new world" (2:274). Significantly enough, in view of recent events, these are "chants of Kansas," and even as they honor the doctrine of states' rights (2:277) it is made quite clear that this new world is going to be a world of free labor: "See, ploughmen, ploughing farms—See, miners, digging mines—See, the numberless factories; / See, mechanics, busy at their benches, with tools—See from among them, superior judges, philosophs, Presidents, emerge, dressed in working dresses" (2:289). So, in his poetry, he colonizes the West, claiming it as free soil for free men, and fashioning it into an artisanal republic. "Workingmen! Workwomen!" he trumpeted in "The Eighteenth Presidency," "these immense national American tracts belong to you; they are in trust with you; they are latent with the populous cities, numberless farms, herds, granaries, groves, golden gardens, and inalienable homesteads, of your successors."[13] In the 1860 *Leaves of Grass* this becomes one of the positively aggressive themes of "Chants Democratic."

Whitman severed his connections with the Democratic party in 1848, never to renew them. He regarded the ruling Democrats of the fifties as contemptible opportunists, enemies of free labor both in the West and in the cities of the East, who were intent on feathering their own nests and maintaining their stranglehold on power. Rapacious self-interest made them "Doughfaces"—malleable men, willing at all costs to placate the South, fearful of the breakup of their profitable Union. These were also, of course, the charges brought by the newly formed Republicans against the Democrats; and this was the view of the Democratic party which led many former Democrats to join the Republican ranks before the end of the fifties. But Whitman, although from well-nigh first to last an unswerving devotee of Lincoln, was never—could never have been—a thoroughgoing Republican.[14] The Whiggish side of republicanism, prominent in its proposals of federal aid for internal improvements, and its policy of protective tariffs, would have been anathema to him; many of the important political factions—nativists and abolitionists as well as Free Soilers—which the Republicans claimed to represent were unpopular with Whitman; and he must have reacted instinctively against the social complacency as well as the thrusting ambitiousness and frank materialism of the Republican ethos.[15]

Deprived, early in the decade, of an editorial platform from which to announce his views, Whitman used the other means at his disposal. His political criticism took the form of verse as well as the unpublished pamphlet concerning the eighteenth presidency, and always his impassioned theme remained the same; that the great human cause of liberty in America had been vilely betrayed by its erstwhile friends. The most obvious, dramatic victims of this betrayal were the Southern blacks, and yet it was not of them that Whitman, who was no abolitionist, was primarily thinking.[16] In his torrential raging against corrupt political leaders, party bosses, office holders, administrators, and the like, Whitman was fiercely objecting to the way in which the ordinary American people—mechanics, farmers, workingmen—had been effectively disinherited; their political will was being frustrated, their vision dimmed.

Recent historians analyzing the aftermath of the Jacksonian revolution have come up with evidence which supports Whitman's often intuitive and anguished claim that the great democratic vision had miscarried. Jacksonian democracy, it is now argued, did not equalize society to the degree that has generally been supposed. Very significant differences remained in status, wealth, and income; political offices continued to be held predominantly by the educated, professional classes; the complexities even of local government demanded an expertise in legislative and administrative matters not easily developed by the ordinary man so that "in public office, experts, not common men, flourished."[17] Extension of the suffrage led not to real social, political, and economic equality but to a cynical use of populist rhetoric by the ruling-class cliques which continued to dominate the major parties. Pessen's analysis of prewar Brooklyn shows that in 1841 one percent of the population owned at least forty-two percent of the wealth, and that the rich were crammed into one square mile west of Fulton Street.[18] Similar evidence from other American cities leads him to the conclusion that "far from being an age of equality, the ante-bellum decades featured an inequality that appears to surpass anything experienced by the United States in the twentieth century.[19]

Sensing these inequalities, Whitman eagerly sought (for his own peace of mind) to blame the still dominant wealthy class for the widespread spirit of gross materialism which prevented the appearance of a genuinely enlightened, humane, and spiritual culture such as he imagined a true democracy would unfailingly be. In fact, his was a definition of the democratic ideal which, as has already been noted, was essentially contrary to the practice of the incoming entrepreneurial capitalism of his period. But rather than confront this fundamental incompatibility, Whitman preferred to blame the manifest shortcomings of his society on those who seemed to him to be monopolizing power—the rich and their agents in party and government. These conspired together to thwart the development of that evolved version of the artisanal republic—in which, for instance, mutuality replaced competition—which he was eventually to be convinced he had experienced in the comradeship of men at war.

In the face of failure many Jacksonian idealists turned, during the fifties, into aristocratic or antipopulist conservatives, but Whitman typically continued to invoke the unsullied nobility of a betrayed people. "How little," he wrote in a crucial letter to the Free Democrat presidential nominee Senator Hale in 1852, "you at Washington—you Senatorial and Executive dignitaries—know of us, after all, how little you realize that the souls of the people ever leap and swell to anything like a great liberal thought or principle." "I know the people," he explained, "I know well, (for I am practically in New York,) the real heart of this mighty city—the tens of thousands of young men, the mechanics, the writers, etc., etc. In all these, under and behind the bosh of the regular politicians, there burns, almost with fierceness, the divine fire which more or less, during all ages has only waited a chance to leap forth and confound the calculations of tyrants, hunkers, and all their tribe."[20]

That flame leapt forth after Sumter, in 1861, and continued to burn fiercely throughout the war—but not without resistance. The war always seemed to Whitman to be less an effort to free the slave than a struggle to liberate the common man, the average Northerner, the quintessential American. He saw it, in a way, as being an artisanal revolution. When he tried to form a picture of the events of 1861, what he saw was an alliance of urban artisan and western farmer in the cause of a new, popular democracy: "I saw you, as one of the workmen, the dwellers in Manhattan; / Or with large steps crossing the prairies out of Illinois and Indiana, / Rapidly crossing the West with springing gait, and descending the Alleghanies" (2:467). Indeed the whole poem, constructed as it is like a verbal poster, is reminiscent of the propaganda art of Russia in the immediate aftermath of the Bolshevik Revolution. It is a poetic rendering of sentiments he had already expressed six years previously in "The Eighteenth Presidency": "I would be much pleased to see some heroic, shrewd, fully-informed, healthy-bodied, middle-aged, beard-faced American blacksmith or boatman come down from the West across the Alleghanies, and walk into the Presidency, dressed in a clean suit of working attire, and with the tan all-over his face, breast, and arms."[21]

> . . . as a strong man, erect, clothed in blue clothes, advancing, carrying a rifle on your shoulder,
> With well-gristled body and sunburnt face and hands—with a knife in the belt at your side,
> . .   .   .   .
> Saw I your gait and saw I your sinewy limbs, clothed in blue, bearing weapons, robust year;
> Heard your determin'd voice, launch'd forth again and again;
> Year that suddenly sang by the mouths of the round lipp'd cannon.   (2:467)

Whitman's thesis was that the Northerners would now at last discover true, or pure, democracy in the very process of defending it. Many saw the war as primarily undertaken to defend the Union, but "Whitman and Lincoln were almost alone among the philosophers of Unionism in giving a strong democratic meaning to the conflict."[22] For him the struggle to preserve the Union was identified with the fight of the people to secure authentic, popular democracy against its enemies both North and South. And Whitman, taking the Southern enemy for granted, was always much more passionately concerned, during as well as before the war, with the struggle within Northern society between what he considered to be its pro- and anti-democratic elements respectively. This aspect of the American Civil War is reflected (albeit unsystematically) in almost everything Whitman wrote about the Secession War, including (most importantly) *Drum Taps*: and yet its presence at several crucial points remains very largely unacknowledged and uninvestigated by critics.

EVERYONE knows that Whitman spent most of the war in Washington as a nurse to the wounded, but few have seriously considered what Washington itself meant to him. For most critics, the city is simply the vague background in a picture which focuses not only intensely but almost exclusively on the poet's hospital experiences. And yet, on the evidence of his writing at the time, the question of what exactly he was to make of Washington concerned Whitman greatly. His initial reaction seems to have been one of outright hostility: "Do not be discouraged," he wrote Moses Lane in May 1863, "I am not even here—here amid all this huge mess of traitors, loafers, hospitals, axe-grinders, & incompetencies & officials that goes by the name of Washington."[23] It is obvious that Whitman was very aware that the nascent Washington was a city unlike any other American city, whose very raison d'être (unlike bustling New York or Boston) was government. It was not incidentally but essentially and entirely an administrative center, and for its population of civil servants and peripatetic senators and congressmen, Whitman seems, initially at any rate, to have had only the profoundest contempt.[24] In his passionate letter to Emerson of January 17, 1863, Whitman wrote of how he had seen

> America, already brought to Hospital in her fair youth—brought and deposited here in this great, whited sepulchre of Washington itself—(this union Capital without the first bit of cohesion—this collect of proofs of how low and swift a good stock can deteriorate—) Capital to which these deputies most strange arrive concentrating here, well-drest, rotten, meagre, nimble and impotent, full of bag, full always of their thrice-accursed *party*—arrive and skip into the seats of mightiest legislation, and take the seats of judges and high executive seats—while by quaint Providence come also sailed and wagoned hither this other freight of helpless worn and wounded youth, genuine of the soil, of darlings and true heirs to me the first unquestioned and convincing western crop, prophetic of the future, proofs undeniable to all men's ken of perfect beauty, tenderness and pluck that never race yet rivalled.[25]

Washington was thus transformed into a powerful symbolic landscape epitomizing that other civil war between the people and their estranged officers and institutions.

In *Specimen Days* Whitman recorded Washington at its nadir, after the Battle of Bull Run, when the remnants of the shattered army dribbled back into the city, mostly "in disorderly mobs, some in squads, stragglers, companies," exhausted, sullen, demoralized. The defeat discouraged the soldiers, but positively encouraged many of the civilians to desert the democratic cause to which they were less than halfheartedly attached:

> The dream of humanity, the vaunted Union we thought so strong, so impregnable—lo! it seems smash'd like a china plate. One bitter, bitter hour—perhaps proud America will never again know such an hour. She must pack and fly—no time to spare. Those white palaces—the dome-crown'd capitol there on the hill, so stately over the trees—shall they be left—or destroy'd first? For it is certain that the talk among certain of the magnates and officers and clerks and officials everywhere, for twenty-four hours in and around Washington after Bull Run, was loud and undisguised for yielding out and out, and substituting the southern rule, and Lincoln abdicating and departing.   (1:29)

And Whitman also explicitly associated the Northern officers, as a class, with such sentiments, even going so far as to blame the defeat itself on their lack of true democratic zeal: "I think this is your work, this retreat, after all . . . Bull Run is your work; had you been half or one-tenth worthy your men, this would never have happen'd" (1:29).

Whitman's early Washington experience confirmed him in his prewar opinion that the people of America were being controlled (and in large measure governed) by a loose but powerful alliance of disunionists and antidemocrats.[26] There was, however, a degree of ambivalence in his feelings about government and its relationship to the people, and this comes out in his mixed reactions to the great (although still unfinished) public buildings of Washington. He included in a letter to his brother Jeff detailed descriptions of "the incredible gorgeousness" of some of the rooms in the Capitol: "By far the richest and gayest, and most un-American and inappropriate ornamenting . . . the style is without grandeur, and without simplicity . . . these days I say, Jeff, all the poppy-show goddesses and all the pretty blue & gold in which the interior Capitol is got up, seems to me out of place beyond any thing I could tell."[27] But very shortly afterward, he could describe the same interiors to the same correspondent simply as "probably the most beautiful rooms, ornamented and gilded style, in the world."[28] The reason for this alternation between pride and distaste appears in the following passage from a letter to his friends Nathaniel Bloom and J. F. S. Gay:

> Washington and its points I find bear a second and third perusal, and doubtless indeed many. My first impressions, architectural etc. were not favorable; but upon the whole, the city, the spaces, buildings etc. make no unfit emblem of our country, so far, so broadly planned, every thing in plenty, money & materials staggering with plenty, but the fruits of the plans, the knit, the combination yet wanting—Determined to express ourselves greatly in a capital but no fit capital yet here—(time, associations, wanting, I suppose)—many a hiatus yet—many a thing to be taken down and done over again yet—perhaps an entire change of base—may-be a succession of changes.[29]

The grand buildings of Washington here assume, in Whitman's eyes, something of the equivocal character of America itself. What is needed to resolve the uncertainty is "an entire change of base," that is, for government to be founded on the uncorrupted popular will, as Whitman fondly imagines that to be.

In the meantime the white palaces are—with one notable exception—whited sepulchers. The exception was, of course, the White House itself, whose influence was potentially powerful enough to redress the balance in favor of the people, and to reestablish them at the very heart of government. Whitman described the building as he saw it by moonlight on February 24, 1863, ravishingly alluring, yet elusive and enigmatic: "Everything so white, so marbly pure and dazzling, yet soft—the White House of future poems, and of dreams and dramas, there in the soft and copious moon—the gorgeous front, in the trees, under the lustrous flooding moon, full of reality, full of illusion . . . the White House of the land, and of beauty and night" (1:41). It is a shimmering image, redolent of romance, almost a mirage, which rises with the purity of yearning from a heart sick of, and a mind soiled by, the sordid realities of both politics and war. But it is a vision which was possible for Whitman only because Lincoln, the people's man, was President.[30] Whitman's dream of a truly democratic America, although still homeless and destined to find its truest home only with the wounded in the hospitals, is at least (and at last) able to attach itself with real conviction to this one redeeming political institution.

The eventual success of the army under Lincoln (the people's army joined with the people's President) worked a transformation, under Whitman's very eyes, in the character of the city of Washington. "Washington," he wrote in 1863, "is having a livelier August, and is probably putting in a more energetic and satisfactory summer, than ever before during its existence. There is probably more human electricity, more population to make it, more business, more light-heartedness, than ever before . . . here she sits with her surrounding hills spotted with guns, and is conscious of a character and identity different from what it was five or six short weeks ago, and very considerably pleasanter and prouder" (1:62). The refined seat of un-representative government, the city whose only business was admin-istration, had at last, not least because of the soldiers from every state in the Union who thronged its streets, become a truly American city, and a genuine national capital. Washington, in the midst of war, had undergone its own social revolution. The army hospitals alone "con-tain a population more numerous in itself than the whole of the Washington of ten or fifteen years ago. Within sight of the capitol, as I write, are some thirty or forty such collections, at times holding from fifty to seventy thousand men. Looking from any eminence and studying the topography in my rambles, I use them as landmarks. Through the rich August verdure of the trees, see that white group of buildings off yonder in the outskirts" (1:66). Such are the new white houses of Washington.

As a result of these changes, Whitman's opinion of the city was completely altered. In October of 1863 he contributed a piece to the *New York Times* doubting "whether justice had been done to Wash-ington D.C." Not only was Washington located on a handsome natural site, the lay out of its streets and buildings now met with his complete approval. They were so extensive and spacious, so "Amer-ican [and] prairie-like," as to make "up to me the absence of the ocean tumult of humanity I always enjoyed in New York."[31] The inhab-itants, too, now seemed to him to possess admirably Western char-acteristics, being generous and casual. Recalling, only to dismiss, the familiar "chorus" of complaints about Washington as the seat of (mal)administration, "the rendezvous of the national universal axe-grinding, caucusing," Whitman proceeds to construct an alternative image of the capital, a composite image in which its compassion for the wounded softens, without weakening, its profile as enforcer of "the imperial laws of American Union and Democracy."[32]

Once again it is in the dome of the Capitol, "this huge & delicate towering bulge of pure white," that he finds a symbol suggestive both of Washington's lofty, resolute power, and its delicate sensibility. Just as the tree was for him a favorite emblem of the personal self-sufficiency for which he yearned, so the dome becomes his image for the central "serenity," the "aplomb" which, in fantasy, he attributes to the Union cause. Here, where Melville found rust, Whitman found immaculate, untarnished metal, signifying democratic America's perfect purity of purpose. Yet his whole response to this crowning glory of democracy and its institutions is imbued with a sense of its (at least apparent) fragility: "A vast eggshell, built of iron & glass, this dome—a beauteous bubble, caught & put in permanent form." If modern engineering can give resilient strength and structure to a dream, then can modern democracy do likewise?

But was the other civil war really won—even if the democratic troops had occupied Washington? Even if the dome firmly surmounted the Capitol? Even if Lincoln occupied the White House? Whitman's letter to James Redpath, of October 21, 1863, shows that he was aware that the enemy was not only still strong and near at hand, but was actually to be found within the gates:

> One of the drifts [of the book Whitman was proposing to write] is to push forward the very big & needed truth, that our national military system needs shifting, revolutionising & made to tally with democracy, the people—The officers should almost invariably rise from the ranks—there is an absolute want of democratic spirit in the present system and officers—it is the feudal spirit exclusively—nearly the entire capacity, keenness & courage of our army are in the ranks—(what has been done has been unavoidable so far, but the time has arrived to discuss the change).[33]

This analysis of the deficiencies of the army is diametrically opposed to the official view, implemented successfully from 1863 onward, that what was needed was "the schooling of the nation in military discipline." Instead, Whitman repeats what he had noted before the war in his *Primer of Words:* "The personnel of the Army and Navy exists in America, apart from the throbbing life of America—an exile in the land, foreign to the instincts and tastes of the people, and of course, soon in due time to give place to something native, something warmed with the throbs of our own life."[34] The "something native . . . warmed with the throbs of our own life" was, of course, supplied by the ordinary soldiers of the Civil War armies who won Whitman's love, admiration, and devotion. But he continued, not only during the war but persistently and loudly thereafter, to criticize the antiquated structure and reactionary spirit of the military hierarchy and its administrators.[35]

Whitman's seething anger, long outlasting the war, found considered and measured expression in that section of *Specimen Days* entitled "A New Army Organization Fit for America" (1:74–75). There he argued that the theory and practice of modern warfare "are not at all consonant with the United States, nor our people, nor our days." They needed to be changed in accordance with the "original, democratic premises" which distinguished the United States from feudal Europe. The primary need was for the authorities truly to recognize, and to act upon the recognition, that "the greatest military power" of the United States resided in an "exhaustless, intelligent, brave and reliable rank and file." With that lesson learnt the future could avoid repeating the disastrous mistakes that had been made during the Civil War, where "probably three-fourths of the losses, men, lives etc. have been sheer superfluity, extravagance, waste." It is a devastating accusation—that the majority of the Northern casualites were killed, in effect, by their own leaders. A simple, central point about the war seemed to Whitman to have been consistently overlooked by its military directors: for virtually the first time in human history (or so he supposed) the army *was* the nation in arms. The soldiers were not conscripts or mercenaries fighting for money or for the interests of another class represented by their officers: the soldiers in this war embodied that for which they were fighting—true democratic equality and freedom—and were fighters in their own noble cause. This was not just another old European war waged by a breed of men with whose character humanity was all too wearily familiar since "the military and caste institutes of the Old World furnished them in choice and selected specimens from a few narrow nurseries, at the expense of the vast majority and of almost continual war" (2:772). And yet it appeared to Whitman that many Union officers had conducted the war on the traditional aristocratic assumption that the soldiers in the field were a limitless and relatively worthless commodity.[36]

To this charge that men had been used as cannon fodder, Whitman added the accusation that they had also been shamefully neglected once they were wounded or ill. The fault here lay not primarily with the officers but with the civilian administrators in the medical bureaucracy. The medical arrangements at the front, governing the transfer of the wounded to the main hospitals, and the care provided in these hospitals themselves, were hopelessly and culpably inadequate. The surgeons and the practical helpers and the nurses Whitman exempted from criticism, but otherwise he was adamant "that there are . . . serious deficiencies, wastes, sad want of system, in the commissions, contributions, and in all the voluntary and a great part of the governmental nursing, edibles, medicines, stores etc." It was partly a fatal muddle, "always plenty of stores, no doubt, but never when they are needed, and never the proper application" (1:84–85), but also partly and far more unforgivably due to the willful, self-interested blindness of the bureaucratic class to the real needs (and status) of the fighting men.[37] It was, in other words, a disturbing indication of how imperfectly democratic a society the North (let alone the South) had so far evolved.

SEVERAL of Whitman's war poems have tended to be neglected precisely because their connection with Whitman's interest in democratizing Northern society has not been fully appreciated. Of course readers of Whitman have always recognized that his love of the ordinary soldiers had a political as well as a deeply personal provenance. He had in any case explained the matter himself: "Before I went down to the Field, and among the Hospitals, I had my hours of doubt about These States; but not since. The bulk of the Army, to me, develop'd, transcended, in personal qualities—and, radically, in moral ones—all that the most enthusiastic Democratic-Republican ever fancied, idealized in loftiest dreams. And curious as it may seem, the War, to me, *proved* Humanity, and proved America and the Modern" (1:323). But special concentration on this theme, which the relevant poems seem to have a power to compel, and which in any case is readily forthcoming from the modern reader, may actually have blinded critics to other important areas of feeling in Whitman's war poetry. This, in turn, may be the reason why so many interesting poems in *Drum Taps* are consistently overlooked or at best underestimated, so that the whole pattern of the collection is falsified and its character misunderstood.

Some of the poems that have suffered most are those at the beginning of *Drum Taps* which deal with the period of the first call to arms. Uneven in quality, and apparently belligerent and chauvinistic in tone, they are not poems one would expect a critic to be immediately attracted to; and indeed, the best that is customarily said of them is that they represent the work of a man who as yet knew nothing of the vile and shocking realities of war.[38] As such, they seem suited to their early place in a collection whose overall design is assumed to have been concisely summarized by Whitman in his original epigraph to *Drum Taps* (later incorporated into "The Wound-Dresser"):

> Arous'd and angry, I'd thought to beat the alarum, and urge
>   relentless war,
> But soon my fingers fail'd me, my face droop'd and I
>   resign'd myself,
> To sit by the wounded and soothe them, or silently watch
>   the dead.   (2:480)

The poems are generally supposed to trace the dramatic (and classic) pattern of the initiation of innocence into the real experience of war—a pattern the modern reader is perhaps predisposed to look for, because it assumed such archetypal proportions in the poetry of World War I. It is the most obvious way in which, as Paul Fussell has pointed out, "the dynamics and iconography of the Great War have proved crucial political, rhetorical, and artistic determinants on the subsequent life."[39] But whatever the merits or demerits of such a reading, one of its attendant disadvantages is that it encourages critics to expect to find real dramatic complexity only in the poems of experience, for which they accordingly reserve their most serious attention. The early poems, in being accepted (or rather tolerated) as records of precombat naiveté and initial national euphoria, are assumed to be simple and jarringly bellicose and as such continue to be effectively ignored.[40]

And yet the early poems are far from simple. They are, in fact, full of that very "conflict . . . between the passions and paradoxes of one and the same [national] identity" to which Whitman, as we have seen, referred. They are, in other words, full of Whitman's hopes and uncertainties about the outcome of the nation's internal struggle to determine the extent and nature of its commitment to democracy. He rejoiced in the commencement of hostilities because it seemed to him to involve the clearest and most uncompromising commitment by the North to the idea, and ideal, of a truly democratic Union— which in turn meant that the North was at last repudiating, and, Whitman hoped, purging itself of, pronounced undemocratic traits in its own character. The rebirth (in the religious sense) and genuine spiritual unification of the North was, to Whitman, an essential pre- lude to the meaningful reunification of North and South and the birth of a genuinely democratic nation.

Whitman was, as he described later in *Specimen Days,* overwhelm- ingly impressed by the period of mobilization. "The volcanic up- heaval of the nation, after that firing on the flag at Charleston, proved for certain something which had been previously in great doubt, and at once substantially settled the question of disunion. In my judgment it will remain as the grandest and most encouraging spectacle yet vouchsafed in any age, old or new, to political progress and democ- racy" (1:24–25). Its significance for him lay, as the title of his de- scriptive paragraph shows, in its being a "National Uprising and Volunteering." The first poem in *Drum Taps,* "First O Songs," wel- comes not only a massing of forces to meet and defeat the South but a revolutionary and explosive assertion of popular democratic will after the frustrations of more than a decade of corrupt and unrepre- sentative government. It was, said Whitman, an immortal proof of democracy, unequall'd in all the history of the past" (1:25). The poem celebrates not the marshaling of a professional force but the completely voluntary gathering of the first true citizen army:

> To the drum-taps prompt,
> The young men falling in and arming;
> The mechanics arming, (the trowel, the jack-plane, the
>   blacksmith's hammer, tost aside with precipitation;)
> The lawyer leaving his office, and arming—the judge leaving
>   the court;

The driver deserting his wagon in the street, jumping down,
   throwing the reins abruptly down on the horses' backs;
The salesman leaving the store—the boss, book-keeper,
   porter, all leaving.   (2:454)

The mixing of the social classes—representatives of the middle class
depicted as sharing the unhesitating enthusiasm of the artisans—is
very important here. It indicates that the real significance of the occasion lies, for Whitman, in the (largely imaginary) spectacle of black-
smiths and drivers standing shoulder to shoulder with judges and
lawyers—those very lawyers whom he had repeatedly singled out,
in "The Eighteenth Presidency," for particularly critical attention as
the enemy of the masses: "Are lawyers, dough-faces, and the three
hundred and fifty thousand owners of slaves, to sponge the mastership
of thirty millions? Where is the real America? Where are the laboring
persons, ploughmen . . ."[41]
   These men, as they dress for war, are aware of the responsibilities
that they are simultaneously assuming; there is sobriety at the heart
of all their enthusiastic preparations:

The new recruits, even boys—the old men show them how to
   wear their accoutrements—they buckle the straps
   carefully.   (2:454)

Such physical delicacy and deliberateness is obviously, in this context,
indicative of a corresponding moral seriousness and determination.
There is an interesting contrast here with Melville, who in *Battle-
Pieces* consistently sees the new soldiers as "boys" ("Moloch's un-
initiate") about to be initiated through carnage into manhood: "Youth
must its ignorant impulse lend— / Age finds place in the rear, / All
wars are boyish, and are fought by boys, / The champions and en-
thusiasts of the state."[42]
   But however genuinely Whitman might revel in playing Homer
to the arming of his democratic heroes, and enjoy singing lustily of
the "manly life in the camp," he could not, even at the beginning,
be a wholehearted or heart-whole supporter of this "just" war. Could
the war after all be so implicitly relied upon to advance the democratic
cause as he understood it? His dislike of war was not only personal
and temperamental but also involved his realization that wars had

historically been the extension and expression of the class antagonism, competing economic interests, and power struggles endemic to European social and political history. Such evidence suggested the spirit of war to be the very antithesis of the spirit of democratic life, and the first stanza of "Beat! Beat Drums!" is alive with Whitman's awareness of this dilemma:

> Beat! beat! drums—Blow! bugles! blow!
> Through the windows—through doors—burst like a force of
>   ruthless men,
> Into the solemn church, and scatter the congregation;
> Into the school where the scholar is studying:
> Leave not the bridegroom quiet—no happiness must he have
>   now with his bride;
> Nor the peaceful farmer any peace, plowing his field or
>   gathering his grain;
> So fierce you whirr and pound, you drums—so shrill you
>   bugles blow.   (2:487)

The inflexibility of the drums' rhythm (imitated in the verse) raises the specter of their intolerance. The poem's power derives from the way in which, to borrow a phrase from Melville, "it spins against the way it drives," and so keeps faith with Whitman's own "conflict of convictions."[43] It incorporates his unflinching recognition of the disturbing fact that peaceful and peace-loving democratic life may itself at times only be preserved through the use of forces which are its very opposite and denial. It also, almost uncannily, registers the imperialism which is part of the imperiousness of the martial spirit.

A democratic war, if not a direct contradiction in terms, was then in Whitman's view a phenomenon in need of careful examination and very special justification, and "Song of the Banner at Daybreak" is his most ambitious attempt at performing this service. It takes the form, as the editors of the *Comprehensive Readers' Edition of Leaves of Grass* have succinctly noted, of a "kind of dramatic colloquy in which the poet, at beginning and end, instructs himself, and is instructed, to sing the idealism of war."[44] The voices in the argument are those of Poet, Pennant, Child, and Father. The case for peace is made by the Father, initially in a reasonable and persuasive manner, but thereafter increasingly in the querulous terms which belong to craven, unprincipled, profit-seeking, business-mad America. Central to his case is the objection that there is nothing, materially, to be gained from war, and this shameful and timorous argument is contrasted with the Poet's exultant claims that what distinguishes this war from all previous human conflicts is that it is fought for a pure abstraction, a true ideal, which is best symbolized by a worthless but omnipotent flag—the Pennant or Banner. The flag claims all American life as its own, to dispose of as it will, because only under its sway could democratic life in all its material and spiritual wealth exist. It represents war as being not only necessary to preserve the Union but also the means of saving the nation's soul (the people having become morally soft and flabby) through the testing and purifying experience of carnage. Only against a dark background can the Banner's stars shine bright again in men's eyes and lives. And so the flag, in a poem which is permeated with a biblical spirit oddly compounded of Old and New Testament elements, speaks to the nation with the terrible voice of the Jehovah of the Israelites. Finally the Poet, obeying the biblical injunction that he allow himself to be led by a little child, is wrought to a pitch of ecstatic, visionary celebration of the "warlike pennant" and banner, "valueless, object of eyes, over all and demanding all—O banner and pennant!" (2:465).

"Song of the Banner at Daybreak" is as poetically unsuccessful as it is morally unpleasant, but it is also Whitman's most sustained attempt at facing his dilemma directly and arguing it out. Thirty years later, only a year or so before his death, he could still see the struggle substantially in the same dilated terms: "And was there not something grand, and an inside proof of perennial grandeur, in that war! We talk of our age's and the States' materialism—and it is too true. But how amid the whole sordidness—the entire devotion of America, at any price, to pecuniary success, merchandise—disregarding all but business and profit—this was for a bare idea and abstraction—a mere, at bottom, heroic dream and reminiscence—burst forth in its great devouring flame and conflagration quickly and fiercely spreading and raging, and enveloping all" (2:706).

And so the second stanza of "Beat! Beat! Drums!" fiercely, even exultantly, exhorts the drums to disrupt the "bargainers' bargains by day" and overwhelm the "business of brokers and speculators"—only for an undercurrent of doubt again to run strongly against the tide of ostensible confidence in the last stanza:

Beat! beat! drums!—Blow! bugles! blow!
Make no parley—stop for no expostulation;
Mind not the timid—mind not the weeper or prayer;
Mind not the old man beseeching the young man;
Let not the child's voice be heard, nor the mother's entreaties;
Make even the trestles to shake the dead, where they lie
    awaiting the hearses,
So strong you thump, O terrible drums—so loud you
    bugles blow. (2:487)

It could be that the vibrant force of the drums reanimates even the dead, after a galvanic fashion; or it may be that they are vulgar intruders, grotesque disturbers of the peace even of the departed. Time was to show how the drums, when they coerced rather than inspired, were harbingers of a postwar society whose authoritarian efficiency contrasted, ironically enough, most unfavorably (by Whitman's own standards) with the prewar liberalism in which he had been so disappointed but of which he was nevertheless a product. But in the meantime the poem, with its two voices, gives quintessential expression to the argument within Whitman's nature between what George M. Fredrickson called, with great acuteness, the "democratic imperialist" and the "democratic humanitarian." The imperialist is the other face of the prewar cosmic poet. He is the Whitman frustrated by a society permeated by materialism, to the point where he passionately wishes to see it cleansed by violence and forcibly regenerated. Always within Whitman there lurked this brutal fantasy of a decisive exercise of power on behalf of the ideal, to extirpate all corruption. It erupts most memorably in the idyllic sounding "Swallows on the River" passage in *Specimen Days:* "Though I had seen swallows all my life, seem'd as though I never before realized their peculiar beauty and character in the landscape. (Some time ago, for an hour, in a huge old country barn, watching these birds flying, recall'd the 22d book of the *Odyssey,* where Ulysses slays the suitors, bringing them to *eclaircissement,* and Minerva, swallow-bodied, darts up through the spaces of the hall, sits high on a beam, looks complacently on the show of slaughter, and feels in her element, exulting, joyous" (1:204–205). There is a Nietzschean, or Yeatsian, cruelty to that "joy." It reminds us that (to mix metaphors very thoroughly) in the beat of the drums Whitman saw the bending of the bow.

A feature of the early *Drum Taps* poems is that they map out the symbolic geography of Whitman's democratic States. He never doubted that the energy of western pioneers, frontiersmen, and settlers could be easily harnessed for war; but the commercial energy and mixed population of the rapidly expanding eastern seaboard cities was of a much more problematic character. Even during his last years he still occasionally brooded over this subject and gave Traubel his weighty, considered opinion on the matter. The "critical factors of the national life in those years lay not in the South alone but north here, too— here more insidiously. I was bred in Brooklyn: initiated to all the mysteries of city life—populations, perturbations: knew the rough elements—what they stood for: what might be apprehended from them: there in Brooklyn, New York, through many, many years: tasted its familiar life. When the War came on I quite well recognised the powers to be feared, understood: and not alone in New York, Brooklyn: in Boston as well: the great cities north, north-west, the very hotbeds of dissent."[45] He was no doubt thinking primarily of the draft riots in New York in 1863. Letters show that he had at first reacted sympathetically, but then, as more detailed news reached him, he turned to a frightened, venomous attack on those he regarded as the unpatriotic scum of the city.[46] At the end of his life, he again told Traubel: "We do not seem to realize, even at this late day, how many loyal men there were at the South—were too of the most tenacious patriotism. And there was New York *halved* too—the very rich and the very poor allied strangely together in Southern sympathies."[47]

But at the time, the initial urban enthusiasm for war after Sumter thrilled and ostensibly reassured a Whitman who had over the previous decade become decidedly wary of urban America. He was moved to a kind of *Nunc Dimittis* by the sight:

> I have witness'd the true lightning—I have witness'd
>   my cities electric;
> I have lived to behold man burst forth, and warlike America
>   rise. (2:485–486)

Yet his unease at such "power unanointed" (in Melville's telling phrase) led him to make of his poetry and of himself a kind of Mirror for the Metropolis:

Behold me! incarnate me, as I have incarnated you!
. . . . .
I chant and celebrate all that is yours—yet peace no more;
In peace I chanted peace, but now the drum of war is mine;
War, red war, is my song through your streets, O
    city! (2:490)

His celebration of New York's power and hungry energy is simultaneously an attempt to claim it for, or at least to persuade it to
identify with, democracy and this righteous war;[48] its commercial
predatoriness is flatteringly metamorphosed, by the potency of song,
into menacing virility:

City of ships!
(O the black ships! O the fierce ships!
O the beautiful, sharp-bow'd steam-ships and sail-ships!)
City of the world! . . .
. . . . .
City of the sea! city of hurried and glittering tides! (2:490)

The very word "city" is there repeated like an honorific title in this
litany of New York's qualities, this ceremony of praise. The poem
is haunting because it is such a blend of shifting emotions. A love
poem in which Whitman pleads for an answering love, it is also a
petition, a prayer, and a challenge: few poems written by Whitman
have more beautifully caught and honestly conveyed the uneasy poise
of his mind between belief in and despair of his democratic society.

THE POEMS of demobilization, which conclude *Drum Taps,* have
also suffered critical neglect, and yet they too are eloquent testimony
to Whitman's involvement in that continuing struggle for a fully
democratic society of which the Civil War had been but a part. In
this unfinished business Whitman came to suspect he would mostly
have to soldier on alone; there could be no demobilization for him.
Hence the interestingly ambivalent attitude he shows toward the disbanding of the armies, in a series of poems which alternate in revealing
faith in the future and profound regret for the irrecoverable intensity
of the comradeship he had known.

The war had, in one sense, done the work Whitman had expected of it. From the raw materials of an imperfectly democratic prewar society it had, indeed, produced soldiers of rare human quality. Moreover, in Whitman's privileged experience, it had created a genuine community in the very spirit of the working people, and in sharp contrast to the economic individualism which was the prevailing ethos of prewar society. Before the war Whitman wistfully imagined, from stolen moments of friendship in his own life, what the spirit of a real social life would be like: "Some carpenter working his ripsaw through a plank—some driver, as I ride on top of the stage,—men rough, not handsome, nor accomplished—why do I know that the subtle chloro-form of our spirits is affecting each other, and though we may encounter not again, have exchanged the right password, and are thence free comers to the guarded tents of each others' most interior love?"[49] War as Whitman knew it, encouraged—indeed, it even forced— men to live together on such intense and intimate terms.

But—and it is a tragic but—Whitman came to suspect that the qualities of men at war were not, after all, the stuff from which a new civilian society could be made. They were inextricably connected with the conditions which produced them. They were the result of "a march in the ranks hard-prest"; hard-pressed, that is, in the sense of men subjected to pressure, under duress, until compressed together into a solid fraternity. Whitman is already unconsciously admitting defeat when he poignantly, because quite unintentionally, gives his wartime poems their curiously retrospective and elegiac quality. The elegy is not for the dead, but for what is, in more senses than one, passing before his very eyes: the only true society Whitman was ever to know.

The demobilization, the return of these citizen-soldiers to civilian life, should, according to the pattern of events foreseen by Whitman at the very beginning of the war, have been the crowning moment of the whole affair. Soldiers, transfigured by their experience, would return to inspire the nation's growth toward a truly egalitarian and fraternal society. But the last poems in *Drum Taps* reveal a Whitman who inclines in several different directions when he tries to anticipate and prepare for the social outome of this war. If the theme of one poem is reconciliation—"beautiful that war, and all its deeds of carnage, must in time be utterly lost" (2:555)—then in another he invokes and dedicates himself to the "spirit of dreadful hours"

(2:542), obviously mistrusting the soft blandishments of peace. His hopefulness, where it appears, is still genuine, not forced or spurious; and all the more substantial now for his having shed his earlier millenarianism and come to trust instead the slow but sure processes of growth, set in motion by the war. He accepts that it may be the very distant future which will reap the harvest of these men's sacrifice:

> To the leaven'd soil they trod, calling, I sing for the last;
> (Not cities, nor man alone, nor war, nor the dead,
> But forth from my tent emerging for good—loosing, untying
> the tent-ropes;)
> . . . . .
> To the far-off sea, and the unseen winds, and the sane
> impalpable air;
> And responding, they answer all, (but not in words,)
> The average earth, the witness of war and peace,
> acknowledges mutely. (2:556–557)

But he also in other poems seems still to anticipate betrayal by the future of the dead and of himself. In "Adieu to a Soldier" he dedicates himself to his lonely mission in an untransformed and uncongenial society:

> Adieu, dear comrade!
> Your mission is fulfill'd—but I, more warlike,
> Myself, and this contentious soul of mine,
> Still on our own campaigning bound. (3:630–631)

The soldiers returned to peace, he is left to keep faith with the dead and with the ideals of the soldiers at war.

The debate between these different views that he was capable of taking of the war's effect on American society was never really concluded, as the following chapters will show. Of his internal voices the only one he officially recognized and sanctioned was that which said, "the War, to me, proved Humanity, and proved America." But poignantly, at the very end of his life, the other voice broke the public silence he had imposed upon it, to ask the bitter question: "Will the America of the future—will this vast rich Union ever realize what itself cost, back there after all?—those hecatombs of battle-deaths" (2:738).

The war had indeed, as Allen Nevins famously put it, become a revolution. But the form of that revolution was not what Whitman had envisaged; instead it took the "shape of anvil, loom and piston."[50] The industrialization of the North involved a complete social revolution, a prominent feature of which was "the replacement of improvisation by plans and organization."[51] On the business front this resulted in the growth of vast corporations and "a sturdy new business system centered in New York."[52] The postwar world was fashioned not in the image of the ordinary rank-and-filers as Whitman knew them but by the spirit of the majors and colonels who, having learned their lessons "of command and organisation," became, after demobilization, efficient and energetic business captains.

HENRY JAMES, in his notoriously uncomprehending 1865 review, did at least grasp an important truth about *Drum Taps,* however badly he misapplied it, when he described Whitman (and of course his collection) as being filled with "a certain amount of *violent* sympathy with the great deeds and sufferings of our soldiers" (my emphasis). And James again saw the right thing (but for the wrong reason) when he deplored the way in which Whitman had allowed himself to be "bullied by the *accidents* of the affair."[53] He had divined the radical spirit which underlies all of this poetry and which demanded (and produced) such revolutionary formal expression. What he was illuminating by the strength and clarity of his objection was what might be called Whitman's "confounded democratic quality of vision,"[54] his refusal to employ the usual hierarchical categories of distinction and classification in order to interpret or evaluate men and events. He proceeded from the conviction that the real war could never be got into the books of those conventional historians and writers who, whatever their principles of social equality, observed the feudal convention of paying attention only to "the official surface-courteousness of the Generals," and "the few great battles" (1:116). And it led to Whitman's determination to be faithful only to the fighting man ("the actual soldier") whose spirit alone had given the war its unique significance, and the infusion of whose spirit could alone produce authentic democratic life in the reunited nation. He would be the soldiers' poet, and his poetry would record not only the war that they knew but, by and large, the war *as* they knew it—confusedly and by glimpses. The poems are arranged to show Whitman, along with the ordinary soldiers, being tumbled, repeatedly yet seemingly at random, upon the reviving truth that in the turbulent darkness of wartime experiences, human qualities are still solidly and steadily at work.

He would claim for himself none of the artist's customary aristocratic privilege of exalted and comprehensive understanding. The renowned Civil War illustrator Theodore Davis once observed wryly that most civilians "seem to have an idea that all battlefields have some elevated spot upon which the general is located, and that from this spot the commander can see his troops, direct all their manoeuvres and courteously furnish special artists an opportunity of sketching the scene."[55] Whitman knew better. Reading Carlyle's *Frederick the Great* late in life, he criticized it for making too much of the set battles. "My experiences on the field have shown me that the writers catch very little of the real atmosphere of a battle. It is an assault, an immense noise, somebody driven off the field—a victory won: that is all. It is like trying to photograph a tempest."[56]

Drum Taps is not only a commemorative and celebratory work, it is also a missionary one; its point of view is both democratic and democratizing. Both in form and content, it is Whitman's most moving attempt to resolve, in favor of democracy (and, one might add, in defiance of the facts), "the conflict . . . between the passions and paradoxes" of the American identity.[57] As such, *Drum Taps* points beyond itself, being the culmination of Whitman's sustained attempt, begun before the war and intensified during those "parturition years," to act as midwife to an American democracy which he conceived of as substantially more than a political system, for "that would describe a portion only. It would need the application of the word extended to all departments of civilization and humanity, and include especially the moral, esthetic, and philosophic departments."[58] And such an ideal surely represents not so much a rejection as an extension of his early, more purely political beliefs.

8 ❧ The Pains and Obligations of Memory

IN OLD AGE Whitman naturally enough had trouble with his memory of what, with studied neutrality, he called the Four Years War. After handing Traubel a letter written during those years, Whitman quizzed him about his reaction to it, before himself confessing: "I don't seem to be able to review that experience, that period, without extreme emotional stirrings—almost depressions . . . I don't want to wipe out the memory: it is clear, sacred, infinitely so, to me: but I would rather not have it recur too frequently or too vividly: I don't seem to be able to stand it in the present condition of my body."[1] And not only in his "present condition." The problem of how neither to succumb to certain memories nor to repress them was a problem with which Whitman had been grappling ever since some of the sights of the war had (to paraphrase Blake) seized his brain with frantic pain.

Of course by 1890 (the date of his remark to Traubel) Whitman had had more than twenty-five years of reviewing "that period," hence the practiced pieties of the authorized version of this past: "It is dear, sacred, infinitely so, to me." But what is touching is that on this occasion these phrases do not conceal, but rather concede, the emotional emergency which originally gave them being. Losing their marmoreal calm, the consoling phrases themselves are reanimated by the threat of desolation. It is almost as if Whitman's mind, in old age, were in danger of losing its long-standing power to construct what Tennyson, in *In Memoriam,* called "the mortal lullabies of pain."[2]

This power of construction is most richly and elaborately evident, as will later emerge, in the greatest of "mortal lullabies," "When Lilacs Last in the Dooryard Bloom'd." But the process, inaugurated by pain, had begun even earlier, as the following passage shows:

—through the p-h-t! pht of the mine—and the bursting of shells, the thud of the great ball falling, and that wild shriek of the rifled powder—though the fields are covered with dying and with dead—and the hospitals crowded long & long with wounded and with sick—out of all that—the like, and the ghastly face, just dead upon that cot outside the tent, and the other covered with a dark grey blanket, and waiting to be buried—for these, and more than these, if more than these there be—if anything more monstrous, more unnatural than these there be . . . Democracy goes on—the modern and America goes on and must and shall go on.[3]

The passage of course has power, and is effective in its immediate purpose, which was to nerve the North to persist in the face of appalling losses. The emphasis is therefore on developing the simple corporate will to outface disaster: democracy "must and shall go on," in spite of the ghastly faces and immobile forms of the dead. But this crude solution to the problem of pain and death naturally left a residue of unresolved feelings, including guilt. It was precisely this brutal contrast between the dead or dying and the ruthlessly on-going society of the living that was, in other moods, to become deeply problematic for Whitman, and the narrative pattern of several of the key poems of *Drum Taps* betrays the structure of this, Whitman's persistent psychological dilemma.

It can be clearly seen in "The Artilleryman's Vision." There the old soldier has a waking dream of being caught up once more in the excitement of war, which anesthetizes not only physical but spiritual pain—the pain of seeing others cut down:

> And ever the hastening of infantry shifting positions—
>   batteries, cavalry, moving hither and thither;
> (The falling, dying, I heed not—the wounded, dripping and
>   red, I heed not—some to the rear are hobbling;)
> Grime, heat, rush—aid-de-camps galloping by, or on a
>   full run.   (2:507)

It is a striking study of the difference between total recall and selective memory—the kind of memory that functions as a protective device which filters out the painful elements in the original situation.

Just as the artilleryman's dream returns him to the very heat of actual battle, insulating him for the moment against its coldly bloody aftermath, so the published poem itself is a sort of fragment cut out of a longer composition in which Whitman had embraced battle experience in its disconcerting totality and had contrasted the euphoria of active combat with the subsequent psychological reaction. That draft registers the monstrously lively, and perversely enlivening, sights and sounds of an actual engagement; the susuration of the rifled ball, the drone of shells, the "rushing whirr of the grape." In the desperate interests of survival, the senses become heightened and are awakened to the finest kinds of aesthetic discrimination, appreciating for instance "the peculiar shriek of certain shells—the thud of the round ball falling in the soft earth." Even the dead seem temporarily to be subsumed within the rich aesthetic of the scene, as they too assume an obliging variety of violently frozen postures:

> The positions of the dead, some with arms raised, poised in
> the air,
> Some lying curl'd on the ground—the dead in every position
> The wild excitement and delight infernal,
> One reach'd forward, with finger extended, pointing—one in
> the position of firing
> (Some of the dead, how soon they turn black in the face
> and swollen!)[4]

That last line, in particular, is masterly in the way it fuses different emotions. There is in it an avidness of curiosity, a bizarre appreciativeness which temporarily overrides the sickening disgust and frank terror that will surface more clearly, and fatefully, later, once the mind and the senses are no longer placed on a war footing, and are no longer so fiendishly alert. In context the phrase "how soon they turn black in the face and swollen" is placed next to, and parallel with the phrase "how proud the men are of their pieces"—a powerful example of the way the disturbed mind, in war, becomes incapable of making vital moral distinctions, and starts instead to make monstrously dispassionate connections.

But the draft does not stay safely within the unnatural world of battle psychology. After the hyperactivity comes the reaction:

> Then after the battle, what a scene! O my sick soul! how the
>   dead lie,
> The wounded—the surgeons and ambulances—
> O the hideous hell, the damned hell of war.
> Were the preachers preaching of hell?
> O there is no hell more damned than this hell of war,
> O what is here? O my beautiful young men! O the beautiful
>   hair, clotted, the faces!
> Some lie on their backs with faces up & arms extended.[5]

The sickness of the soul is not only physical revulsion, and not even only spiritual terror, it is also caused by guilt—guilt at one's own previous murderous excitement.

Compared, then, with the original draft, "The Artilleryman's Vision" can be seen to deal with a post-guilt fantasy; the merciful fantasy of still being fully licensed by the nature of the occasion to pass on, to press on regardless, in "devilish exultation." But the more enduringly satisfying fantasy for Whitman incorporates an opportunity to return, in which the living faithfully seek out, reclaim, and honor the dead. That is what happens in "Vigil Strange," where the father, having sped onward in the battle, returns to find the body of his son, to keep vigil, and to perform the last rites of love.

Regarded naturalistically, it is of course an extremely untypical, not to say unlikely event. But the whole point lies in its unreality. Like any protective fantasy it derives much of its compelling emotional force from its relationship with that terror which it has been designed to replace, or at least conceal. The underlying, and as it were sustaining, terror in this case is Whitman's well-documented dismay at the corpses left unclaimed on the battlefield, which were so quickly disfigured and rendered unrecognizable by putrefaction. Elsewhere, as best he could, he tried to rescue one or two of them from the ignominy of mere decay. So, in the *Brooklyn Daily Union* of September 22, 1863, he commemorated, and thus brought back to mind, one Benjamin D. Howell, aged eighteen: "This is the name of one of Brooklyn's lost and dead. Like many others, his young life given for his country, his death unknown at the time, & his corpse never recovered . . . I give this as a specimen of hundreds, nay, thousands of cases, all over the land. How many there are, even in Brooklyn; cases of our young men who have died a soldier's death on the field, or elsewhere, & their corpses left forever undistinguished & unrecovered."[6]

A related fantasy, again a psychological defense, appears at the end of "A March in the Ranks." Whitman hears "outside the orders given, *Fall in, my men, fall in*," and prepares to leave "the impromptu hospital" in the woods, and all its sickening sights and smells:

> But first I bend to the dying lad—his eyes open—a half-smile
> gives he me;
> Then the eyes close, calmly close, and I speed forth to
> the darkness.   (2:494)

Here the living receive the blessing of the dying (and therefore implicitly of the dead). This absolves them from guilt (for surviving) and from fear (of death). Such is the restorative power of this moment that a march which, before halting, had been "A route through a heavy wood, with muffled steps in the darkness, / Our army foil'd with loss severe, and the sullen remnant retreating," is pointedly resumed as a speeding forth in the darkness. But with him Whitman carries, as he later desperately wished the speeding postwar American to carry, the memory of life's debt to the seriously wounded and the dead.

The hospital location in "A March in the Ranks" is consciously described in aesthetic terms, a somber use of the picturesque:

> Entering but for a minute, I see a sight beyond all the pictures
> and poems ever made:
> Shadows of deepest, deepest black, just lit by moving candles
> and lamps,
> And by one great pitchy torch, stationary, with wild red
> flame, and clouds of smoke.   (2:494)

Once again the original draft—a prose sketch, this time, based on the reminiscence of an actual soldier—was a rather grimmer, untidier affair. The retreat had included a "stumbling over bodies of dead men in the road," and the scene in the church was simply "horrible beyond description"—which brings out the careful ambivalence of tone of the printed version: "I see a sight beyond all the pictures and poems ever made" (2:494). The wounded are simply "bloated and pale"—

contrast "the youngster's face is white as a lily" (2:494)—and instead of the manfully restrained "occasional scream or cry" heard in the poem, there were the frankly "despairing screams and curses of some."[7] In contrast to the prose sketch, therefore, the aesthetic coherence of the poetic scene is evidence that the heroic dignity and solemn lineaments of the occasion have been imprinted indelibly upon the mind and will pass into intelligible memory. That, indeed, is depicted as already happening during the war itself; Whitman recovers the scene in retrospect. And so the "dying lad's" half-smile has both a dramatic and a moral appropriateness—it closes and clinches a theatrical scene which is also a spiritual "tableau."

Indeed *Drum Taps* is full of these "tableaus of life" which are also frequently "the groupings of death" (3:688). In reproducing such scenes, Whitman believes himself to be working to the deeper spiritual aesthetics, rather than the surface realism, of wartime life itself. But we might now argue somewhat differently and suggest that there are many occasions in *Drum Taps* when Whitman uses his aesthetic perceptions specifically in order to exclude other, more painful perceptions. "Cavalry Crossing a Ford" is an attractive little visual set piece, a design composed exclusively of contrasting colors and attitudes, allowed to stand as an unqualified record of brave color and pageantry. As such, the sketch has its truth—a truth which painterly writers like Whitman (here) and like Isaac Rosenberg during the First World War were capable of registering, while more single-mindedly morally engaged writers like Wilfred Owen perhaps were not. There are, after all, occasions when war does aspire to the condition of parade.[8]

But it does not hold that visible shape for long, and when Whitman wrote his prose version of this sketch, for inclusion in *Specimen Days*, he contrasted the spectacle of the departing troop with the sorry arrival of a very different procession: "How inspiriting always the cavalry regiments. Our men are generally well mounted, feel good, are young, gay on the saddle, their blankets in a roll behind them, their sabres clanking at their sides. This noise and movement and the tramp of many horses' hoofs has a curious effect upon one. The bugles play— presently you hear them afar off, deaden'd, mix'd with other noises. Then just as they had all pass'd, a string of ambulances commenc'd from the other way, moving up Fourteenth street north, slowly wending along, bearing a large lot of wounded to the hospitals" (1:54).

One might sternly insist that the prose exposes the prowar ideology concealed within the apparently innocent aesthetic of the poem, but it is more important, in the context of the present discussion, to appreciate the way the prose passage brings out the very different psychology behind the poetic version. It shows how Whitman deliberately narrows his sights, for the duration of the piece, to prevent noticing precisely the sort of harrowing contrast admitted into the prose—a contrast that, very late in life, he was to admit to Traubel he had always found a particularly haunting aspect of real, or at least realistic, wartime "aesthetics." "One of the great lessons of the war was, to see the regiments go out fresh—then after a long, long, long time trail back—defile the old way once more. It was solemn, gigantic, in what it suggested."[9]

"A March in the Ranks" is probably more representative than "Cavalry Crossing a Ford" of the sort of scene Whitman generally liked to compose out of the materials of war, because it shows how he set out honestly to include and to handle pain and suffering. As Whitman was well aware, however, always beyond the masterly, mastering composition of scenes such as this, the "theater" of war stretched unmanageably, disturbingly, over "the fields covered with dying" and many a "ghastly face, just dead." A fragment from this period gives the (probably accidental) impression of an unnerved mind, rendered virtually incoherent by the prospect of widespread devastation: "After a feverish battle perhaps next Day, (or 2 days)—the field and for a great distance around him & then the dead & wounded—blood, corpses, fragments, the dying, in some spots very thick—the cloud comes over the scene—it rains sometimes for hours—heaven looking, they lie in all attitudes—some shot through the heart—the dead lie mostly on their backs—they swell & bloat—they turn black & discolored—some falling holding the gun in their hand, just as . . ."[10]

The world's exhilarating expanse, stretching out of sight represented "branching vistas" for the early Whitman, and it was again, significantly, the restoration of those vistas that signified for him the ending of the war:

In the freshness, the forenoon air, in the far-stretching circuits
   and vistas, again to peace restored,
In the fiery fields emanative, and the endless
   vistas beyond. (2:556)

But during the war itself this expansive delight in "vista" was psychologically impossible both for observers like himself, and for the participants themselves. A poem such as "An Army Corps on the March" can therefore be read as a tragic parody of the vista, or open-road, poem:

> The swarming ranks press on and on, the dense brigades
>   press on;
> Glittering dimly, toiling under the sun, the dust-cover'd men,
> In columns rise and fall to the undulations of
>   the ground.   (2:551)

No individualizing, invigorating detail of face, color, or sound can escape to meet the senses of the observer from "An Army Corps on the March"; an anonymous density of dust-covered men applying themselves as one body to the task, the sheer physical effort, of this grueling war. Amoeba-like the corps adapts itself from within to the changing environment, alert to every kind of danger, adjusting itself to meet it as imperceptibly as it molds itself to the contours of the land it traverses. Sensitized in the extreme to certain limited stimuli, the body of men is correspondingly desensitized to all those aspects of life which are irrelevant to its present purpose. And with its "cloud of skirmishers in advance" the corps is the embodiment of what might be called a state of justifiable paranoia, in which the imagination is entirely given over to mistrust and fear. Short though it is, the poem is a sadly eloquent comment on what has become of the song of the open road.

Nevertheless, even if vista is impossible in wartime, Whitman's yearning for it cannot be repressed. Instead it is displaced from land to sky, as "Bivouac on a Mountain Side" beautifully illustrates. The army is there halted above a spreading, fertile plain, but the campfires and the shadowy forms of the men actually carry the eye through the picture from the valley up to the sky, and so serve as a bridge to the mind, opening it to the calming and expanding influence of the stars: "And over all, the sky—the sky! far, far out of reach, studded with the eternal stars" (2:526). Similarly the father, in "Vigil Strange," addressing his dead son, remembers how he "Bared your face in the starlight—curious the scene—cool blew the moderate night-wind; / Long there and then in vigil I stood, dimly around me the battle-field spreading" (2:492). Bathed in night the silent battlefield mirrors the quiet vista of what he elsewhere calls "those buoyant upper oceans" of the sky. Whitman took the poetry of Gray and Collins, as well as Milton, with him to the Washington hospitals,[11] and he becomes in *Drum Taps* the Il Penseroso of the war, fond of what Collins called the "religious gleams" of twilight, and the subdued aerial expanses of moonlight and starlight.

These were desperately necessary perspectives for a Whitman who knew that the land which had once supplied him with vista was now encumbered with "the mad, determin'd tussle of the armies." The phrase comes from his remarkable attempt to convey, in *Specimen Days*, the savage confusion of the fighting in the Battle of Chancellorsville (Second Fredericksburgh). As far as I know, it is his only sustained attempt to penetrate beyond what, by comparison, was— at least metaphorically speaking—the well-lighted place of the hospitals, to the violent darkness of the battlefield itself. It was precisely the obscure, extensive nature of the nighttime skirmishing at Chancellorsville that particularly excited Whitman's imagination. Who, he asks, can "know the conflict, hand-to-hand—the many conflicts in the dark, those shadowy-tangled, flashing moonbeam'd woods—the writhing groups and squads—the cries, the din, the cracking guns and pistols—the distant cannon—the cheers and calls and threats and awful music of the oaths—the indescribable mix—the officer's orders, persuasion, encouragements—the devils fully rous'd in human hearts" (1:47). This is anti-vista writing with a vengeance. As Whitman warns at the outset of his descripton, he intends "to give just a glimpse of the scrimmage": "a moment's look, in a terrible storm at sea—of which a few suggestions are enough, and full details impossible" (1:45). So this is also, in a way, anti-tableau writing, since there is no question of these snatched scenes operating as condensations and spiritual clarifications of the savage world of encounter from which they are taken.

"The many conflicts in the dark, those shadowy-tangled, flashing moonbeam'd woods" (1:47): the Chancellorsville piece strongly contrasts with Whitman's general emphasis on maintaining good marching order. Similar battle scenes awoke the tragic visionary in a Melville already predisposed to believe that men were "turned adrift into war."[12]

None can narrate the strife in the pines,
A seal is on it—Sabbaean lore!

Obscure as the wood, the entangled rhyme
But hints at the maze of war. [13]

Whitman customarily preferred to stress not the maze but the "sweet-est comradeship and love, threading its steady thread inside the chaos." Most of his writing about the war is, as is well known, carefully strung along that thread. But this description of Chancellorsville is a fascinating exception, and in letting go of the thread, Whitman is plunged into unknown and dangerous territory and confronts the ambivalence of the qualities displayed by men in war: "brave, deter-min'd as demons."

There is no uplifting moral pattern Whitman can claim to discover in the fighting itself. In describing it he uses instead a pattern of dramatic contrasts—employing an aesthetic language not, as in "A March in the Ranks," to suggest spiritual illumination, but as the disturbing vernacular of amoral excitement. Calm nature—"the early summer grass so rich, and foliage of the trees"—sensually heighten the carnage: "the red life-blood oozing out from heads or trunks or limbs upon that green and dew-cool grass." Pity and horror simply play a part in the drama of conflicting and frankly confused emotions: "Then the camps of the wounded—O heavens, what scene is this?—is this indeed *humanity*—these butchers' shambles? . . . Such is the camp of the wounded—such a fragment, a reflection afar off of the bloody scene—while over all the clear, large moon comes out at times softly, quietly shining. Amid the woods, that scene of flitting souls—amid the crack and crash and yelling sounds—the impalpable perfume of the woods—and yet the pungent, stifling smoke" (1:46–47).

The whole passage is a serious and powerful exercise in theatrical effects—a theatricality which, Whitman implies, half conceals and half reveals the thing itself. Historiography, lacking this theatrical sense, cannot reveal the turbulent passions at the heart of the war. Literature, by contrast, while it can be the theater of passion, still threatens to misrepresent the sheer scale, if not the nature, of the anarchic passional life of conflict. So, toward the end of what is inescapably a set piece, Whitman tries to avoid closure and endeavors to create the sinister equivalent of his branching peacetime vistas. To this end, he uses the familiar rhetorical device of advertising the im-possibility of doing what he's doing ("What history, I say, can ever give—for who can know . . . Who paint the scene? . . . Who paint the irrepressible advance . . . Who show . . . ?"), and the technique of literary impressionism ("the cries, the din, the crackling guns and pistols—the distant cannon—the cheers") in order to suggest the impetus of a reality which carries on, and takes over where the writing stops.

But he cannot allow himself to end there, leaving his writing opening on to anarchy. Having permitted himself to experience more of the bloody disorder of the war than ever, perhaps, before, he begins to grope again for the thread inside that chaos, eventually finding it in "the irrepressible advance of the second division of the Third Corps, under Hooker himself, suddenly order'd up—those rapid-filing phantoms through the woods . . . to save (and it did save) the army's name, perhaps the nation as there the veterans hold the field" (1:48). In gratefully imagining the advent of these soldiers, Whitman reverts to a bedrock image—one of those reassuring images which were fundamentally necessary to him because they represented matter crystallizing out of the nebulous, and order consolidating out of chaos. The troops move "there in the shadows, fluid and firm," like ambiguous phantoms that eventually materialize into the solid embodiments of solidarity.

Place this passage on Chancellorsville in the context of the passages which flank it in *Specimen Days,* and it becomes clear both why Whitman should have embarked on this uncharacteristic re-creation of the actual conditions of combat, and how in the aftermath he was left saddened and depressed. The preceding section describes those badly wounded in the battle of Chancellorsville arriving at the landing, at the rate of up to a thousand a day. The patient silence of their endurance affected Whitman deeply. It is no wonder he was moved, perhaps as much by guilt as by sympathy, to participate imaginatively in the circumstances in which these wounds had been incurred.

In the passage already examined he therefore enters into the fury of the fighting, but once it is over Whitman stays behind in imagination on the field to picture the "unnamed, unknown" soldier who dies, by the thousand, alone after "the battle advances, retreats, flits from the scene, sweeps by": "the last lethargy winds like a serpent round him—the eyes glaze in death—none recks" (1:49). Here there is no father (except, in a way, for Whitman himself) to seek out the body and keep vigil, and so he "crumbles in mother earth, unburied and unknown" (1:49). "The unnamed lost," as Whitman wrote later, "are ever present in my mind." It was particularly important that he should seek them out in imagination so as to "embalm" them in memory, and so at least to preserve them from the devouring worm of oblivion.

It was when considering those thousands abandoned to the degradation and the loneliness of anonymous suffering and death that Whitman could be most deeply shaken in his faith. He was liable to see with his unwilling mind's eye "the ghastly face, just dead upon that cot outside the tent: and the other covered with a dark gray blanket, and waiting to be buried." In "A Sight in Camp in the Daybreak Gray and Dim" he confronts himself with three forms "on stretchers lying, brought out there, untended lying, / Over each the blanket spread, ample brownish woolen blanket, / Grey and heavy blanket, folding, covering all" (2:496). Here, for a moment, all those who are dead appear to Whitman to have been abandoned, left to their death, regardless of whether they had actually been left to die. They are "untended lying," and the rest of the poem is given over to Whitman's tending, and attending to, those dead, as "with light fingers I from the face of the nearest, the first, just lift the blanket." He gazes into the ghastly faces of the dead, and so restores to them their individual features, their human identities, even though their actual names, personalities, histories, remain concealed from him. Recognition of them as comrades is offered as an acceptable substitute for the impossible act of personal recognition:

> Who are you, elderly man so gaunt and grim, with well-
> grey'd hair, and flesh all sunken about the eyes?
> Who are you, my dear comrade?   (2:496)

Here again it is instructive to refer to the prose passage which is the precursor of this poem. There Whitman affects to approve of the matter-of-fact way in which corpses are treated. "Death is nothing here," he informs us, adding that anyone stepping out of the tent to wash their face first thing in the morning is liable to see "a shapeless extended object," under a blanket on a stretcher. Necessity dictates that the dead should be efficiently disposed of, without "useless ceremony." "The stern realities of the marches and many battles of a long campaign make the old etiquets [*sic*] a cumber and a nuisance."[14] In fact, as Glicksberg notes, under these circumstances there was no practicable way of burying the dead except to dig long lines of trenches, and to detail men to heap corpses in them. In this way "chances of future recognition were thus lost." While the prose records a businesslike acceptance by Whitman of this unavoidable, utilitarian arrangement, the poem's approach is, of course, quite different. It is Whitman's attempt to humanize an inhuman situation and to enact his own little private "ceremony" to demonstrate a continuing, human solidarity between the living and the dead.

When set in this way against the background of Whitman's anguished pre-occupation with the "untended" dead, this little poem's touching episode of encounter becomes an allegory of one of the most important ways in which Whitman's memory of war was to operate. The war exacted tributes of memory of at least two kinds from Whitman, and these were intimately interconnected, although the one mostly involved a voluntary, the other an involuntary act of remembrance. The first followed from Whitman's determination to convey to the future something of the true nature, the deep human significance, of wartime events that would otherwise be dishonored by being inadequately, inauthentically remembered, or casually forgotten. In this connection critics have usually followed Whitman himself in emphasizing his admiring memories of the spiritual courage displayed by the men both in action and under the appalling conditions prevailing in the hospitals. There were, however, more darkly compelling reasons than this for discharging the duty of remembering, as we shall see. He was trying to admit the dead into the community of the living; trying to stare the ghastly faces of the dead back into answerable, human shape, by recognizing their sacrifice.

But beyond this voluntary exercise of memory, and therefore beyond Whitman's own certain control, lay those other memories which threatened his mental equilibrium. During his grueling period of service in the hospitals, Whitman had himself anticipated the return of present events as racking future recollections: "Mother, I see such awful things—I expect one of these days, if I live, I shall have awful thoughts & dreams—but it is such a great thing to be able to do so some real good, assuage these horrible pains & wounds, & save life even—that's the only thing that keeps a fellow up."[15]

It is, of course, as "The Wound-Dresser" that Whitman made, in his poetry, his most determined effort to move voluntarily among these memories, and to recover these events for consciousness in their full emotional color. He has to stoop to this dark, buried truth, entering upon these memories of the seriously wounded as he approached the wounded themselves: on "hinged knees." But "The Artilleryman's Vision" can also be examined in this context, as a fascinating example of an alternative strategy for dealing with "vision [that] presses upon me" (2:506). The poem has already been read as a sort of protective fantasy, in which Whitman imagines war memories returning not as nightmares but with all the anesthetizing excitement of the occasion, the blood-heat of the moment, still intact, so that "the falling, dying, I heed not—the wounded, dripping and red I heed not—some to the rear are hobbling" (2:507). But the fantasy may also have served the additional function of allowing Whitman to express, through the invented character of the artilleryman, the feeling of resentment that is almost always a hidden ingredient in such sympathetic devotion as he himself had unfailingly shown to his patients. It is, as Simone Weil penetratingly remarked, "a phenomenon [that] is as automatic as gravitation. Our senses attach all the scorn, all the revulsion, all the hatred which our reason attaches to crime, to affliction. Except for those whose whole soul is inhabited by Christ, everybody despises the afflicted to some extent, although practically no one is conscious of it."[16]

Of course, Whitman himself never actually sought to live out that aggressive fantasy or to act out those scornful feelings. Moreover, he knew from the experience of others as well as from personal experience that visions of a very different and deeply disturbing kind were in reality much more likely to press upon an ex-combatant's mind. While working in the attorney general's office in Washington, during the immediate postwar years, Whitman continued to visit the soldiers in the remaining military hospitals: "the old dregs & leavings of the war, old wounds, brokendown sick, discharged soldiers, who have no place to go, etc."[17] In letters he spoke not only of their lingering festering wounds ("youth & hope struggling against fate—but the latter, alas! almost always conquering at last") but of the delirium, which caused them to see "such sights & terrible things."[18] Even during the war itself, he had reported to his mother that "one new feature is that many of the poor afflicted young men are crazy, every ward has some in it that are wandering—they have suffered too much, & it is perhaps a privilege that they are out of their senses—Mother, it is most too much for a fellow, and I sometimes wish I was out of it—but I suppose it is because I have not felt first rate myself."[19]

In view of Whitman's loud emphasis throughout his later years on the melancholy satisfactions of his nursing experiences, it is important to note one point. While his letters at the time certainly confirm that he did indeed repeatedly find impressive evidence among the men of a courage that alone could give meaning to suffering, his correspondence also records occasions when he came close to breaking down under the cumulative weight of his oppressive experiences. When he heard, on March 22, 1864, that a new offensive had begun, it was with dread he anticipated the inevitable consequences:

> O mother, to think that we are to have here soon what I have seen so many times, the awful loads & trains & boat loads of poor bloody & pale & wounded young men again—for that is what we certainly will, and before very long—I see all the signs, getting ready in the hospitals etc.—it is dreadful, when one thinks about it—I sometimes think over the sights I have myself seen, the arrival of the wounded after a battle, & the scenes on the field too, & I can hardly believe my own recollection—what an awful thing war is—Mother, it seems not men but a lot of devils & butchers butchering each other.[20]

It is true he was not entirely himself at this time, since he was about to succumb to the prostrating sickness which forced him to suspend his work in the hospitals for several months. But it is also very probably true that he succumbed physically because he was already emotionally drained and mentally undermined.

Although he was careful to convey an impression, in his published writings about the war, of an unwavering confidence in the predestined victory of the North, and therefore of his undeviating support for the war effort, some of his reactions at the time were far from being so assured. One letter in particular, to his mother, shows the unremitting struggle that was then going on within him: "Mother, one's heart grows sick of war, after all, when you see what it really is—every once in a while I feel so horrified & disgusted—it seems to me like a great slaughter-house & the men mutually butchering each other—then I feel how impossible it appears, again, to retire from this contest, until we have carried our points—(it is cruel to be so tossed from pillar to post in one's judgment)."[21] No wonder his patience snapped during an argument with his great friend, the fiery abolitionist William D. O'Connor, causing him to say bluntly "my opinion is to *stop the war now*," and to add, with more than a hint of bitterness, that "in comparison with this slaughter I don't care for the niggers."[22]

Just as in *Calamus* he had created, out of his lonely yearnings, the antithetical image of the self-sufficient live oak, standing in its pride of singleness, so later in *Drum Taps* he imagined an authoritative figure possessed of an imperturbability that contrasted with his own emotional perturbations, and who perhaps helped to calm them:

> I saw old General at bay;
> (Old as he was, his grey eyes yet shone out in battle
>   like stars;)
> His small force was now completely hemmed in, in his works;
> He call'd for volunteers to run the enemy's lines—a
>   desperate emergency;
> I saw a hundred and more step forth from the ranks—but two
>   or three were selected;
> I saw them receive their orders aside—they listen'd with
>   care—the adjutant was very grave;
> I saw them depart with cheerfulness, freely risking
>   their lives.   (2:521–522)

As time wore on, even his nursing couldn't sustain him quite as it had. Previously he had been able to convince himself that the spirits of the men had illuminated their suffering bodies from within, but now "the only comfort is that I have been the cause of some beams of sunshine upon their sufferings & gloomy souls & bodies too."[23] Weil offers us a distinction that is useful to bear in mind: the distinction between ordinary suffering and affliction. "In the realm of suffering, affliction is something apart, specific and irreducible. It is quite a different thing from simple suffering. It takes possession of the soul and marks it through and through with its own particular mark, the mark of slavery."[24] In other words, affliction eats into the soul and devours it. Whitman's very survival in those Washington hospitals had depended on his capacity to see what men underwent there as suffering, and not as affliction. He needed to believe that suffering could not touch the souls of these men with anything except nobility, however it might torture their bodies. It is therefore particularly moving to find him here noticing, in "their gloomy souls," the mark of the slave on those soldiers who were for him the great representatives of American freedom.

In this mood he began for the first time to notice, or perhaps to admit he noticed, the increasing callousness with which the wounded were treated and "how even the dying soldier's money [is] stolen from his body by some scoundrel attendant, or from some sick ones, even from under his head, which is a common thing."[25] When, on top of "the agony I see every day" he saw all this, then, he admitted to his mother, "I get almost frightened at the world." It is surely very close to being the most heartrending sentence Whitman ever permitted himself to write.

These memories were the "vultures of the mind." And they did not pass away with the years. As we have seen, Whitman was in old age periodically shaken by "extreme emotional stirrings—almost depressions" rising from the buried life of the war years. They were responsible for his celebrated eruption on December 13, 1888, when he burst out to Traubel against "that whole damned war business," which was "about nine hundred and ninety nine parts diarrhoea to one part glory." He agreed with Sherman that war was hell, and concluded with a curse every bit as impassioned and every bit as impotent as those of Lear: "God damn the wars—all wars: God damn every war: God damn 'em! God damn 'em!"[26] So time shook Whitman's "fragile frame at eve / With throbbings of noontide."

IF THERE WERE, then, these lurking, lacerating memories which followed Whtman through the postwar years, there were also specific obligations of memory which he felt deeply obliged to honor. He became preoccupied with the responsibility of producing an appropriate personal and national memory out of the war, and was in turn also haunted by the possibility of failure in these respects. Such a failure would have been tantamount to a betrayal of the dead, and their sacred trust.

In the *Drum Taps* collection "The Wound-Dresser" affords a particularly fascinating example of the complexities of Whitman's developing interest in memory. Poetry is so often supposed to offer emotions not in their pressing immediacy but as "recollected in tranquillity" that it is worth remarking how opposite to this is the relationship of both poetry and memory to feelings in this poem. As

Whitman explained in a letter to his mother: "When I am present at the most appaling [sic] things, deaths, operations, sickening wounds (perhaps full of maggots), I do not fail, although my sympathies are very much excited, but keep singularly cool—but often, hours afterward, perhaps when I am home, or out walking alone, I feel sick and actually tremble when I recal [sic] the thing & have it in my mnd again before me."[27] The vital lesson that Whitman the orderly had to learn, as he mentions in *Specimen Days,* was to control his emotions; not to act impulsively out of his own store of feeling, but to regulate his reactions, adjusting them to the varying nature and needs of his patients. He also in *Specimen Days* warns against entering a ward unwarily: it is imperative to guard one's emotions and to prepare one's mind and senses for all disgusting and harrowing eventualities (1:53). A nurse had to observe the same discipline as a soldier. It is important to recognize how expressive "The Wound-Dresser" is of such guardedness and tact, essential "hospital wisdom" as Whitman called it. Throughout the poem Whitman in his wisdom acts as Virgil to the reader's Dante in this visit to the underworld: "Whoever you are, follow me without noise and be of strong heart."[28] But what the poem, through the device of memory, allows Whitman to do is precisely what as a nurse on the ward he could not do: to contemplate the scene in its full emotional color; to exclaim as well as to act—as he could not when his effectiveness depended on his ability to suppress his feelings and to conceal them even from himself. His travel into an imaginary future becomes his means of penetrating into the emotional recesses of present experience.

But this only partially explains the elaborate structure of memory in this poem. It derives equally from Whitman's imperative need to view the war steadily in the light of his responsibility to the future to bear true witness to its character and meaning. The primary importance of the Civil War lay for Whitman in its significance for the American future—much of its justification depended, in short, on its successful transmutation into national memory. This made him especially sensitive to the possibility that the future might betray the war and its soldiers by disregarding or squandering their legacy. If that happened it would not, Whitman determined, be for the want of a poet to act as conveyer and interpreter of this present to that future. He, like Melville as Hart Crane imagined him, knew that dead men's bones "bequeath an embassy."[29] In "Not the Pilot" Whitman represents himself as the composer of a "march for These States," and in the 1871 version he supplies "a battle call, rousing to arms, if need be—years, centuries hence" (2:446). But "The Wound-Dresser" offers a different and less bellicose image of himself and of the war, one born of a different conception of his future audience.

That ideal future audience is here identified as being "the young men and maidens that love me" (2:480), and who beg him to speak to them as yesterday's witness. But Whitman can also realistically and fearfully imagine a different future, in which "the world of gain and appearance and mirth goes on, / So soon what is over forgotten, and waves wash the imprints off the sand." He and his kind might be left alone to "enter the doors" of memory, "in silence, in dream's projections" (2:480). The incommunicability, the terrible privacy and public unavailability of wartime memories, was something which clearly troubled Whitman. His own war poetry, as he admitted in *Specimen Days,* was an attempt at the impossible, an attempt to convey to noncombatants what the war had really been like, and what therefore it should mean to Americans (*Prose Works,* 1:115–118). Even when a society does remember and honor the casualties of war, there is still a gulf set between the public language of official commemoration and the terms privately known only to the participants. As late as 1888, over twenty years after the cessation of hostilities, and only four years before his death, Whitman was himself still liable to invasion by what he called "interpolation sounds." During the sonorous solemnities of the service held to commemorate General Philip Sheridan, there came "to me . . . interpolation sounds not in the show— plainly to me, crowding up the aisle and from the window, / Of sudden battle's hurry and harsh noises—war's grim game to sight and ear in earnest" (3:738). The musical pieties of the occasion are disturbed by the jarring dissonance of the noises inside Whitman's own head.

But it was not only nightmare that Whitman impotently yearned to share with others, it was also vision. That part of him, and of America, that lay in the past, was the best part as well as the worst. *Drum Taps* was its epitaph. Elegiac stanzas for a dead Whitman, a Whitman who had come truly alive only in the comradeship of war. This is a feeling dispersed throughout the collection, a feeling which Whitman seems to have felt not only after the event, but at the time, which perhaps best explains the peculiar timbre of these poems, in which the present is poignantly felt to be passing so rapidly that already, even in the experiencing, it is irrecoverable, unrepeatable, past.

Yet memory can still, of course, recover something from such loss. In "As Toilsome I Wander'd" Whitman takes a positively Wordsworthian pleasure in the consolations of memory, finding in it a capacity for providing a ruminative refuge, a hope for future years:

> Long, long I muse, then on my way go wandering;
> Many a changeful season to follow, and many a scene of life;
> Yet at times through changeful season and scene, abrupt,
>   alone, or in the crowded street,
> Comes before me the unknown soldier's grave—comes the
>   inscription rude in Virginia's woods,
> *Bold, cautious, true, and my loving comrade.*   (2:509–510)

And Whitman was indeed to draw, during the difficult postwar years, upon his sweetly elegiac memories in precisely this way. Even during the personally dark days of the seventies, he could speak of his "Memoranda of the War Years" as transcribed "in order to partially occupy and off-set days of strange sickness, and the heaviest affliction and bereavement of my life."[30]

Whitman's pride in his wartime experience was matched only by his anger and contempt for unsympathetic noncombatants, and his dumb, ominous suspicion that they might comprise the majority of the American nation. Himself transfigured—"I have been born of the same as the war was born" (2:500)—he felt profound distaste at a complacently untransfigured world. His "noli me tangere" rings out in "To a Certain Civilian," and "Not Youth Pertains to Me," for "I have nourish'd the wounded, and sooth'd many a dying soldier" (2:528). He felt distinguished, identified, by his immediate past experience. He was made precious by his memories. And behind his distaste lay a fear of the consequences of that reassimilation to civilian life which, like an unknown fate, awaited the soldiers and himself. That fear, and the hope which accompanied it, provoked his long meditations on the process of demobilization and the resumption of peacetime living.

There is in Whitman by the end of *Drum Taps* an almost overwhelming urge, an overriding psychological need, to trust anew life's primal sanities and primary antiseptics; to offer himself up without qualification to its abundant creative energies, and to acknowledge the claim of "the average earth" upon the fundamental human affections. There is, in short, a healing impulse to forget. But there are also deep scruples and misgivings. One such is the suspicion that in order to keep faith with such an immoderate past, a man must pledge himself to it and dedicate his life to the remembering and perpetuating of its spirit. "Spirit Whose Work is Done" is therefore a Shelleyan prayer to the "spirit of dreadful hours" to renew its work in Whitman; to make him its instrument and so save him from the soft (and softening) blandishments of peace. "Leave me your pulses of rage! bequeath them to me! fill me with currents convulsive!" (2:543). "Reconciliation," by contrast, is a prayer for necessary healing forgetfulness and preservation from the bitterness of unforgiving memories. "Beautiful that war, and all its deeds of carnage, must in time be utterly lost" (2:555). The successful reconstruction of the Union of States, whereby they might be "anneal'd into a living Union," depended, as Whitman very early understood, upon acceptance of yesterday's enemy as today's friend. Paradoxically, it was a process which could be conceivably easier for those who had actually fought in the opposing armies, since not only had they been bled of their hostilities, they also had shared memories and a common past in war. They could appreciate that if "my enemy is dead," then "A man divine as myself is dead" (2:556).

"The dead, the dead, the dead—*our* dead": what—thinking of the way war had called them together from all walks of life and all the states of a vast continent, he marvelously called the "varieties of the *strayed* dead"—haunted Whitman constantly (1:114). And most of all he thought of the unidentified and the unlocated bodies. "Today there lie buried over 300,000 soldiers in the various National army cemeteries, more than half of them (and that is really the most significant and eloquent bequest of the War) mark'd unknown" (2:614). "The unnamed lost," he admitted, were "ever present in my mind." He was appalled by what the Welsh poet Alun Lewis has called "the gradual self-effacement of the dead." Love and justice alike required that they be not forgotten, that their deaths should somehow or other be honored (and therefore redeemed) by proper personal and national memory. This task of "justifying the past" became for Whitman a psychological necessity and a mission; he would write "the psalms of the dead." The accusatory twisted shapes, those grotesques of memory, demanded attention:

> Look down, fair moon, and bathe this scene;
> Pour softly down night's nimbus floods, on faces ghastly, swollen, purple;
> On the dead, on their backs, with arms toss'd wide. (2:519–520)

The dead are magicked into sleep. Or, as he more famously and explicitly phrased it later, "They themselves were fully at rest—they suffer'd not" (2:538). But to swathe them in peace would not fully pacify them, nor would they be silenced by silence.

One solution to this clamorous problem was, of course, to make good compost of their bodies—"To the leaven'd soil they trod, calling, I sing, for the last" (2:556). The future of "the infinite dead" (1:114) is supposedly secure, for the land remembers, and there is not a breathing of the common wind that will forget them. Lincoln himself is, we shall see, given the same rich and successful treatment in "When Lilacs Last in the Dooryard Bloom'd."

The little masterpiece of this kind in *Drum Taps,* though, is "Pensive on Her Dead Gazing"—a poem in which Whitman generates an eloquence that is like a gorgeously decorated shroud, designed to obscure, and ultimately obliterate, the foulness of slaughter. One of the great "buried" themes of *Drum Taps* is the guilty physical revulsion felt by Whitman at the stink of corpses, the stench of wounds and diseases, and all the noxious contamination of war. Disgust, or at least distaste, is a hidden attribute of the style itself, as it tends always, like a funeral ceremony, toward the grandiloquent and the stately. And from time to time the cleansing function of this ritual of language is tacitly admitted by the poems themselves. This is notably the case in "Reconciliation," where the "word" is used by Whitman to signify "that the hands of the sisters Death and Night incessantly softly wash again, and ever again, this soil'd world" (2:556): once the "corpse" of all this carnage has been washed clean, then it can be kissed by Whitman and visited again with love. And here, in "Pensive on Her Dead Gazing," the earth, having "absorbed" the bodies, transforms their grossness into air: "O years and graves! O air and soil! O my dead, an aroma sweet! / Exhale them perennial, sweet death, years, centuries hence" (2:527). There the aroma of the transmuted corpses allows Whitman finally to conceive of death itself as "sweet."

Read on this personal level, then, the poem is one which—through the medium of the poetry itself—enables Whitman to transform foul memories into fair, as perhaps he hopes time itself will conclusively do in his future case. On the one hand, the poem indeed can be understood as an attempt to influence time in that very direction—a piece of white verbal magic. On the other hand, if one emphasizes, in reading, the national significance of the piece, then it can be seen to be profoundly concerned with another problem of memory. Mother America's beseeching cry to the earth is actually Whitman imploring America itself: "Absorb them well O my earth, she cried, I charge you lose not my sons, lose not an atom" (2:527). If, as has frequently been suggested, the Whitman of "Song of Myself," fascinated by his studies in Abbott's Egyptian museum, partly modeled the poem on Isis' search for Osiris, then surely in "Pensive on Her Dead Gazing" the same story is given a somber new lease of life. Here "the Mother of all," gazing distraught on the "torn bodies" of the dead, enjoins the earth to collect every dismembered particle of their being, so as eventually to restore them completely to life, as the very "breath" of the future. This, of course, is Whitman's prayer to the nation: to assimilate not only the dead soldiers, but also what they had died for, so completely that even business America would become the dead, incorporated. But, radically uncertain of his sociey, he substitutes the reliable trope of nature for the unreliable actualities of the nation. Given the unresolved tensions within Whitman, at this historical juncture, it is no wonder the poem opens with such a strange conjuncton of terms—where America (and, by implication, Whitman) gazes on the dead both with a (would-be) calm "pensiveness," and with "desperation": "Pensive, on her dead gazing . . . / Desperate, on the torn bodies, on the forms covering the battle-fields gazing" (2:526).

Similar signs of strain are to be found in "The Return of the Heroes," the poem which is easily the most ambitious of all Whitman's "demobilisation" poems. Originally known as "A Carol of Harvest, for 1867," it was preceeded, in the 1876 edition, by an interesting author's note: "In all History, antique or modern, the grandest achievement yet for political Humanity—grander even than the triumph of THIS UNION over Secession—was the return, disbanding, and peaceful disintegration from compact military organization, back into agricultural and civil employments, of the vast Armies, the two millions of embattled men of America—a problem reserved for Democracy, our day and land, to promptly solve" (2:590). He was not thinking of anything as mundane as the finding of employment for a huge new labor force. The problem he had in mind for Democracy to solve, was how to carry over into civilian life the virtues and qualities exhibited by men in war; how to produce a land fit for heroes to live in, a land worthy of those who had died. The emphasis falls, for Whitman, on the word "land." For one thing, as the 1871 version of the poem shows, he was already beginning to dissociate himself from urban life: "A song of the good green grass! / A song no more of the city streets; / A song of farms—a song of the soil of fields" (3:590). For another, he places his faith not so much in agricultural life, as in the land itself—the "lavish brown parturient earth," which is seen as both the source and the image of the generous society Whitman imagines postwar America to be.

"The Return of the Heroes" is the counterpart to "First O Songs for a Prelude." The one celebrates the making of a nation-at-arms out of a pacific society, the other celebrates the return of the heroic soldiery to "the true arenas of my race—or first or last, / Man's innocent and strong arenas" (3:595). Whitman uses his rhetorical skills to overcome what was in historical fact an intransigent social problem so that the transition from soldier to civilian is made to seem a natural process. The "fields of battle" are simply replaced by the "fields" of the West; war gives way to the "life giving wars" of man with his environment; men-at-arms turn into wielders of "better weapons," and so on. Above all, the soldiers are made to "melt," to "dissolve," to "resolve . . . back again"; they are completely absorbed, along with their heroic qualities, into the social landscape.

It is the dream Whitman sets against the immediate postwar reality, the dream by which henceforth he had to live in order to escape despair. "Return of the Heroes" chronicles unforgettably the publicly forgotten armies of the wounded and the dead which continued to march silently through Whitman's mind. He had to convince himself that the quality of life in postwar America somehow gave meaning to their sacrifice, and in that sense honored and remembered it. His poetry had, in this respect, to supply the manifest deficiencies of contemporary history:

For an army heaves in sight—O another gathering army!
Swarming, trailing on the rear—O you dead, accruing army!
O you regiments so piteous, with your mortal diarrhoea! with
    your fever!
O my land's maimed darlings! with the plenteous bloody
    bandage, and the crutch!
Lo! your pallid army follow'd!

7

But on these days of brightness,
On the far-stretching beauteous landscape, the roads and lanes,
    the high-piled farm-wagons, and the fruits and barns,
Should the dead intrude?

Ah, the dead to me mar not—they fit well in Nature;
They fit very well in the landscape, under the trees and grass,
And along the edge of the sky, in the horizon's far margin.

Nor do I forget you, departed;
Nor in winter or summer, my lost ones;
But most, in the open air, as now, when my soul is rapt and
    at peace—like pleasing phantoms,
Your dear memories, rising, glide silently by me.   (3:593)

These specters, then, are actually bidden to the feast, honored guests
at harvest thanksgiving. Here indeed, it might be supposed, the problem, and the dead, are finally put to rest. But Whitman remains
troubled by "Old War Dreams":

In clouds descending, in midnight sleep, of many a face
    of anguish,
Of the look at first of the mortally wounded—of that
    indescribable look;
Of the dead on their backs, with arms extended wide,
        I dream, I dream, I dream.

Of scenes of nature, the fields and the mountains;
Of the skies, so beauteous after the storm—and at night the
    moon so unearthly bright,

Shining sweetly, shining down, where we dig the trenches and
  gather the heaps,
> I dream, I dream, I dream.   (2:551)

This is "Reconciliation" minus the copula, the connecting, restorative link between pure sky and soiled, war-torn earth. The source of the enduring trouble is here precisely defined in that yawning gulf of a stanza division. In other poems the peaceful land is reconciled to war (and becomes the means of reconciling Whitman himself to deaths in battle) through the consolation that blood is being shed only in order that life may be lived more abundantly. But not so here, for Nature remains the blank, uncomprehending opposite of war. It is a perception anticipated in "Come Up from the Fields, Father," where the desolate figure of the mother in the rawness of her sorrow totally obscures any possibilities of healing in the landscape behind her. She is a kind of bitter parody of Ceres as, "where apples ripe in the orchards hang and grapes on the trellis'd vines," she "longs with one deep longing . . . To follow, to seek, to be with her dead son." (2:488, 489) So too was Proserpine seized by death, "which cost Ceres all that pain / To seek her through the world."[31] Ceres, however, succeeded in bringing Proserpine, and with her summer and harvest, back into the world for six months of the year.

What we have, then, is one of the profoundly significant occasions when Whitman was unconvinced by his own metaphors—those central metaphors by which he performed the necessary miracle of transforming death into life. These were almost invariably metaphors of natural process; and by substituting nature for culture, natural life for social and political life, Whitman was able to guarantee the fertile perpetuation of the dead. But the trope had something of the saving lie about it. The presence of the dead was, after all, far less credibly visible in postwar American society than in the pregnant contours of nature. It was far from certain that this cynical national prosperity was indeed what they had died for. There was, in other words, the uneasy possibility that they were indeed forgotten, betrayed not only by men's memories but also by their deeds. At best they were but ingloriously remembered.

This was the fact which Whitman resolutely denied and gingerly confronted for years. Out of his dilemma (and perhaps out of his guilt) came the determination, of whose origin he was only partly aware, to make his work, and even his life, a kind of monument to that ignominiously forgotten war. "Forth from the war emerging, a book I have made" (2:656); "my book and the War are one" (3:628); "the whole Book, indeed revolves around that Four Years' War, which, as I was in the midst of it, becomes, in *Drum Taps*, pivotal to the rest entire."[32] These are the remarks which will be examined, along with their implications, in the final chapter of this book. Such an anxious overstatement of his case by the poet is paralleled by the man, writing at the very end of his life: "Then behind all, the deep-down consolation (it is a glum one, but I dare not be sorry for the fact of it in the past, nor refrain from the dwelling, even vaunting here at the end) that this late-years palsied old shorn and shell-fish condition of me is the indubitable outcome and growth, now near for 20 years along, of too over-anxious, over-continued bodily and emotional excitement and action through the times of 1862, '3, '4, and '5" (2:738). Personal history is there simplified, purified, and improved into myth. In his own body Whitman bears the lurid stigmata of that war's sacrifice, as in his mind he has borne the burden of its memory. In memory the nurse pressed ever closer to the soldiers themselves, until in the end he was representing himself as having virtually been one of them, implicitly claiming far more frontline experience than his history could in fact corroborate: "I went down to the war fields in Virginia (end of 1862), I lived thenceforward in camp—saw great battles and the days and night afterward—partook of all the fluctuations, gloom, despair, hopes again arous'd, courage evoked—death readily risk'd—*the cause* too—along and filling those agonistic and lurid following years . . . the real parturition years . . . of this henceforth homogeneous Union. Without those three or four years and the experiences they gave, 'Leaves of Grass' would not now be existing" (2:724).

There are, not surprisingly, a few stray signs in the late poetry that Whitman felt some guilt at having survived, and survived for so long, when so many young men had died in their prime. This may well have contributed to his evidently pressing need to regard himself, and to be regarded, as a man who had, as it were, been wounded in action. "I should like all my friends to understand from me—all of them—that the succession of whacks, as I call them, to which I have been subject these last fifteen years, is the result of two or three years of great exposure during the critical period of the War."[33] He constructed, in self-defense, a gnarled work in praise of "True Conquerors," "Old soldiers from campaigns, with all their wounds, defeats and scars; / Enough that they've survived at all—long life's unflinching ones!" (3:718). Yet self-accusation still persisted. "Brave, brave were the soldiers (high named today) who lived through the fight," he wrote in his old age, "but the bravest pass'd to the front and fell, unnamed, unknown" (*Leaves of Grass*, 3:697). The sadness lies in the unfair disparity between the "high named" and the "unnamed." Whitman himself, we recall, had acquired a name of sorts in the American world of letters, and achieved success of a kind, if only a succès de scandale. Perhaps it was partly by way of reparation that he dedicated a late poem "To those who've failed, in aspiration vast, / . . .To all cut off before their time, / Possess'd by some strange spirit of fire, / Quench'd by an early death" (3:696). The case is, however, complicated by his suppressed tendency to think of his own life and work as a failure, down to the very end.

But if, as I suspect, Whitman knew the guilt of the survivor, he also knew, upon his return from "that backward world" of barbarism, the near hysterical joy of the survivor:

> Away with themes of war! away with War itself!
> Hence from my shuddering sight, to never more return, that
>   show of blacken'd, mutilated corpses.   (3:619)

His prose could be vibrant for a new beginning: "The Four Years' War is over—and, in the peaceful, strong, exciting, fresh occasions of Today, and of the Future, that strange, sad war is hurrying even now to be forgotten. The camp, the drill, the lines of sentries, the prisons, the hospitals—(ah, the hospitals!)—all have passed away— all seem now like a dream. A new race, a young and lusty generation, already sweeps in with oceanic currents, obliterating the war, and all its scars, its moulded graves, and all its reminiscences of hatred, conflict, death. So let it be obliterated."[34]

His confidence, too, could pass for genuine. The war was the nation's rite of passage: "all the hitherto experience of The States, their first Century, has been but preparation, adolescence, — and . . . this Union is only now and henceforth [since the Secession War] to enter on its full Democratic career."[35] The war, as he was never tired of intoning, "to me, *proved* Humanity, and proved America and the Modern" (*Prose Works*, 1:323). Even so, one might be permitted to doubt whether such conclusive "proof" was good for Whitman the poet. One could even venture further, and wonder whether he might not here, as elsewhere, be protesting just a little too much. It seems conceivable that the war planted an unfortunate but understandable equation in Whitman's mind: to doubt America was to cast a slur on the dead, to doubt the adequacy of their sacrifice. Psychologically, Whitman simply could not afford to do this. It would have been more than his emotional life was worth. As a result, he was as much condemned as committed to optimism. His fixed belief in the future was in this sense a belief in the historical resurrection of the dead, and a return to (or the return of) the past. That future could, of course, be deferred indefinitely to accommodate a persistently unsatisfactory present, but never canceled. For that would be to destroy the dead. Culture had eventually to conform to nature before the metaphor could work. But the whisper of doubt found a louder voice in the end, at the last: "Will the America of the future—will this vast rich Union ever realise what itself cost, back there after all?—those hecatombs of battle-deaths" (2:738).

WHITMAN early suspected that before life could be persuaded to imitate his mythic art, he would first have to vanquish history, that "huge Mississippi of falsehood" as, Whitman delightedly noted, Matthew Arnold called it (*Prose Works*, 1:271). It was the historians' history that Whitman hated—or, as he put it, "those puerilities often called history" (1:327) which dealt with the contingent rather than the necessary. Whitman himself believed profoundly in the divine logic of national history, that it had a providential shape or destiny which it fulfilled, "maybe unconscious of itself" (1:327). "What the technists called history" seemed to him merely empirical according to his own definition of empiricism: "an acquaintance with a number of isolated facts, yet not of the subtle relation and bearing of them, the meaning—their part in the ensemble—the instinct of what they prove."[36]

For Whitman the historians' history had, in the war, been disproved, defeated by history itself. His visionary nationalism was now a confirmed historical religion, founded on particular historical events which in their turn engendered an apocalyptic national history whose end was prophesied (and indeed prefigured) in its beginning. He himself was, of course, the New Historian. "I sh'd be tickled enough," he wrote to his friend Dr. Richard Bucke in 1888, "if I c'd think I had indeed skimm'd some of the *real cream* of the American History of the last 15 years and preserved it here."[37] And, of course, after his fashion and according to his light he had. "There is a tally-stamp and stage-result," he wrote in a preface that same year, "of periods and nations, elusive, at second or third hand, often escaping the historian of matter-of-fact—in some sort the nation's spiritual formative ferment or chaos—the getting in of its essence, formulating identity— a law of it, and significant part of its progress . . . My going up and down amidst these years, and the impromptu jottings of their sights and thoughts, of war and peace, have been in accordance with that law, and probably a result of it. . . . In certain respects . . . I therefore launch forth the divisions of the following book as not only a consequent of that period and its influences, but in one sort a History of America, the past 35 years" (2:732). His duty as poet, and true historian, as he wrote elsewhere, was to get at "this something . . . rooted in the invisible roots, the profoundest meanings of that place, race or nationality; and to absorb and again effuse it, uttering words and products as from its midst" (2:411). This he had done to America in, and through, the war whose history was indeed for him a continuing revelation.

Exalted his view of history may be, but it depends intimately on the power, indeed the special potency, of memory. "Already," he wrote in anguish in 1874, "the events of 1863 and '4, and the reasons that immediately preceded, as well as those that closely followed them, have quite lost their direct personal impression, and the living heat and excitement of their own time, and are being marshalled for casting, or getting ready to be cast, into the cold and bloodless electrotype plates of History" (1:310). He would combat this process by the only effective means: that prose, and in particular poetry, which he had already used to overcome the cold and bloodless electrotype plates of conventional literature. In that way could memories be broadcast, and the present and future put in touch (that sense so vital to Whitman) with the real "interior history" of the past.

But always the shadow of the irrecoverably lost fell across Whitman's mind, the sad lesson taught him by his own memory. "Think how much, and of importance, will be—how much, civic and mil-

itary, has already been—buried in the grave, in eternal darkness"
(1:118). In 1886 Whitman wrote a passage which is a touchingly
murky, even distorted, reflection of "The Wound-Dresser." "Already
a new generation begins to tread the stage, since the persons and
events of the Secession War," and Whitman admits to fancying that
near future when "the men and deeds of that contest have become
somewhat vague and mythical." He imagines himself, an unknown
"ancient soldier sitting in the background as the talk goes on, and
betraying himself by his emotion and moist eyes—like the journeying
Ithacan at the banquet of King Alcinoüs, when the bard sings the
contending warriors and their battles on the plains of Troy":

(So, from the sluices of Ulysses' eyes
Fast fell the tears, and sighs succeeded sighs.)   (2:603)

It is almost as if he were listening to his own poems, and as if they
were his own and yet not his own; as the war both was and was not
an experience communicable to these listeners.

The war and Whitman's subsequent memories had, after all, created
in him a complex experience of history. As he advanced in years, so
in some ways he seems, contrary as we shall see to his expressed
wishes, to have grown somewhat less confident that retrospect would
inevitably be obediently echoed by prospect. Interestingly enough,
there are very early signs of this other perspective in a wartime letter
Whitman wrote about the prospective *Drum Taps*. Referring to the
already existing *Leaves of Grass*, he remarks how there "are some
things in it I should not put in if I were to write now, but yet I shall
certainly let them stand, even if but for proofs of phases passed away."[38]
If one's past life can include "phases passed away," then what about
the life of a nation? Memory had shown Whitman how present might
be sundered from past. What people had been and done might not
easily predict what they would be and do, and so memories of the
past became urgently precious, precisely because that past would
never be repeated in the future. During his last years he developed
an endearing habit of bravado in the face of the ineluctable, a stoicism
that was at once suited to the irremediable years of sickness he suffered, and to all that had, along with health, disappeared never to
return. Traubel particularly remarked on Whitman's delight in reeling
out a couplet from Horace, in the Dryden translation: "Not heaven

itself upon the past has power, / But what has been has been—and I have had my hour."[39]

When Whitman launched his poetic attack on his arch rival and enemy, that hated profaner of sacred national truth, the historian, the worst taunt he could aim at his opponent was "You who celebrate bygones" (2:307). Yet, however unwillingly, Whitman was to find himself in old age the increasingly lonely custodian of memories unwanted by the nation; relics, like himself, of a bygone age. Unbeknown to himself, time had made him too a celebrator of bygones, so much so that he even constructed, in "Twenty Years," his own fascinating little version of the Rip Van Winkle story. He began to respond sympathetically to pieces like the following, printed in a magazine, in which the mutability of certain art forms, such as dance and theater, was elegiacally discussed: ". . . after hearing some great performance, we leave the theatre and think, 'Well, this great thing has been, and all that is now left of it is the feeble print upon my brain, the little thrill which memory will send along my nerves, mine and my neighbors, as we live longer the print and thrill must be feebler, and when we pass away the impress of the great artist will vanish from the world' " (2:591). So, too, in *Sands at Seventy*, Whitman composed his own tribute to "The Dead Tenor" whose voice had once and unforgettably thrilled him.

It is very apparent that into Whitman's poems of old age there creeps, alongside the well-established habit of looking always to the present and future as the blithely perfect fulfillment of the past, a new and deeply moving contrary tendency to recognize aspects of the past as irretrievably lost. While admirably refusing to decline into a fond remembrancer, and continuing to insist that old men should be explorers, he was silently overtaken by his past as he neared his three score and ten and began to "live largely on memory" (*Prose Works*, 2:712). He wrote an affectionately wondering poem about this new propensity: "How sweet the silent backward tracings! / The wanderings as in dreams—the meditations of old times resumed—their loves, joys, persons, voyages" (3:701). And in "The Pallid Wreath" such feelings produced a poem which, compared with the rest of Whitman's work, is a quietly revolutionary piece of work. It confesses Whitman's antiprogressive, or reactionary attachment to the departed past, his Hardyesque impulse still to treasure the faded flowers in an old funeral wreath:

Are the colors, vitalities, dead?
No, while memories subtly play—the past vivid as ever;
For but last night I woke, and in that spectral ring saw thee,
Thy smile, eyes, face, calm, silent, loving as ever.   (3:734)

In similar mood he discovers a new sympathy for the Indians who are being wiped off the face of what was their American earth. "Yonnondio," he tells us, is the Iroquois term meaning "lament for the aborigines," and he proceeds to expand the word into a dirge. As is appropriate to one who had loved Macpherson's poem in his youth, a melancholy Ossianic vision descends on him. He sees Indians "flitting by like clouds of ghosts, they pass and are gone in the twilight, / (Race of the woods, the landscapes free, and the falls! / No picture, poem, statement, passing them to the future)" (3:717). And in that nightmare vision of a people annihilated, obliterated, their very existence erased even from memory, the darkest of Whitman's fears rise to the surface. How can what he most cherishes from the past, his perishable memories of those other white warriors of the Civil War, survive intact to the future, unless a "picture, poem, statement" is fashioned to convey them? In the ending of "Yonnondio" can be heard the anguish of responsibility felt in this respect by an American poet, the keeper of the language of the white tribe, as he listens with foreboding to what once was living, communal speech, and is now reduced to a single unintelligible, extinguishable, sound:

A muffled sonorous sound, a wailing word is borne through
   the air for a moment,
Then blank and gone and still, and utterly lost.   (3:717).

It is not, of course, the actual decay of the English language that Whitman fears, but the failure to shore words against the ruin of the American memory of the dead. Of this emotion was born one of the most haunting, and haunted, of his late poems, "A Twilight Song." It takes its rise not only from memories of the war in general, but, with poignant particularity, from Whitman's still inconsolable grief for "the countless buried unknown soldiers, / Of the vacant names, as unindented air's and sea's—the unreturn'd" (3:742). In the face of life's unspeakable atrocities, poets, not unnaturally, still find a consolation in words. "I write it out in a verse," says Yeats, taking notable comfort from the naming by name of the Easter Rising dead, and it is the denial to unknown warriors of this final rite of identity, which would be a dignified rite of passage from one world to the next, that wounds Whitman into writing "A Twilight Song." The poem is his attempt to fill in "the vacant names," to indent them in matter more pertinent and permanent than air and sea. In his memory they are returned:

> (Even here in my room-shadows and half-lights in the
>   noiseless flickering flames,
> Again I see the stalwart ranks on-filing, rising—I hear the
>   rhythmic tramp of the armies;)
> You million unwrit names all, all—you dark bequest from all
>   the war,
> A special verse for you—a flash of duty long neglected—your
>   mystic roll strangely gather'd here.
> Each name recall'd by me from out the darkness and
>   death's ashes,
> Henceforth to be, deep, deep within my heart recording, for
>   many a future year,
> Your mystic roll entire of unknown names, or North
>   or South,
> Embalm'd with love in this twilight song.   (3:742–743)

After reading this piece in the *Century* magazine, where it first appeared, a contemporary perceptively remarked "that Whitman was evidently more moved by war subjects than any others." Understandably enough Whitman demurred.[40] He even explained to Traubel that the piece was "not formidable—it is merely a song of memory of dead soldiers—Oh! the many! many! many!—unknown."[41] But the final emotional exclamation unmistakably gave the lie to his affected unconcern about what he had claimed was "merely a song."

"A Twilight Song" is Whitman's last substantial attempt to exercise his memory in order to bring the forgotten dead of the Civil War to the unconcerned attention of the living. The circumstances that turned the prophet into an embalmer are spelled out in the late preface to *Goodbye My Fancy*, where Whitman writes of a war "back there," far distant from a present which is wholly unappreciative of "these hecatombs of battle-dead." And "of those times," he defiantly concedes, "this whole book is indeed finally but a reminiscent memorial from thence by me to you" (2:738).

But such was the self-rectifying balance of optimism in Whitman's temperament that the melancholy memorializer was to the last reassured by the historian of the "future-founding" past. "Only that historian," wrote Walter Benjamin, "will have the gift of fanning the spark of hope in the past who is firmly convinced that *even the dead* will not be safe from the enemy if he wins."[42] Saving the dead from the enemy was certainly an obligation, and it became almost an obsession for the later Whitman; which is why, by drawing on personal memory, he sought repeatedly to bring sparks of hope out of the past to kindle the present and illuminate the future.

THE TRAUMAS of memory and the obligations of memory: Lincoln's death, as the war drew to its close, stirred up feelings of both kinds in Whitman, and it was out of them that he composed the greatest of all his "mortal lullabies of pain":

> When lilacs last in the door-yard bloom'd,
> And the great star early droop'd in the western sky in
>   the night,
> I mourn'd—and yet shall mourn with
>   ever-returning spring.   (2:529)

It begins with this delicate emphasis on mourning as an exercise of memory which, as he put it in a much later elegy, is also a form of faithfulness: "Then after burying, mourning the dead (Faithful to them found or unfound, forgetting not, bearing the past, here new musing)" (3:744). The association of mourning with faithfulness leads, however, to a psychological problem well known to Victorian England (most notoriously to Victoria herself) and equally familiar to "Victorian" America; the dilemma that to cease mourning comes to appear to the bereaved as a form of unfaithfulness, an abandonment of the departed. This was a problem acutely felt by Whitman, as we have already seen, in relation to the dead of the war—particularly the "unfound" dead—and it accounts for important features of the opening lines of the poem.

In particular, it explains Whitman's emphasis on a mourning which is guaranteed perpetuation: "I mourn'd . . . and yet shall mourn with ever-returning spring." That line relies not on the shrill and vulnerable "will" of determined personal endeavor, but on the quietly ineluctable "shall" of nature's own dictation. The natural world has been made the custodian and guarantor of a grief which will return as surely, and as regularly, as the lilacs bloom. Whitman places his faith (and his faithfulness) not in himself and his own feelings, but in the strange constancies of the lilac and the star, which are proof against what Wyatt, long before, had called the "strange fashion of forsaking."

> O ever-returning spring! trinity sure to me you bring;
> Lilac blooming perennial, and drooping star in the west,
> And thought of him I love. (2:529)

In the spring landscape the picture of the mourning mind will perennially revive. But the corollary is that grief is controlled and limited by being localized—by being guaranteed the location of a place in time, its due season. The resulting emotional balance is prophesied in the beautiful symmetry of a single poetic line: "I mourn'd . . . and yet shall mourn with ever-returning spring."

Readers of the poem have always, and properly, responded to the seemingly inexhaustible symbolic power of the lilacs. And yet, if Whitman's later note on the subject is to be credited, it was as metonymy rather than as metaphor that he himself read them: "I remember where I was stopping at the time, the season being advanced, there were many lilacs in full bloom. By one of those caprices that enter and give tinge to events without being at all a part of them, I find myself always reminded of the great tragedy of that day by the sight and odor of these blossoms. It never fails" (2:503). It seems particularly perverse of Whitman to deny the obvious metaphorical implications of the lilacs, since earlier in the same passage he had admitted that for him Lincoln's assassination as the spring was flowering signified the tragic marring of the most propitious of occasions—the concluding of the Four Years War. But there is more than perversity at work here. What Whitman wanted to establish was that it was the death of Lincoln that had given to the lilacs their distinctive color of loving memory, as surely as it was (according to myth and to poetry) the death of Adonis that had once and for all produced the purple anemone. The lilacs can function for Whitman in this respect as a welcome synecdoche of the whole American landscape, which in turn serves as a trope for the American people. In the intensely private, personal miracle of the lilacs, the postwar Whitman is to find the public faith to preserve him from the "malady of the quotidian."

The symptoms of this malady are everywhere apparent in the midst of Whitman's protestations of his healthy confidence that postwar America would indeed remember in its practice the pain and sacrifice to which it owed its existence. It was difficult to discover in the mundane busyness of the civilian population signs that the American people had been transfigured by war, and so Whitman habitually preferred the trope of a transformed landscape: "To the leaven'd soil they trod calling I sing for the last" (2:556). "When Lilacs" is fertile in variations on this trope, and begins, as we have seen, with a particularly poignant personal variation on the theme. The lilacs themselves, and by extension the whole landscape of the American spring, has been changed, changed utterly and irrevocably, for Whitman himself.

He wrote the poem within a couple of months of Lincoln's assassination, long before his confidence that his mourning would prove lilac-perennial could be put to the actual test of time. But it eventually survived that test triumphantly. Appropriately enough, one of the best and most beautiful of his postwar poems turned out to be a "Warble for Lilac-Time," first published in 1871. Throughout, the emphasis is on the lilac's unique capacity to remind Whitman simultaneously of life and of death, and of the internal connection between them. With all his perception safely grounded in, and controlled by, this knowledge—an explicit knowledge of death, and an implicit acknowledgement of Lincoln and the Civil War dead—Whitman proceeds to gather his emotionally freighted souvenirs of spring: "The tranquil sunny haze, the clinging smoke, the vapor, / Spiritual, airy insects, humming on gossamer wings, / Shimmer of waters with fish in them, the cerulean above" (3:600). Armed and fortified by these experiences, and confessing a "restlessness after I know not what," Whitman unloosens his feelings:

> —Gathering these hints, the preludes—the blue sky, the grass,
> the morning drops of dew,
> (With additional songs—every spring will I now strike up
> additional songs,

Nor ever again forget, these tender days, the chants of Death
  as well as Life;)
The lilac-scent, the bushes and the dark green,
  heart-shaped leaves,
Wood violets, the little delicate pale blossoms
  called innocence,
Samples and sorts not for themselves alone, but for
  their atmosphere,
To tally, drench'd with them, tested by them,
Cities and artificial life, and all their sights and scenes,
My mind henceforth, and all its meditations—my recitatives,
My land, my age, my race, for once to serve in songs,
(Sprouts, tokens ever of death indeed the same as life,)
To grace the bush I love—to sing with the birds,
A warble for joy of Lilac-time.   (3:601)

Why on earth, one can only wonder, are these marvelously poignant lines not better known? It is after all a passage brimming with emotion—or rather, with many emotions—and the reference to "When Lilacs" is of course central to them all: "the lilac-scent, the bushes" with "dark green, heart-shaped leaves." For Whitman personally the memory of Lincoln's death, and all the deaths that preceded it, has paradoxically restored to him a sense of the creation's perennially innocent renewal of itself in beauty: "the morning drops of dew . . . Wood violets, the little delicate blossoms called innocence." The violets, it will be remembered, "peep'd from the ground" in "When Lilacs," and spotted "the gray debris." And Whitman's response to the "morning drops" is very similar to that of another soldier poet, Edward Thomas, who wrote of how, at reveille, troops woke to "the dew that covers / The print of last night's lovers," and to "this earth new-born."[43]

But when he then tries to bring contemporary life to the test of these revelations, it is clear that the lilacs on the one hand, and "cities and artificial life" on the other, don't "tally" at all. It was to be Whitman's bitterly repeated postwar experience that his land, his age, his race did not so much "grace" as disgrace "the bush I love." And never again would his birdsong be the same.

From 1879 onward, whenever health and circumstances permitted, Whitman kept the day of April 14 sacred to the memory of Lincoln, never failing to mark the occasion with a public lecture, at which he usually spoke from behind a table decorated with lilacs. Even when old, ailing, and scarcely able to walk, he insisted on performing this ritual as if his very life depended on it (as in a way no doubt it did): "I feel pledged to it—not to you but to myself . . . I hope to be identified with the man Lincoln, with his crowded, eventful years— with America as shadowed forth into those abysms of circumstances. It is a great welling up of my emotional sense: I am commanded by it: only a severe chastisement could hold me from my contract."[44]

In circumstances such as this, the word "memory," as ordinarily used, seemed to him inadequate, as he explained to Traubel when talking not about Lincoln but about his dead friend William O'Connor and his wife. They "occupy a large place in my memory—not in my *memory* alone, but in that larger life—my emotional, sympathetic, poetic, life—which has most importantly commanded me."[45] "Memory" in this larger, augmented sense, was always what "commanded" Whitman when commemorating Lincoln. And it was the gift of this memory (not only for the President himself, but for "his crowded, eventful years" of war) that, as Whitman's lecture makes clear, he believed Lincoln had bestowed, through the manner and occasion of his death, on the nation. It is an astonishing lecture, which demands close attention. From the outset, Whitman contrasts the real, solemn drama of the assassination of Lincoln ("the leading actor in the stormiest drama known to real history's stage") with the silly posturings of the actors on the theater stage. But it is not the actual incident of the assassination itself that constitutes the authentic drama; rather, it is the expressive power of the event within its historical setting:

> The immeasurable value and meaning of that whole tragedy lies, to me, in senses finally dearest to a nation, (and here all our own)—the imaginative and artistic senses—the literary and dramatic ones. Not in any common or low meaning of those terms, but a meaning precious to the race, and to every age. A long and varied series of contradictory events arrives at last at its highest poetic, single, central, pictorial denouement. The whole involved, baffling, multiform, whirl of the secession period comes to a head, and is gather'd in one brief flash of lightning–illumination—one simple, fierce deed. Its sharp culmination, and as it were solution, of so many bloody and angry problems, illustrates

those climax-moments on the stage of universal Time, where the historic Muse at one entrance, and the tragic Muse at the other, suddenly ringing down the curtain, close an immense act in the long drama of creative thought, and give it radiation, tableau, stranger than fiction.   (2:507–508)

The death of Lincoln is, then, the artistic masterpiece of Clio, a distinctively American tragedy which affords the people a unique experience of their historical and historic identity. It is the last, and infinitely the greatest of those tableaux which the war had offered Whitman, and which he reconstituted as poetry in *Drum Taps*. But when he came to deal in poetry with this culminating death, it was not with the "tableau" of the actual assassination that he dealt, but with the emotional aftermath of that tableau—its "radiation."

It is indeed Clio—the Clio that Whitman denied could ever be content with being the muse of the mere historian—who is the muse of important sections of "When Lilacs Last in the Dooryard Bloom'd." The stately ceremoniousness of the poetry is, in Charles Tomlinsons's words, a "style [which] speaks what was seen," and "not a voice / Wearing a ruff,"[46] because Whitman actually saw the ordinary human and natural world of America, during the period immediately following the murder, assume the elevated dignity of ritual and portent, through the inspiration of the great historical event which itself "condensed a Nationality." The land, at least temporarily, incarnated Lincoln (and his soldiers) as Lincoln had incarnated it. Even Whitman's otherwise overmastering grief in the second section respects, in its stylized expression, the somber theatrical decorum of the occasion.

All the Muses were of course the daughters of Memory, but Whitman takes the unconventional step of also making Clio the *mother* of Mnemosyne, since she has produced a "special event, incisive enough to mark with deepest cut and mnemonize, this turbulent nineteenth-century of ours" (2:509). The poet of "When Lilacs" seeks to become the father, as Clio is the mother, of national memory. In so doing he tacitly admits his old fear that American history in the careering postwar period would prove too unruly for Clio to handle alone; and that by the end of the century the national character would have no memory, and bear no sign, of its beginning in the years of war. If so, then his poem might still have the power to remind the American people of what once, in mourning Lincoln, they had remembered.

Gathering in memory of Lincoln, the whole of the United States stands revealed to itself as reunited by his war. But the "union welded in blood" needs to be even further secured by the "cement of a death" (*Prose Works*, 2:508)—which is what that slow progress of the coffin across half a continent partly signifies in the poem. Not only does it bind the living together, most important of all for Whitman it binds the living to the dead—to *all* of the dead, as Whitman emphasizes. It reveals the soil of America to be now "leavened soil." What the death of Lincoln had done to Whitman's lilacs, this cortege does to the breast of the whole land: it transforms a continent into the sorrowing landscape of memory, which will eventually, later in the poem, with Whitman's help, become a great, growing joyous garden of remembrance.

This, surely, is the meaning of the marvelous passage where Whitman chooses "pictures" to decorate the walls of Lincoln's tomb. He attempts to build a conventional sepulcher but is defeated by "the scenes of life" that lead him back out to life itself: "Lo! body and soul! this land! / . . . The varied and ample land" (2:534). This tomb is a mausoleum without walls. The "burial house" is no tomb but is the American land itself, adorned as it is with "pictures of growing spring, and farms, and homes," and simultaneously the poem itself becomes not a memorial but a vista. So he avoids the claustrophobia, and the claustrophobic sense of finality with which, in "Hush'd Be the Camps Today," another elegy for Lincoln, he responded to the burial: "Sing, to the lower'd coffin there; / Sing, with the shovel'd clods that fill the grave—a verse, / For the heavy hearts of soldiers" (2:523). In the later version these lines assumed an even grimmer aspect, with their reference to the "invaulting" of the coffin, and the "clos[ing] of the doors of earth upon him" (2:523).

As an elegy which is, in many ways, a criticism of the genre of elegy, "When Lilacs" is, of course, full of moments when established conventions metamorphose into radically new practices implying a new view of death. The cornucopia of spring blossoms and green branches which are poured on the coffin, revises in the very act of recalling, the traditional ritual of placing, as for example in Collins's poetry, fresh flowers on the corpse "to waste and wither in their prime." Yet if there is, throughout the poem, a prejudice against indulging in the traditional melancholy practice and practices of mourning, it is nevertheless through admitting his grief that Whitman wins his way to joy.

Lincoln's death seems to have awakened two equally strong, but diametrically opposed feelings in Whitman. There was, probably first, the anguished feeling that Lincoln had been killed in the very spring-time of the "new" nation's life; and there was, probably second, the feeling that by dying, even more than by living, Lincoln might contribute to that spring growth, might even be able to advance the spring into the settled maturity of summer. The seasonal image is appropriate because it is used by Whitman himself in the poem. Indeed, in one important section (the fifth) he is able to contain both these emotions within one carefully enigmatic description of the spring land through which the corpse travels in its coffin. In fact the section is so structured as to send us, the readers, traveling hopefully "over the breast of spring," before the grotesque realization comes that we are in truth following a corpse. But there is also, in passing, the other realization that all of this life has sprung up out of death—"Passing the yellow-spear'd wheat, every grain from its shroud in the dark-brown fields uprising" (2:530). Moreover, when rereading the poem it is natural to bring to "the violets [peeping] from the ground, spotting the gray debris," a memory of the later mention of the "debris and debris of all the slain soldiers of the war" (2:539), and so to discover everywhere in Whitman's response to the spring's innocence his unacknowledged experience of carnage.

It was after all in the very month of Lincoln's death, April 1865, that Whitman responded to the spring by writing the following fragment of verse, which was never published, probably because it was overtaken by events and became transposed into a passage from the great elegy:

> I heard
>   The blue birds singing
> I saw the yellowish green where it covered the willows
> I saw the eternal grass springing up
> The light of the sun on the bay—the ships, dressed with
> I saw on the ships the profusion of colors
> I knew of the fete, the feasting
> —Then I turned aside & mused on the unknown dead
> I thought of the unrecorded, the heroes so sweet & the tender

The young men
The returned—but where the unreturned
I thought of the unreturned, the sons of the mothers.[47]

There, too, as in the elegy, the relationship between the dead and burgeoning life is profoundly equivocal—Whitman being uncertain whether the renewal of life is a callous affront to the dead, or whether in it they are themselves, after a fashion, reborn.

Then, in the next two sections of "When Lilacs," these two strands of feeling, of loss and of hope, are more clearly separated out. The sixth section moves into "dirge" before culminating in the sprig of lilac which is as much a refusal to mourn as it is a token of Whitman's loss, and the seventh takes up some of the very phrases and gestures of sorrow of the preceding section, in order to translate them into joy. The dirges that were poured around the coffin are replaced by the roses, lilies, and above all the lilacs which "with loaded arms I come, pouring for you, / For you, and the coffins of all of you, O death" (2:531–532). The reason for Whitman's excursion into this sudden emotional parenthesis is fascinating to note, because it shows how complex and many are Whitman's allegiances of memory in "When Lilacs." He interrupts his mourning for Lincoln in order to assure the other (jealous?) dead that they are not forgotten; that they, too, are all included. And as the conclusion of the poem clearly shows, he has the slaughtered soldiers very particularly in mind.

Throughout the poem, Whitman is careful to speak not of his emotions, but of the different calls made *upon* his emotions by lilacs, star, and bird. This is not simply a sophisticated literary or psychological device; it actually reflects the pull on Whitman of different and sometimes conflicting voices of obligation. The eighth section is where, in the approach of the star, Whitman begins to recognize Lincoln's need and claim to be remembered—not only in the private obsequies of the lilac, or the brief pageant of state funeral, but in a broader, more permanent way. No longer associated simply with raw grief, the star is remembered by Whitman as having singled him out, even before the event, for some obscurely intimate reason that only now can he begin to divine. In the lustrous star Lincoln the man gently beseeches to be singled out from the anonymous coffins of death and to be remembered: and in reply Whitman is moved to construct and to adorn that private burial house which, as has been seen, turns in the process into the whole public domain of America.

The foregrounding of Lincoln in this way may well have taken place against the background of Whitman's previous association of the evening star with the multitudinous dead. In a note, written on February 28, 1865, in the same, small, white hospital notebook which he later used for notes on Lincoln's death, Whitman recorded the following scene: "the brilliant silver moon, & close by it the evening star—of intoxicating softness, largeness & beauty—a night of nights, the air so fresh &—the crowds of the avenue, the lights beaming, the windows—approach the Capitol—the slits in the dome—rising out of the dark shadow—& the slain lit up."[48] There the stark juxtaposition of the living and the dead, with the implied indifference of the former to the fate of the latter, is reminiscent of that extraordinary scene in *Little Dorrit* (book 2, chapter 1) where "the living travellers [think] little or nothing of the dead" who are in the next room.

In the seventh section Whitman had honored death with the carefully conjoined epithets "sane and Sacred," while postponing the full exploration in chant of his complex instinct so to address it. As bestowed upon death in its original context (where it is neighbor to the phrase "fresh as the morning") the title suggests that in its delicately fertile office, death rejuvenates life by cleansing it. But when death is next addressed in similar terms (in section 14) the emphasis now falls instead on death's great mercies of annihilation. Although the advent hymn of the hermit thrush certainly soars in dark-edged joy to rapturous praise, it should not be forgotten that it is still a "reedy song, / Loud human song, with voice of uttermost woe":

> I bring thee a song that when thou must indeed come,
>   come unfalteringly.
>
> Approach, encompassing Death—strong Deliveress!
> When it is so—when thou has taken them, I joyously sing
>   the dead.   (2:536)

The quickly dead are there very clearly, and pointedly, distinguished from the slowly dying. If the song in its entirety is more than an invitation to death—if it is a passionate invocation, a pressing petition, even a desperate courtship—then that is because Whitman is trying to effect a transition from life to death which will be so

mercifully abrupt as virtually to eliminate the grim interlude of pro-
tracted suffering. So mesmerized have critics been by the obvious
parallels between this song and that of the bird in "Out of the Cradle"
that they have usually failed to consider the possibility that the truly
revealing analogue (and emotional source) of this passage may be
found elsewhere, in "The Wound-Dresser":

> On, on I go,—(open, doors of time! open, hospital doors!)
> The crush'd head I dress, (poor crazed hand, tear not the
>   bandage away;)
> The neck of the cavalry-man, with the bullet through and
>   through, I examine;
> Hard the breathing rattles, quite glazed already the eye, yet life
>   struggles hard;
> (Come, sweet death! be persuaded, O beautiful death!
> In mercy come quickly.   (2:481)

No wonder Whitman sets to calling easeful death by many a soft
name in "When Lilacs." Yet behind the courtesies and the impassioned compliments of the song, lies not only the raw pressure of
painful memories, but also the solace of other memories from the
same source; "one finds, as I have the past year, that our feelings &
imaginations make a thousand times too much of the whole matter—
Of the many I have seen die, or known of, the past year, I have not
seen or heard of *one* who met death with any terror."[49] On both counts
the path down to the swamp may be said to have passed directly
through the hospitals.

This song is at once the greatest of Whitman's "mortal lullabies
of pain," and a carol of joy to the "dark mother," and as such it
initiates and controls a very important psychological process. By
approaching death from the direction of the suffering lives for which
it is a welcome release, he has enabled himself to approach that other,
previously unthinkable and unspeakable, subject of his poem, the
dead soldiers, without mental revulsion. Those repressed memories,
which were perhaps the subconscious raison d'être of the poem, its
ghostly subtext as it were, can now be released, first as nightmare
and then as healing dreams. Protected from pain by his song, which
sustains and directs him, Whitman permits himself those very vistas
of war which he had so scrupulously avoided during wartime: "my

sight that was bound in my eyes unclosed, / As to long panoramas of visions. / I saw the vision of armies . . ." (2:538).

The notion of sight having been bound in the eyes—as if the eyes had been prevented from telling the brain what they had recorded, and so had themselves been actually deprived of the active power of seeing, which comes only when the ocular organs act as the mind's eye—is an astonishing one. And this remarkable image for the psychological mechanism of repression is reinforced by another word of equal psychological percipience: "unclosed." It perfectly suggests the relief that follows the effort of negating the mind's determined negativeness.

But there can, of course, be no final solution or resolution of Whitman's acute emotional difficulties. "Ashes of Soldiers" shows signs of his continuing struggle with those morbid elements war had introduced into his imagination. His effort there is again to transform the offensive stench rising from the battlefields into perfume. Translated into the grim prose of psychological realities, this means that, his sensibility having been violated by the war's horrors, he tries to heal it by believing that the slaughtered soldiers, who had themselves been animated by patriotic love, will give rise in their death to an answering love on the part of the living; a love which will constitute both a recognition and a justification of their sacrifice. Love "solve[s] all, fructif[ies] all with the last chemistry," so as to "make all wholesome" (2:512). And yet the noisome bodies of the dehumanized dead were still to be found lying inertly at the bottom of his mind to the very end of his life, as tortured lines from the "Preface Note to Second Annexe" (1891) testify: "those hot, sad, wrenching times—the army volunteers, all States,—or North or South—the wounded, suffering, dying—the exhausting, sweating summers, marches, battles, carnage—those trenches hurriedly heap'd by the corpse-thousands, mainly unknown" (2:738).

The great concluding verse paragraph of "When Lilacs" makes it clear that memory is what has always been at issue in this poem: "Yet each I keep, and all; retrievements out of the night" (2:539). The phrases are capacious enough, in their suggestiveness, to include those several different aspects of memory with which Whitman has been so painfully concerned, and to recognize the many ways in which his seminal images have ministered to the manifold needs of memory. Lilac, star, and song are now his keepsakes. In preserving for him the vividness and somber richness of his slow initiation into the life-illuminating mysteries of death, they continue to allow him to recall, to admit, the slain dead to mind, without the fear of being mentally prostrated. In that sense they serve not only as keepsakes, but also as keepsafes—keeping Whitman safe from the emotional anarchy with which such memories used to threaten him. At the same time, they stand as, and for, a different kind of security. They jointly secure a future for the dead in Whitman's memory, securing him (and them) against the treacheries of time:

> Comrades mine, and I in the midst, and their memory ever I
>   keep—for the dead I loved so well;
> For the sweetest, wisest soul of all my days and lands . . . and
>   this for his dear sake;
> Lilac and star and bird, twined with the chant of my soul,
> With the holders holding my hand, nearing the call of
>   the bird,
> There in the fragrant pines, and the cedars dusk
>   and dim.   (2:539)

Of course the strength of these "twined" images is the strength of the integrated psychological experience for which they now stand. And at the very point where his experience finally became integrated—down there in the swamp—Whitman, as these lines for the first time so movingly reveal, discovered the faces of his "comrades" in those strange figures of death who walked each side of him, "and I in the midst, and their memory ever I keep—for the dead I loved so well." The "dead" is, in one sense, the dead person of Lincoln. But in another sense the word represents, as does Lincoln himself in this poem, *all* the dead whom Whitman had, as he here so artlessly admits, "loved so well." In "When Lilacs Last in the Dooryard Bloom'd" their memory is, as the later version firmly has it, "ever to keep."

9 ✑ My Book and the War Are One

WHEN IN 1888 he appended a short note to his *Complete Poems and Prose*, Whitman took advantage of the opportunity to present his lifetime's work to "some reader of a far-off future age" as specifically "a missive sent from Abraham Lincoln's fateful age" (2:733). As he speaks of himself as one who "came on the stage too late for personally knowing much of even the lingering Revolutionary worthies—the men of '76," it immediately appears that his frustrated wish to have been in on the legendary beginnings of the original American experiment is now to some extent satisfied by his treating the Civil War, in which after all he had so memorably participated, as itself a beginning—not of America per se of course, but of the modern democratic union of states. This was the creation myth Whitman propounded as the real meaning of events he was convinced were in need of rescue from "that false and distant thing," "that fetish," history. And during the last twenty-five years of his life a great deal of his energy went into constructing and publicizing this saving national legend.

Interestingly enough, it was his encounter, as a young man, with a few remaining veterans of the War of Independence, "The Last of the Sacred Army," that had first alerted him, in the forties, to the need to foster certain national memories. It was a traumatic shock for him to realize that the last of young America's living links with its founding fathers was about to be severed, and Whitman returned repeatedly to the theme in his editorials, over a period of years, in an obviously disturbed state of mind. On December 18, 1846, he regretted the loss of another of these veterans, "for while they are with us, the scenes of the Liberty-birth are to our mind as vivid as the light . . . often, with our whole heart, have we thanked God that we were vouchsafed this communion with these men—the instruments wherewith He built up this freest nation of the earth." Their passing, he felt, left America vulnerably exposed, orphaned in effect: "the only mementos left to Americans of their Freedom's battle-days, will be History and our blessed Institutions."[1] Eventually his awareness of this danger was to be partly what spurred him into song.

In another of these editorials he admitted that "we love to seize these occasions of awakening the purest patriotism—the more needed in the too-much selfishness of political contests, now."[2] As progressive Brooklyn, irreproachably active in its pursuit of wealth, either grubbed up or covered over the dead bones of the prison ship martyrs, Whitman did not know whether to laugh or to cry—whether to exult at this new manifestation of the old democratic spirit, or to mourn nervously the passing of the heroic age. So when a proposal was made to clear away the monument to Captain James Laurence, hero of an Anglo-American skirmish of 1813, he wrote: "we confess, for our part, to a kind of horror at any thing that seems like disturbing the ashes, or the mortal resting place, of the departed."[3] "Nothing more becomes a nation," he wrote in the *Democratic Review* in 1842, "than paying its choicest honors to the memory of those who have fought for it or labored for its good . . . No: it is well that the benefactors of a state be so kept alive in memory and in song, when their bones are mouldering."[4] Following the Civil War Whitman resolved to make his own body of poems, retrospectively where necessary, into precisely such enduring songs of commemoration. *Leaves of Grass* became a monumental work, designed to rivet wayward America's attention to "that time of glory."[5]

Already in the forties, when he tried to plant "the bright example" of the dead independence fighters "in the firm foundation of the nation's love,"[6] Whitman turned instinctively to poetry to accomplish his purpose. His ode, to be sung to "The Star Spangled Banner," spoke of American earth "sanctified" by the soldiers' blood, and asserted that "In memory still / We have placed our hearts, and embalmed there forever! / The battle, the prison-ship martyrs and hill."[7] Similarly, in the gloomy crisis of 1861, he sought reassurance in "The Centenarian's Story"—a poem in which a "volunteer of 1861–2" is inspired by the ancient's visionary recall of Washington and his troops.

As his story ends, the narrator feels that "the past and present have interchanged" and experiences himself as "connector," both of present with past, and of present with what the past guarantees will be "a great future" (2:473). Having had the person of Washington made so vivid to him, Whitman, in the person of the narrator, determines to "preserve that look as it beam'd on yon rivers of Brooklyn" (2:474). It is a suggestive sentence. "Look" here means both the expression on Washington's face, and his glance—the way he looked at Brooklyn and the America beyond, because what Whitman wants to preserve, and to make his own, is Washington's vision of America. For Whitman (and all modern Americans) this means seeing the sacrifice on which their modern democracy was erected: "Ah, hills and slopes of Brooklyn, I perceive you are more valuable than your owners supposed; / . . . Encampments new! in the midst of you stands an encampment very old, / Stands forever the camp of the dead brigade" (2:474).[8]

If Whitman went into the war with his eyes firmly fixed on the preservative sight of that "dead brigade," the emblem of Washington's America, then of course he came out of the war with that vision at once vindicated and somberly updated. Wherever he looked he now saw the "camps of green" (2:508), and the "mystic army" of the dead. Although he himself could never lose sight of what he had recently seen, his task was to "preserve that look" for the rest of America. He had to be the poet as "connector," effecting an "interchange" between past and present.

There are even poems where, in pursuit of this aim, he himself assumed a "centenarian's" role—becoming, in "The Wound-Dresser," an "old man coming among new face," and identifying, in "The Dying Veteran," with "a queer old savage man, a fighter under Washington himself" (3:722). But, of course, his governing strategy was ultimately far more ambitious: it was to turn *Leaves of Grass* itself into a veteran's testimony, into a centenarian's song, as it were. The lengths to which he was prepared to go in order to achieve this—in order to convert the desultory events of a sometimes disobliging past into this supreme fiction—can be gauged from the description he offers of his work as "a missive sent from Abraham Lincoln's fateful age." It is a remark which falls demonstrably short of the actual, unsatisfactory, historical truth, since most of Whitman's poetry, including practically all his greatest poems, was already written and published before Lincoln had come either to his personal attention or to public eminence. This is a historical discrepancy Whitman could not actually deny. But he could, and did, try sometimes to blur the unfortunate fact in the higher interests of an ideal view of personal and national history which, during his last years, he was particularly concerned *Leaves of Grass* as a whole should embody. The work of revising his poems accordingly became for Whitman a historical mission of historic importance, and it began with the adjustments he started to make, even before the war had properly ended, to his prewar poetry.

What he chose in the process to remove from *Leaves of Grass* can sometimes be as eloquently and as poignantly expressive of his hospital experiences as what, in an attempt to identify himself totally with them, he decided to add. From the 1860 version of "So Long," for instance, he drained all the emotion specifically belonging to what later he touchingly called "the poems of the morning" (*Prose Works*, 2:727). Originally one resonant line had read: "I remember I said to myself at the winter-close, before my leaves sprang at all, that I would become a candid and unloosed summer-poet" (2:448). Acting under the sobering influence of subsequent circumstances, Whitman cut this, and with it all mention of a summer world, proceeding instead to acknowledge the solemn new dimensions his life had acquired: "I have sung the body and the soul, war and peace have I sung, and the songs of life and death" (2:449). Meanwhile, balanced against this example of the way war had somewhat abated the younger Whitman's exuberance, are signs of a determinedly burgeoning confidence in the future, based now supposedly not, as previously, on his own solitary, visionary undertakings, but on what he has been privileged to see, in the interim, of his fellow men:

> Myself unknowing, my commission obeying, to question it
>   never daring,
> To ages and ages yet the growth of the seed leaving,
> To troops out of the war arising, they the tasks I have
>   set promulging.   (2:451)

The 1860 version of that last line had been infinitely lonelier, for all the enforced self-sufficiency of Whitman's then bardic prognostications: "To ages, and ages yet, the growth of the seed leaving, / To troops out of me rising—they the tasks I have set promulging" (2:451).

However minor they may be, these changes, like all the others originally proposed by Whitman in his *Blue Book*, testify to that general reluctance, so deeply characteristic of his later years, to let bygones be bygones, to leave the poetry he had written in the past still at liberty to speak, uncensored and unrevised, for the different person he once had been. He even tried to alter parts of that Ur-poem of the early *Leaves of Grass*, "Song of Myself," in the light of his war service. But the emotions that sometimes became implicated in the attempt tended to complicate matters intensely:

> The real or fancied indifference by some man or woman
>   I love,
> The sickness of one of my folks or of myself, or ill-doing or
>   loss or lack of money, or depressions or exaltations,
> Battles, the horrors of fratricidal war, the fever of doubtful
>   news, the deaths of my friends, mortally wounded,
>   fitful events;
> These come to me days and nights and go from me again,
> But they are not the Me myself.[9]

This version of the familiar passage never officially saw the light of day. After penciling it in the margins of his *Blue Book*, Whitman was overcome by second thoughts and struck out that mention of "the deaths of my friends, mortally wounded." Perhaps it was his instinct for public relations, his constant sensitivity to the image he was projecting, that saved him from thus appearing callous. More likely he found that the tender state of his feelings simply would not allow him to carry off such an outrageous rhetorical flourish after all. He may very well have attempted this verbal maneuver in the first place only as a psychological ploy, since the most familiar of the defensive mechanisms to which we commonly resort under stress is that of shutting down the emotions, so as to maintain an inner, "unnatural," detachment. Whitman may consequently have tried to avail himself of an existing passage in "Song of Myself" which seemed to allow, and even to encourage, him to take that sort of self-pro-tective attitude toward circumstances that were threatening to destroy his very integrity as an individual, only to find that he could not after all convincingly dissociate himself from his harrowing wartime experiences.

Elsewhere, it was upon these very same painful experiences that Whitman drew in order to add emotional depth to a passage which had previously been rather theoretical and shallow:

> With music strong I come, with my cornets, and my drums,
> I play not marches for victors only—I play great marches for
> conquered and slain persons
> . . . I beat and pound for the dead,
> I blow through my embouchures my loudest and gayest
> for them.[10]

To achieve these accents of sincerity he had first to remove from the original version those touches of bombast that betrayed his lack of the experiences to which he so glibly laid claim. Out went references to "hero marches," either for victors or slain, along with the easy bravado of "triumphant drums" for the dead. The result is the urgent tension in the tautened sentence: "I beat and pound for the dead" (is there, one wonders, a sidelong glance here at "Beat! Beat! Drums," the poem in which he had called the living to arms at the outbreak of war?). There is also a moving reliance on the "music strong" not only of literal cornets and drums, but "my cornets and my drums," which are clearly those of Whitman's own verse. He settled initially on a different adjective for distinguishing this music, choosing to maintain, with reference to his own wartime transformation, that it was "with music new" he came. But he was psychologically in need of receiving much more from his music than this, if it was to bear the strain of his recent encounters with death, and so it was upon "music strong" he eventually settled, as indeed it was upon the strength of his poetry's music that he came to rely.

Precisely because the *Blue Book* revisions were produced under the influence of such very recent events, they occasionally afford fascinating glimpses of the ways Whitman was finding for bringing his feelings under better control. He had presciently imagined, in the prewar "Song of Myself," what it must be like to participate in battle (in this case recalling an old-time naval exchange), and to hear "the hiss of the surgeon's knife, the gnawing teeth of his saw, / Wheeze, cluck, swash of falling blood, short wild scream, and long dull tapering groan" (1:58). So affected had he then been by this vividly constructed fictional scene, that he had broken off, exclaiming "O Christ! This is mastering me! / Through the conquered doors they crowd. I am possessed" (1:58). Not surprisingly, this was a passage with which he was able to identify with almost uncanny directness when he returned to it for revision purposes during his hospital service. Yet in his later response there seems also to have been a strong measure both of personal and of poetic opportunism. On the one hand he saw his chance to add the weight and authenticity of wartime experience to those already potent lines, while on the other he took advantage of the established power which allowed the existing poetry to speak his newly acquired feelings for him; so relieving himself of the painful necessity of tapping his still raw emotions directly:

> Oh Christ! This is mastering me!
> Through the conquered doors they crowd. I am possessed . . .
> The days I live, the passions immense,
> The bloody vindictive battles, with thousands falling, or
>   throes of peace or war,
> What powerful emotion present or past, all become mine and
>   me every one—and they are but little,
> I become as much more as I like.[11]

Although these revisions were not destined to survive into print, Whitman made sure elsewhere that his wartime credentials were indeed properly presented to the public in "Song of Myself":

> The soldier camp'd, or upon the march, is mine;
> On the night ere the pending battle, many seek me, and I do
>   not fail them;
> On the solemn night (it may be their last,) those that know
>   me, seek me.   (1:78)

This is one of the few, modest details left in the final published version of "Song of Myself" to bear witness to the assiduous attention the poem had received from Whitman toward the end of the war as part of his exercise of personal reassessment and re-presentation. For fuller public evidence, therefore, of the comprehensiveness of Whitman's wish, and the voraciousness of his need, to redefine himself at this time by taking very pointed account of his period in the hospitals, it is better to turn to "By Blue Ontario's Shore."[12] This is a piece that had in 1856 been constructed, not altogether satisfactorily, out of the 1855 preface, and in this case the wartime updating work is extensive, since it includes the addition of several complete sections, as well as many single lines and phrases. Some of the modifications are suggested, and sometimes rejected, in the *Blue Book* margins, while others were made at some later stage, but before the first postwar appearance of the poem on the printed page in the 1867 annex to *Leaves of Grass*. Most significant of all is Whitman's decision not only to alter the whole tenor of the piece, but to announce this at the outset by providing an introduction which makes it appear as if the whole work had originated in—had even been irresistibly dictated by—the war:

> As I wandered the Prairies alone or at night,
> As I mused these nights and days, and of peace restored and
>   the dead that return no more,
> A Phantom, gigantic, superb, with stern visage, arrested me,
> *Chant me a poem*, it said, *that breathes my native air alone,*
> Chant me a song of *the throes of Democracy*;
> Democracy, the destined conqueror—yet treacherous lip
>   smiles everywhere,
> And death and infidelity at every step.[13]

The lines capture several aspects of Whitman's disturbed postwar psychology. In particular, they register his dread awareness of the dead "that return no more," except to haunt him, until he manages to subsume their ghosts within the larger phantom presence of that reassuringly authoritative Spirit of America for whom he sings his cathartic song. This connection between the dead and the phantom is again made elsewhere in the *Blue Book*, when Whitman, drafting in pencil an early version of "Over the Carnage," includes the line, "Thus cried the Phantomic voice rising over the carnage, rising over the dead I in anguish mourn."[14] Private anguish is controlled by a providential view of national history, but for once the assumption of this elevated perspective does not automatically induce Olympian calm, as instead new anxieties appear concerning the threats to democracy. In the opening lines these threats are, of course, seen as powerless in the long term, since democracy is predestined to conquer. But in the next revision, a few lines later, there is no mistaking the raw accents of a discovered fear: "O mother! O sisters dear! / If we are lost, no victor else has destroy'd us; / It is by ourselves we go down to eternal night" (1:191). What surfaces here is the unsettling anxiety whose buried life in Whitman's postwar writing was briefly examined in the previous chapter. Self-betrayal might yet lead the States to self-destruction, in which case, as it went down "to eternal night," America would visit upon its dead soldiers a second more terrifying descent, this time into total oblivion.

One way of combating these fears was for Whitman to consign them to the recent past, by treating the late war as the decisive final engagement with the enemies of democracy, both North and South. This explains the otherwise uncharacteristic venom of his attack on the already conquered enemy, and the unseemly gloating over the defeated, found in the additional lines which became the seventh section of the augmented poem:

> . . . your foot on the neck of the menacing one, the scorner,
>   utterly crush'd beneath you;
> The menacing, arrogant one, that strode and advanced with
>   his senseless scorn, bearing the murderous knife;
> Lo! the wide swelling one, the braggart, that would yesterday
>   do so much!
> To-day a carrion dead and damn'd, the despised of all
>   the earth!
> An offal rank, to the dunghill maggots spurn'd.   (1:197)

This is the kind of pamphleteering rant to which Whitman not infrequently resorts when some of the more unpleasant facts of the American case penetrate his carefully nurtured protective faith and hurt him to the quick. Ineffectual and bombastic to the point of absurdity when taken out of its social and political context, when studied within that context such a diatribe assumes quite a plaintive and affecting air, as the record of Whitman's vulnerability to the outrages of profane history.

Emotion, then, runs high in some of these *Blue Book* revisions to the piece that became known as "By Blue Ontario's Shore,"—so much so that Whitman sometimes decided against making it public. "How dare these petty piddling little creatures write poems for America, for our armies, and the offspring begotten of them?"[15] he penciled in at one point, revealing in the process his desperate wish to have America identify itself totally and exclusively in the future with his own version of its wartime self. Associated with this effort to monopolize history was his construction, in poetry, of a mythic version of his own wartime self:

> . . . sped to the camps, and comrades found and accepted
>   from every State . . .
> (Upon this breast has many a dying soldier lean'd to breathe
>   his last,
> This arm, this hand, this voice, have nourish'd,
>   rais'd, restor'd,
> To life recalling many a prostrate form.   (1:205)

But most touching of all is the attempt to project himself in imagination beyond his limited wartime experiences, in order to endure, if only vicariously, the sights and sounds of actual battle. "Angry cloth I saw there leaping! / I stand again in the leaden rain, your flapping folds saluting" (1:200). The details that follow are rather stereotyped, literary, and melodramatic—until, that is, he comes to his great unavoidable subject, the dead:

> Now the corpses tumble curl'd upon the ground,
> Cold, cold in death, for precious life of you,
> Angry cloth I saw there leaping.   (1:201)

Whenever elsewhere he mentions the battlefield dead, he tends to see them in his horrified mind's eye as sprawled grotesquely on their backs. But here, in a poem that wants to represent the pains of war as the birth throes of democracy, the corpses assume a fetal position even as they tumble into the rigors of death and are seized by its cold rigidities.

As Whitman tries to provide his nation and himself with a new beginning in war, by furnishing his poem with a new opening, so by supplying it with a new conclusion does he try to secure the future for his prophetic vision. His would-be vaunting lines are nevertheless everywhere penetrated and deeply humanized by the humility of doubt: "I know not what these plots and deferments are for; / I know not fruition's success—but I know that through war and peace your work goes on, and must yet go on" (1:209). (In 1881 that phrase was changed to "war and crime".) Suddenly, Whitman is pierced by the devastating possibility that even his poetry may, after all, have been playing him false: "O my rapt song, my charm—mock me not!" (1:210). His temporary fear is that although the power to control and determine events may have been a prerogative of the bards of the past, it could yet be denied to the poets of the questionable American future. Concealed in his vatic language are very real, intelligent, prescient anxieties. "The War," he insists in 1871, "the war is over"; and when he repeats the sentence as if mesmerized by its implications, only two lines later, there can be no mistaking the misgivings that mingle with the exultation. War was one thing, peace is quite another, whose outcome is as yet undecided. "The slavery contest is settled— and the war is long over—yet do not those putrid conditions, too many of them, still exist? still result in diseases, fevers, wounds— not of war and army hospitals—but the wounds and diseases of peace?" (*Prose Works*, 2:430). Thus Whitman's call in 1867 is for "bards of the marching armies," and then in 1871 for

> bards of the latent armies—a million soldiers
>   waiting ever-ready,
> Bards towering like hills—(no more these dots, these pigmies,
>   these little pipping straws, these gnats, that fill the hour, to
>   pass for poets;)
> Bards with songs as from burning coals, or the lightning's
>   fork'd stripes
> . . . bards for [later "of"] the war. (1:210–211)

His verse becomes a sorcerer's magic spell for conjuring up the bards needed to defeat the menace of mundane history: "You, by my charm, I invoke!" (1:211).

But as he walked the broad majestic days of peace, Whitman was to be forced further and further away in his poetry from objective historical realities, inward toward what he called "my realities / . . . The rapt promises and lumine of seers—the spiritual world—these centuries-lasting songs, / And our visions, the visions of poets, the most solid announcements of any" (2:318). Shortly after the war he demonstrated the confidence in America that had become a positive article of faith with him by omitting the lines which originally concluded "As I Walk": "After the rest is done and gone, we [the poets] remain. / There is no final reliance but upon us, / Democracy rests finally upon us, (I, my brethren, begin it,) / And our visions sweep through eternity" (2:318). Retained only until the 1871 edition, they were thereafter removed, perhaps because Whitman felt that such an embattled visionariness was ill-suited to the complete confidence he now professed to have in his newborn society. In fact, for the rest of his life he could place little reliance on anyone or anything except his own, increasingly attenuated visions.

WHITMAN'S REVISION of what in the process became "By Blue Ontario's Shore" was aimed therefore at presenting a vision, for want of which his people would surely die, and for the sake of which he was convinced a whole generation of Americans had already been killed. As, however, the nation proceeded to give itself up ever more enthusiastically to the pleasures of unbridled materialism during the postwar period, Whitman had to decide whether to cleave to the deterministic certainties of a vision purchased supposedly beyond all doubt and to all eternity by the death of thousands of young men, or whether to concede that the American future had been thrown wide open, once more, to question, its direction still to be decided by the actions of the present. There was never any doubt which attitude Whitman would take. But in choosing the protective confidence of certainty he disabled himself from grappling seriously, as a poet, with American life in its postwar form.

Moreover, the greater the disparity, during that period, between the widely differing realities of fact and faith, the more urgent became Whitman's need to construct in his work, and particularly in his poetry, an alternative, satisfactory history in which the events of personal and national life were consistently referred back to, and faithfully construed in terms of, the war. The results could sometimes be grotesque to a degree which sadly illustrates the distorting angle at which, by then, Whitman was forced to stand to historical truth. Consider his reaction to the justified massacre of Custer and his troops by the Indians at Little Big Horn, on June 25, 1876. The incident becomes, in Whitman's treatment of it, a late, vivid instance, in unpropitious times, of the distinguished spirit Custer and countless others had shown during the Civil War ("thy many battles in which never yielding up a gun or color"). From this welcome episode Whitman draws the comforting lesson that the shaping spirit of American history is always silently at work:

> As sitting in dark days,
> Lone, sulky, through the time's thick murk looking in vain
>   for light, for hope,
> From unsuspected parts a fierce and momentary proof,
> (The sun there at the centre though conceal'd,
> Electric life forever at the centre,)
> Breaks forth a lightning flash.   (3:654)

Although the darkness of those days was in part personal, since he had recently lost his mother, and been himself crippled by a paralytic stroke, the reference is also clearly to the moral corruption of the social and political life of the seventies. By and large, Whitman much preferred that his poetry not concern itself with this unsavory mess, but he did contrive on one occasion to find an outlet for his bitter store of disillusion. By the simple expedient of adding a single line at the start—"The War is completed—the price is paid—the title is settled beyond recall" (1:260)—he converted the early poem "Respondez" into a blistering assault on postwar spiritual sloth. In this particular instance our realization that a prewar poem has been so easily commandeered for this purpose adds much more to than it detracts from the force of the attack. It brings to the piece a desolate air of déjà vu; a cynical sense of plus ça change; which directly militates against the claim so regularly advanced by Whitman, the very sine qua non of his faith, that the war had changed America completely and for all time. This simple, almost casual, readjustment or recycling of "Respondez" is Whitman's unintentional concession to those social, economic, and political forces which were actually at work fashioning nineteenth-century America, totally unaffected by the war mystique he was at that time so diligently cultivating. Into the body of his prewar poem he inserted four of the most blisteringly honest lines he wrote about the postwar nation. What price he paid in pain for such frankness one can only guess:

Stifled, O days! O lands! in every public and
   private corruption!
Smother'd in thievery, impotence, shamelessness,
   mountain-high;
Brazen effrontery, scheming, rolling like ocean's waves around
   and upon you, O my days! my lands!
For not even those thunderstorms, nor fiercest lightnings of
   the war, have purified the atmosphere.   (1:261)

Later, as he approached seventy, he found in "The Dying Veteran"
a more cunning, and perhaps self-saving, way of expressing—incog-
nito, because in the assumed character of "a queer old savage man,
a fighter under Washington himself"—his violent dissent from the
way American life had gone. It is Whitman's own version of a wild
old wicked man, and aware that the poem amounts to an assault on
his age's sensibilities, he prefaces it with an apology:

Amid these days of order, ease, prosperity,
Amid the current songs of beauty, peace, decorum,
I cast a reminiscence—(likely 'twill offend you,
I heard it in my boyhood).   (3:722)

A likely story. This studiously courteous opening is, like the piece
in its entirety, fraught with ambivalent emotions. Under the proffered
apology lie layers of defiance and sarcasm which Whitman challenges
the reader to discover, while preferring not to admit their existence,
even to himself. There follows a deathbed scene touched by the gro-
tesqueness of satiric farce. Around the old fighter's bed are gathered
"sons, daughters, church-deacons, lovingly tending him," all "sharpening their sense, their ears, towards his murmuring, half-caught
words." What they hear is not an old man gently blessing, and making
his peace with, this world as he departs it, but the scandalously un-
abated passion of a primitive war cry: "Let me return again to my
war days . . . Away with your life of peace!—your joys of peace! /
Give me my old wild battle-life again!" (3:723). Such a dismissal of
the dwarfish, knavish present in favor of the heroically immoderate
past is very much a cri de coeur arising out of Whitman's own embattled isolation.
   On only one occasion, however, did Whitman fully disclose the

potential extent of his alienation from postwar society. "Thou Mother With Thy Equal Brood" is in any case an interesting poem, since it includes so many perfect examples of the trick Whitman developed after the war of turning up the volume of his rhetoric in order to drown out the noise of his doubts. But it is truly memorable for the mad audacity of two lines tucked away somewhere amongst its many pretentions:

> (Thy soaring course thee formulating, not in thy two great
> wars, nor in thy century's visible growth,
> But far more in these leaves and chants, thy chants,
> great Mother!)   (3:639)

Here Whitman is driven to the final, desperate extremity of renouncing the whole world of nineteenth-century America in order to gain its soul. America is no longer recognized as having authentic existence outside what Whitman authorizes in his poetry. He made the same point in *Democratic Vistas*: "It may be, a single new thought, imagination, abstract principle, even literary style, fit for the time, put in shape by some great literatus, and projected among mankind, may duly cause change, growths, removals, greater than the longest and bloodiest war, or the most stupendous merely political, dynastic, or commercial overturn" (2:366). There is a pathos in these revealing examples of Whitman's loss of faith even in his wartime experiences, and his essential reliance, in this crisis, upon nothing except his own leaves and chants.

That such an incipiently schizoid conclusion is not repeated elsewhere in the poetry is due partly to the sustaining ties of loyalty and obligation which continued to attach Whitman to his wartime comrades. Viewed in this way, they can be seen to provide a valuable defense against the manic-depressive state which the postwar American environment was always threatening to induce in him. No better example can be had of the protection against the desolating intrusion of the present which Whitman sought and found in memories of wartime, than the following passage from "Ashes of Soldiers":

> But aside from these, and the marts of wealth, and the
> crowded promenade,

Admitting around me comrades close, unseen by the rest,
    and voiceless,
The slain elate and alive again—the dust and debris alive,
I chant this chant of my silent soul, in the name of all
    dead soldiers.

Faces so pale, with wondrous eyes, very dear, gather
    closer yet,
Draw close, but speak not.

Phantoms of countless lost!
Invisible to the rest, henceforth become my companions!
Follow me ever! desert me not, while I live.

Sweet are the blooming cheeks of the living! sweet are the
    musical voices sounding!
But sweet, ah sweet, are the dead, with their
    silent eyes.   (2:511)

This is the 1871 version. The 1865 version differs from it in several significant details. The earlier reference was not to "marts of wealth and the crowded promenade" but to the much gentler "crowd's hurrahs, and the land's congratulations." There was no reference either to "the slain elate and alive again—the dust and debris alive," perhaps because Whitman's need to resurrect the dead had not yet been made urgent by his embittering experience of the postwar years. Similarly, there was no desolate mention of the "Phantoms of countless lost," only of "Phantoms, welcome, divine and tender!" (2:511).

Whitman's feeling of solidarity with this spectral company assembling protectively around him, reminds us, surely, of the *Calamus* poem, "These I Singing in Spring," and the *Drum Taps* poem, "By the Bivouac's Fitful Flame." What is notable, about "Ashes," this last in a series of such ruminative invocations, is that here the silence of the phantoms is not so much an inevitable corollary of their ghostliness, as a state to which they are urgently enjoined by a Whitman who wants to keep their presence a secret. Any self-betraying noise they made would, certain as cockcrow, cause them to melt away into the bustle of the world, having lost along with secrecy their power to fortify him against the assault of the public day. Only in the silent eyes of the dead does Whitman have authentic existence, and yet there is the accompanying fear that if the dead were to speak directly to and through him, then the spell of need which bound them to his living self would be broken, and they would depart.

Whereas the 1865 *Drum Taps* version of the poem opened quite straightforwardly ("One breath, O my silent soul, / A perfum'd thought—no more I ask, for the sake of all dead soldiers"), subsequent editions actually began with a passage mustering a spectral army to defend Whitman against both the defections of memory and the incursions of the postwar years:

> Ashes of soldiers South or North,
> As I muse, retrospective, murmuring a chant in thought,
> Lo! the war resumes—again to my sense your shapes,
> And again the advance of armies.
>
> Noiseless as mists and vapors,
> From their graves in the trenches ascending,
> From the cemeteries all through Virginia and Tennessee,
> From every point of the compass, out of the countless
>   unnamed graves,
> In wafted clouds, in myriads large, or squads of twos or
>   threes, or single ones, they come,
> And silently gather round me.   (2:510)

The purpose of friendship, Emerson had written in a sentence which throws a strong light on *Calamus*, is that it allows us to "weave social threads of our own, a new web of relations: and, as many thoughts in succession substantiate themselves, we shall by and by stand in a new world of our own creation, and no longer strangers and pilgrims in a traditionary globe."[16] Very much a "stranger and pilgrim" in American society once the war had ended, Whitman naturally sought refuge in a world of his own creation, which he populated with his wartime friends—for "love is not over—and what love, O comrades!" Yet he liked to think of this withdrawal only as preparatory to a new advance. Stepping back from the wasteland present into the secret company of the departed was for Whitman the essential part of a fertility ritual, or process of spiritual transmutation, whereby he believed that by dying to his old self he could become a "fountain, / That I exhale love from me wherever I go, like a moist perennial dew, / For the ashes of all dead soldiers South or North" (2:512).

Cisterns contain; fountains overflow. It was most unusual for the postwar Whitman to identify with the trustful bounty of a fountain. More typically he thought of himself as involved in a tenacious holding operation—obdurately persisting in the face of all discouragement. Along with Whitman's sensitivity to the changed American scene there went, after all, a certain durability which should not be underestimated. Outside of his poetry he preferred to attribute this quality of resilience to the sanguine temperament he had inherited from the Dutch side of his family. Yet in the poetry itself he chose to see it in terms of the persistence into later life of the militant determination developed in him by the war years: "Weave in! weave in, my hardy life! / Weave, weave a soldier strong and full, for great campaigns to come; / . . . the need goes on, and shall go on—the death-envelop'd march of peace as well as war, goes on; / For great campaigns of peace the same, the wiry threads to weave" (2:524). There is a hard gloss to this poem, corresponding to the almost brazen confidence Whitman is deliberately attempting to assume, whereas "Lessons" approaches a similar conclusion from the opposite direction, by openly admitting the vulnerable soft body of feeling which underlies this protective carapace:

> There are who teach only the sweet lessons of peace
>   and safety;
> But I teach lessons of war and death to those I love,
> That they readily meet invasions, when they come.   (3:607)

The invasions referred to are obviously not of a physical but of a psychological nature, disturbing mental intrusions such as he himself had suffered during the war, and from whose devastating effects he wishes to protect others. It is, after all, surely significant that, outside of *Calamus*, the most desperately broken state of mind Whitman ever revealed in his poetry was in a poem he allowed to appear once only, in *Sequel to Drum-Taps*:

> Not my enemies ever invade me—no harm to my pride from
>   them I fear;
> But the lovers I recklessly love—lo! how they master me!

Lo! me, ever open and helpless, bereft of my strength!
Utterly abject, grovelling on the ground before them.   (2:546)

It was never reprinted, and therefore disappeared from sight—even from the sight of many of the recent interpreters of Whitman's work.

In spite, or perhaps because, of his sensitivity, Whitman wanted to produce an ardent, battle-hardened civilian population, which would be equal to the arduous task of sustaining its responsibilities to the dead. "Pioneers! O Pioneers!" is probably his most emotionally complex attempt at conveying this last aspiration, and it is a pity the poem should have been so frequently used by critics simply as a convenient source of thematic material. First appearing in the 1865 *Drum Taps*, it should be regarded as an important demobilization poem, whose every line is held in vibrant tension between the divergent feelings of hope and fear. Nowhere, for instance, is the nervous ambivalence of Whitman's reaction to the outbreak of peace better expressed than in the edgy opening of the second verse: "For we cannot tarry here, / We must march my darlings" (2:475). The danger is that the resting nation will be overcome by peace, and by what the poem at first lightly mocks as "delectations sweet, / . . . the cushion and the slipper . . . riches safe and palling . . . tame enjoyment" (2:478). Then fear takes hold of Whitman and spawns monstrous images of gross self-indulgence; of corpulent sleepers and gluttonous feasting. True safety can, under such circumstances, only be found through courting that nobler, spiritually invigorating danger which Whitman urges his people actively to invite by their determined, unresting onward march. Alarmed and excited in roughly equal measure by the prospects of peace, Whitman makes a determined and ambitious poetic effort to translate the simple purposefulness of the war effort into civilian terms, by applying the metaphors of soldiering to postwar life.

Not only did the West seem naturally to provide him with a way of life congenial to this strenuous imagination, it had the additional advantage of being the region which had provided the greatest of presidents in the wartime Lincoln, who had been so invincibly combative on behalf of human rights and freedoms. The western states had also, in his opinion, provided the best combatants—many a "tan-faced prairie boy" (2:507) such as he had seen in the hospitals would be among the "tan-faced children" of his western crusade. Moreover, as we have already seen, the war had been in part, for Whitman, concerned with the winning of the West for free labor, free men. In other words, the movement westward seemed to be impelled by the very same spirit in which the war had been triumphantly fought, and so it offered Whitman hope and reassurance. And although he had hymned the West before the war, in what appears, at first glance, to be virtually identical terms, it would nevertheless be more accurate, as well as much more interesting, to see "Pioneers! O Pioneers!" not as simply additional to an established series of western-movement pieces, but as a new departure specifically occasioned, indeed demanded, by the Civil War.

What particularly distinguishes the poem in this respect is the attitude it takes toward the past, which in turn significantly affects the view it offers of the future. From the outset of his poetic career, Whitman had been fond of representing America as the culmination of all previous cosmic and human history, but not until the postwar period did this belief acquire a very special, rich, dark timbre. "All the rest on us depend," he declares in "Pioneers! O Pioneers!" Yet, although he can refer disparagingly to "the elder races" that have been outdistanced, and the past that is blithely being left behind, the weight of the emotion falls decisively elsewhere:

> See, my children, resolute children,
> By those swarms upon our rear, we must never yield or falter,
> Ages back in ghostly millions, frowning there behind
>   us urging,
>   Pioneers! O Pioneers!
>
> On and on, the compact ranks,
> With accessions ever waiting, with the places of the dead
>   quickly fill'd,
> Through the battle, through defeat, moving yet and
>   never stopping,
>   Pioneers! O pioneers!   (2:476)

Concealed in that reference to the "ghostly millions" from "ages back" is an anguished awareness of those victims of the recent past, the dead of the Civil War. Indeed "left behind," they now come swarming upon the rear, frowningly urging America to live up to their sacrifice. The American dream (on which the poem also obviously draws) becomes the only escape from this newly acquired American nightmare of a ghostly past which could be appeased only by having its expectations fulfilled. Whitman is himself accurately recognizing the mixture of feelings within him and his poem when he cries "O I mourn and yet exult—I am rapt with love for all, / Pioneers! O pioneers!" (2:476). And, unawares, he prophesies his marginal future situation with bleak clarity in lines such as these: "I too with my soul and body, / We, a curious trio, picking, wandering on our way, / Through these shores, amid the shadows, with the apparitions pressing" (2:477).

Such a homeless wandering was very much the disconsolate plight of the postwar Whitman. "Wandering at morn, / Emerging from the night, from gloomy thoughts—thee in my thoughts, / Yearning for thee, harmonious Union! thee, Singing Bird divine!" (3:669). This 1876 poem derives additional power from its darkly ironic links of phrase and image with the Civil War poetry. At the end of *Sequel to Drum Taps* Whitman had, after all, depicted himself as "forth from my tent emerging," and as stepping confidently into the day, "in the freshness the forenoon air, in the far-stretching circuits and vistas again to peace restored" (2:556). But peaceful America was providing him with more smothering nightmares than ever the war had done, so there was now no escape route opening like a vista out from the present—only the fool's paradise of hope deferred to infinitely future prospects. Instead of being stretched out before him "in fiery fields . . . emanative" America appeared to be "coil'd in evil times . . . with craft and black dismay—with every meanness, treason thrust upon thee" (3:669). The referential ambiguity of the world "coil'd" is very important. It is probably meant to refer to an America whose innocent strength has been caught in the throttling coils of evil. But it could also mean that the Union is itself a serpent "coil'd in evil times"—the phrase thus registering, unintentionally, Whitman's fear that evil may not only be thrust upon America but may have entered into the very constitution of his society.

Of all the silent allusions in this poem to his previous work, the most moving is surely that to the hermit thrush of "When Lilacs Last in the Dooryard Bloom'd." That bird is transmuted, as it were, into this "singing thrush, whose tones of joy and faith ecstatic, / Fail not to certify and cheer my soul" (3:669). Although that other bird had indeed sung, unforgettably, darkling, it is this singing thrush which is most like Hardy's "Darkling Thrush," in whose song the poet heard a blessed hope "of which he knew but I was unaware":

> There ponder'd, felt, I,
> If worms, snakes, loathsome grubs, may to sweet spiritual
>   songs be turn'd,
> If vermin so transposed, so used, so bless'd may be,
> Then may I trust in you, your fortunes, days, my country;
> —Who knows but these may be the lessons fit for you?
> From these your future Song may rise, with joyous trills,
> Destin'd to fill the world.   (3:669–670)

The more difficult Whitman found it to stomach postwar society, the more emphasis he placed on the excellent digestive system of American democracy.[17] A letter sent to Bucke, just two years before his death, shows this image being used and the nebulous piety that went with it: "they have evidently great inward intestinal agitation & unsettledness in Great Britain, (we too here in America, but our belly is so large)—then the unsettledness on the Continent too—as dear Mrs G[ilchrist] said we are all 'going somewhere' indeed—I suppose the dyspeptic Carlyle would say 'Yes, to hell'—But per contra old black Sojourner Truth was always saying 'God reigns yet I tell you.' "[18] Dyspeptically speaking, it would perhaps be a kindness to Whitman to regard the endearing humor in this letter as an admision of the falseness of its philosophy.

Elsewhere, though, he regularly advanced the same philosophy without benefit of humor, and with the utmost seriousness, yet still without succeeding in turning it into a substantial faith. Certainly it was never strong enough to sustain a credible poetry. Of course, Whitman had always been devoted to the future, but now he became positively addicted to it, like any habitual drug taker. If he could find no room for the Civil War dead in the American present, he could always find plenty of room for them there. As he admitted, in what was the frankest remark he ever made on the subject, "that I have not gain'd the acceptance of my own time, but have fallen back on fond dreams of the future—anticipations—('still lives the song, though Regnar dies') . . . is all probably no more than I ought to have expected" (2:712–713). This altered relationship to the future was, naturally, the result of his altered relationship to his own time. In the

1855 preface he had accurately seen that "past and present and future are not disjoined but joined. The greatest poet forms the consistence of what is to be from what has been and is . . . he places himself where the future becomes present" (2:443). There was a sense, explored in the opening chapters of this book, in which his early poetry was indeed placed precisely there, when he found his inspiration "in real objects today, symptoms of the past and future" (2:456). But as he later sadly noted, "Only to the rapt vision does the seen become the prophecy of the unseen" (2:486). The loss of that "vision" was not, however, an inexplicable psychological disaster, nor was it entirely the result of his physical and mental prostration. Whitman lost his grip on his world because, for social, political, and economic reasons, it had assumed a shape which he simply could not grasp. As has already been seen, his kosmos was a historically specific myth and could not survive the disappearance of the unique set of conditions which had brought it into being.

Whitman, then, dwindled from a poet into "a mere prophet." The phrase, complete with its unexpected, diminishing adjective, occurs in Larkin's study of Carlyle—a work which pleased Whitman enormously precisely because it included such comments. "Little as some of his critics imagine it," wrote Larkin, who had been Carlyle's secretary for ten years, "his heart was sick of perpetually exhorting and admonishing. He longed to be doing something, instead of, as he says, eloquently writing and talking about it; to be a kind of king or leader in the practical activities of life, not a mere prophet, forever and forever prophesying."[19] Whitman reacted enthusiastically to these words, because they seemed to him to apply very exactly to himself. They "may," he told his young friend, "be applied to my life and may be used as in some byways an explanation of my addiction to the trades and my apprenticeship to the life of the hospitals during the War." It is an extraordinarily suggestive remark, but for my purposes it is enough to note the way Whitman here recognizes that the "trades," and the "hospitals" had in the past saved him from what had now become his fate. The old, socially disengaged poet was indeed "forever and forever prophesying."

This is not to suggest, however, that in the process he entirely gave up the futile attempt to engage with contemporary society. "Wert capable of war—its tugs and trials?" he admonished the nation, then "Be capable of peace, its trials; / For the tug and mortal strain of nations come at last in prosperous peace—not war" (3:640). It was much easier for him to persuade himself that the America of the muscularly enterprising West was, in his understanding of the phrase, "capable of peace" than it was for him to make the scandalously prosperous East out to be a country fit for wartime heroes to live in. "Song of the Exposition" is the work produced by a rapidly tiring poet as he nobly fails to prove equal to the strain of making spiritual sense of the booming (and sometimes slumping) seventies. Instead, the real significance of the poem lies elsewhere, in its attempt to will the unheeding present into taking its preordained place in the mythic historical design which Whitman insisted had been inaugurated by the war. While all too eager to replace memories of that "hell unpent and raid of blood" with welcome appreciation of "thy undaunted armies, Engineering!" (3:619), he also shows a real counterbalancing anxiety that modern America will prove only too successful in putting the recent cost of conflict out of its mind. Psychologically incapable of leveling what amounts to a very damaging accusation directly at American life, he addresses his feelings instead to the Union flag:

> And thou, thy Emblem, waving over all!
> Delicate beauty! a word to thee, (it may be salutary;)
> Remember, thou hast not always been, as here today, so
>   comfortably ensovereign'd;
> In other scenes than these have I observ'd thee, flag.   (3:623)

Having irrevocably banished bloodstained memories only a few stanzas earlier—"Away with themes of war! away with War itself!" (3:619)—he now recalls them in an attempt to remind America of its debt and its destiny. The poem ends with a solemn ceremony of reconsecration, in which, as the "measureless wealth" of the States is rededicated to the mystic Union, the nation renews its covenant with its recent dead.

During the immediate aftermath of war, Whitman signaled his concern about the developing social situation by devoting a complete section in *Leaves of Grass* to "Marches Now the War is Over" and to "Bathed in War's Perfume," as well of course as to *Drum Taps*. With the passage of time, such sections came to seem less appropriate, but when they were subsequently dismantled, and the pieces scattered throughout *Leaves of Grass*, the intention was not to diminish the influence of the war on the collection. On the contrary, Whitman was rearranging his poems in accordance with his developing contention that the war was an all-pervasive influence in *Leaves of Grass*. It was a philosophy he worked out with ingenuity as well as emotion in "To Thee Old Cause." The war, he argued, was fought in the name and for the sake of the grand old cause of Liberty—"a strange, sad war—great war for thee" (3:628). As this cause, predating the war, had always been acknowledged in America to be the nub of national life, so too all of Whitman's poetry, having been steadily devoted from the beginning to the liberties for which America essentially stood, could in this sense justifiably be said to have been written, regardless of the date of composition, in the same spirit as the Civil War had actually been fought:

> Around the idea of thee the strange sad war revolving,
> With all its angry and vehement play of causes,
> (With yet unknown results to come, for thrice a
>   thousand years,)
> These recitatives for thee—my Book and the War are one,
> Merged in its spirit I and mine—as the contest hinged on thee,
> As a wheel on its axis turns, this Book, unwitting to itself,
> Around the Idea of thee.   (3:628)

It has already been established that Whitman had been working quite wittingly, had indeed gone to considerable trouble, to make sure his book was extensively and prominently marked by the war. Equally important, though, is the contrary idea advanced here, that the whole volume turns unwittingly "around the idea of thee." The claim is that *Leaves of Grass* had unawares prophetically anticipated the conflict, by voicing from the beginning the issues for which thereafter the war was fought; and furthermore that, following the cessation of hostilities, whenever his poetry had not consciously taken its bearings from those years, it was nevertheless being unconsciously determined by the experiences Whitman had undergone at that time.

A very beautifully personal example of the way such experiences could well up gently, and fill a poem almost unawares, can be found in the short piece, so sadly neglected by critics, called "By Broad Potomac's Shore." Being so little known, it deserves to be quoted in full:

By broad Potomac's shore—again, old tongue!
(Still uttering—still ejaculating—canst never cease this babble?)
Again, old heart so gay—again to you, your sense, the full
    flush spring returning;
Again the freshness and the odors—again Virginia's summer
    sky, pellucid blue and silver,
Again the forenoon purple of the hills,
Again the deathless grass, so noiseless, soft and green,
Again the blood-red roses blooming.

Perfume this book of mine, O blood-red roses!
Lave subtly with your waters every line, Potomac!
Give me of you, O spring, before I close, to put between
    its pages!
O forenoon purple of the hills, before I close, of you.
O smiling earth—O summer sun, give me of you!
O deathless grass, of you!   (3:649)

Virtually without acknowledging it, this poem goes right back to Whitman's period, some six or seven years before, in the Washington hospitals "by broad Potomac's shore." During that period, as the lacerating daily duty of ministering to the wounded had grown almost unbearable to him, Whitman had turned, for relief, to the beauties of the surrounding countryside. "Mother," he wrote on October 6, 1863, "it is lucky I like Washington in many respects, & that things are upon the whole pleasant personally, for every day of my life I see enough to make one's heart ache with sympathy & anguish here in the hospitals, & I do not know as I could stand it, if it was not counterbalanced outside."[20] Several years later, in this poem, he finds that the Washington landscape is no longer appreciatively remembered as the antidote to carnage. Rather, it is the very epitome of what, gentled by memory, is now precious and dear to Whitman about the suffering he witnessed. The "blood-red roses" of the Potomac are his Roses of Picardy. It is what he had wished for in "Ashes of Soldiers." "Up from the foetor arising," up from the stench of the battlefield, comes the sweet scent to "Perfume all—makes all wholesome." Love "solve[s] all, fructif[ies] all with the last chemistry" (2:512).

But when he refers to the war's comprehensive influence on *Leaves of Grass*, it is not of such intimate instances as this that Whitman is primarily thinking. Instead, he is suggesting that every detail of the collection proves, in retrospect, to have been produced in either conscious or unconscious obedience to an omnipotent law, so that the completed *Leaves of Grass* itself offers a compelling example of the force of ineluctable destiny in American history. With reference to the history of the second half of the nineteenth century, the collection acts as a sacred text, disclosing the providential pattern of meaning which had become so difficult to perceive in the apparently aimless chaos of actual events. Having started out as a prophet proposing to "project the history of the future," Whitman now regards himself in an opposite but complementary light, as (to borrow Hazlitt's famous paradox) the prophet of the past.

Leaves of Grass is finally offered to the reader by Whitman as a collection of poems that together describe an exemplary life—a life which is the embodiment of the hidden, or "interior," spirit of nineteenth-century American history. Had he not already used the phrase elsewhere, he could very well have given to the complete *Leaves of Grass* the subtitle "Specimen Days," meaning an apparently random series of personal occasions from which nevertheless a consistently underlying general law could be inferred. It was this word "specimen" that he used in the note at the end of his *Collected Poetry and Prose* (1888), when insisting that he could not "let my momentous, stormy, peculiar Era of peace and war, these States, these years, slip away without arresting some of its specimen-events—even its vital breaths— to be portray'd and inscribed from out the midst of it" (2:734). His sense of slippage, and of the intangible, permeates the whole sentence. Of course, by then the war had been recorded in a spate of journals and books. Personal reminiscences and official histories poured from the presses, to be devoured by a large popular readership. As Whitman observed, rather tartly, "statistically and descriptively our times are copiously noted and memorandised with an industrial zeal" (*Prose Works*, 2:734). That word "industrial" reeks of his distaste for the whole enterprise and reveals the connection he made between the new, mechanical age's dehumanized methods of mass production, and its crass inability to recapture the subtle "flame-like" atmosphere of the Civil War, or to understand its significance. An aficionado of the indirect approach, he quietly despised current attempts to nail the ghost of that past by hammering straightforwardly away at the documentary evidence. All of those proliferating books, he told Traubel, were no more than an expression of "the mania of this decade." "The historian is not yet born: the voice of those times—the historic voice [has] not yet spoken." Although he would not on this occasion presume to regard himself as being that "historian," he certainly thought of himself in *Leaves of Grass* as one who came "with insignia to know, to tell."[21]

The seminal part played by the war in determining the quality and character of American life during the nineteenth century and on to the future, was, in Whitman's opinion, perfectly illustrated in his own particular case. Speaking in "A Backward Glance" of his own development as a poet, Whitman laid great stress on the crucial contribution made by the Civil War to his personal and artistic growth:

> It is certain, I say, that, although I had made a start before, only from the occurrence of the Secession War, and what it show'd me as by flashes of lightning, with the emotional depths it sounded and arous'd (of course, I don't mean in my own heart only, I saw it just as plainly in others, in millions)—that only from the strong flare and provocation of that war's sights and scenes the final reasons-for-being of an autochthonic and passionate song definitely came forth . . . Without those three or four years and the experiences they gave, "Leaves of Grass" would not now be existing. (2:724)

At the very end of this passage Whitman is moved to extend his creation myth to include *Leaves of Grass* itself, going so far as to claim that, like modern American history, it owes its very existence to the Civil War—although only a few sentences earlier he had put the point much more cautiously when asserting that, although *Leaves of Grass* might not owe its actual existence to the war years, it had nevertheless found its very reason for being in them. And when he chose to describe himself in his seventy-first year as "some old broken soldier, after a long, hot, wearying march, or haply after battle, / Today at twilight, hobbling, answering company roll-call, *Here*, with vital voice, / Reporting yet, saluting yet the Officer over all" (3:733), he was also pointing out, for the last time, that he continued to owe his mature identity to his identification with his wartime comrades. He himself, like his book, had become one with the war. But if *Leaves of Grass* was, in a way, the verbal tribute which he laid along with "wreaths of roses and branches of palm," on the graves of all dead soldiers, North or South, then, like the floral offering, it was placed there "not for the past alone," but "for meanings to the future" (3:722).

~ Notes

Introduction

1. Wallace Stevens, *Collected Poems* (London: Faber and Faber, 1959), p. 150.
2. Jim Perlman, Ed Folsom, and Dan Campion, eds. *Walt Whitman: The Measure of His Song* (Minneapolis: Holy Cow! Press, 1981).
3. Charles Tomlinson, *Selected Poems, 1951–1974* (Oxford: Oxford University Press, 1978), p. 128.
4. Horace Traubel, *With Walt Whitman in Camden* (New York: Rowman and Littlefield, 1961), 3:383.
5. Ibid., 3:538.

1. A Critical Situation

1. Horace Traubel, *With Walt Whitman in Camden* (New York: Rowman and Littlefield, 1961), 1:25.
2. Ibid., p. 25.
3. Arthur Golden, ed., *Walt Whitman's Blue Book* (New York: New York Public Library, 1968), 1:166.
4. Albert Feuillart, ed., *The Prose Works of Sir Philip Sidney* (Cambridge: Cambridge University Press, 1963), 3:45–46.
5. Edward K. Spann, *Ideals and Politics: New York Intellectuals and Liberal Democracy, 1820–1880* (Albany: State University of New York Press, 1972), p. 137.
6. *Ideals,* p. 130. As Spann succinctly puts it: "The capitalists won; the average individual person lost." Over the longer period, however, these campaigns on behalf of popular rights did "serve to strengthen the American liberal tradition," and contributed to the development of an ultimately more equitable and humane society (*Ideals,* p. 108).
7. Spann, *Ideals,* p. 105.
8. Ibid., p. 112.
9. Sean Wilentz, *Chants Democratic: New York City and the Rise of the American*

Working Class, 1788–1850 (New York and Oxford: Oxford University Press, 1984), pp. 128–129.

10. Whitman had taken his own educational responsibilities as an editor very seriously and striven to establish a bond of intimacy between himself and his readers: "There is a curious kind of sympathy (haven't you ever thought of it before?) that arises in the mind of a newspaper conductor with the public he serves. He gets to *love* them. Daily communion creates a sort of brotherhood and sisterhood between the two parties" (Emory Holloway, ed., *The Uncollected Poetry and Prose of Walt Whitman,* London: Heinemann, 1922, 1:115). Not only, though, was he eventually thwarted in his aim by the very nature of this modern mass-communication, party-dominated medium, he also came to feel that the very language of newspapers was false and stilted. "No vibration of the living voice in the living ear" was possible, such as he therefore aimed to achieve in his poetry (Emory Holloway and Ralph Adimari, eds., *New York Dissected by Walt Whitman,* Folcroft: Folcroft Library Editions, n.d.; reprint of New York: Rufus Rockwell Wilson, 1936; p. 59).

11. Cleveland Rogers and John Black, eds., *The Gathering of the Forces* (New York: Putnam, 1920), 2:79.

12. Ibid., 2:79.

13. This passage first appeared in "Thou Vast Rondure," a poem completed in 1868 and published in April 1869. In "When the Full-Grown Poet Came" Whitman wrote more fully about the poet as the "blender, uniter" of nature ("the round impassive Globe, with all its shows of Day and Night") and the Soul of Man (3:651).

14. The influence of Paine on Whitman has been sensibly discussed by Margaret M. Vanderhaar, "Whitman, Paine, and the Religion of Democracy," *Walt Whitman Review* 16 (1970):14–22. But she relies on selections from Paine's writings, and so misses many of the intriguing parallels that can be drawn between Whitman's philosophy and ideas advanced not only in *The Age of Reason* and *Common Sense,* but also in the second part of the *Rights of Man*—where, after all, the United States is his model of constitutionalism. The following gives some idea of his outlook: "As America was the only spot in the political world where the principles of universal reformation could begin, so also was it the best in the natural world. An assemblage of circumstances conspired not only to give birth, but to add gigantic maturity to its principles. The scene which that country presents to the eye of a spectator has something in it which generates and encourages great ideas. Nature appears to him in magnitude. The mighty objects he beholds act upon his mind by enlarging it, and he partakes of the greatness he beholds" (*The Rights of Man,* London: J. M. Dent, 1969, p. 152).

The most thoroughgoing of Whitman's own assessments of Paine is his short essay "In Memory of Thomas Paine" (*Prose Works* 1:140–142). For Paine's decisive contribution to the struggle to establish an independent, democratic America, see Eric Foner, *Tom Paine and Revolutionary America* (New York and Oxford: Oxford University Press, 1976).

15. Isaac Krammick, ed., *Common Sense* (Harmondsworth: Penguin, 1981), p. 65.
16. Holloway, *Uncollected Poetry,* 1:261, 167.
17. Traubel, *Camden,* 2:142–143.
18. Wilentz, *Chants Democratic,* pp. 14–15.
19. This whole background is admirably discussed, and its relationship to literature ingeniously interpreted, in Carolyn Porter, *Seeing and Being: The Plight of the Participant Observer in Emerson, James, Adams, and Faulkner* (Middletown, Conn.: Wesleyan University Press, 1981). See particularly chap. 3, "Emerson's America."
20. Wilentz, *Chants Democratic,* p. 55. As will be clear from the references, my discussion of the artisanal world in these next paragraphs is very deeply indebted to this superb study. Joseph Jay Rubin summarizes as follows those aims of the Working Men's Party (1829), which probably won support from Walter Whitman, Sr.: "He wanted to work for ten hours rather than from sunup to sundown, to have his wages secured by a strong mechanic's lien and payment in specie. As a potential entrepreneur he sought easier credit; as a father he wanted a future for his sons and daughters" (*The Historic Whitman,* University Park: Pennsylvania State University Press, 1973, p. 21).
21. Traubel, *Camden,* 2:352.
22. Wilentz, *Chants Democratic,* p. 102.
23. The influence of his early background on Whitman's development should not, however, be underestimated. Rubin has pointed out, and documented, the way "the carpenter's son and long-time journeyman followed the struggle of mechanics and artisans to raise wages and reduce hours" (*Historic Whitman,* pp. 150–153).
24. See Rubin, *Historic Whitman,* p. 49.
25. Traubel, *Camden,* 1:79.
26. Charles I. Glicksberg, ed., *Whitman and the Civil War* (Philadelphia: University of Pennsylvania Press, 1933), p. 48.
27. Ibid., p. 58.
28. Wilentz, *Chants Democratic,* p. 301.
29. While he was in New Orleans, Whitman saw two sights which may have influenced the writing of this passage. On the one hand, he saw slaves being displayed for auction and read detailed descriptions of those physical attributes which in some cases fetched a high price (Rubin, *Historic Whitman,* p. 190). On the other hand, he also experienced the delights of "Dr Collyer and his Living Models—twenty specialists in nude posturing" (Rubin, *Historic Whitman,* p. 194). In his poem Whitman deliberately applies to the former the standards of aesthetic appreciation reserved for the latter.
30. Emory Holloway, ed., *Walt Whitman: Complete Verse and Selected Prose* (London: Nonesuch Press, 1938), p. 595.
31. Wilentz, *Chants Democratic,* p. 263.
32. Glicksberg, *Civil War,* p. 59.
33. Justin Kaplan seems to have finally scotched the rumor, assiduously cultivated by Whitman himself in later years, that he turned his hand to carpen-

tering at this time. In fact, he was a contractor—and a particularly efficient bookkeeper, as Kaplan points out (*Walt Whitman: A Life,* New York: Simon and Schuster, 1980, p. 160); thus vindicating the phrenologist Fowler who suggested that Whitman might prove to be a good accountant. Perhaps his love of inventories should be connected to this unexplored side of his complex character!

34. These circumstances, and Whitman's reaction to them, have been very well summarized by Rubin (*Historic Whitman,* pp. 298–299). It is worth noticing that the *Crayon* at this time "defied commercial fate and offered [its] stricken countrymen the gospel of beauty as a cure for the hollowness of 'money-pride.' " Not only was that Whitman's message to the Brooklyn Art Union in 1851, it is also one important element in the 1855 "Song of Myself," as the following chapter will attempt to show.

35. Rubin, *Historic Whitman,* p. 299.

2. Self-Possession and Possessive Individualism

1. Thomas Stone, in *The Dial* (New York: Russell and Russell, 1961), 4:275.
2. A. S. B. Glover, ed., *Shelley's Selected Poetry, Prose and Letters* (London: Nonesuch Press, 1951), p. 13. For Fromm's treatment of this distinction, see *To Have or To Be* (New York: Harper and Row, 1976).
3. Emory Holloway, ed., *The Uncollected Poetry and Prose of Walt Whitman* (London: Heinemann, 1922), 2:67. It is worth noting that this is the early notebook in which Whitman first tried out, in prose and in verse, some of the material eventually included in the 1855 "Song of Myself."
4. Horace Traubel, *With Walt Whitman in Camden* (New York: Rowman and Littlefield, 1961), 2:77–78.
5. Terence Hawkes, *Structuralism and Semiotics* (London: Methuen, 1977), p. 27.
6. *The Riverside Edition of Emerson's Complete Works* (London: Routledge, 1883), 2:85–86.
7. C. J. Furness, ed., *Walt Whitman's Workshop* (New York: Russell and Russell, 1964), p. 45.
8. Ibid., p. 46.
9. Ibid., p. 45.
10. Traubel, *Camden,* 3:81.
11. Emerson, *Riverside Edition,* 1:280.
12. Ibid., 2:58.
13. Holloway, *Uncollected Poetry,* 2:68. Whitman was, however, no advocate of free love. His editorial views on marriage could even be unimpeachably conventional in their sentimentality. See for instance the section "Women—Sex—Marriage" in Emory Holloway and Vernolian Schwarz, eds., *I Sit and Look Out* (New York: AMS Press, 1966). The extract from "The Marriage Tie" is particularly worth noting: "The sacredness, the divine institution of the marriage tie lies at the root of the welfare, the safety, the very existence of every Christian nation. Palsied be the hand, blistered the tongue that

would make one movement to defeat its holy purposes, or to weaken its binding nature by a single breath!" (114).

14. Emerson, *Riverside Edition,* 1:222.
15. Furness, *Workshop,* p. 45.
16. Ibid., p. 46.
17. Theodore Parker, in *The Dial* (New York: Russell and Russell, 1961), 1:68.
18. G. K. Newcomb, in *The Dial* (New York: Russell and Russell, 1961), 3:113–114.
19. R. W. Emerson, in *The Dial,* 1:146–147.
20. Denis Donoghue, *Connoisseurs of Chaos* (London: Faber and Faber, 1966), p. 28.
21. Holloway, *Uncollected Poetry,* 1:44–45.
22. G. J. Barker-Benfield, "The Spermatic Economy: A Nineteenth-Century View of Sexuality," in Michael Gordon, ed., *The American Family in Social-Historical Perspective* (New York: Saint Martin's Press, 1978), pp. 374–402. For further information on the same subject, consult Harold Aspiz, "Walt Whitman: The Spermatic Imagination," *American Literature* 56 (1984):379–395; and Myrth Jimmie Killingsworth, "Whitman's Love-Spendings," *Walt Whitman Review* 26 (1980):145–153. The latter points out that "economic metaphor came to be associated in the middle-class mind with the physiology of male sexuality; careful finance became the metaphor for 'careful love' " (p. 146).
23. Geoffrey Keynes, ed., *Blake: The Complete Writings* (London: Oxford University Press, 1966), p. 217.
24. Holloway, *Uncollected Poetry,* 1:245.
25. Stone, in *The Dial,* 4:277.
26. Yehoshua Arieli, *Individualism and Nationalism in American Ideology* (Cambridge, Mass.: Harvard University Press, 1964), p. 101.
27. Emerson, *Riverside Edition,* 1:237, 239.
28. William Wordsworth, *Poetical Works,* ed. Thomas Hutchinson and Ernest de Selincourt, reprint ed. (London: Oxford University Press, 1969), p. 738.
29. Blake, *Complete Writings,* p. 123.
30. Holloway, *Uncollected Poetry,* 1:111.
31. Charles Olson, *The Maximus Poems* (New York: Jargon/Corinth Books, 1960), p. 42.
32. F. H. Hedge, in *The Dial* (New York: Russell and Russell, 1961), 1:178.
33. Holloway, *Uncollected Poetry,* 2:68.
34. Anthony Beale, ed., *D. H. Lawrence: Selected Literary Criticism* (London: Heinemann, 1961), pp. 86–87.
35. Traubel, *Camden,* 2:126. There is an amusing footnote to this in an editorial Whitman wrote for November 13, 1858: "In our business affairs, as in our political action, we are too much addicted to what sensation newspapers would call 'splurges'—we attempt to get rich by bold speculation instead of a long course of steady industry . . . To all these habits and tendencies the practice of chess is likely to act as a corrective. There is probably no other amusement which demands such patience, such intense and long-continued

exercise of the faculties of combination and analysis" (Holloway and Schwarz, *I Sit and Look Out,* p. 110).

36. The influence of Lamarck on Whitman is a subject which has been extensively researched, as Gay Wilson Allen has shown in *The New Walt Whitman Handbook* (New York: New York University Press, 1975). Its relevance to "Song of Myself" has been discussed by David Charles Leonard, "Lamarckian Evolution in Whitman's 'Song of Myself,' " *Walt Whitman Review* 24 (1978):21–28. There is also a particularly thorough account of the matter in Harry Gershenowitz, "Whitman and Lamarck Revisited," *Walt Whitman Review* 25 (1979):121–123; and in the same writer's "Two Lamarckians: Walt Whitman and Edward Carpenter," *Walt Whitman Quarterly Review* 2 (1984):35–39. In chap. 4 ("The Geological Timetable: Rocks") of *Nature and Culture: American Landscape and Painting, 1825–1876* (New York: Oxford University Press, 1980), Barbara Novak gives an excellent summary of the geological controversies of the day and explains their interest for artists and writers, Emerson included. He clung to Louis Agassiz's spiritual, teleological version of natural history and wrote an intriguing little note entitled "Consolations for readers of Darwin" (quoted in Novak, p. 280).

Edward Hitchcock's view of the cosmos, also quoted in Novak, is so similar to that which stood in the background of all Whitman's utterances on American democracy that it is worth recording here in full: "It appears that one of the grand means by which the plans of the Deity in respect to the material world are accomplished is constant change: partly mechanical, but chiefly chemical. In every part of our globe, on its surface, in its crust, and we have reason to suppose, even in its deep interior, these changes are in constant progress . . . In short, geology has given us a glimpse of a great principle of *instability,* by which the *stability* of the universe is secured; and at the same time, all those movements and revolutions in the forms of matter essential to the existence of organic nature are produced. Formerly, the examples of decay so common everywhere were regarded as defects in nature; but they now appear to be an indication of wise and benevolent design—a part of the vast plans of the Deity for securing the stability and happiness of the universe."

37. See Madeleine Davis and David Wallbridge, eds., *Boundary and Space: An Introduction to the Work of D. W. Winnicott* (Harmondsworth: Penguin, 1983).
38. Ibid., pp. 55–56.
39. I am very grateful to my friend and colleague John Turner for drawing Winnicott's work to my attention. There is also useful material on this subject in Anthony Storr, *The Dynamics of Creation* (Harmondsworth: Penguin, 1983).
40. Holloway, *Uncollected Poetry,* 1:64.
41. I am not at this point concerned to argue that Shelley directly influenced Whitman's thinking in these matters, but the possibility of debts incurred has been entertained by Roland A. Duerksen, "Similarities between Shelley's 'Defence of Poetry' and Whitman's 1855 Preface: A Comparison," *Walt Whitman Review* 10 (1964):51–60; and "Markings by Whitman in His Copy of Shelley's Works," *Walt Whitman Review* 14 (1968):147–151.

42. For a subtle and imaginative treatment of this theme, see the chapter on Whitman in Lewis Hyde, *The Gift: Imagination and the Erotic Life of Property* (New York: Random House, 1983).

43. This is what he had in mind when he wrote of the "true noble expanded American character" in the following terms: "It is to be poor, rather than rich—but to prefer death sooner than any mean dependence. Prudence is part of it, because prudence is the right arm of independence" (Holloway, *Uncollected Poetry*, 2:63).

44. Blake, *Complete Writings*, p. 229.

45. Ibid., p. 228.

46. Emerson, in *The Dial*, 2:149.

47. Edward Pessen, *Jacksonian America* (Homewood, Ill.: Dorsey Press, 1969), p. 34. For "the Jacksonian character: a contemporary portrait of American personality, traits and values," see chap. 4 of this book. Whitman's feelings about his money-making society were further complicated by his own family's involvement in business, and his mixed reactions to that, as has been shown by Ivan Marki, *The Trials of the Poet* (New York: Columbia University Press, 1976), pp. 63–64.

48. Holloway, *Uncollected Poetry*, 1:124.

49. Wilentz, *Chants Democratic*, p. 4.

50. The difference between these two stages has been usefully summarized by Raymond Williams in *Culture* (Glasgow: Fontana, 1981).

51. Wilentz, *Chants Democratic*, pp. 5, 6.

52. For a full discussion, see Edward Pessen, *Most Uncommon Jacksonians* (Albany: State University of New York Press, 1967).

53. Wilentz, *Chants Democratic*, p. 107.

54. See Michael Lebowitz, "The Jacksonians: Paradox Lost," in B. J. Bernstein, ed., *Towards a New Past* (London: Chatto and Windus, 1970), pp. 65–89. Actually Lebowitz is here disputing this view of the schizophrenic Jacksonian, supposedly split between the Old Republic personality and the New Acquisitive Man. But the paradox fits Whitman, nevertheless. For a description of the new capitalist ethos of the immediate prewar era, see Eric Foner, *Free Soil, Free Labor, Free Men* (Oxford: Oxford University Press, 1970).

3. Inhabiting the Kosmos

1. Gay Wilson Allen, for instance, explains the word as follows: "In 'Song of Myself' Whitman called himself a 'Kosmos,' perhaps meaning that his 'greatest poet' in the 1855 Preface is an all-inclusive system, independent of outside forces. His preference for the Greek spelling . . . which came from Sanskrit *cad*, 'to distinguish one's self,' indicates emphasis on independent order and harmony as an attribute of his own 'divinity' " (*The New Walt Whitman Handbook*, New York: New York University Press, 1975, p. 343). As several critics have noted, the publication in America of translations of Alexander von Humboldt's *Cosmos* had made the word, and the idea, current in the fifties.

2. David Allen and Warren Tallman, eds., *The Poetics of the New American Poetry* (New York: Grove Press, 1979), p. 160.

3. See Bruce Collins, "The Ideology of the Ante-Bellum Northern Democrats," *Journal of American Studies* 11 (1979):103–121.

4. Edward Pessen, *Most Uncommon Jacksonians* (Albany: State University of New York Press, 1967), p. 165.

5. For a full discussion of Leggett's economic theories and an outline of his life, see Richard Hofstadter, "William Leggett, Spokesman of Jacksonian Democracy," *Political Science Quarterly* 5 (1943):581–594. There are informative chapters on Leggett in Marvin Meyers, *The Jacksonian Persuasion* (Stanford: Stanford University Press, 1957); and E. K. Spann, *Ideals and Politics: New York Intellectuals and Liberal Democracy, 1820–1880* (Albany: State University of New York Press, 1972).

6. Emory Holloway, ed., *The Uncollected Poetry and Prose of Walt Whitman* (London: Heinemann, 1922), 1:124.

7. Joseph Jay Rubin, "Equal Rights in the Foreground," in K. W. Cameron, ed., *Scholars' Companion to the American Renaissance,* 1st ser., vol. 2, pt. 4 (Hartford: Transcendental Books, 1977), pp. 20–23.

8. Horace Traubel, *With Walt Whitman in Camden* (New York: Rowman and Littlefield, 1961), 2:308.

9. Ibid., p. 84. See also his defense of free trade and attack on the "malevolent" spirit of the tariff in ibid., 1:99.

10. This, of course, was the standard belief of all idealistic liberals. William Cullen Bryant argued that "without the corporate power derived from government, there could be no monopolies, no encouragement to violate the laws of nature, no privileged protection from the will of the community. In a society composed exclusively of individuals, no man or no group of men could with impunity interfere with the laws of trade or violate the interests of the people. The result would be a truly republican society" (Spann, *Ideals,* p. 106). Unlike Bryant's, however, Whitman's idealism had a strongly artisanal flavor to it.

11. Compare Spann's comment on Bryant: "Nowhere was the prophet more disappointed than in his hopes that Americans would be content with individual status, for few ambitious men could resist the temptation to acquire corporate power in the face of the growing opportunities and complexities of urban-commercial life" (*Ideals,* pp. 107–108). By contrast, and much more realistically, Parke Godwin "and other utopians saw competition in existing society as turning man against man in a war that encouraged selfishness, brutality, and the drive for dominance" (ibid., p. 146).

12. Pessen, *Uncommon Jacksonians,* p. 172.

13. Marvin Meyers, *Jacksonian Persuasion,* p. 155.

14. Emory Holloway, ed., *Walt Whitman: Complete Verse and Selected Prose* (London: Nonesuch Press, 1938), p. 593.

15. Although the most comprehensive and sophisticated consideration by far of this change as it affected New York is to be found in Wilentz's work, there are other studies that may also be profitably consulted, including chap. 1 of

Pessen's *Most Uncommon Jacksonians* and the useful summary provided by Charles A. Glaab and Theodore Brown in *A History of Urban America* (New York: Macmillan, 1976). Several features of the poetry that I comment on here have already been splendidly discussed by Leo Marx under the heading of "pastoralism" in *The Machine in the Garden; Technology and the Pastoral Ideal in America* (New York: Oxford University Press, 1964).

16. Lawrence Buell, *Literary Transcendentalism: Style and Vision in the American Renaissance* (Ithaca, N.Y.: Cornell University Press, 1973), p. 186.
17. Traubel, *Camden,* 3:224.
18. Horace Traubel, *With Walt Whitman in Camden,* vol. 6, ed. Gertrude Traubel and William White (Carbondale: Southern Illinois University Press, 1982), p. 132.
19. Holloway, *Uncollected Poetry,* 2:250–252.
20. Traubel, *Camden,* 1:42.
21. Emory Holloway and Vernolian Schwarz, eds., *I Sit and Look Out* (New York: AMS Press, 1966), pp. 71, 72.
22. After the war Whitman became understandably more alarmed than ever at the tensions within society, blaming it on "wolfish parties" that owned "no law but their own will, more and more combative, less and less tolerant of the idea of ensemble and of equal brotherhood" (2:399–400). Troubled, he harked back to an old Long Island character remembered by his mother— a memory that may perhaps have helped Whitman devise a role for himself as a poet: "She was known by the name of Peacemaker. She was well toward eighty years old, of happy and sunny temperament . . . She had come to be a tacitly agreed upon domestic regulator, judge, settler of difficulties, shepherdess, and reconciler in the land" (2:401).
23. Sean Wilentz, *Chants Democratic: New York City and the Rise of the American Working Class, 1788–1850* (New York: Oxford University Press, 1984) p. 109.
24. E. K. Spann, *The New Metropolis: New York City, 1840–1857* (New York: Columbia University Press, 1981), p. 18.
25. Ibid., p. 112.
26. Ibid., pp. 42–43.
27. Ibid., p. 43.
28. *The Riverside Edition of Emerson's Complete Works* (London: Routledge, 1883), 3:25.
29. Elsewhere in the preface, Whitman imagined "the poets of the kosmos" as effecting a revolution of values that would be tantamount to a reorganization of society on a more equitable, even egalitarian, basis: "They are of use— they dissolve poverty from its need, and riches from its conceit. You large proprietor, they say, shall not realize or perceive more than any one else. The owner of the library is not he who holds a legal title to it, having bought and paid for it" (2:450). But of course this was a strictly poetic arrangement, a change that would conveniently occur without any actual redistribution of property.
30. Emerson, *Riverside Edition,* 3:40.

31. A full and extremely knowledgeable account of Coleridge's convictions at this early stage of his complicated intellectual career can be found in the editors' introduction to Lewis Patton and Peter Mann, eds., *Lectures 1795 on Politics and Religion*. Vol. 1 of *The Collected Works of Coleridge* (Princeton: Princeton University Press, 1971).

32. E. H. Coleridge, ed., *The Poetical Works of S. T. Coleridge* (London: Oxford University Press, 1974), p. 113.

33. Ibid., pp. 113–114.

34. Ibid., pp. 114–115.

35. Another passage from *Democratic Vistas* is full of pathos, as Whitman sees what had once been vista turned into an infinitely receding future prospect, a Pisgah sight: "Though not for us the joy of entering at last the conquer'd city—not ours the chance ever to see with our own eyes the peerless power and splendid *eclat* of the democratic principle, arriv'd at meridian, filling the world with effulgence and majesty far beyond those of past history's kings, or all dynastic sway—there is yet, to whoever is eligible among us, the prophetic vision, the joy of being toss'd in the brave turmoil of these times— the promulgation and the path, obedient, lowly reverent to the voice, the gesture of the god, or holy ghost, which others see not, hear not—with the proud consciousness that amid whatever clouds, seductions, or heart-wearying postponements, we have never deserted, never despair'd, never abandon'd the faith" (2:391). The whole passage is strikingly similar—and most suggestive in its similarity—to the famously mosaic conclusion of Arnold's essay "The Function of Criticism at the Present Time": "That promised land it will not be ours to enter, and we shall die in the wilderness: but to have desired to enter it, to have saluted it from afar, is already, perhaps, the best distinction among contemporaries; it will certainly be the best title to esteem with prosperity" (*Essays*, London: Oxford University Press, 1914, p. 36).

4. Crossing Brooklyn Ferry

1. John Wilmerding, *Audubon, Homer, Whistler and Nineteenth-Century America* (New York: Lamplight, 1978), p. 8.

2. Peter Redgrove, *Dr Faust's Sea-Spiral Spirit and Other Poems* (London: Routledge and Kegan Paul, 1972), p. 31.

3. The phrase is borrowed from Emyr Humphreys, whose book *The Taliesin Tradition* (London: Black Raven Press, 1983) traces Taliesin's ancient and continuing role in Welsh history and culture. A famous notebook entry makes clear how Taliesin was reborn in Whitman in the guise of an American transcendentalist: "The soul or spirit transmits itself into all matter—into rocks, and can live the life of a rock—into the sea, and can feel itself the sea—into the oak, or other tree—into an animal, and feel itself a horse, a fish, or bird—into the earth—into the motions of the suns and stars—A man only is interested in anything when he identifies himself with it" (Emory Holloway, ed., *The Uncollected Poetry and Prose of Walt Whitman*, London:

Heinemann, 1922, 2:64). Whitman's boasting can also, of course, be viewed within a strictly native context of braggart frontier humor, as Constance Rourke so memorably demonstrated many years ago, in *American Humor: A Study of the National Character* (New York: Doubleday, 1953).

4. Redgrove, *Dr Faust*, p. 27.

5. I do not at all mean to suggest that these painters influenced Whitman; I am only suggesting that an interesting parallel can be made between their use of light and his. As far as we can tell, their work was unknown to Whitman, although this was a period when he was associating very closely with Brooklyn artists, even taking some painting lessons himself, and preaching the need for native American art (Justin Kaplan, *Walt Whitman: A Life,* New York: Simon and Schuster, 1980, pp. 167–168). This interest in painting had been characteristic of Whitman since his youth (Joseph Jay Rubin, *The Historic Whitman,* University Park: Pennsylvania State University Press, 1973, chap. 17), and was to remain, and perhaps intensify, in his old age. A particular favorite by then was Millet, as F. O. Matthiessen has shown in *American Renaissance* (Oxford: Oxford University Press, 1974). He also expressed great enthusiasm for the new American art of Thomas Eakins (see Elizabeth Johns, *Thomas Eakins: The Heroism of Modern Life,* Princeton: Princeton University Press, 1983, chap. 6). There is a useful summary of this artistic context in Kent Blaser, "Walt Whitman and American Art," *Walt Whitman Review* 24 (1978):108–118. Whitman's influence on modern American art has been scintillatingly discussed by Max Kozloff, "Walt Whitman and American Art," in E. H. Miller, ed., *The Artistic Legacy of Walt Whitman* (New York: New York University Press, 1970), pp. 29–53.

6. See her contribution to John Wilmerding, ed., *American Light: The Luminist Movement, 1850–1875* (New York: Harper and Row, 1980).

7. Barbara Novak, *Nature and Culture: American Landscape and Painting, 1825–1875* (New York: Oxford University Press, 1980), p. 43.

8. Wilmerding, *American Light,* p. 11.

9. A. S. B. Glover, ed., *Shelley's Selected Poetry, Prose and Letters* (London: Nonesuch Press, 1951), p. 348.

10. Ibid., p. 342.

11. John Bauer, in Wilmerding, *American Light,* p. 12.

12. In Leon Edel, ed., *The Complete Tales of Henry James* (London: Rupert Hart-Davis, 1962), 1:127.

13. Harold Aspiz has provided a most illuminating interpretation of this poem "Faces," explaining it with reference to the popular nineteenth-century pseudoscience of physiognomy. See *Walt Whitman and the Body Beautiful* (Urbana: University of Illinois Press, 1980).

14. Arthur Geffen has recently provided a full and subtle account of Whitman's passion for the ferries, as part of an explanation of why the poet never celebrated the technological marvel of the building of Brooklyn Bridge ("Silence and Denial: Walt Whitman and the Brooklyn Bridge," *Walt Whitman Quarterly Review* 1 [1984]:1–11). To the reasons he advances, I would add the suggestion that Whitman was too attached to an independent Brooklyn ever

to welcome the constructing of a bridge that virtually tied it to its bigger partner and rival, New York (see chap. 6 below).

15. E. K. Spann, *The New Metropolis: New York City, 1840–1857* (New York: Columbia University Press, 1981), p. 203.

16. See Thomas L. Brasher, *Whitman as Editor of the "Brooklyn Daily Eagle"* (Detroit: Wayne State University Press, 1911).

17. Spann, *New Metropolis*, p. 187.

18. Novak, in Wilmerding, *American Light*, pp. 27–28.

19. Holloway, *Uncollected Poetry*, 1:169.

20. Ibid., p. 168.

21. Quoted in Rubin, *Historic Whitman*, p. 351.

22. Brasher, *Whitman as Editor*, pp. 52–53.

23. Rubin, *Historic Whitman*, p. 350.

24. Emory Holloway and Vernolian Schwarz, eds., *I Sit and Look Out* (New York: AMS Press, 1966), p. 145.

25. Holloway, *Uncollected Poetry*, 1:262, 264.

26. Wallace Stevens, *Collected Poems* (London: Faber and Faber, 1959), p. 520.

27. Novak, in Wilmerding, *American Light*, pp. 25-26.

5. The Nature of American Society

1. Raymond Williams, *Problems in Materialism and Culture* (London: Verso, 1980), pp. 70–71.

2. For Whitman's relationship to de Tocqueville, see Keith Monroe, "Tocqueville, Whitman and the Poetry of Democracy," *Walt Whitman Review* 26 (1980):52–58.

3. From J. M. Robson, ed., *Essays on Politics and Society*, vol. 18 of *The Collected Work of John Stuart Mill* (London: Routledge and Kegan Paul, 1977), p. 195.

4. Ibid., pp. 143, 148.

5. Ibid., p. 219.

6. Ibid., p. 263.

7. Anthony Beale, ed., *D. H. Lawrence: Selected Literary Criticism* (London: Heinemann, 1961), p. 154.

8. Charles Wright, *Country Music: Selected Early Poems* (Middletown, Conn.: Wesleyan University Press, 1982), p. 36.

9. Wallace Stevens, *Collected Poems* (London: Faber and Faber, 1959), p. 234.

10. O. B. Bunce, in William Cullen Bryant, ed., *Picturesque America* (New York: Appleton, 1874), 2:547. A footnote in *Specimen Days* records Whitman's objections to "those who will laud the specially picturesque—the chasm, the cliff, the mountain-peak." On that occasion, though, he conflates the picturesque with the sublime and criticizes the cult of the awesome: "I don't want to be awed only by the shows of Nature—not merely to admire—I want to be dilated, strengthened and soothed, not kept at a distance" (1:208).

11. For Wordsworth's complex feelings towards the picturesque see Martin Price's

valuable essay, "The Picturesque Moment," in Frederick W. Hilles and Harold Bloom, eds., *From Sensibility to Romanticism* (New York: Oxford University Press, 1965), pp. 259–292.

12. William Wordsworth, *Poetical Works,* ed. Thomas Hutchinson and Ernest de Selincourt, reprint ed. (London: Oxford University Press, 1969), p. 576.

13. Bryant's was not, of course, by any means the first book to treat America as a rich source of the picturesque. Notable predecessors had been Joshua Shaw, *Picturesque Views of American Scenery* (1820); William Guy Wall, *The Hudson River Portfolio* (1828); William Bartlette, *American Scenery* (1840); and the book *Lotus Eating*, with drawings by Kensett (1852). Lisa Fellows Andrus has pointed out that by the 1850s "there was even a standard circuit taken by artists and tourists of the picturesque spots in the mountains of New York State and New England" (in John Wilmerding, ed., *American Light: The Luminist Movement, 1850–1875,* New York, Harper and Row, 1980, pp. 31–56).

14. Bryant, *Picturesque America,* 1:iii.

15. Ibid., 2:96.

16. Ibid., 2:50.

17. Ibid., 1:110.

18. Ibid., 1:200.

19. Brian Jay Wolf, *Romantic Re-vision* (London: Oxford University Press, 1969), p. 11.

20. A. S. B. Glover, ed., *Shelley's Selected Poetry, Prose and Letters* (London: Nonesuch Press, 1951), p. 34.

21. Lawrence, *Selected Literary Criticism*, p. 163.

22. In fact, they could usefully be discussed as picturesque in the sense Whitman used the phrase when referring to the unappreciated vividness of scenes from ordinary American working life. During his crossing of the Alleghenies, on his way south to New Orleans in 1858, he recorded the glimpses he saw of such natural "pictures." "They might, it seems to me," he concluded, "afford first rate scenes for an *American* painter—one who, not continually straining to be merely second or third best, in *imitation*, seizes original and really picturesque occasions of this sort for his pieces" (Emory Holloway, ed., *Uncollected Poetry and Prose of Walt Whitman,* London: Heinemann, 1922, 1:185–186).

23. Whitman himself put this contrast most uncompromisingly—even if at the same time he phrased it in rather conventional and precious language—in his Brooklyn Art Union address (1851). "Among such a people as the Americans, viewing most things with an eye to pecuniary profit—more for acquiring than for enjoying or well developing what they acquire—ambitious of the physical rather than the intellectual; a race to whom matter of fact is everything, and the ideal nothing—a nation of whom the steam engine is no bad symbol—he does a good work who, pausing in the way, calls to the feverish crowd that in the life we live upon this beautiful earth, there may, after all, be something vaster and better than dress and the table, and business

and politics." He then proceeds to tell the story of a Persian poet who, when challenged to prove his usefulness, replied by asking what use had a rose: " 'To be beautiful, to perfume the air,' answered the man of gains. 'And I,' responded the poet, 'am of use to perceive its beauty and to smell its perfume' " (Holloway, *Uncollected Poetry*, 1:241).

24. Bernard Rosenthal, *City of Nature* (Newark: University of Delaware Press, 1980). Christopher Mulvey has contrasted the indifference of Americans to the beauty of their own country with the appreciation of it shown by visiting English tourists (*Anglo-American Landscapes,* Cambridge: Cambridge University Press, 1983).

25. Barbara Novak, "The Double-Edged Axe," in *Art in America* 64 (1976):44–50.

26. Gary Snyder, *Myths and Texts* (New York: New Directions, 1978), p. 4.

27. Novak, "Double-Edged Axe," p. 45.

28. Coincidentally, there was a very slight personal connection between Whitman and George Pope Morris, author of this song. When he was an apprentice, he had some of his pieces published in Morris's paper, the *New-York Mirror* (Justin Kaplan, *Walt Whitman: A Life,* New York: Simon and Schuster, 1980, pp. 79–80). Later, when Whitman's criticism of visiting English actors and actresses embraced Ellen Tree, the *Mirror,* in playful protest, produced its own, modified, version of the popular favorite: "Whitman, Spare That Tree!/By A Puff Critic" (Joseph Jay Rubin, *The Historic Whitman,* University Park: Pennsylvania State University Press, 1973, p. 163).

29. Basil Hall, quoted in Nicolai Cikovsky, Jr., " 'The Ravages of the Axe': The Meaning of the Tree-stump in Nineteenth-Century American Art," *The Art Bulletin* 61 (1979):611–626.

30. Thomas Cole, quoted in "Double-Edged Axe," p. 48.

31. Gustave de Beaumont, quoted in Rosenthal, *City of Nature,* p. 68

32. Pointing out that it was written not long after Whitman was paralyzed and moved to live with his brother George in Camden, New Jersey, Allen argues persuasively that the poem is very much an account of Whitman's own shattered condition at this time (*The Solitary Singer,* New York: Macmillan, 1955, p. 457).

33. The cryptic quality of these opening lines has been noticed by Linda Peavy, " 'Wooded Flesh and Metal Bone': A Look at the Riddle of the Broad-Axe," *Walt Whitman Review* 20 (1974):152–154, but she has not drawn the same conclusions as I have. For a completely different reading of the poem, see Dorothy M. T. Gregory, "The Celebration of Nativity: 'Broad-Axe Poem,' " *Walt Whitman Quarterly Review* 2 (1984):1–11.

34. Merritt Y. Hughes, ed., *John Milton: Complete Poems and Major Prose* (New York: Odyssey Press, 1957), pp. 228–229.

35. Ray Allen Billington, *Westward Expansion: A History of the American Frontier* (New York: Macmillan, 1974), p. 263.

36. Wordsworth, *Poetical Works,* p. 147.

37. For further information on this and every other aspect of the lumber industry, consult Billington's comprehensive study, *Westward Expansion*.

6. Manahatta–New York

1. Morton White and Lucia White, *The Intellectual versus the City* (Cambridge, Mass.: Harvard University Press, 1962), p. 2.
2. Oscar Handlin, *The Historian and the City* (Cambridge, Mass.: Harvard University Press, 1963), p. 19.
3. E. K. Spann, *The New Metropolis: New York City, 1840–1857* (New York: Columbia University Press, 1981), p. 342. E. H. Miller has taken an opposite view: "It has been said too loosely and too often that Whitman is the first of the urban poets . . . The settings of his greatest poems are almost invariably rural" (*Walt Whitman's Poetry: A Psychological Journey*, New York: New York University Press, 1968, p. 32). There have been several important recent discussions of Whitman's treatment of urban life. Especially valuable are James L. Machor, "Pastoralism and the American Urban Ideal: Hawthorne, Whitman and the Literary Pattern," *American Literature* 54 (1982):329–353; and Peter Conrad, *The Art of the City: Views and Versions of New York* (Oxford: Oxford University Press, 1984).
4. Horace Traubel, *With Walt Whitman in Camden*, vol. 6, ed. Gertrude Traubel and William White (Carbondale: Southern Illinois University Press, 1982), p. 201.
5. For Whitman's connections with these movements, see Joseph Jay Rubin, *The Historic Whitman* (University Park: Pennsylvania State University Press, 1973), and "Equal Rights in the Foreground," in K. W. Cameron, ed., *Scholars' Companion to the American Renaissance,* 1st ser., vol. 2, pt. 4 (Hartford: Transcendental Books, 1977), pp. 20–23. A detailed history of the workingmen's movements is to be found in Edward Pessen, *Most Uncommon Jacksonians* (Albany: State University of New York Press, 1967), and in Walter Hugins, *Jacksonian Democracy and the Working Class* (Stanford: Stanford University Press, 1960).
6. Emory Holloway, ed., *The Uncollected Poetry and Prose of Walt Whitman* (London: Heinemann, 1922), 1:93.
7. Ibid., 2:265.
8. For the background to this idea in Romantic philosophy consult A. O. Lovejoy's discussion of the "principle of plenitude," in *The Great Chain of Being* (Cambridge, Mass.: Harvard University Press, 1936), passim.
9. The Brooklyn of Whitman's childhood was in any case a kind of halfway house between the urban and the rural. He himself recalled how "the population was then between 10,000 and 12,000. The character of the place was thoroughly rural" (2:774).
10. Although, of course, he did like to imagine himself as a far-from-anonymous figure in the general urban crowd. In a particularly splendid piece of self-advertisement he observes himself from a distance as one of the thronging

masses: "Tall, large, rough-looking man, in a journeyman carpenter's uniform. Coarse, sanguine complexion . . ." (Emory Holloway and Ralph Adimari, eds., *New York Dissected by Walt Whitman,* Folcroft: Folcroft Library Editions, n.d.; reprint of New York: Rufus Rockwell Wilson, 1936; p. 130).

11. C. J. Furness, ed., *Walt Whitman's Workshop* (New York: Russell and Russell, 1964), p. 61.

12. In the same way, and for related reasons, he pleaded for Long Island to be called "Paumanok." This would be a distinctive name, "which would by time and association become a sound of pride and convey the idea of home." Its beauty would be appropriate to the beauty of the great, growing, city of Brooklyn, while simultaneously it would commemorate "the great nation of the lenni-Lenape, or Delawares, of which stock the aborigines of this region were a part" (Holloway, *Uncollected Poetry,* 2:274).

13. It would be interesting to consider the influence of this word, derived from medical theories of the time concerning disease prevention, on Whitman's view of the social mobility that characterized modern America. Compare his use of it to justify (rather reluctantly, it should be noted) the practice of mass migration on May 1 of every year, as the whole of New York and Brooklyn seemed to be moving house at once: "The sanitary effects of the moving institution makes some recompense for the evils. The whitewash, the clean house, the thorough ventilation, purification, carpets shook, everything dusted and sent through the open air—these are all good" (Emory Holloway and Vernolian Schwarz, eds., *I Sit and Look Out,* New York: AMS Press, 1966, p. 126).

14. Horace Greeley, quoted in Spann, *New Metropolis,* p. 73.

15. Whitman did register displeasure at this in his rather tediously whimsical essay-writing style: "While upon the subject, let us in confidence reader, just whisper to you that we are no friend to thoroughfares that are rigid and right-angular. The checker-board principle applied to laying-out a town is our abomination . . . Much more do we prefer the winding and curvicular arrangement. We like to come upon new shows—to turn a bend, and behold something fresh. Uniformity! Why it's the taste of the vulgar. Nature hath nought of it" (Rubin, *Historic Whitman,* p. 348). This was a reaction very much in keeping with the urban landscape theories of his contemporary Calvert Vaux.

16. Spann, *New Metropolis,* p. 16.

17. Horace Traubel, *With Walt Whitman in Camden* (New York: Rowman and Littlefield, 1961), 2:71.

18. Thomas Paine, *Rights of Man* (London: J. M. Dent, 1969), p. 214.

19. Quoted in Spann, *New Metropolis,* p. 16.

20. Hayden White, quoted in Sam B. Girgus, *The Law of the Heart: Individualism and the Modern Self in American Literature* (Austin: University of Texas Press, 1970), p. 54.

21. E. H. Miller, ed., *Walt Whitman: The Correspondence* (New York: New York University Press, 1961), 2:53.

22. Ibid., 2:52.

23. Ibid., 2:55.
24. Holloway, *Uncollected Poetry*, 1:154.
25. Charles I. Glicksberg, ed., *Whitman and the Civil War* (Philadelphia: University of Pennsylvania Press, 1933), p. 48.
26. Bayard Still, ed., *Urban America* (Boston: Little Brown, 1974), pp. 146–147. In the early nineteenth century the voluntary fire companies had chiefly been manned by the respectable middle class, property owners who turned out to defend property. But by the 1830s "the fire laddie was becoming a new social type in Jacksonian New York" (Sean Wilentz, *Chants Democratic: New York City and the Rise of the American Working Class, 1788–1850,* New York: Oxford University Press, 1984, pp. 257–263). He was now, typically, one of the lower classes, a "mechanic" intensely proud to be a member of the local brigade, and demonstrating the physical prowess and daring which entitled him to a place among the elite of working-class culture. Inter-company rivalry was intense, and sometimes violent. Kaplan has drawn attention to the many fires in Brooklyn and New York (which suffered twice as many as the London of the same period) that affected Whitman directly, culminating in the destruction, in 1849, of his own printing shop and newspaper office (*Walt Whitman: A Life,* New York: Simon and Schuster, 1980, pp. 109–110). As he noted, "Whitman and other practiced observers acquired after a while a sort of firebug discrimination" (p. 109). But there was more to his interest in fires than that, as Harold Aspiz has shrewdly remarked: "His concern for injured firemen, like his compassion for wounded soldiers, fed on the psychological-sexual interplay of violence and suffering" (*Walt Whitman and the Body Beautiful,* Urbana: University of Illinois Press, 1980, p. 62). By 1858 Whitman had taken to visiting injured firemen in various New York hospitals.
27. Traubel, *Camden*, 2:87–88.
28. Spann, *New Metropolis*, p. 94.
29. Holloway and Schwarz, *I Sit and Look Out*, p. 82.
30. Ibid., p. 83.
31. The whole sorry history of the repeated attempts made to remedy the deplorable housing situation in New York is expertly summarized in Spann, *New Metropolis*, chap. 7.
32. Holloway and Adimari, *New York Dissected*, pp. 89–102.
33. A good example of his campaigning is the *Brooklyn Eagle* editorial (1849) on working women (Holloway, *Uncollected Poetry*, 1:137). Jeff's letters to his brother after his marriage suggest that his wife Mattie was sometimes employed as an outworker, making shirt fronts for New York manufacturers. She apparently found it taxing work. Jeff told Walt on April 6, 1863, that Mattie "has no work and has not had hardly since you were away, and I am glad she has not" (Dennis Berthold and Kenneth M. Price, eds., *Dear Brother Walt: The Letters of Thomas Jefferson Whitman*, Kent, Ohio: Kent State University Press, 1984, p. 45).
34. Holloway and Schwarz, *I Sit and Look Out*, p. 73.
35. Ibid., p. 84.

36. Thomas Pinney, ed., *The Essays of George Eliot* (London: Routledge and Kegan Paul, 1968), p. 270.
37. Daniel Curry, quoted in Spann, *New Metropolis,* p. 42.
38. For a sociologist's appreciation of this side of Whitman, see V. W. Turner, *The Ritual Process: Structure and Anti-Structure* (London: Routledge and Kegan Paul, 1968), p. 203.
39. Spann, *New Metropolis,* p. 42.
40. Greeley, quoted in ibid., p. 179.
41. Rubin, *Historic Whitman,* p. 323.
42. Ibid., p. 241.
43. Holloway, *Uncollected Poetry,* 2:252. Very interesting conclusions about the social, political, and economic power of the wealthy in the Brooklyn of this period have been drawn by Edward Pessen in *Riches, Class and Power before the Civil War* (Boston: D. C. Heath, 1973).
44. Holloway, *Uncollected Poetry,* 1:262.
45. Ibid., 1:262.
46. Ibid., 2:253.
47. Holloway and Schwarz, *I Sit and Look Out,* p. 145.
48. Holloway, *Uncollected Poetry,* 1:262.
49. Ibid., 1:262.
50. Charles Tomlinson, *Selected Poems, 1951–1974* (Oxford, Oxford University Press, 1978), p. 133.
51. Robin B. Hoople also sees the 1860 version as a crucial step in Whitmans's changing attitude to the city: "Walt Whitman and the City of Friends," in K. W. Cameron, *Scholars' Companion* 1, pt. 4, pp. 45–51.
52. E. H. Miller believes there is a nostalgia for pastoral society in *Calamus* (*Whitman's Poetry,* p. 150).
53. The Jeffersonian tradition of anti-urbanism that is relevant here is discussed by White and White, *Intellectual versus the City;* and by Robert A. Dahl, *Pluralist Democracy in the United States* (Chicago: Rand McNally, 1967). And there is a particularly useful survey in Leo Marx's work, *The Machine in the Garden* (New York: Oxford University Press, 1964).
54. Miller, *Correspondence,* 2:74.
55. Ibid., 1:269.
56. Ibid., 1:180.
57. Traubel, *Camden,* 6:313–314.
58. Charles Glaab and Theodore Brown, *A History of Urban America* (New York: Macmillan, 1983), pp. 36–37.
59. Miller, *Correspondence,* 2:97.
60. Ibid., 1:342. This letter also continues very interestingly: "Only the majestic & moving river & rapid sea-water scenery & life about the islands, N.Y. and Brooklyn tower into larger proportions than ever. I doubt if the world elsewhere has their equal, or could have, to me—The waters about New York & west end of Long-Island are real sea-waters, & are ever-rolling & rushing in or out—never placid, never calm—surely they please this uneasy spirit, Me, that ebbs & flows too all the while, yet gets nowhere, & amounts to nothing—".

61. Theodore Dreiser, *An American Tragedy* (London: Constable, 1932), p. 4.
62. The phrase quoted is that William James uses to describe a world inadequately served by the "shiveringly thin wrappings" of transcendental idealism (*A Pluralistic Universe*, London: Longmans, Green, 1909, p. 136).
63. Traubel, *Camden*, 6:195.
64. Ibid., 3:44.
65. Ibid., 3:177.
66. Ibid., 1:38.
67. Ibid., 2:29.
68. Miller, *Correspondence*, 3:118.
69. Ibid., 4:299.
70. Ibid., 2:60.

7. The Other Civil War

1. Emory Holloway, ed., *Walt Whitman: Complete Verse and Selected Prose* (London: Nonesuch Press, 1938), p. 592.
2. Ibid., pp. 588, 587, 589.
3. George M. Fredrickson, *The Inner Civil War* (New York: Harper and Row, 1968), pp. 8–9. In calling it a period of "cosmic optimism," Fredrickson points out that this widespread anti-institutionalism was not simply an unconsidered form of utopianism but a pertinent expression of the spirit of a capitalistic society in a period of unprecedentedly rapid economic and geographical expansion.
4. For an explanation of why, nevertheless, the Democratic party of the fifties continued to satisfy the political aspirations of large numbers of Northerners, see Bruce Collins, "The Ideology of the Ante-Bellum Northern Democrats," *Journal of American Studies* 11 (1979):103–121. But elsewhere he points out that there was during that decade much more dissatisfaction with, and many more defections from, the political party system than historians have generally recognized. See "Community and Consensus in Ante-Bellum America," *The Historical Journal* 19 (1976):640–646.
5. Holloway, *Complete Verse*, p. 589. The "negative liberalism," or mistrust of state power, which characterized Democratic ideology, and of which the Locofoco philosophy was an extreme version is illuminatingly discussed by Lee Benson in *The Concept of Jacksonian Democracy* (Princeton: Princeton University Press, 1961), chap. 5.
6. Quoted in Joseph Jay Rubin, *The Historic Whitman* (University Park: Pennsylvania State University Press, 1973), p. 141.
7. "The Racial Attitudes of the New York Free Soilers" is a very thorough survey by Eric Foner, in *Politics and Ideology in the Age of the Civil War* (Oxford: Oxford University Press, 1980), chap. 3.
8. Rubin, *Historic Whitman*, p. 204.
9. Emory Holloway, ed., *The Uncollected Poetry and Prose of Walt Whitman* (London: Heinemann, 1922), 1:171.
10. Foner has also examined the labor movement's attitudes toward both free soil and abolition (*Politics and Ideology*, chap. 4).

11. Holloway, *Uncollected Poetry,* 1:172.

12. For instance, Rubin has pointed out that as a reaction to the 1854 slump "Benton, in a well-attended lecture, gave his pragmatic solution for easing the suffering of city dwellers—a transcontinental railroad to carry them to free land so spacious that twenty million families could homestead there" (*Historic Whitman,* p. 299). For an excellent discussion of the homestead movement in the forties and fifties, including the safety-valve theory, see Henry Nash Smith, *Virgin Land: The American West as Symbol and Myth* (New York: Vintage Books, 1950).

13. Holloway, *Complete Verse,* p. 595.

14. Foner has interestingly noted that "Lincoln's Union was of self-made men. The society he was attempting to preserve was, in this respect, also premodern—the world of the small shop, the independent farm, and the village artisan" (*Politics and Ideology,* p. 32).

15. This description of early republicanism relies heavily on the classic study by Eric Foner, *Free Soil, Free Labor, Free Men* (Oxford: Oxford University Press, 1970), especially chap. 1; and on Joel H. Silbey, *The Transformation of American Politics, 1840–1860* (Englewood Cliffs, N.J.: Prentice-Hall, 1967). The complacency of the Republicans is well characterized by Collins, "Ideology," p. 117.

16. A convenient summary of Whitman's attitude toward blacks can be found in Daniel Aaron, *The Unwritten War: American Writers and the Civil War* (New York: Alfred Knopf, 1973), pp. 59–62.

17. This is demonstrated by Collins, "Community and Consensus," pp. 654–658.

18. Edward Pessen, *Riches, Class and Power before the Civil War* (Boston: D. C. Heath, 1973), p. 42.

19. Ibid., p. 42. This is a view in substantial agreement with those labor leaders of the twenties and thirties, whose social views interested both Whitman and his father, that America was "the land of class conflict" (Edward Pessen, *Most Uncommon Jacksonians,* Albany: State University of New York Press, 1967, p. 174).

20. E. H. Miller, ed., *Walt Whitman: The Correspondence* (New York: New York University Press, 1961), 1:40. This letter also includes a sentence that anticipates Whitman's mixed wartime reactions to his city: "At this moment, New York is the most radical city in America. It would be the most antislavery city, if the cause hadn't been made ridiculous by the freaks of the local leaders here."

21. Holloway, *Complete Verse,* p. 587.

22. Fredrickson, *Inner Civil War,* p. 56. Daniel Aaron agrees that Whitman's interpretation of the war was unique. See *Unwritten War,* chap. 4, especially "Sounding the Tocsin."

23. Miller, *Correspondence,* 1:99.

24. In this and other respects it is worth comparing Whitman's impressions of Washington with those of William Russell only a year or so previously; recorded in Fletcher Pratt, ed., *My Civil War Diary* (London: Hamish Hamilton, 1954), pp. 17–46, 188–268.

25. Miller, *Correspondence*, 1:69. Emerson, predictably, seems to have shared Whitman's initial dislike of Washington, "that least attractive [to me] of cities" (ibid., 1:66).
26. So strong and enduring was this feeling that he included sentiments and phrases from "The Eighteenth Presidency" in *Democratic Vistas* (after the war), when mentioning his antebellum "doubt and gloom." He attributed these criticisms, though, to "a foreigner, an acute and good man," while admitting that they corresponded to his "own observations" (2:386).
27. Miller, *Correspondence*, 1:75.
28. Ibid., 1:76.
29. Ibid., 1:82.
30. For Whitman's view of Lincoln see Aaron, *Unwritten War*, pp. 69–72.
31. Charles I. Glicksberg, ed., *Whitman and the Civil War* (Philadelphia: University of Pennsylvania Press, 1933), p. 29.
32. Ibid., p. 31. Whitman was already slowly moving toward the position (afterward confirmed by his own experiences as a Washington clerk) which he eventually outlined to Traubel during their discussion of Washington officialdom: " 'From my experience at Washington I should say that honesty is the prevailing atmosphere.' Somebody laughed. Whitman stubbornly resumed: 'Let me explain that. I do not refer to the swell officials—the men who wear the decorations, get the fat salaries (they are mostly dubious enough, though not all): I refer to the average clerks, the obscure crowd, who after all run the government: they are on the square. I have not known hundreds—I have known thousands—of them. I went to Washington as everybody goes there prepared to see everything done with some furtive intention, but I was disappointed—pleasantly disappointed' " (Horace Traubel, *With Walt Whitman in Camden*, New York: Rowman and Littlefield, 1961, 1:148). It is noticeable that in *Democratic Vistas* clerks have already been admitted to the ranks of noble, average Americans: "the floating, uncommitted electors, farmers, clerks, mechanics, the masters of parties" (2:399).
33. Miller, *Correspondence*, 1:171.
34. William White, ed., *Walt Whitman: Daybooks and Notebooks* (New York: New York University Press, 1978), 1:734. For the military authorities' views on discipline, see Fredrickson, *Inner Civil War*, chap. 4.
35. Glicksberg provides a useful summary of Whitman's views on hospital mismanagement during the war, including an article which appeared in the *Brooklyn Daily Eagle*, March 13, 1863 (*Unwritten War*, pp. 166–169).
36. The shooting of an inoffensive young soldier, William Grover, for desertion, seemed to Whitman to be a vividly ugly example of the callousness of both military and civilian authorities. "O the horrid contrast & the sarcasm of this life—to know who they really are that sit on judges benches, & who they perched on the criminal's box—to know. While all this gaud & tinsel shines in people's eyes amid the countless officers straps, amid all this show of general stars, & the bars of the captains & lieutenants—amid all the wind & puffing and infidelity—amid the swarms of contractors and their endless contracts, & the paper money—and out from all this—stalks like a phantom that boy, not yet nineteen years of age" (Glicksberg, *Civil War*, p. 127).

37. Whitman opposed all institutionalized response to suffering (Fredrickson, *Inner Civil War,* pp. 106–107). Justin Kaplan gives an excellent summary of Whitman's relationship to the various medical agencies in *Walt Whitman: A Life* (New York: Simon and Schuster, 1980), chap. 14.

38. This is the assumption made, for instance, by James E. Miller in his influential reading of *Drum Taps* (*A Critical Guide to Leaves of Grass,* Chicago, Chicago University Press, 1957, pp. 219–225).

39. Paul Fussell, *The Great War and Modern Memory* (Oxford: Oxford University Press, 1977), p. ix.

40. The fullest and most balanced discussions of *Drum Taps* have tended to appear in those works which compare Whitman's response to the war with that of other combatants and noncombatants. See Aaron, *Unwritten War,* pp. 56–74, especially pp. 66–69; and Fredrickson, *Inner Civil War,* pp. 90–97. John Snyder's book, *The Dear Love of Man* (Mouton: The Hague–Paris, 1975) also merits a special mention, since it seems not to have received the general attention it deserves.

41. Holloway, *Complete Verse,* p. 589.

42. Hennig Cohen, ed., *The Battle-Pieces of Herman Melville* (London: Yoseloff, 1964), p. 43.

43. Ibid., p. 40.

44. Harold Blodgett and Sculley Bradley, eds., *Comprehensive Reader's Edition of Leaves of Grass* (New York: New York University Press, 1965), p. 285.

45. Traubel, *Camden,* 3:205.

46. Compare his letter of July 15, 1863 (Miller, *Correspondence,* 1:117) with that of August 18 (ibid., 1:136). In Berthold and Price's edition of Jeff's correspondence there are several informative pages on the draft, including letters to Walt on the subject (Dennis Berthold and Kenneth M. Price, eds., *Dear Brother Walt: The Letters of Thomas Jefferson Whitman,* Kent, Ohio: Kent State University Press, 1984, pp. 63–67).

47. Horace Traubel, *With Walt Whitman in Camden,* vol. 6, ed. Gertrude Traubel and William White (Carbondale: Southern Illinois University Press, 1982), p. 172.

48. There is a detailed account of New York's attitude toward the whole question of secession during this period in S. D. Brummer, *The Political History of New York State during the Civil War* (New York: Columbia University Press, 1911). Whitman rejoiced in the upsurge of patriotism following Sumter but continued to have doubts about the city, as his letters, as well as the poems, show. "Well, dear comrades," he wrote to his friends in Washington during his brief visit to New York in November 1863, "it looks so different here in all this mighty city, every thing going with a big rush & so gay, as if there was neither war nor hospitals in the land. New York & Brooklyn appear nothing but prosperity & plenty" (Miller, *Correspondence,* 1:180).

49. White, *Daybooks,* 3:765.

50. Allen Nevins, *The War for the Union* (New York: Scribner, 1960), 2:528.

51. Ibid., 2:310.

52. Ibid., 2:511.

53. M. Shapira, ed., *Selected Library Criticism* (Harmondsworth: Penguin, 1968), p. 25.
54. Joseph Conrad, *Lord Jim* (Harmondsworth: Penguin, 1968), p. 76. Marlow's other wry remarks are also relevant: "My weakness consists in not having a discriminating eye for the incidental—for the externals—no eye for the hod of the rag-picker or the fine linen of the next man . . . A confounded democratic quality of vision which may be better than total blindness but has been of no advantage to me, I can assure you. Men expect one to take into account their fine linen. But I never could get up any enthusiasm about these things" (pp. 75–76).
55. Theodore Davis, quoted in Stephen W. Sears, ed., *The American Heritage Century Collection of Civil War Art* (New York: American Heritage Publishing Co., 1974), p. 125.
56. Traubel, *Camden*, 2:52–53.
57. There is pathos in Whitman's continuing references, after the war, to the unresolved contradictions of American society—its democratic principles, embodied in its political structure, being negated by the undemocratic spirit of so much of its social and economic life. He had no choice but to defer the resolution of this "conflict" to an ever more distant future, where America would eventually become "a compact whole, uniform, on tallying principles. For how," he plaintively asked, "can we remain divided contradicting ourselves, this way?" (2:409).
58. C. J. Furness, ed., *Walt Whitman's Workshop* (New York: Russell and Russell, 1964), p. 152.

8. The Pains and Obligations of Memory

1. Horace Traubel, *With Walt Whitman in Camden* (New York: Rowman and Littlefield, 1961), 3:111.
2. Christopher Ricks, ed., *The Poems of Tennyson* (London: Longmans, 1969), p. 926.
3. C. J. Furness, ed., *Walt Whitman's Workshop* (New York: Russell and Russell, 1964), pp. 61–62.
4. Charles I. Glicksberg, ed., *Whitman and the Civil War* (Philadelphia: University of Pennsylvania Press, 1933), p. 122.
5. Ibid., p. 123.
6. Emory Holloway, ed., *The Uncollected Poetry and Prose of Walt Whitman* (London: Heinemann, 1922), 2:28–29.
7. Glicksberg, *Civil War*, pp. 123–124.
8. There is an interesting study to be written, someday, of Whitman's use of pictures and tableaux in his Civil War writings. His notes on this period are studded with references to "the picturesque scene of a battery drill on the open plains" (Glicksberg, *Civil War*, p. 71), or to the "picturesque scene" spread "down below . . . The countless baggage wagons, with their white roofs, the numerous strings of mules, the railroad locomotive, the broad spread of slopes and hills winding their way over the railroad track, and

making a huge S towards the river" (ibid., p. 73). Simple enough these compositions may be, but Whitman's aesthetic reactions can also extend to disturbing observations like the following—reminiscent of passages in Owen's poetry:

> the profuse beauty of the young men's hair, damp with the spotted blood,
> their shining hair, red with the sticky blood,—clotted with spots of blood—
> the shining beauty of the young men's hair dampened with clots of blood. (ibid., p. 123)

9. Horace Traubel, *With Walt Whitman in Camden,* vol. 6, ed. Gertrude Traubel and William White (Carbondale: Southern Illinois University Press, 1982), p. 483. See, too, Whitman's letter on the subject of the cavalry troop: "I tell you it had the look of *real war*—noble looking fellows—a man looks—feels so proud on a good horse, & armed. . . . Alas, how many of these healthy handsome rollicking young men will lie cold in death, before the apples ripe in the orchards" (E. H. Miller, ed., *Walt Whitman: The Correspondence,* New York: New York University Press, 1961, 1:114).

10. Glicksberg, *Civil War,* p. 164.
11. Traubel, *Camden,* 6:254.
12. Hennig Cohen, ed., *The Battle-Pieces of Herman Melville* (London: Yoseloff, 1964), p. 98.
13. Ibid., p. 101.
14. Glicksberg, *Civil War,* p. 74.
15. Miller, *Correspondence,* 1:224.
16. Simone Weil, *Waiting on God,* trans. Emma Craufurd (London: Fontana, 1959), p. 81.
17. Miller, *Correspondence,* 1:276.
18. Ibid., 1:283, 324.
19. Ibid., 1:231.
20. Ibid., 1:204.
21. Ibid., 1:115.
22. Quoted in Justin Kaplan, *Walt Whitman: A Life* (New York: Simon and Schuster, 1980), p. 291.
23. Miller, *Correspondence,* 1:206.
24. Weil, *Waiting on God,* p. 76.
25. Miller, *Correspondence,* 1:205.
26. Traubel, *Camden,* 3:293.
27. Miller, *Correspondence,* 1:157.
28. Whitman took Davidson's 1857 translation of Dante's *Inferno* to the hospitals (Glicksberg, *Civil War,* p. 73). In his frequent references to the "hell" of war, this work is constantly at the back of his mind. During the course of his powerful letter to Nathaniel Bloom and J. F. S. Gray he mentions that "not old Greek mighty ones, where man contends with fate, (and always yields)—not Virgil showing Dante on & on among the agonized & damned, approach what here I see & take a part in" (Miller, *Correspondence,* 1:82). Yet

in this particular context, what Whitman is actually experiencing is a kind of harrowing of hell, a defiance of, which becomes a victory over, its power. The young men, holding themselves "cool and unquestioned master above all the pains and bloody mutilations," become Herculean heroes of the world of the spirit. On behalf of America, they face, and outface, the terrors of death: so that Whitman, like the Christian poets ("Death, thou shalt die!") can scoff, incredulously, at his former fears. "This then, what frightened us all so long!" (ibid., p. 82).

29. Hart Crane, *The Complete Poems and Selected Letters and Prose,* ed. Brom Weber (London: Oxford University Press, 1968), p. 34.
30. Walt Whitman, *Comprehensive Reader's Edition of Leaves of Grass,* ed. Harold Blodgett and Sculley Bradley (New York: New York University Press, 1965), p. 746.
31. John Milton, *Complete Poems and Selected Prose,* ed. Merritt Y. Hughes (New York: Odyssey Press, 1957), p. 284.
32. *Reader's Edition,* p. 750.
33. Traubel, *Camden,* 3:204.
34. *Reader's Edition,* p. 743.
35. Ibid., p. 748.
36. William White, ed., *Walt Whitman: Daybooks and Notebooks* (New York: New York University Press, 1978), 3:670.
37. Miller, *Correspondence,* 4:258.
38. Ibid., 1:247.
39. Traubel, *Camden,* 2:142.
40. Ibid., 6:386.
41. Ibid., 6:311.
42. Walter Benjamin, *Illuminations,* ed. Hannah Arendt, trans. Harry Zohn (London: Cape, 1970), p. 257.
43. Edward Thomas, *Collected Poems* (London: Faber and Faber, 1965), p. 21.
44. Traubel, *Camden,* 6:353.
45. Ibid., 6:135.
46. Charles Tomlinson, *Selected Poems, 1951–1974* (Oxford: Oxford University Press, 1978), p. 8.
47. Glicksberg, *Civil War,* p. 128.
48. Ibid., p. 166.
49. Miller, *Correspondence,* 1:225.

9. My Book and the War Are One

1. Cleveland Rodgers and John Black, eds., *The Gathering of the Forces* (New York: Putnam, 1920), 1:93.
2. Ibid., 1:76.
3. Ibid., 1:86.
4. Emory Holloway, ed., *The Uncollected Poetry and Prose of Walt Whitman* (London: Heinemann, 1922), 1:77–78.
5. Rodgers and Black, *Gathering of Forces,* 1:90.

6. Ibid., 1:89.
7. Ibid., 1:76.
8. After the war Whitman reverted in *Democratic Vistas* to this theme of the founders. Marveling at the events that had made the States—"They hasten, incredible, blazing bright as fire . . . when I con them, I feel, every leaf, like stopping to see if I have not made a mistake, and fall'n on the splendid figments of some dream. But it is no dream" (2:409)—he pondered the dilemma of the present: "We stand, live, move, in the huge flow of our age's materialism—in its spirituality. We have had founded for us the most positive of lands. The founders have pass'd to other spheres—but what are these terrible duties they have left us?" (2:409).
9. Arthur Golden, ed., *Walt Whitman's Blue Book* (New York: New York Public Library, 1968), 1:27.
10. Ibid., 1:46.
11. Ibid., 1:80–81.
12. The different versions of "By Blue Ontario's Shore" have been examined by Gary A. Calbert, "Whitman's Revisions of 'By Blue Ontario's Shore,' " *Walt Whitman Review* 23 (1977):35–45.
13. Golden, *Blue Book*, 1:108.
14. Ibid., 1:351.
15. Ibid., 1:109.
16. *The Riverside Edition of Emerson's Complete Works* (London: Routledge, 1883), 2:186.
17. Compare Whitman's use of the image in *Democratic Vistas*: "And as, by virtue of its kosmical, antiseptic power, Nature's stomach is fully strong enough not only to digest the morbific matter always presented, not to be turn'd aside, and perhaps, indeed, intuitively gravitating thither—but even to change such contributions into nutriment for highest use and life—so American democracy's—" (2:282).
18. E. H. Miller, ed., *Walt Whitman: The Correspondence* (New York: New York University Press, 1961), 4:370.
19. Henry Larkin, quoted in Horace Traubel, *With Walt Whitman in Camden* (New York: Rowman and Littlefield, 1961), 2:241.
20. Miller, *Correspondence*, 1:157.
21. Horace Traubel, *With Walt Whitman in Camden*, vol. 6, ed. Gertrude Traubel and William White (Carbondale: Southern Illinois University Press, 1982), p. 370.

❧ Index